Christianity as a World Religion

D1081310

Also available from Bloomsbury:

The Study of Religion, George D. Chrissides and Ron Geaves

Christianity as a World Religion

Sebastian Kim and Kirsteen Kim

B L O O M S B U R Y
LONDON · NEW DELHI · NEW YORK · SYDNEY

Bloomsbury Academic

An imprint of Bloomsbury Publishing Plc

50 Bedford Square	1385 Broadway
London	New York
WC1B 3DP	NY 10018
UK	USA

www.bloomsbury.com

First published in 2008 by the Continuum International Publishing Group Ltd
Reprinted by Bloomsbury Academic 2013

British Library Cataloguing-in-Publication Data
A catalogue record for this book is available from the British Library.

ISBN: HB: 978-0-8264-9840-3
PB: 978-0-8264-9841-0

Library of Congress Cataloging-in-Publication Data
A catalog record for this book is available from the Library of Congress.

Kim, Sebastian C. H.
Christianity as a world religion/Sebastian Kim and Kirsteen Kim.
p. cm.
Includes bibliographical references and Index.
ISBN 978-0-8264-9840-3 – ISBN 978-0-8264-9841-0 1. Christianity. I. Kim, Kirsteen. II. Title.
BR121.3.K56 2008
270–dc22
2007047407

Typeset by Fakenham Photosetting Limited, Fakenham, Norfolk
Printed and bound in Great Britain

Contents

Acknowledgements

The authors wish to acknowledge the people in the following institutions and organizations around the world through whom they have gained insight into Christianity as a world religion:

All Nations Christian College, UK
Commission on World Mission and Evangelism, World Council of Churches
Cross-Cultural Missionary Training Institute, South Korea
Department of Theology and Religion, University of Birmingham, UK
Faculty of Divinity, University of Cambridge, UK
Faculty of Education and Theology, York St John University, UK
Fuller Theological Seminary, USA
Global Network for Public Theology
Henry Martyn Centre, Cambridge Theological Federation, UK
International Association for Mission Studies
(and British and Irish Association for Mission Studies)
Presbyterian College and Theological Seminary, South Korea
Union Biblical Seminary, India
United College of the Ascension, UK
Yale–Edinburgh Group for Non-Western Christianity

We also wish to thank Rebecca Vaughan-Williams and Tom Crick and Joanna Kramer of Continuum for their initiative and work for this project.

Christianity as a world religion

1

Christianity is regarded as a world religion in the ideological sense that it is deemed to be worthy of equal respect in the public sphere, along with other world religions such as Islam, Hinduism, Buddhism and Judaism. This reflects the recognition accorded to (certain forms of) Christianity by politicians or academics, but this designation does not reveal anything about how or where Christianity is expressed on the ground, which is the main interest of this book. According to Tomoko Masuzawa, the term 'world religion' was first used in the late nineteenth century to express the confidence of European Christians of the period that Christianity was the universal religion or religion of the world. Today, although Christianity remains the largest religion, including about a third of the world's population, the sense is more from the language of plurality and diversity: that Christianity is one of a group of trans-regional religions, all of which can be called 'world religions'. Both uses reveal their origins in Western classification of 'the rest'. The classification also privileges systems of belief that have a literature and recorded history (Masuzawa 2005: 23, 29, 3–4). In describing Christianity as a world religion, we do not mean either to privilege Christianity above other religions, or necessarily to classify or ally it with others. We wish to discuss many other meaningful senses in which Christianity may be described as a world religion, which have more to do with the nature of Christianity and its different expressions around the world.

We put forward the following ways in which Christianity may be properly described as a 'world religion':

- Topographically, Christianity is spread across the globe and is not just the religion of one region
- Theologically, Christianity claims to be universally applicable and locally inclusive
- Geographically, Christianity has always been widespread and practised locally in different communities across the world

- Socio-politically, the worldwide presence of Christianity today is not primarily the result of attempts by powerful churches to replicate themselves worldwide but the result of indigenous response and grassroots movements
- Historically, Christianity does not have one single strand of development, one centre, or a linear history but is diffuse, locally divergent and adapted to different contexts
- Structurally, Christianity is trans-national, and Christians around the world are connected to one another through many different structures and networks

In this introductory chapter we will discuss each of the ways in which Christianity can be considered a world religion to set the framework for later discussion. In the next five chapters we will investigate Christianity as a world religion by taking a regional approach, looking at Christianity as it is expressed on each continent. Although we set the Christianity in each continent in its historical perspective, the focus is on contemporary belief and practice. We will analyse contemporary Christianity not only in terms of numbers and phenomena, but in terms of its presence in society. Taking into account issues of culture and politics, we will look at the distinctive forms of worship and theologies of Christians, and the interaction of churches with the wider society and the other religions in each part of the world. Although inevitably much more information is available about those areas of the world where there are large Christian communities, we try to include regions where Christians are few, and the experience of Christians who are small minorities. Sometimes the term 'world Christianity' is used in the West to mean 'non-Western Christianity', in which case it comprises (usually the exotic) instances of Christian faith in 'the global South', in Asia, Africa and Latin America. We include Europe and the United States, on the basis that Christianity in the contemporary West must be part of the picture if we are to understand the full dynamics of Christianity.

By considering the nature of its local presence and relations, and its self-understanding, we hope to see better the nature of contemporary world Christianity. We are not saying that this continent-by-continent approach is the only way to look at world Christianity, but we find that it clarifies that world Christianity is not merely a product of Western expansion but the result of local initiative, and it corrects an imbalance in most studies of Christian history and theology published in the West, which tend to include

Christianity in Africa, Asia and Latin America only at the end. We do not ignore Christianity in Europe and North America – there is a chapter on each – but we try to show that they are part of an interconnected phenomenon with multiple centres and diverse manifestations. All our research is necessarily hampered by our own human limitations: it is mainly conducted through the medium of English; our own knowledge and contacts – worldwide though they are – cannot be fully representative; and we were not able to devote as much time as this project justifies. We apologize to Christians who do not recognize themselves in our portraits, but we hope that by combining in ourselves Asian and European perspectives we have done some justice to the study of world Christianity.

Topography: mapping Christianity

It is estimated that about one-third of the world's population is Christian. In the year 2000, Christians were fairly equally distributed around the globe: 29 per cent were in Europe, 25 per cent in Latin America, 18 per cent in Africa, 16 per cent in Asia and 11 per cent in North America. These figures represent Christian majorities in Latin America and Africa, but the population of Asia is so large that Christians make up less than 9 per cent of the whole (Barrett 2001: 12–13). The statistics by continent disguise a more complex picture at national and local level. In Latin and North America, Christians are distributed throughout, but the Christian map of Africa is strikingly weighted to the sub-Saharan section of the continent. All the countries from Congo southwards are majority Christian, with the exception of Botswana, Mozambique, Tanzania and Madagascar. West African countries have large numbers of Christians and Muslims, but countries in north Africa have almost no Christians. Egypt and Sudan have large Christian minorities, and Ethiopia is largely Christian. The Christian map of Asia (as defined by the United Nations) is very patchy. Armenia, Cyprus and Georgia in the far west and the Philippines in the far east are predominantly Christian. South Korea and Vietnam have relatively large Christian minorities. Absolute figures give a different perspective, however. The Republic of Singapore has about 12 per cent Christians, about 440,000 in all; but the 13 per cent of its huge neighbour Indonesia who call themselves Christian number 28 million people. Numbers of Christians in India are put at 62 million and in China are estimated to be 90 million. Although geographically removed from Europe, many Christians of European descent are found in North America, Australia, New Zealand and South Africa. However, as a result of migration, the Christian populations of all these countries – and of Europe – are undergoing a 'darkening' (Tiénu 2006: 40), as Christianity is no longer the faith only of the white populations.

The label 'Christian' is difficult to define and attach, and therefore numbers of Christians can only be educated guesswork. The *World Christian Encyclopedia* (Barrett 2001) represents the most long-term, extensive and comprehensive attempt to collate statistics pertaining to world Christianity. It is conducted among the churches, so it attempts to measure the faith at the grassroots as well as institutionally. This is one reason why its figures may be more generous to Christians than some other sources, such as local census results (especially where Christians are in a minority) or the CIA Factbook. However, another reason is that the *Encyclopedia* has an agenda to promote a particular kind of Christian growth, represented by the idiosyncratic category of 'Great Commission Christians', which attempts to single out the relatively few believed to be actively trying to fulfil the mandate for world evangelization (Barrett 2001: 28). The *Encyclopedia* divides Christians into several categories according to denomination and according to 'trans-megabloc groupings'. In the former category, we recognize the Orthodox churches and the Roman Catholic Church and consider the others under the broad label of 'Protestant'. We also refer to two trans-continental Christian movements, Evangelicalism and the Pentecostal–charismatic movement, which we will discuss below. What counts as membership of any of these groups is also a difficult question. It may mean, at one end of the spectrum, fulfilling the requirements of baptism and confirmation in the largest of all trans-national organisations, the Roman Catholic Church. Or, at the other end, it may mean occasional participation in a local group.

The relation between the Christian label and Christian belief and practice is also complex. The adjective 'Christian' may be used in many different senses to refer to a kind of morality based on the Sermon on the Mount, certain cultural traits, membership of a particular community, belief in certain doctrines or participating in certain ritual activities (see, for example, the discussion in Davie 1994). 'Christian' may or may not indicate regular Christian practice. In some European countries, such as Denmark, Norway and Sweden, where citizens automatically belong to the national church unless they opt out, levels of baptism and confirmation of children are also high, but regular church attendance is as low as 3 per cent. In many places in Africa and Asia, being a Christian implies regular attendance at worship and church events, and also a high level of giving – many churches expect a tithe (10 per cent) of income. In some countries, especially in the Middle East, being known as a Christian brings a high social cost. The decision to become or remain a Christian may be a private matter, for example in North America and South Korea, but elsewhere – in India for example – it may be a badge of ethnic or caste identity and a matter of status in law. Counting numbers is a starting point but it is a very rough guide to the Christian-ness of any part of the world.

Theology: Christianity as essentially worldwide

Mark Juergensmeyer points out that (almost) all religions are found in diaspora and that religion 'has always been global, in the sense that religious communities and traditions have always maintained permeable boundaries. They have moved, shifted, and interacted with one another around the globe'. Religion is spread by the movement of people. Whether a religion stays within the diaspora community or spreads beyond it depends on the external circumstances but also – and perhaps more importantly – upon the nature of the religion itself: whether it makes a universal appeal and/or a personal invitation. Christianity is generally one of those religions which outsiders can convert to, and are invited to convert to (2003: 5, 7). Christianity is also a religion spread by proselytizing as well as by migration and globalizing processes (cf. Rudolph 1997: 1). It claims theological universality and local inclusivity.

The missionary nature of Christianity was much discussed in the wake of the colonial period as the extent of the complicity of Christian missionaries with colonial oppression was revealed. Missionaries were, perhaps unfairly, made to carry much of the blame for the cultural aspects of imperialism, to the extent that some church leaders among the colonizers and the formerly colonized repudiated the term 'mission' altogether. Others engaged in rethinking its meaning and Christian relations with those outside the community in general by looking at the biblical and church traditions and the history of missions. The balance of the conclusions, as presented by South African mission theologian David Bosch in a widely acclaimed publication (1991), is that Christianity is essentially missionary, but that mission in the way of Jesus Christ is not in power but in weakness (2 Cor. 13.4). It is primarily the multifaceted witness to the nature of God, as revealed in Jesus Christ, which is an integral part of Christian living and inherent in the nature of the church. 'Mission' (derived from the Latin '*mitto*', 'I send') is first and foremost the action of God in sending Jesus Christ into the world (John 3.16), but Jesus' disciples also understand themselves to be sent into the world (Mt. 28.18–20; Mk 16.15–18; Lk. 24.46–48/Acts 1.8; Jn 20.21–23) for its salvation. The salvation that is proclaimed and demonstrated by the Christian community is available to all and comprehensive of the whole of life (Col. 1.19–20). It unites people of different ethnicity, social status and gender (Gal. 3.23) (see also Senior and Stuhlmueller 1983; Legrand and Barr 1990).

The instinct of Christians to share their faith was encouraged by some of the conditions in which Christianity arose (Goodman 1994) and formalized by certain decisions made by the church. For example, at the Jerusalem Council (Acts 15) in about 48 CE, it was resolved that Gentiles (or Greeks) were equally members of the church with the original Jewish members on the basis that they had also received the Holy Spirit. Only the moral demands of the law of Moses, summed up by Jesus Christ as love of God and neighbour (Mt. 22.36–40; Mk 12.28–31), not the external requirements of circumcision and the food laws, were considered binding. The new community of both Jews and Greeks called 'Christians' (Acts 11.26) was characterized by a willingness to 'contextualize' or re-express its faith and life in different situations and societies (Dunn 2006: 333; cf. 1 Cor. 9.22). The decision of the Council was also an endorsement of the mission of the Apostle Paul to the Gentiles (cf. Gal. 2.9). Since few other Jews responded to the gospel, the church took on an increasingly Gentile nature (cf. Rom. 9.1–5). Second, although the first Christians worshipped at the temple in Jerusalem (Acts 3), which continued to have great significance for them (2 Cor. 8–10; Rom. 16.23–27; 15.16), this was no longer possible for Christians, or Jews, after the desecration and destruction of the Temple by the Romans in 70 CE. Instead, Rome and Constantinople became the premier centres for Christianity, and distance from Jerusalem was not a limitation on the spread of the faith. The two religions had separated from one another by the end of the first century, but Christians include the Hebrew Bible (Old Testament) in their Bible, and the place of the Jewish people, and their faith, in Christian theology remains a topic of intense debate until today. Third, the public criterion for inclusion in the Christian community became baptism in the name of God, the Father, Son and Holy Spirit, which signified (among other things) a participation in the dying and rising of Jesus Christ to a new life of obedience made possible in the Holy Spirit. Baptism was a simple ceremony, inclusive of women, who played a prominent role in the church, and inexpensive for a community which included many poor people. Although not always confirmed in practice, in these and other ways Christianity was affirmed as unlimited by ethnicity, geography or socio-economic status, and therefore had the potential to spread through all communities worldwide.

Geography: Christianity as a world religion in the first millennium

In 1900 the *World Christian Encyclopedia* estimates that 70 per cent of all Christians were to be found in Europe, but around the middle of the twentieth century a significant moment occurred after which Christianity could no longer be described statistically as a 'European religion'. Concluding his seven-volume study of the spread of world Christianity in 1945, Kenneth Scott Latourette declared that Christianity had now spread worldwide for the first time (Latourette 1971: 419), and in 1964 the mission historian Stephen Neill claimed that Christianity had now become a universal religion in a way that it never had been before (Neill 1964: 15). However, Christianity's recession in Europe and its growth in Africa, Latin America and the Pacific is only the most recent example of the changing landscape. In the first three centuries, Christianity moved from a Jewish setting in Palestine to a Hellenistic–Roman one and it also took root among the 'barbarians' beyond the Roman empire in all directions: in Europe, Africa and Asia. Christian numbers have grown and declined in different times and places over the past two thousand years. For example, as renowned mission historian Andrew Walls points out, Egypt and Syria were once almost 'axiomatically Christian', and Arabia once had Jewish tribes and Christian towns (Walls 2002: 29), while Europe was once synonymous with all that was anti-Christian. At no time in its history has Christianity been the religion of one people group or been practised uniformly in one language according to identical rites. It has always been geographically widespread and practised locally in different communities across the world.

Several histories of world Christianity have been published in recent years (including Dowley 1990; Hastings 1999a; McManners 2002; Norris 2002; Spickard and Cragg 1994). The most outstanding is *History of the World*

Christian Movement (Vol. I, 2001), edited by Dale Irvin and Scott Sunquist, which was prepared by a group of scholars from many different regions and traditions of Christianity and is supported by collected readings (Coakley and Sterk 2004). What they show is that Christianity spread not only to the west but in all directions, so that by the end of the first millennium it had become the faith of people as far south as Ethiopia, as far north as Moscow, as far west as Ireland and as far east as China. Although the biblical historian Luke's view that the church spread outwards from Jerusalem to Judaea and 'the ends of the earth' (Acts 1.8) is correct in so far as Christianity started from a certain point at a certain time, it needs to be taken together with his emphasis on the diversity of communities which had received the gospel, even in the first century, indicated by the variety of peoples in Jerusalem at Pentecost who heard the gospel in their own native language (Acts 2.6). The role of those who received the message is evident by the variety of local forms Christianity took, which made agreement on matters of doctrine at the ecumenical church councils of the first five centuries impossible and led to disputes among Christians. Furthermore, while there were missionaries, known in this period as 'apostles' or 'patron saints', who deliberately carried the message to different lands, it was also spread by traders, slaves and migrants. In many, perhaps most, cases the spread of the faith was 'accidental' and communities who had happened to hear the message then themselves requested clergy to come and instruct them further.

In the east, Christianity was established in Damascus and Antioch in Syria in the first century (Acts 9.1–6; 11.19–26), and the manual for leaders of local churches in Syriac, known as the *Didache*, shows that Christianity was rural as well as urban and in a distinctively Semitic form. The Syrians rejected the Greek-dominated Christianity of the Mediterranean churches which stressed the union of the two natures of Christ, adopting what is commonly but erroneously called the 'monophysite' view. In the sixth century, the churches were invigorated by the mission movement based in Edessa led by Jacob Baradeus (hence the name 'Jacobite'). The Syriac gospel was established in Nisibis in Persia before the fourth century where, under political pressure from the Shah to distance themselves from Rome, the Persian, or 'East Syrian' (or Assyrian), church adopted the (misnamed) 'Nestorian' or 'dyophysite' view, which tends to distinguish the divine and human nature in Christ. It may be that the first Christian in India was Thomas, one of the twelve disciples of Jesus, but it is more likely that the ancient Orthodox Christians of India, who call themselves 'St Thomas' Christians, are descended from the church established by a Persian merchant, Thomas of Cana, who settled in the area of Cranganore (modern Kodungallur) in Kerala in about 350. It was the Persian form of Christianity which travelled along the trade routes across Asia to Afghanistan, North India, Sri Lanka, China, Tibet and Indonesia. By 600 the Persian church already included members of nomadic tribes such as the Huns and Turks, who lived in the north-east of the country in cities on the Silk Road to China. In the sixth to the tenth centuries the Persian church maintained a chain of monasteries in the cities along the road to China in what are now Uzbekistan, Kazakstan and Tajikistan, and supported Christian communities as far afield as Tibet, Yemen and northern Mongolia. The furthest communities of East Syrian Christians of which we have knowledge (from archaeological and written records) were in T'ang dynasty China in the seventh to ninth centuries.

To the south, the Christian community in Alexandria was certainly established very early (cf. Acts 18.24) and soon developed a distinctive allegorical method of biblical interpretation favoured by the philosophers there. Christian Gnosticism, which regarded Jesus as a spiritual figure who only appeared to take on bodily form, had strong characteristics of the Egyptian mystery religions and influenced the famous Alexandrian theological school. The Egyptian masses, the Copts, did not adopt the creed of Chalcedon, preferring to express their national identity through a 'monophysite' theology. The ascetic community life practised in the deserts of Egypt became the basis for the pattern of monasticism found across the Christian world. There were certainly Christians further south in Ethiopia in the second century (see also Acts 8.26–40). In the mid-fourth century the king of Axum became a ('monophysite') Christian and the scriptures were translated into the Ethiopian language of Ge'ez. The land of Nubia, between Egypt and Ethiopia, adopted Chalcedonian Christianity in the sixth century.

The book of Acts and the letters of the Apostle Paul describe how he travelled westward and the gospel was received (and sometimes not received) in Asia Minor (modern Turkey), which was known for its prophets and the third-century charismatic movement known as 'Montanism' or the 'New Prophecy' which erupted there (cf. 1 Cor. 12–14). The Greek Orthodox Church regards as its foundation charter the visit of Paul to Athens (Acts 17). Since the people of Asia Minor and Greece were not Semitic, the Christianity of this region gradually became Hellenized. At the end of the third century, King Tiridates III of Armenia was baptized and the national church elected its own patriarch or *catholicos*. Within a century or so, the scriptures had been translated into the Armenian language. Its neighbour Georgia was Christianized from Greece in the fourth century and maintained the Chalcedonian orthodoxy, but the Armenian Church adopted the 'monophysite' position. There was already a church in Rome before the Apostle Paul wrote to it or was taken there in chains (Acts 27–28). The extent of Christian presence at the heart of the empire became clear in 64 CE when the emperor Nero executed hundreds. From Rome the Christian faith could rapidly be disseminated further west into Europe and south into north Africa through the excellent communications network of which it was the centre. There were churches as far apart as Lyons (modern France) in 177 and Carthage (north Africa) in 180. The need to present a united front to the authorities, and, after the conversion of the emperor Constantine in 313, the role of Christianity as the official religion of the empire encouraged its systematization, but the local rooted-ness of the church was seen as the cultural and linguistic tensions within the empire between the Latin west and the Greek east gradually split the church into Roman Catholic Christianity and (Byzantine) Orthodox Christianity. The theologians who defined Roman Christianity – who were almost all north Africans – wrote in Latin, and from Augustine onwards were unable to understand the Greek of the ecumenical councils. The loss of imperial lands east of Asia Minor to Muslim armies by 634 meant that the Orthodox faith no longer spread eastwards. However, the Slavs and the Bulgars, who from the sixth century moved into territory north of Constantinople, adopted Christianity in the ninth century. A church gradually came into existence in the lands of the Rus people, north of the Black Sea, and in the eleventh century Vladimir built a strong Russian national identity on the basis of Orthodox Christianity.

While Orthodox Christianity spread northwards, Roman Catholicism spread north and westwards. The migrants and invaders who settled within the Roman empire's borders – Germanic tribes and the Visigoths in Italy – adopted Catholic Christianity, and after the fall of the empire the church became a unifying force, preserving its language especially through Jerome's translation of the Bible into Latin, the Vulgate. The tribes of northern Europe tended to respond to the Christian faith en masse, especially when they were convinced that the Christian God was more powerful than their own gods. Celtic Christianity spread from Ireland eastwards to Britain and the continent of Europe, and possibly even west across the Atlantic, although these Christians deferred to the Roman model in the seventh century. On the continent of Europe, Clovis, king of the Franks, in what is now Germany, France and Spain, was baptized a Catholic around 500, and under their emperor Charlemagne the Franks forced the Saxons of what is now northern Germany to be baptized on pain of death. In the tenth century, the Saxons expanded their power and Christian faith northwards into Denmark, south to Italy and east into Poland. The Vikings who had first raided Christian settlements spread the faith back to Scandinavia in the ninth and tenth centuries, but the people of Finland opted for Christianity only in 1300. In the year 1000, after long deliberations of the elders of the community and shamanistic-style divinization, the people of Iceland opted to become Christians.

Society and politics: world Christianity as globalization from below

World Christianity is one example of how the contemporary world is globalized, both in the sense of the extension of one entity across the entire globe and also in the sense of time and space being compressed within a network (cf. Schreiter 1997: 8). Contemporary world Christianity, like other world religions, is both an agent of globalization and a product of it. However, the relationship of world Christianity to processes of globalization is not straightforward. The spread of Christianity is often tied to the expansion of Europe and the rise of North America. But, as we have just seen, Christianity is not inherently a European religion. As in the first millennium, the worldwide presence of Christianity today is not primarily the result of attempts by powerful churches to replicate themselves worldwide but the result of indigenous response and grassroots movements.

Globalization is generally understood as a top-down homogenizing process determined, from the point of view of the right, by markets or, from the perspective of the left, by political hegemony (cf. Vásquez and Marquardt 2003: 2). However, the motives and goals of religious globalization, in so far as it is a conscious process, may have little in common with the motives and goals of economic or political globalization (cf. Muzaffar 1998: 179). Although the spread of Christianity cannot be disconnected from matters of economics and politics, sociologist Roland Robertson's work on cultural globalization, which he sees as 'at least as old as the rise of the so-called world religions two thousand and more years ago' (Robertson 1992: 7), may be more relevant. Such cultural processes of globalization do not necessarily follow the same global flows as capital and power (Robertson 1992:

96). Robertson's work shows that there may be many cultural globalization processes going on, arising from multiple centres, and interrelating with one another. Peter Berger and Samuel Huntington agree with Robertson that there are 'many globalizations' (2002: title), and furthermore, Berger recognizes that these include some popular movements that are not in the service of the dominant global players. The main example he gives is the fastest-growing Christian movement, Pentecostalism (Berger and Huntington 2002: 7–8). However, Berger (in Berger and Huntington) still wishes to see all globalizing movements as in some respects responses to the dominant globalization from America. In his careful study of religion and globalization (1994), Peter Beyer takes issue with this, arguing that globalization 'is more than the spread of one historically existing culture at the expense of all others. It is also the creation of a new global culture with its attendant social structures, one which increasingly becomes the broader social context of *all* particular cultures in the world, including those of the West' (1994: 9). What may have been set in train by events in the West has knock-on effects that inexorably alter the situation of all. With the recognition of this 'reflexivity' of global movements (Beck, Giddens and Lash 1994), the question of who started it becomes increasingly irrelevant. Moreover, David Martin questions whether movements of globalization always begin from the dominant world power. In his study of Latin American churches, Martin contrasts the conscious, planned expansion of the Catholic Church and the 'unsponsored' growth of Pentecostalism (Martin 2002: 5; quoting David Lehman), and concludes that faith 'creates a mobilization from the bottom up by "unlearned and ignorant men"' (Martin 2002: 6). Also drawing on studies of the Americas, Manuel Vásquez and Marie Marquardt, in common with others, recognize a 'globalization from below', which is not about 'domination and homogenization' but about 'resistance', 'heterogeneity' and 'negotiation' at the grassroots (2003: 3). This is much closer to the pattern for the spread of early Christianity as suggested in the New Testament. Beyer further draws attention to the fact that religion is not only a culture but also a social system, although he tends to give priority to the former. As a social system, world Christianity is the church, or communions of churches, which may be structured institutionally in the public sphere or privately, and may be both locally rooted and trans-national. Christianity exists in communities as well as institutions, it consists of many movements, which may be elite or popular, and faith is not only a matter of word and thought but also of deed and material acts. It is spread by people, agents whose actions are dependent on many contingent events. The globalization of Christianity – as both culture and system – is a fact, and theories of globalization help to analyse the processes involved, but it is 'a complex, historically contingent cluster of processes involving multiple actors, scales, and realms of human activity' (Vásquez and Marquardt 2003: 3).

From the point of view of Christian missiology, Dana Robert points to the 'irony' that historians who saw world Christianity as an arm of European imperialism failed to notice that in the post-colonial period colonial churches were actually growing much more rapidly in Asia, Africa and Latin America than ever before. Because Christianity is more a people's movement than a political one, they failed to notice 'that growth among the grass roots did not mirror the criticisms of the intellectual elites' (Robert 2000: 53). With this scenario in mind, Lamin Sanneh attempts to make a distinction between 'world Christianity' as 'the movement of Christianity as it takes form and shape in societies that previously were not Christian' and 'global Christianity', which he takes to refer to 'the faithful replication of Christian forms and patterns developed in Europe'. In this model, 'world Christianity' represents a grassroots movement, while 'global Christianity' is seen as the result of a more intentional, political attempt to spread particular institutions across the world (2003: 23). World Christianity is a 'globalization from below' as opposed to 'an imposition from the world's great powers' (Carpenter 2005: vii). In practical terms, this is an impossible distinction because 'global Christianity' often gives rise to 'world Christianity' as local churches become independent of foreign control, and what was brought from Europe (or elsewhere) becomes 'contextualized'. And syntactically, the term 'world Christianity' is also not free from connotations of being monolithic or culturally uniform. But what Sanneh wishes to emphasize by preferring the term 'world Christianity' (Carpenter 2005: 24) is 'the indigenous discovery of Christianity rather than the Christian discovery of indigenous societies' (Sanneh 2003: 10). This is an attempt we support. A great deal of attention has been paid to the intentional spreading of Christianity from centres of power, especially in the last two centuries. In this book we prefer to concentrate on the way the faith has been received, and how in different world contexts believers have made it their own.

History: Christianity as contextual

Historically, because of its open invitation and universal appeal, Christianity did not remain a religion in diaspora or the faith of enthusiastic missionaries, but over two thousand years the Christian faith spread in a disorganized way to include new peoples. Christianity does not have one single strand of development, one centre or a single history, but is diffuse, complex and polycentric. Christianity has had multiple centres from the time of Jesus, when the focus was divided between Jerusalem and Galilee. It later developed in different patriarchates: Rome, Constantinople, Antioch, Alexandria, Baghdad and so on. Christianity today is also polycentric, although theologians from Africa, Asia and Latin America complain that their colleagues in the West have yet to appreciate this (e.g. Tiénu 2006). As well as Rome, Athens and New York, major Christian hubs today include Lagos, Seoul, Bangalore and São Paulo. Furthermore, Christianity has exhibited a remarkable ability to adapt to many different global settings far from its original homeland. It has changed internally as a result of encounters with different cultures so that it is now 'ambicultural as the faith of multiple language users straddling national and social boundaries' (Sanneh 2005: 214), and 'the largest world religion is in fact the ultimate local religion' (Robert 2000: 56).

As a result of this diversity, one of the early ecumenical Christian debates was about the canon of Scripture, or what should be included in (or rather excluded from) the Bible. For the Christian church the compilation of the Bible was a secondary activity, an 'accident' rather than the 'substance' of apostolic witness (H. Chadwick 2002: 34), which was to the 'living Word', Jesus Christ. Nevertheless, with more than thirty gospels alone in circulation, there were disputes about which were authoritative, and church leaders began to find it necessary to list those that they believed were traceable to the early apostles and whose contents were in keeping with the teaching of the church leaders. The New Testament documents were in Greek, but it was also decided to include the books of the Jewish canon, the Hebrew Bible. Therefore the Christian Bible represents within itself two different linguistic-cultural perspectives. Over the first five centuries ecumenical agreement was reached that the four gospels attributed to Matthew, Mark, Luke and John were authoritative, together with thirteen letters attributed to Paul, the Acts of the Apostles, the first letter of Peter and the first letter of John. The status of the Epistle to Hebrews, James, 2 John, 3 John, 2 Peter, Jude and Revelation continued to be debated, and different sections of the church operated with slightly different canons. It is of great significance for Christianity as a world religion that the churches accepted four parallel accounts of Jesus' life and ministry and set them side by side. These cover the same ground of Jesus' ministry and passion but vary in the traditions they include, present the material differently, and do not always agree on historical detail, or even sometimes on theological meaning. The Gospels are attributed to different disciples and plainly represent the views of different parts of the church. Though there are a few examples within the text of attempts to reconcile conflicts between these accounts, and the Syrian church used the *Diatessaron*, a single combined gospel, for at least two centuries, a plurality of Christian theologies was retained with the one Bible (Dunn 2006).

On the basis of its spread across Africa, Lamin Sanneh argues that Christianity as a religion exhibits 'translatability', which is in marked contrast to its main rival for African religious allegiance, Islam (Sanneh 1989: 211–38). That is, whereas Muslim religious observance and instruction is everywhere in Arabic because it is the original Arabic version of the Qur'an which is regarded as the final authority for faith, Christian missionaries translated the Bible and liturgy and developed vernacular expressions of the faith. Sanneh regards this as a pattern in the spread of Christianity worldwide ever since the decision to adopt Hellenistic culture. It is striking that, in contrast to Islam, most Christians have appropriated the local name for God, for example. However, Sanneh neglects the extent to which the church, having expressed the gospel in Greek language and thought, then resisted further contextualization. It is true that the whole Bible and liturgy were translated into Latin in north Africa and into Syriac by the fourth century. In the first millennium they were also translated into Coptic in Egypt, Ge'ez in Ethiopia, and into Armenian, Slavonic, and at least portions into Chinese. But at many points the churches have resisted vernacularization. The missionaries Constantine-Cyril and Methodius, who were sent from Constantinople in 683 to evangelize the Slavs, were supported by the Greek Church in their efforts to translate Christian literature, but opposed by Frankish bishops, who regarded Latin (or possibly Greek and Hebrew) as the only proper language for the liturgy. In 867 their protestations were overruled by the Roman pontiff, but the Franks prevailed eventually, and by the end of the ninth century the Moravian church was increasingly Latinized. While the Greeks encouraged locally autonomous churches, wherever the Roman Catholic Church was established, Latin was maintained as the language of scripture and worship as a sign of the universality of the church. Translation of the Bible into the tongues of northern Europe was a precipitating factor in the Protestant Reformation of the sixteenth century, but the Roman Catholic Church nevertheless maintained its policy worldwide right until after the Second Vatican Council of 1962–5. Looking back over Christian history, it seems that the urge to translate the gospel into local terms is always in tension with the desire to express Christian unity by having a common language.

Focus on translatability, a linguistic term, also neglects other dimensions of what is necessary if a religion is to be owned by people of a different culture. When Martin Luther complained about the 'Babylonian captivity' of the church of his day (1520), he was referring to matters of doctrine. Similarly, from the perspective of many Third World theologians and their representatives, the Western churches, even the Protestant ones, have not overcome their 'Latin captivity' (Boyd 1974) or the captivity of their doctrine to the categories of Greek thought in which it was first formulated (e.g. Samartha 1991), or the Western garb in which it was promulgated (e.g. Mbiti 1971), or the context of power and privilege in which it has been developed (e.g. Segundo 1976). When Christianity takes root in a new cultural context, it is not only the outward form of the faith which is affected – as the translation model might imply – but also its content that is challenged and reshaped in that setting. Not only is Christianity adapted to the new context, but there is a deeper-level and long-term interaction between the new faith and its new cultural surroundings which results in fresh expressions of the Christian gospel (e.g. Bediako 1992). Christianity is not imported as a package, but the local people encounter the person of Jesus Christ for themselves and respond according to their own cultural patterns and thought forms (e.g. Koyama 1974). The analogy often used is that of a seed planted in a new soil, which takes from the soil as well as bringing something new (Coe 1976).

Stephen Bevans (1992) has classified the processes by which the church has become rooted, or 'contextualized', in diverse cultures. In addition to the translation model, he lists four others: anthropological, praxis, synthetic and transcendent. Whereas the translation model is concerned primarily to preserve Christian identity, while taking cultural change seriously, the anthropological model is concerned to protect the cultural identity of a person of Christian faith. This model takes seriously the dignity of all human beings and the integrity of their cultures, and depends on the belief that the image of God can be found in them. In it local symbols are used to express the faith and develop a distinctively African or Filipino or Roma expression of Christianity. The dangers of this approach are cultural idealism, which identifies the gospel with the culture and may have disastrous results – as in the case of the folk church of Nazi Germany – and cultural relativism, which cuts off believers from the wider Christian community. Whereas the anthropological model tends to focus on the cultural symbols of the context, the praxis model emphasizes Christian living, particularly in view of the socio-economic realities of the context. It aims to see the transformation of the society to more closely conform to the ethical imperatives of the kingdom of God, of justice and moral uprightness. By its nature, the praxis model will raise challenges to the political status quo in any locality, and in its activism may lose sight of the gospel of peace that it proclaims. The synthetic model aims to respect both the Christian tradition and the local heritage and issues; it sets up a dialectic between scripture and culture, and between local church and world Christianity. As a middle way, it is in danger of not being forceful enough when a prophetic voice is needed, and of being undiscerning and therefore open to manipulation. The transcendental model seeks an authentic experience of Christ in a particular context, and expects that it is shared with others as part of universal human experience. The aim is integral human spirituality, which is inspired by Christ but may easily cross the usual religious divisions, although its claims to universality may be questioned.

Bevans recognizes all these approaches in contemporary Christian thought as it relates to social and cultural change. Each of the other models regards contextualization as a two-way process in which Christianity changes culture and context reshapes Christian faith and understanding. That this mutual interaction does indeed represent what is happening is shown by the influence of Christian values, often mediated through Westernization, worldwide, and also by the tensions within trans-national and trans-cultural church bodies. In summary, Christianity is 'a religion made to travel' (Cox 1996: 102) because it allows for a plurality of beliefs and practices. Though change is often resisted, Christianity has shown a great propensity to be re-expressed in different contexts, through a number of different methods of 'contextualization'.

Structure: trans-national forms of Christianity

As Susanne Rudolph has pointed out, 'Religious communities are among the oldest of transnationals' and today they are vigorous creators of trans-national civil society (Rudolph 1997: 1). Christianity is locally expressed but it is also connected together through many organizations and networks. Throughout this book we will be referring to five main streams of Christianity: Orthodox, Roman Catholic, Protestant (mainline and independent) and the trans-denominational categories of Evangelical and Pentecostal–charismatic. The origins of all of these, with the exception of the last, are associated with particular parts of the world and will be explained in these contexts. 'Orthodox' and 'Roman Catholic' refer to churches which arose in the first centuries in Europe, Africa and (in the first case) West Asia, and 'Protestant' we will use to refer to all the churches descended from the Reformation in Europe in the sixteenth century. We will use 'Evangelical' to refer primarily to a movement, originating in trans-Atlantic movements in the eighteenth, nineteenth and twentieth centuries, and expressed in certain churches (or denominations) and also by movements within Protestant churches. The newest and most difficult term to define is Pentecostal–charismatic, which we will consider in some detail below and in several of the following chapters. Here we will introduce the terms briefly from the point of view of observable differences between them today.

These five transcontinental forms of Christian church can be roughly divided into three by their forms of worship. In the Roman Catholic Church and Orthodox churches, priority is given to the sacraments, or outward signs of inward grace: Baptism, Confirmation or Chrismation, the Eucharist, Ordination to the priesthood, Confession, Anointing the sick, and Matrimony. The central part of worship is the sacrament of the Eucharist: the ritual re-enactment by the priest and people of the death and resurrection of Jesus Christ and the impartation of its efficacy for salvation by the distribution of bread and wine. In many churches the Eucharist – often referred to by Catholics as 'Mass' – is performed daily. Though there may be services of worship without participation in the Eucharist, the obligation of believers is to partake at least weekly. Both Catholic and Orthodox encourage the use of visual symbols in worship. The Orthodox churches particularly use icons, sacred pictures; the Roman Catholic Church statues. Both single out certain individuals after death for saintly status and both give special veneration to the Virgin Mary. The Orthodox Churches and the Roman Catholic Church both have a continuous historical, theological, liturgical and organizational development going back to the first church. After Christianity became the religion of empire, the churches took on a modified form and structure of imperial institutions which is reflected in costumes worn by the priests and the forms of the liturgy, and also in the fact that the priests are exclusively male. The most readily identifiable difference between the two traditions is organizational. The Roman Catholic Church has a hierarchical structure with a single centre in Rome, where the Pope, the successor of St Peter, is regarded as the head of the whole church worldwide, and universal teaching is promulgated to be applied in all contexts. The Orthodox churches are linguistic and ethnic groups in eastern Europe, Egypt and the horn of Africa, and West and South Asia. Each linguistic or ethnic church has its own patriarch. This arrangement carries with it the danger of ethnic conflict (Labi 2004: 190), but ideally the churches meet in council to decide matters pertaining to the whole church, and the patriarch of Constantinople is recognized as *primus inter pares*. Both Roman Catholic and Orthodox churches claim apostolic succession – that is, bishops (who are celibate) are consecrated by other bishops in an unbroken line to the first disciples – and affirm the creeds of the first ecumenical councils of the church, but the two churches drifted apart after the council of Chalcedon (451) and have been divided in practice since the rise of Islam, and formally since 1054. The differences between them are mainly cultural, but there is a difference in the way each understands the relations within the Trinity. This difference is reflected in their preferred creeds: the Apostles' Creed in the West and the longer Nicene-Constantinopolitan Creed in the East.

The vast majority of Protestant churches also celebrate the Eucharist, although they may refer to it as 'Holy Communion' or (especially the Evangelical churches) 'The Lord's Supper', but they generally accept only two sacraments: Communion and Baptism. Some Protestant churches maintain the traditional pattern of daily Eucharist, but most celebrate it less frequently – some only twice a year (or not at all in the case of the Quakers). This is because in Protestant churches equal importance is given to the 'preaching of the Word', usually by means of a sermon. The relative importance is indicated in the church architecture by the positions of the pulpit (or lectern) vis-à-vis the altar or (as many Protestants refer to it) the 'communion table'. It is also shown in the order of the service of worship. As their name implies, the Protestant churches were originally a protest movement, which aimed to reform the Roman Catholic Church in Europe in the sixteenth century. The Reformation had many aspects and resulted in Christians within lands ruled by different monarchs being separated into different churches. Theologically, the Reformation emphasized *sola gratia, sola fide, sola scriptura*: God's grace or initiative in revelation toward humankind as the only ground for knowing God; faith, rather than religious ritual, as the way to approach God; and the Bible rather than the Pope as the authority for teaching and formulating doctrine. There were several different leading figures. The theology of Martin Luther, a German, is the basis for the Lutheran churches of Germany and Scandinavia. Another German, Huldrych Zwingli, founded the Swiss Reformed Churches. The French reformer John Calvin became the leading theologian of the Reformed or Presbyterian churches; the Scottish Reformer John Knox was an associate of Calvin. The English Reformation had more of the nature of a political compromise, although it had religious antecedents. The theologians of Anglicanism (or Episcopalianism in North America), such as Thomas Cranmer, followed Luther more closely. Generally speaking, the Reformed churches represent a more thoroughgoing reformation of worship than the Lutheran and Anglican churches, which have retained (or can choose to retain) more of the form of Catholic worship, such as a strong emphasis on the Eucharist, a priestly role for their 'ministers' and an ornate sanctuary. The Reformed churches stripped the churches of many of the things they regard as non-essential in order to focus on the Word. Buildings are relatively (and sometimes very) plain in style; there is less emphasis on the celebration of the sacraments and more on preaching. There were also more radical Reformation groups such as the Anabaptists (whose main representatives today are Mennonites). Subsequent protest movements in Europe and North America led to the formation of the Society of Friends (Quakers), Methodist churches, Baptists, and other denominations, many of which will be mentioned later. The Ecumenical movement is a Protestant-initiated movement to unify the churches, begun in the early twentieth century.

Evangelical churches may be described as Protestant churches in which the sermon, not Holy Communion, is the climax of worship. However, the term 'Evangelical' covers a wide variety of meanings. First, it may simply refer to any Christian with a special concern to convey the 'good news' (*euangellion* in Greek). Second, it may be a general term for Protestants, which avoids the negative connotation of 'protest'. This is the usual meaning in continental Europe. In Britain and North America and countries influenced by these countries in Africa and Asia, 'Evangelical' often has a third, more restricted meaning referring to groups, churches and organizations that are related historically and/or theologically to the Pietist or Methodist revivals in the eighteenth century and subsequent 'Evangelical revivals'. The Evangelical theology resulting from these has four chief characteristics: conversionism – the need for individual change of life (being 'born again') because of sin; activism – through evangelistic and missionary efforts; biblicism – attaching a special importance to the Bible as authority for belief and conduct; and crucicentrism – belief in Christ's death on the cross as of central significance for human salvation (Bebbington 1989: 2–17). Evangelicalism in this sense does not necessarily correspond with particular denominations – although some denominations such as Baptists are generally Evangelical – but is a badge of orthodoxy within other churches. It may also be a label for independent local congregations. But there are Anglican evangelicals, for example, who stress personal holiness through prayer and Bible study as well as mission within the wider Anglican Church. Sometimes the term Evangelical is confused with 'Fundamentalist', but this is best reserved for a particular twentieth-century movement within Evangelicalism. There are some Evangelicals who reject charismatic styles of worship (see below), but in many cases Pentecostal–charismatics adopt an Evangelical theology. So, fifth, 'Evangelical' may be a term for 'Pentecostal'. In Latin America, *Evangelicos* is a general name for Protestant, but most of the Christians referred to by the term are Pentecostals.

In churches affected by the Pentecostal–charismatic movement, worship is distinguished by emphasis not on the Eucharist, or the Word, but the Spirit. When they meet, Pentecostal worshippers anticipate 'the immediate presence of God' by the power of the Spirit. Although there is usually a leader preacher at the service, his (or possibly her) role is to excite the congregation and call for a response. Because it is 'immediate', every member of the congregation is open to receiving a 'gift of the Spirit' to contribute to the worship service (Anderson 2004: 9). And because the presence and work of the Spirit cannot be controlled, the events of the service are (or appear to be) spontaneous and the constituent parts of the worship (the hymns, prayers, sermon) are not written down but are performed according to a more flexible oral tradition. Bodily movements of various forms – such as swaying, dancing and clapping – may be expected, prayer may be very loud and simultaneous, and ecstatic behaviour occurs in many cases. Manifestations of the Spirit in the congregation, such as dreams and visions, are taken seriously. Tangible results of prayer are expected in personal life, including bodily healing and prosperity (Hollenweger 1997: 18–19). In parts of the world where there is a strong awareness of a world of spirits, exorcism and prayer for victory over evil spirits may be an important part of the worship. In many cases, Pentecostals are groups of poor people without influence in society, except in numbers. They meet in the open air, in homes or rented rooms, although some large churches have constructed their own church buildings, some of which seat thousands. Pentecostalism is 'a potent mixture of the premodern and the postmodern, of the preliterate and the postliterate, of the fiesta and the encounter group' (Martin quoted in Cox 1996: 110). Because of various 'revivals' and 'charismatic movements', these features of worship may also be found in churches which – or meetings of Christians who – are otherwise Protestant, Catholic or Orthodox. There is a worldwide movement of Catholic Charismatic Renewal, for example, which has remained within the Church of Rome. In Africa the indigenous churches of the 'spirit type' and also the 'prosperity type' may be termed 'Pentecostal' or 'charismatic'. The term 'Pentecostal' can therefore refer to any one or all of three 'branches': denominations named 'Pentecostal', charismatic renewal movements, and indigenous churches in Africa, Asia and Latin America that show Pentecostal-type features (Hollenweger 1999: 33–4). This usage is problematic (see Anderson 2004: 166–83) and so we will try and distinguish these different meanings.

Study Questions and Further Readings

- In what sense is Christianity a world religion?
- How does the changing demography of the Christian population worldwide influence the dynamics of world Christianity?
- How does the spread of Christianity relate to other globalizing processes?
- In understanding world Christianity, what is contextualization and why is it important?
- What are the distinctive characteristics of Catholic, Orthodox and Protestant churches and Evangelical and Pentecostal–charismatic Christianities?

Bevans, S. B. and R. P. Schroeder (2004), *Constants in Context: A Theology of Mission for Today*. Maryknoll, NY: Orbis.

Hastings, Adrian (ed.) (2000), *A World History of Christianity*. London: Cassell.

Irvin, D. T. and S. W. Sunquist (2001), *History of the World Christian Movement. Vol I: Earliest Christianity to 1453*. Maryknoll, NY: Orbis.

Jenkins, Philip (2002), *The Next Christendom: The Coming of Global Christianity*. Oxford: Oxford University Press.

McManners, J. (ed.) (2002), *The Oxford History of Christianity*. Oxford: Oxford University Press.

European Christianity 2

Europe has a long Christian history, and two of the earliest forms of Christianity originate from European centres: Roman Catholicism and (Greek) Orthodoxy. The first Protestant churches also were born later in European contexts. These three different ecclesial cultures, or theological paradigms, roughly correspond to south, east and northern Europe. Christian experience in Europe is distinct from that in most other parts of the world in one obvious way: it was in Europe that (some) churches shared political power in what was known as Christendom. The precedent for an inter-dependent relationship between church and state was set in Rome 300 years after the birth of Christianity. Such an arrangement is not necessarily integral to Christianity – and some Christian commentators regret that development, believing it has compromised the church and inhibited its prophetic role – but it carried over into the Byzantine and Holy Roman Empires in Europe. Questions of church and state loom large for European churches, especially as those relations have been challenged by another powerful movement which has its origins in Europe: modernity. Each of the three forms of Christianity has encountered modernity in a different way and, brought together in a new united Europe, they each find themselves in an unfamiliar situation.

Orthodox Christianity: Trinity and unity

The Christians of Europe fall under the ancient patriarchates of Rome and Constantinople, which, although they both ratified the early councils, from Jerusalem to Chalcedon, gradually separated due to cultural, political and economic factors, until in 1054 a papal delegation to Constantinople excommunicated the ecumenical patriarch – and the action was reciprocated. The patriarch of Constantinople continued to preside over further 'ecumenical' councils, and the Orthodox Church regards itself as 'the church of the seven councils', the first and the last being at Nicaea (modern Turkey) in 325 and in 787. The councils systematized Christian thought in the language and culture of the Hellenistic world. Through the councils, the Orthodox Church came to understand God as Trinity in three distinct but interpenetrating Persons, each playing a different but complementary role in the salvation of the world. The church reflects their communal nature and is the channel through which the whole world is gathered up into Christ – crucified and risen, human and divine – and through which the energies of the Holy Spirit invigorate the world. As a result of the iconoclastic controversy, the church stressed the unity of spiritual and material, soul and body, heaven and earth. The unity of all things is expressed in the unity of divine and human in Christ, in the transformation of the elements in the Eucharist, in the unity of material and spiritual in the icons, and in the unbroken fellowship of God's people. It is an all-embracing vision in which salvation is understood as the divinization of human beings and the whole creation. Because the Oriental Orthodox churches of Asia and Africa that did not ratify Chalcedon did not participate in the later councils, and also because from the seventh century the patriarchates of Alexandria, Antioch and Jerusalem came under Muslim rule, the patriarchate of Constantinople came to be without rival in the Byzantine church, although its territory was much reduced and Constantinople or Byzantium was itself under threat from Muslim armies. Nevertheless, in the Middle Ages the splendour of Byzantium was legendary. Church and state were interdependent, as soul and body, and the whole was understood to be 'heaven on earth' (Ware 1993: 41, 35). It was also totalizing since everything was included within the reach of the church; in practice it was imperialist.

The Byzantine Church saw itself as universal but so did the Church of Rome, and gradually the latter became the more powerful. When, threatened by Turkish forces in the late eleventh century, the Byzantines requested help from the pope, the leaders of the crusading army imposed Latin rites on the eastern churches and even appointed Latin bishops over the existing Orthodox ones. There were skirmishes between Christians, and in 1204 a largely French army sacked and burned Constantinople itself, appointed a pro-Latin patriarch and stripped it of its wealth. The West held Constantinople for 57 years. It continued to try and force a union of the two churches under Rome, and the pope's emissaries even tried to incorporate churches of Africa and Asia, resulting in Uniate churches practising Eastern liturgical rites but in communion with Rome. The antics of the West undermined rather than strengthened Constantinople, which was eventually taken by the Ottoman Turks in 1453 and renamed Istanbul.

During several centuries within the Ottoman Empire, Christians had a respected status as a *millet*, a protected religious minority, but could only integrate by conversion to Islam. Since Muslim rulers did not distinguish religion and politics, the Orthodox Church became a civil as well as religious institution, a situation which persisted in Turkey until 1923 and in Cyprus until 1977. In this way Greek identity was preserved, but at the expense of the church being bound up with Greek nationalism (Ware 1993: 89). As a result of their experience under Muslim rule, and also their experience of attempts by other churches to proselytize them, the Orthodox churches have spoken out strongly against mission which aims at conversion. This stance is also integral to Orthodox theology – although not always reflected in practice – and consistent with their criticism of the western churches (Catholic and Protestant) for emphasizing Christology to the exclusion of theology of the Holy Spirit. Looked at from the perspective of the Spirit, as Greek Orthodox theologian Petros Vassiliadis explains, 'true evangelism is not aiming at bringing the nations or people of other faiths into our religious "enclosure" but seeks to "let" the Holy Spirit use both us and those to whom we bear witness to bring about the kingdom of God' (1998: 100–1). Witness and service are central to Orthodox understanding of mission, and these are exemplified in the liturgy (literally 'work of the people') which is integral to the meaning of orthodoxy (literally 'right worship') (Bria 1986).

While the other Orthodox churches were under the Ottomans, a Russian empire, centred on Moscow, emerged from the Mongol rule that had been imposed upon the Rus since 1240. Under the Mongols the church had held the Russian peoples together, particularly through the monasteries, which were closely integrated into community life. An alternative spirituality, Hesychasm ('keeping stillness'), also thrived in the fourteenth and fifteenth centuries, and it was monks and monastic communities who pioneered the expansion of Russian settlement 600 miles north of Moscow to the White Sea. Since Rome was regarded as heretical and Constantinople as infidel, having capitulated to the Turks, the Russian Orthodox Church began to see itself and the nation as the sole remaining protector of Orthodoxy, and Moscow as 'the Third Rome'. The church gained a great deal of territory, despite the protests of the 'Non-possessors', and church and state became very closely integrated, especially under Ivan IV, the Terrible, in the sixteenth century. During this time Russia had largely cut itself off from both the West and the other Orthodox churches, but during the seventeenth century, and especially under Peter the Great, several Western influences came in. First, Peter's reformation of the church incorporated some additional Westernization of the political structures: the church was subordinated to the state, the patriarch was deposed, and a church council was effectively ruled by the emperor's representative. Secondly, Enlightenment learning attracted the intelligentsia of the Orthodox churches, and the seminaries borrowed Western models and taught Latin, scholastic thought and rationalism. However, the rise of Romanticism convinced many intellectuals to return to the roots of their own tradition and sparked a Hesychast revival in nineteenth-century Russia based at the monastery at Optino (Hackel 2002: 551–3). The power of this mystical and eremitic spirituality based on the repetition of the 'Jesus prayer', 'Lord Jesus Christ, son of God, have mercy on me, a sinner', soon spread throughout the Orthodox world through the monasteries, including the great Greek monastic centre on Mount Athos. Thirdly, when Peter the Great expanded Russian territory over vast tracts of central Asia and Siberia as far east as the Pacific Ocean, he followed a Western model in using missions to convert conquered people. Under Catherine the Great in the late eighteenth century, the Russian empire also expanded westward to incorporate parts of the then greatly enlarged Poland, bringing in Orthodox Ukrainians and Byelorussians, whose churches the Russians incorporated into the Orthodox Church. In the mid-nineteenth century, missionaries went to evangelize Muslim tribes in the Volga and Ural regions and, following Western patterns of evangelism beyond national territory (and in accordance with national interests), by 1899 missions had been established in Persia, China, Japan and Korea, with continuing work in Alaska – by now US territory, where the Russian Orthodox Church continues to be strongly represented today. Inside Russia, the church began a Bible Society in 1814 and established various charitable organizations.

Meanwhile the other patriarchates within Turkish lands had resented the fact that the Turks gave Constantinople jurisdiction over them as well, and so at the end of the nineteenth century as the Ottoman empire gradually broke up, nationalist Greeks, Bulgarians, Serbs (with Russian support) and Romania demanded autocephalic (self-governing) status. The Greeks were first to attain it in 1821. The attempt to bring the remaining Greeks of the Ottoman empire within the Greek state led to the massacre of thousands by Turks in Smyrna in 1922, although a Greek community was allowed to remain in Constantinople with the ecumenical patriarch. In Greece today, the Orthodox Church is strongly supported by the state, and Greeks are overwhelmingly Orthodox. After the First World War, the collapse of the Russian and German empires led to new Orthodox churches coming into being in Poland, Finland, Lithuania, Latvia and Estonia, some linked to Constantinople and others to Moscow, and the Orthodox world became largely a collection of national churches. The rise of national churches has left the Ecumenical Patriarch in Constantinople with very limited jurisdiction, and the Turkish authorities now question the patriarchate's status and presence.

Despite Peter the Great's attempts at Westernization, in the nineteenth century the Russian Orthodox Church, burdened by state bureaucracy and suffering from corruption, tended to maintain tradition without relating it to modernity. As the twentieth century dawned, there was widespread anticlericalism, fuelled by the westernized and Marxist-influenced intelligentsia. However, in 1917 on the eve of the Bolshevik revolution the Russian Church took advantage of the weakness of the government to put in place the vision of *sobornost'* which the theologian Aleksei Khomiakov had outlined in the nineteenth century: a conciliar administration of patriarch, bishops, clergy and laity, in recognition that tradition is 'guarded by the totality, by the whole people of the Church, which is the Body of Christ'. Events later that year meant that most of these plans were never implemented. The new state espoused militant atheism and persecuted the church to an unprecedented extent. By the beginning of the Second World War there was not a single monastery or convent left, barely 100 places of worship were left open in the whole country, and hundreds of thousands of Christians had been liquidated (Hackel 2002: 552, 558). The church was forced into silence in public; its life was limited to cultic activities at the most; its icons were burned. Nevertheless, at the height of Stalin's purges in 1937, millions in the Soviet Union risked their livelihoods and lives to answer 'yes' to a census question asking whether they believed in God. Only with Soviet entry into the Second World War did the government recognize the patriotic value of the church, which came out in support of the state and thereby bought itself some reprieve. Orthodox churches also suffered under Fascism. During the Second World War, Orthodox Serbs in Croatia were forcibly converted to Catholicism as part of a policy of genocide, and 350,000 who resisted were slaughtered. In the aftermath of the Second World War, many more European Christians found themselves under Communist regimes. Particularly during Nikita Khrushchev's rule, repression was renewed in the Union of Soviet Socialist Republics and also in the Eastern bloc, especially in Bulgaria and Romania. Christian solidarity across political borders meant that churches were one of the main means by which, during the Cold War, people of East and West could have contact with one another. The Keston Institute in Oxford monitored the abuse of human rights on the other side of the Iron Curtain, and 'Brother Andrew' (Anne van der Bijl) smuggled Bibles to underground churches. Christian delegations from Communist countries were sometimes permitted to attend conferences, but not to reveal the situation of the churches there (Walters 1999: 316). The churches of the two Germanys were able to maintain the closest contact and they jointly prepared for the unification which eventually came in 1989. In this period of enforced interiority, as the churches were 'aligned ... with Isaiah's Man of Sorrows as never before', Russian Orthodox priest and scholar Sergei Hackel testifies that worship gained 'exceptional dignity and power' (Hackel 2002: 559, 562), but with few if any young people being brought up in the church and trained for ministry the damage inflicted on the ancient religion was not to be easily undone.

Although there was influence from the West, most of the Orthodox peoples of central and eastern Europe, whether in Russia or in the Ottoman Empire, had quite a separate history from the rest of Europe. In particular, most did not experience the effects of the Enlightenment or industrial revolution to the extent that western Europeans did until, in the twentieth century, they were mediated to them through atheistic Communism. This very negative experience of modernity, together with the strength of the Orthodox tradition, maintained through centuries of minority status under Muslim rule or atheistic regimes, means that Orthodox Christians are only now, in the context of European unity, coming to terms theologically with the post-Enlightenment intellectual climate (Vassiliadou 2006: 271–2), and there are many hardline Christians who refuse any compromise with it or relations with other churches.

Roman Catholic Christianity: Christ and church

The Roman Catholic Church long pre-dates the medieval construct of 'Christendom', but involvement with Christendom has had a lasting effect on the church, which continues to reflect its structures and draw on the teaching of its Scholastics today. The basis of the theology of the church was developed by Augustine of Hippo (354–430), who was trained in Roman law, largely separately from the deliberations of the Greeks. His theology differed from that of the east most significantly in the role given to the Holy Spirit, whom he described as the 'bond of love' between the Father and the Son. Augustine began therefore from the unity of God and the church in Spirit. Acutely aware of his own sinfulness and in dispute with Pelagius, Augustine stressed the necessity of grace for salvation – or justification, which he connected particularly with the sacrifice of Christ. And in dealing with the Donatists of north Africa who criticized the Roman church for compromising its faith, Augustine defended it as made holy by the blood of Christ, and taught that outside it there was no salvation. In contrast to the Orthodox, Augustine separated the earthly city from the city of God and allowed for a world outside the church, which needed to be converted. Where the Orthodox tended to totalitarianism, Catholicism tended (contrary to its name) to exclusivism.

Rome had the greatest claim to apostolic authenticity, being associated with saints Peter and Paul, and the Catholic Church regarded itself as the only true church. Although an earlier pope had been forced to turn to Charlemagne for support, the continued political division of Europe meant that Latin Christianity was the only cohesive cultural force. As the power of the church grew in the Middle Ages, the church came out from under the protection of local lords in many parts of Europe and became a pan-(western) European body. It assumed temporal as well as spiritual powers, and the hierarchy took the initiative in Christianizing Europe, changing the laws, institutions and customs to conform more closely to the law of Christ – as they understood it. Within the boundaries of this 'notionally unbroken Christian territory', alternative forms of public worship were not permitted and idolatry, blasphemy and heresy were not tolerated (Walls 2002: 198). People were baptized into the church in childhood, and households contributed a tenth of their income, a 'tithe', to the church. In return, the church pronounced forgiveness, interceded with God for the people, and in the name of God legitimized rulers, governments and systems of justice. However, alongside the church hierarchy is the monastic tradition. In the west, church and monastery are not as closely integrated as they are in the Orthodox Church, and the spirituality of the religious orders tends to be subordinated to the theology of the church (Comblin 1989: 36–8). In the medieval period, a new form of monasticism appeared in the west. The great monasteries of the earlier period, which were, at their best, beacons of learning and culture and a source of material and medical help for the poor, were not adaptable to the needs of the growing towns, nor suitable to accompany an increasingly outgoing church. This led to the emergence of orders of friars, such as the Franciscans and Dominicans, who followed a mendicant model of ministry (cf. Lk. 10.7), and a division between church and mission which is reflected today in Protestant churches as well.

The growth in power of the church led to triumphalism, as shown by the splendour of medieval church buildings in western Europe which displayed the wealth and pomp of a church that behaved in many ways like the imperial government of Rome, which it had come to replace. The papal bull *Unam Sanctam* of Pope Boniface VIII in 1302 asserted that there was only one, holy, catholic and apostolic church, outside which there was no salvation. Christ appointed one head of that church, St Peter, and the pope is his successor, to whom all human beings must be subject if they wish to obtain salvation. Furthermore, the church has not only spiritual but also temporal power, just as Peter also held the sword (Mt. 26.52) (Irvin and Sunquist 2001: 480). With its increasing power, the church came to see itself as 'mother' to the faithful, particularly in its teaching role (Ward and Evans 1999: 110) and 'king' in its 'fullness of power' (Morris 2002: 217). It assumed an increasingly hierarchical structure, a militaristic posture and a juridical theology. The self-assertion of the church was a proclamation of a new society in Europe in which the old pagan past was rejected and the kingdom of God and millennial light (cf. Hastings 1999b: 335) was instituted on earth. But this was not only so that the people of Europe and other church leaders knew where they stood, it was also due to an external enemy. Although different Muslim empires were involved, Islam was perceived to be the enemy which had conquered many Christian lands, including near ones such as Spain, Portugal and southern Italy, and was threatening Constantinople, until it fell in 1453, and Vienna until turned back in 1683. It was the spread of Islamic rule that turned Europe into 'Christianity's main base' (Davies 1996: 257) for the next thousand years. And it was while fighting together in the Crusades, away from their own communities, that Europeans began to express a common identity as 'westerners', 'Christians' or members of 'Christendom'.

At first, Europeans viewed Islam as a new heresy that needed correction by the church for its denial of the crucifixion and Christian beliefs such as the Trinity, and its rejection of the authority of the church. But Islam defined itself over against Christianity (and Judaism) as the pure faith of Abraham and God's last testament with humanity, and so gradually Christians came to regard Islam as lying outside the Christian tradition altogether. By the logic of Christendom therefore, Muslims had no place in Christian territory, and rulers anxious to channel the energies of the warrior class encouraged Christians to participate in driving Muslim rulers out of what had once been Christian lands, beginning with the Iberian peninsula and Sicily. Christian rulers fought these campaigns in the name of Christ and received the church's blessing, but when in 1095 Pope Urban II called for a military campaign under the sign of the cross to recover the Holy Land because 'God wills it', this marked an unprecedented step, as for the first time war was made part of the task of the church – and Augustine's distinction between the church and the kingdom of God was lost (Burrows 1996: 123). Material gain was a major incentive for many crusading knights, but the series of crusades over two centuries were supported by the populations of Europe for religious reasons: as a form of pilgrimage (Johns 2002: 177) and 'the ultimate form of penance' (Irvin and Sunquist 2001: 396). The church very soon lost control of crusaders' activities, and all manner of atrocities were committed against Muslims and Jews in the name of Christianity in an episode that continues to bring disgrace to the name of Christ and the symbol of the cross. The ongoing political fallout in a globalized world is often not appreciated by Christian missionaries, who identify their organizations or activities as a 'crusade', although several international organizations have taken steps to change this designation in recent years.

The Crusaders had not intended to convert Muslims, and indeed hardly any such attempt seems to have been made until the thirteenth century (Armour 2002: 87), when Francis of Assisi, who was known for his holy life, extended his preaching to include Muslims. Since they did not respond and the only result was Christian martyrdoms, in the fifteenth century the Franciscan John of Segovia suggested a shift in Christian–Muslim relations from the goal of conversion to encouraging dialogue about matters of mutual concern and an emphasis on the common ground shared by the two faiths. Ironically, it was during the Crusades that Arab learning, building on the ancient civilizations of the Mediterranean and West Asia, was filtering into the universities established (on an Arab model) in Spain. The great Scholastic theologian Thomas Aquinas drew on Arabic translations of Aristotle as well as Arabic scholarship itself. Aquinas' distinction between natural law, deduced from empirical evidence, and God's law, made known by revelation, allowed him to benefit from Islamic learning while also arguing against Islam itself, and laid the foundations for secular scientific enquiry.

The final crusade ended in 1291, and there was no significant European presence in the Holy Land again until the twentieth century, although Eastern Christians continued to live there. However, not only had Islam been decisive for European identity (Davies 1996: 258), it also shaped the medieval church and aspects of Catholic theology. The crusading mentality continued in western Christendom in two ways. First, it was turned inward against Jews and heretics within Europe and against new groups deemed heretical, such as the Waldensians in Italy and the Cathars in south-eastern France. In the fifteenth century, the pope was supported in repressive measures by the rulers of the European powers: Spain and Portugal. The Inquisition was set up by Queen Isabella of Spain initially to root out Jews, but this was soon extended to exposing all heresy. When biblical justification of force was called for, it was found in Lk. 14.23, where the disciples are to go to the poor of 'the highways and byways' and 'compel them to come in'. At the turn of the twelfth century, Dominic Guzmán tried an alternative way to counteract heresy: by preaching in word and by demonstrating a pure Christian life in deed. The Dominicans, or Order of Preachers, developed a theology that stressed the connection between reason and faith, and therefore promoted scholarship, but they also became heavily involved with the Inquisition. Second, the crusading mentality was harnessed to spread Christianity, especially to the territories which emerging European nations were gaining in Africa and the Americas after discovering alternative ways of reaching Asia. That the last Muslim kingdom in Iberia fell in 1492, the same year as Columbus was looking for Asia, underlines the way in which the Portuguese acquisition of colonies in Africa (from 1415) and the Spanish conquest of the Americas were, in their minds, a continuation of the *reconquista*.

In the next few centuries, the growth of Europe as a world power and of Christianity across the world went largely hand in hand. The aggressive seizure of the lands of Latin America cannot be blamed on Spain and Portugal alone. It was, as Latin American church historian Enrique Dussel points out, part of a greater European enterprise as part of the mercantile economy which developed into the global capitalism of today (1990: 32–3). It was also the product of an older feudal system in which the earthly lords and the Lord God were believed to be working together for the furtherance of the honour of both (Dussel 1990: 36). During the overthrow of the Moorish kingdoms, the *conquistadores* were rewarded by being granted (by the Spanish or Portuguese crown) the conquered land and the labour of those living in it, 'in trust' (*encomienda*). The same applied in the Americas (Wiarda 2001: 57, 63) and on a global scale. *Encomienda* also became the basis of the system of 'patronage' set up in the sixteenth century to stop the squabbling of Spain and Portugal over territory, when Pope Alexander VI drew a line on the world map from the North to the South Pole, declaring that colonies to the east of it, including Brazil and Africa, were under the jurisdiction of Portugal and those to the west belonged to Spain. The papacy was left with almost no power in the newly discovered lands; the monarchs were not only given sovereignty but also charged with baptizing the people, incorporating them into the Christian church. Missionary priests – mainly Franciscans and Dominicans at first, with their corresponding women's orders – were used to Christianize new territories before the church was established.

There was no shortage of recruits, as sixteenth-century Spain saw a renewal of spirituality which produced famous mystics including John of the Cross, Teresa of Avila and Ignatius Loyola (founder of the Jesuits) (Hastings 1999b: 329). At Spain's new universities, neo-Scholastics defended the conquest by appeal to Aristotle and natural law, to which the church and theology were subordinated (Richard 1990: 63). They argued that the indigenous people were 'slaves by nature', and justified armed conquest and subjugation. This approach was translated by missionaries into the *tabula rasa* or 'clean slate' approach, eradicating the expression of traditional customs and beliefs in order to inculcate what they believed was the Christian way of life. However, many missionary friars and some bishops tried hard to protect the people from the predations of the colonists and traders, and protested the treatment of the indigenous people (Gutiérrez 1990: 2, 5; Salinas 1990). The most outstanding example was Bartholomé de las Casas, who campaigned for the rights of the Indians for fifty years. Francisco de Vitoria at the University of Salamanca provided academic grounding for Las Casas' work, both by producing an evaluation of Indian culture and by disputing that the conquest constituted a 'just war'. Some justice was obtained for the Indians – although much too late – but Vitoria's work laid the groundwork for the later development of European concepts of human rights. When the drastic decline in the Indian population led to a shortage of labour, there was no comparable debate in Europe about whether Africans could be enslaved. Already the myth that Africans were the descendants of Ham, who was apparently cursed by his father Noah to be the 'lowest of slaves' (Gen. 9.18–29; 10.6), allowed for a biblical justification to be made for the practice, and led to the development of the anthropology of the 'negro' as suitable for slavery because they were savage and barbarous (Hurbon 1990: 91, 96).

By the sixteenth century, new powers were emerging in Europe north of the

Alps, in Holland, France, Britain and the princedoms of Germany. The papacy was weak, increasingly Italian and unable to correct obvious abuses of religion, and yet the church demanded allegiance and commanded huge wealth that was the envy of secular rulers and accrued from exploitation of the peasants. The uncompromising church could not relate to the aspirations of the people of northern Europe, who were experiencing the beginnings of the capitalist economy, increasingly well informed by printed material, and craving for self-determination. Peasant uprisings, new religious movements and outspoken criticism of the church signalled the rise of Protestantism. In response to the crisis of the Reformation, the 'counter-' or 'Catholic' Reformation initiated at the Council of Trent (1545–63) refuted Protestant doctrine. Although it recognized the biblical testimony as to the priority of grace and the response of faith for justification, it stressed the ongoing dimension of justification and the importance of the tradition of the church for salvation. With regard to the church's inner life, new disciplines were imposed and abuses stopped, but with regard to the outside, the council signalled a restoration, which affirmed the unique sacramental role of the Catholic Church and the authority of its hierarchy (Küng 1995: 483, 493). Furthermore, this restoration was implemented politically and militarily where possible, with disastrous results for the peace of Europe.

In this time of Catholic renewal, several new religious orders were founded, including the Society of Jesus or Jesuits, which Ignatius, a former soldier, conceived on a military model, although the military exercises and battles were now conducted on a 'spiritual' plane. Highly educated men in a central organization engaged with contemporary philosophy in Europe and also constituted a mobile and flexible 'force' to be 'sent' – the Jesuits were the first to use the term 'mission' in this sense – by the pope (not a local ruler) wherever in the world they were needed. The main theatre of Jesuit activity outside Europe was Asia, where conditions were very different from those in the Americas. European conquest of the great empires of Moghul India or China was not (at this time) considered, much less attempted, therefore 'it was necessary to accommodate the Christendom idea to political and military reality' (Walls 2002: 199). Through Alessandro Valignano in the sixteenth century, 'the gentle way', which required missionaries to explain the Christian gospel in a manner appropriate to the cultural context, became Jesuit policy in Asia, and in 1622 the church set up the new Sacred Congregation for the Propagation of the Faith to try to stop mission activity being perceived as an arm of foreign power. Following this policy, Matteo Ricci identified with the

Confucian scholars, or literati, in China. However, Ricci's decision that the Confucian practice of ancestor veneration was a social rather than a religious act, and therefore compatible with Christian faith, was criticized in the seventeenth century, particularly by Dominican missionaries entering China who saw it as a compromise with pagan religions. When these concerns were taken back to Europe they erupted into what became known as the 'Rites Controversy', which pitted the Portuguese Jesuits against French Jansenists, who were much more negative toward human nature and culture. Pope Clement XI's decision in 1715 against the rites contributed eventually to papal suppression of the whole Jesuit order for forty years from 1773. The Rites Controversy shows that in addition to the paradigm of 'missionary war' (Bosch 1991: 236) followed by the church both within and outside Europe, there was another paradigm of 'radical inculturation' (Burrows 1996) at work, which followed the Apostle Paul's advice to be 'all things to all people' (1 Cor. 9.22). This broke away from the Rome-centred, or Eurocentric, mindset and, anticipating the 'culture principle' of later cultural anthropology, approached other societies and new movements 'from within' (Bevans and Schroeder 2004: 203). Of course, this accommodation depended on the separation Jesuits perceived between what was 'cultural' and 'religious'; there was no accommodation in the latter sphere. Though the church hierarchy rejected inculturation, William Burrows argues that the 'radical inculturation paradigm' continued to be widely practised by Catholic workers on the ground, until eventually it resurfaced in the twentieth century (1996: 131).

Protestant Christianity: Bible and society

In the face of an inflexible church, the people of northern Europe inculturated the gospel for themselves in a new theology and a new form of church known as Protestantism, in which many of the new churches were closely linked to their different linguistic, ethnic and national identities. The Protestant paradigm, as articulated by Martin Luther, an Augustinian monk, in Germany beginning in 1517, did not depart from the juridical approach of Augustine and Scholastic theology, or from the Catholic doctrines of the Trinity and Christology, but it took a new source of authority. Luther opposed the teaching of the pope with that of the Christian Scriptures (*sola scriptura*).

Reading Paul's letter to the Romans in the context of the church's sale of indulgences, Luther argued that salvation was the free gift of God, received by faith alone, and therefore not dependent on human effort or accumulated merit (*sola gratia*). Unlike the medieval Scholastics, who had great confidence in human ability, particularly human reason, Luther returned to the theology of Augustine and stressed the complicity of all human beings in the sin of Adam. He emphasized that, in Christ, God had acted unilaterally to restore the sinner to relationship with Godself. All that was necessary for salvation, therefore, was for the individual to receive the free gift of salvation by an act of free will and personal trust in Jesus Christ ('justification by faith'; *sola fide*). This personal act was essentially independent of the church; justification was on the basis of the completed work of Jesus Christ rather than any ongoing sacrifice ('the priesthood of all believers'). He clarified therefore that it is not the role of the church to grant salvation, but primarily to give instruction as to how salvation may be received and lived out. Consequently, Protestants reduced the sacramental role of the church and priesthood, laying emphasis on the priest's role in preaching the Word of God. Although Protestants formed new churches, they continued to believe – like Catholics – that the doctrine they held was absolutely true and universally applicable (Bosch 1991: 240). For leading Reformers it was not the Bible itself but its interpretation by church leaders educated and ordained in their Reformation tradition that was binding on the faithful, but other more radical leaders gave greater freedom to the Spirit and to individual interpretation, and therefore the biblical text itself assumed greater importance.

When the reforms suggested proved unacceptable to the Catholic Church, the Reformers became hostages as European monarchs and local rulers assumed responsibility for reforming the church, and at the same time submitted it to their jurisdiction. Since leadership of the Protestant churches was bound up with the interests of local powers, and neither could conceive that there could be more than one true church or one true doctrine within a defined territory, Catholic rulers persecuted Protestants and vice versa, and Europe entered a period of wars, which devastated life and property across the western part of the continent from Britain to Poland and Germany to Italy for more than a century. Since each ruler took a particular religious view, these were later dubbed 'Wars of Religion'. Eventually a workable solution was found in the Peace of Westphalia in 1648, by which each region should follow the religion of its ruler. So England was recognized as Anglican, Scotland as Presbyterian, Scandinavia as Lutheran, Poland, France, Austria and lands to the south as Catholic, parts of the Netherlands and Switzerland as Reformed, and most other German-speakers as under Lutheran rule. As this suggests, these 'established' churches maintained a close relationship between church and state. In most cases, church taxes were collected by the state, clergy paid by the state and appointments controlled by the state.

Despite the close church–state relationship, the Peace of Westphalia was the first 'breach' of the principle of Christendom (Walls 2002: 211); in fact, as nation-states grew, Christianity became increasingly nationalized. The only self-consciously trans-national churches were the Roman Catholic Church and some radical Protestants such as the Anabaptists who, as their name implies, did not accept the validity of the baptism of the Roman Catholic or any other church, and insisted that believers be baptized again. They were seen as a particular threat because they wandered, in family and community groups, trans-nationally across Europe, preaching the gospel in obedience, believing that 'the earth is the Lord's, and all that is in it' (Ps. 24.1). This attitude infuriated the leaders of the established churches, who regarded the Anabaptists as encroaching on their territory (Bosch 1991: 245–7; Walls 2002: 37). As well as breaching the territorial unity of Christendom, the Peace of Westphalia also signalled an important stage in the secularization of Europe. International relations were no longer conducted on the basis of religion; the state was the dominant actor (Thomas 2005: 33). Furthermore, the understanding was that the established churches would support their state and curb any religious enthusiasm that might disturb the peace of Europe. Dissenters, radicals and independents who set up their own churches and interpreted the Bible in their own way were dealt with ruthlessly as enemies of the state, and those who did not conform to the established religion were denied opportunities for government service. The search for freedom to practise the religion of their choice was the reason many groups migrated to North America in the seventeenth and eighteenth centuries. The effect of the Reformation was to establish separate churches in Europe which defined themselves (or redefined themselves in the case of Catholicism) against one another, rather than in terms of the world in which they were set (Bosch 1991: 248–9). The antagonized differences between Catholics and Protestants were exacerbated by the politicization of religion, and any possibility of an early reconciliation was prevented by the structure of the nation-states. The Protestant churches understood themselves as maintaining and correcting the faith of the nation in which they were established. They renounced violence as a means of Christianization, and relied instead on the proclaimed Word of God to effect the change they expected to see in individuals and – especially in the case of John Calvin – the transformation of society.

From the turn of the eighteenth century a series of movements of religious renewal among Protestants led to new initiatives not always under the direct authority of the national churches. Because they deepened the faith of those involved, the revivals brought them together and separated them in this respect from others who had not experienced renewal. So these movements for 'real' Christianity challenged the assumption that everyone within Christendom was Christian, and also encouraged trans-national – and therefore trans-church – activities, and even churches (cf. Walls 2002: 211–14). Some of these activities were directed locally and others globally, but the same individuals tended to be involved. The first type of renewal movement was Pietism in the seventeenth century, a movement which 'combined the joy of a personal experience of salvation with an eagerness to proclaim the gospel of redemption to all' (Bosch 1991: 252). Beginning from the work of Philipp Jakob Spener within the Lutheran church of Germany, it spread across northern Europe, and also overseas, beginning in Tranquebar, South India. Pietism marked the emergence in Protestantism of Christian organizations – at first within the churches, but separate from their hierarchies and with alternative sources of funding. These took the form of voluntary societies, which became the Protestant, activist equivalent of the religious orders, which could address the shortcomings and limitations of the church. They are typical of Protestant missionary method – both as part of and parallel to denominational structures – to the present day (Walls 1996: 241–54). The catalyst for this development was the need of the church overseas, and the first examples were the societies set up in 1699 and in 1701 by Thomas Bray, an Anglican clergyman, to propagate Christian knowledge (SPCK) and the gospel (SPG) 'in foreign parts'; that is, among the inhabitants of the American colonies, both Europeans and Native Americans and slaves (O'Connor 2000: 11, 21), the link between religion and territory being maintained (Bosch 1991: 244–5; Walls 1996: 246). Bray's missionaries were ordained clergy, always men, and – unlike Catholic priests – usually married with families.

The second type of renewal movement, known as Evangelicalism, was influenced by Pietism but became a transatlantic phenomenon. The 'Evangelical revival' in Britain (1735–45) was led by John Wesley and George Whitefield, both Anglican priests, who carried it to the USA. Wesley's Anglo-Catholic faith led him to seek spiritual perfection by self-denial, and so he dedicated himself to serve with SPG in the American colony of Georgia. Crossing the Atlantic on the boat home after only three years, feeling he had failed, Wesley was impressed by the spiritual vitality of a group of Moravian missionaries – a Pentecostal-type group, the result of an intense and radical revival. Through them he experienced for himself a more 'affective' or emotional expression of faith. Returning to ministry in Britain, Wesley's passion became to revive the Church of England, which he saw was failing to reach and care for the urban poor. His watchword, 'the world is my parish', referred primarily to his challenge to the established church, but it also signalled a willingness to 'go into all the world', which Evangelicals later put into practice, and a catholic spirituality. The direct effect of Wesley's work was Methodism, which separated from the Church of England (in the American colonies and then in Britain) and became another Protestant denomination, so named because of the methodical prayer and Bible study in small groups that the Methodists organized. Unlike the others, it was not the established church of any nation. Evangelicals in general, in awareness of personal sinfulness, practised a strict moral code and, grateful for the grace of God shown in Jesus Christ, they sought to share the good news by preaching, teaching and taking practical steps to improve society. Pietism and Evangelicalism 'conditioned the earnestness of what in England was called the Victorian ethos' (O. Chadwick 2002: 351). And the voluntary societies they established were quintessentially modern in their structures and their pragmatic outlook.

Modern Europe: cross and flag

Modernity is a complex phenomenon, the result of social, scientific and industrial revolutions led by northern European peoples, mainly French, British and German, but resourced by lands far from Europe. Although developments in Europe profoundly influenced other parts of the world, Europe also absorbed ideas from elsewhere (for examples see Ramachandra 2006: 219–22) and was changed by them. Medieval church scholarship and the encouragement to literacy and intellectual freedom encouraged by the Protestant Reformation may both be regarded as contributing to the emergence of modernity but, although the established churches continued to be powerful institutions for most of this period, they were now subject to secular rulers; and in the development of science and philosophy on a secular basis, the initiative moved away from Christians, who were increasingly put on the defensive. Modernity brought new challenges for the (now several) churches of Europe, particularly in terms of their task, thought and morality.

The form of European faith which most thrived in early modernity was Evangelicalism. Further transatlantic Evangelical revivals or awakenings continued into the mid-nineteenth century and resulted in a loose grouping of denominations or groups within denominations who identified themselves as 'Evangelicals' and shared four common characteristics: (1) conversionism: the need for individual change of life – being 'born again' – because of sin; (2) activism: through evangelistic and missionary efforts; (3) biblicism: attaching a special importance to the Bible as authority for belief and conduct; and (4) crucicentrism: belief in Christ's death on the cross as of central significance for human salvation (Bebbington 1989: 2–17). Each revival produced a new wave of voluntary societies for work at home and overseas. The most prominent social result of the first revival was the abolitionist movement. British Quakers, a breakaway group from the English Puritans, in the late eighteenth century formed a loose coalition with the Clapham Sect, a group of Anglican Evangelical activists, and others including freed slaves such as Olaudah Equiano (Eversley 2004). Even after William Wilberforce steered a bill for the abolition of slave-holding through Parliament in 1807, the campaign continued in order to eradicate slave-trading, and spread across the world, becoming a major motive for nineteenth-century missionary activity, particularly in Africa. Abolitionists from Britain and the US established the two west African colonies of Sierra Leone (1787) and Liberia (1822) (respectively) as homelands for freed slaves. They then tried to penetrate the interior to improve conditions for Africans so that there would no longer be any economic incentive for slave-trading, and also to reach with Christianity populations who might otherwise become Muslims (Robinson 2004: 71; Sanneh 2000; Ward 1999: 231). The campaigns against slavery were closely linked with movements to bring the slave-holders and other colonists to the Evangelical faith (because they would then give up slavery) and to bring the gospel of liberation to the enslaved and others in the colonies.

A second Evangelical revival at the end of the eighteenth century led to a mushrooming of voluntary societies for overseas mission. Among the European societies were the London Missionary Society (1795), the Church Missionary Society (1799), the British and Foreign Bible Society (1804), the Netherlands Missionary Society (1797), the Basel Mission (1816), the Danish Missionary Society (1821), the Berlin Missionary Society (1824), the Swedish Missionary Society (1835) and the North German Missionary

Society (1836). But the archetypal 'modern mission' is the Baptist Missionary Society (Stanley 1992), founded in 1792 by William Carey who then went to India as its first missionary. Carey argued that explorers, traders and missionaries of other churches were already going overseas, and in the wake of the advances in knowledge and technology of the Enlightenment, it must be practically possible to do; and also that modern Christians were mandated by Jesus' Commission to the first apostles (Mt. 28.18–20) to take the gospel to 'all nations'. Being a Baptist who rejected the established church, by which Baptists had only been tolerated since 1689, Carey's aim was not to revive the faith of the colonists but to convert people and found new separate local churches, only loosely linked together. These churches would then be more dependent on the mission than the parent denomination. Carey's ministry was ambitious, typical of the era and centred on a compound in the Danish colony of Serampore. This exemplified 'Christian' or European living, provided a safe haven for converts and accommodated Carey's work. This comprised codifying Indian languages, Bible translation, printing, and initiatives in education, healthcare and agriculture. Such voluntary societies, in which the Bible did not always go with the flag (Stanley 1990), were much less easily contained by the Protestant churches than the religious orders of the Catholic model (which were formed within some Protestant denominations as well). The autonomy of the societies, combined with the nation-bound nature of most Protestant churches, led to a greater separation between church and overseas missions than was possible in the Catholic Church, in which the church outside Europe was an extension of the one church.

In 1865, under the influence of the Holiness revival movement of the late nineteenth century, James Hudson Taylor, a member of the independent Brethren, founded the first of a new generation of 'Faith Missions', the China Inland Mission (now OMF International). Taylor introduced a number of innovations (Fielder 1994: 33). For example, the society was non-denominational but required missionaries to sign a statement of faith; the aim of the mission was not to plant churches but only to convert individuals, and then leave it to them to organize churches; his society would not clash with established missions by soliciting funds but would be supplied 'by faith alone'; it undertook a specialist task where there was not already a church – in this case, mission to inland China; calling rather than qualifications qualified the missionary; missionaries were expected to identify with the people, so as not to put any unnecessary barriers in the way of the gospel; single women and wives were treated as co-workers; and Taylor insisted that the work in

China should not be directed from London but on the ground in China. Soon other independent societies were begun to do specialized mission work in particular regions, such as the North Africa Mission (1881) and the Sudan Interior Mission (1900), which borrowed from Taylor's methods. The Faith Missions were particularly influenced by a pre-millennialist theology that the world would soon be destroyed and only believers would be saved – hence Taylor was not greatly concerned about long-term civilization. The divide that opened up at the end of the nineteenth century between 'evangelism' and 'social action' was reflected in the different structures of the Faith Missions, which grew particularly in the United States, and the denominational agencies.

Carey epitomized the modern Protestant mission paradigm (Bosch 1991: 239–43), which began with awareness of the need of the 'heathen', who were regarded as calling out for Europeans to 'come over and help us' (Acts 16.9), and the motive of obedience to 'the Great Commission'. Although missionaries were the first cultural anthropologists, and were instrumental in preserving cultures and languages threatened by globalizing forces, they generally intended to use that knowledge to persuade people to convert, and, with notable exceptions, the two activities of converting and civilizing were largely synonymous because Pietistic Christian faith had strong implications for moral behaviour and way of living. Missionaries were increasingly co-opted by colonial governments as a cheap way of 'civilizing' their populations by providing education and healthcare, and introducing Western standards of hygiene, agricultural methods and other technologies. Whereas some missionaries challenged colonial policy, most, as people of their time, did not question colonialism itself. Earlier Catholic and Protestant missions had been more willing to ordain local people as clergy. In the first half of the nineteenth century, Henry Venn of the Church Missionary Society developed the 'three-self' missionary strategy. Under this plan, local churches established by missions were encouraged to be self-governing, self-supporting and self-propagating, eventually obviating the need for missionaries and leading to the 'euthanasia of the mission'. However, under the influence of social Darwinism, and as even the culture of China began to crumble before the onslaught of modernity, with notable exceptions later missionaries increasingly doubted the character and ability of 'the natives'. Furthermore, having better resources, more personnel and the long view of the imperialist, they did not regard indigenization as a priority. Missionaries, who were portrayed as heroes at home, also neglected to give credit to the role of local evangelists in the growth of churches overseas. A rare protest against colonialism in the church came from Roland Allen, an SPG missionary in China, who unfarourably compared contemporary mission methods to the pattern established by the apostle Paul, whose confidence in the power of the Holy Spirit to guide new believers, and willingness to let them discover their new faith for themselves, contrasted strongly with the paternalism of the missions (Allen 1956).

Protestant societies first emerged at a time when Catholic missionary activity was not so strong because of the weakening of Spain and Portugal, the suppression of the Jesuits and other factors. However, at the beginning of the nineteenth century a renewal of Catholic mission was stimulated particularly by the revival of French spirituality – in the form of devotion to the Sacred Heart, the Virgin Mary and the Sacrament – and French political power in the Napoleonic era. New French missionary orders were founded for men and for women, such as the Society of the Sacred Heart (1800), the Sisters of St Joseph of Cluny (1807) and the Oblates of Mary Immaculate (1816–26). Other developments were the restoration of the Jesuit order in 1814, the reconstitution of the SCPF in 1817 and the renewal of older congregations such as the Franciscans and Dominicans. From 1831 until the turn of the century, a series of popes supported modern mission work (Bevans and Schroeder 2004: 222), which was no longer limited to Catholic-ruled places, but planted churches as well as evangelized society. And the second half of the nineteenth century saw the founding of another raft of new Catholic organizations, including the Spiritans (1848), Comboni Fathers (1864) and the White Fathers (1868). With so many different groups in the 'mission fields', there was inevitably competition between them in some regions. These problems tended to be worked out locally by a system of 'comity', or agreement between the mainline groups to divide up territory and work in different areas. The inter-denominational (Protestant) missionary conference at Edinburgh in 1910 to discuss cooperation on the 'mission field' (i.e. outside Europe) led eventually to closer working relationships between the churches in Europe. Almost all the organizations mentioned in this section still exist today, some in a modified form, and the paradigms they grew out of still manifest themselves.

Modern Europe: faith and reason

British church historian Owen Chadwick sees the experience of the churches in Europe in the nineteenth and twentieth centuries as one of 'attack' and 'persecution', which undermined their confidence as bearers of Christianity to other parts of the world (2002: 349). Those which had authority and privileges saw them stripped away in the interests of progress and commerce, and in some cases misrepresentation, suppression and outright persecution were used against Christians to advance vested interests. The churches deserved much of the criticism directed against them for their collusion with unjust government, self-interested attempts to preserve their privileges, abuse of the trust placed in them, intransigence, lack of respect for popular opinion, and attempts to gain popularity at the expense of truth. However, they were also the victims of ideological and commercial agendas. Whatever the rights and wrongs of the matter, in many respects the churches felt themselves to be under attack; they found themselves marginalized in public life, and on the defensive. The 'attack' was first on the church's doctrines and then on its morals. Both were challenged by the rise of modernity: doctrine by the new intellectual approaches of modern science, and morality by the new social context of democracy and capitalism.

The effect of the Enlightenment, or Age of Reason, on the European elite (the thinking of the peasants was probably little affected (Heimann 1999: 461)) was profound. In western Europe, the self-proclaimed 'enlightened ones' of the seventeenth century blamed the turmoil of wars since the Reformation on something called 'religion', which was increasingly separated from public life and was defined by the Peace of Westphalia as a body of beliefs rather than as a religious community (Thomas 2005: 25). The solution to European problems and the means to achieve 'tolerance' was therefore deemed to lie in playing down the differences in doctrines of Catholicism and Protestantism and emphasizing the developments in empirical science that seemed to offer 'universal truths' that all 'rational men' would be bound to agree upon. However, since scientific method could not prove any of the basic Christian creedal statements of the incarnation and exaltation of Jesus Christ, the lowest common denominator of Deism was all that was left for Enlightenment thinkers; Christian doctrines became matters of conjecture and could not be classed among the 'facts' on which all must agree. Furthermore, the Enlightenment subtly altered the basis of Western thought, putting it out of step with almost every other society in the world. No longer was religion assumed true unless proved otherwise; by the nineteenth century the burden of proof had shifted from the doubter to the believer (Heimann 1999: 458, 466–70).

Further intellectual challenges for Christians arose in the nineteenth century. The opening of the universe to scientific investigation and its explanation in terms of laws which did not need recourse to God removed the category of the 'sacred' from philosophical thought. The Bible and the church were demystified and laid open to study not only by the methods developed within Christian tradition but by secular methods of historical science. When the Bible was read, along with other ancient texts, by F. C. Bauer and others of the Tübingen school, what struck the scientific eye tended to be internal contradictions, uneven style and unprovable claims rather than God-given truth and guidance. Charles Darwin's *The Origin of Species* removed the need for belief in God one stage further by filling in many of the 'gaps' for which God had been invoked before and providing scientific explanation for the 'wonders of creation'. His *The Descent of Man* reduced human beings to the purely material and questioned the existence of what Christians called 'the soul'. 'Natural theology' was now replaced by 'natural science' or just 'Science' (with a capital 'S') (Heimann 1999: 497), and this seemed to be in opposition to something called 'religion', which was as obscure and subjective as Science was clear and objective.

In the face of aggressive scientism, which declared Christianity to be 'untrue', or at best superseded by science, Christians took refuge in one of four positions: traditionalism and modernism, evangelicalism and liberalism. The first two were most pronounced in Catholicism and the second pair in Protestantism. In the strong climate of anticlericalism in France, French Roman Catholic theologians were the first to question the motives of 'the Lights'. Discussion centred on whether or not miracles occurred. The Archbishop of Lyons, A. de Malvin de Montazet, argued that scientists who dismissed miracles on the grounds that the laws of nature could not be broken were not being objective and examining the historical evidence, and further refined the methods for verifying reported miracles (Heimann 1999: 471). The challenges of biblical criticism and the theory of evolution were not as threatening to Catholic theology, which was based first and foremost on the traditions of the church, and which acknowledged an ongoing revelation. Catholic traditionalists therefore defended the church and its historic teaching from what was also an attack on its political power. The church asserted its doctrinal authority and further centralized power in the Vatican. In the 1864 *Syllabus of Errors* the church declared itself against most aspects of the modern world, and at the first Vatican Council in 1869–70 Ultramontanists triumphed when the Pope was declared 'infallible'. Catholic theologians who wished to uphold the faith but in dialogue with the modern world were regarded with the suspicion that they were falling into agnosticism, and in 1907 Pius X labelled them 'modernists'. The future John XXIII, later to open the church to modernity, was cast under a cloud in this period.

While many Catholics retreated into church tradition and looked to the authority of the pope to support them, Protestants read their Bibles and rediscovered aspects of the experience of the early church in the movements known as Pietism, Methodism and Evangelicalism. These movements, like Romanticism, represented a rejection of dependence on reason as the only arbiter of truth. Rather than law or logic, they stressed the unpredictable and the amazing work of God. However, they did not reject reason altogether, but to the sources for theology recognized by Enlightenment thinkers – scripture, tradition and reason – they added the category of experience (the 'Wesleyan quadrilateral'). Pietists and Evangelicals tended to separate life into different spheres: a natural world, in which the laws of nature pertained, and a spiritual world in which God intervened directly in matters to do with morality, guidance and personal salvation (Hilton 1988: 8, 16–17). Methodism particularly gave rise to all sorts of 'enthusiastic' behaviour, often among the new industrial working class, the apparent irrationality of which called forth scorn from the 'enlightened' establishment, who were supposedly tolerant. There were similarities between the behaviour of the Protestant Evangelicals and the Jansenists in the Roman Catholic world. It was not only the uncontrolled behaviour of the latter and their unreasonable assertions of untested miraculous occurrences which caused their suppression by the church authorities in the 1730s. The Jansenists also taught that the philosophies of the Enlightenment were 'pagan' and anti-Christian.

The strength of the initial reaction of Western church leaders against the movements of the Spirit showed the extent to which they were under pressure in eighteenth-century society to conform to Enlightenment reason. However, the shock felt by the establishment at the horrors of the French Revolution, which attempted the complete overthrow of traditional society, de-Christianization and construction of a new society based on pure reason – and in which hundreds of priests and lay Christians were killed – drove those European elites who remained in power back into the arms of religion. For leaders of Protestant nations – Christian and Deist – the faith, and especially the morality, of the Spiritual and Evangelical movements offered an attractive alternative to the chaos of revolution. The Evangelicals were also an essential force in the growth of the capitalist economy, as Max Weber was later to argue. For the leaders of Catholic nations, traditionalism prevailed.

During the nineteenth century European states took steps to protect their established churches as a bulwark against revolution. In France the restored empire made peace with the Roman Catholic Church, and a revival of popular spirituality followed. In Prussia in 1817, the Reformed and Lutheran churches were brought together to form a single Evangelical Church supported by the state. As well as the Evangelical movements, in England and Germany there were reactions against them, which aimed to restore a pristine version of the faith through Anglo-Catholicism (the Tractarian or Oxford movement) and neo-Lutheranism.

However, the leading Protestant theologians of Germany and Britain, who were schooled in their best universities, generally supported what was seen as 'progress' and tried to work out a compromise that took into account the latest intellectual developments while preserving as much of traditional doctrine as possible. Nineteenth-century Liberals encouraged open debate and the use of critical methods to read the Bible and examine Christian doctrines. Their faith was not undermined since, following the lead of the German thinker Friedrich Schleiermacher, they tended to play down Christian doctrine and give greater importance to the experience of faith. However, the results of their enquiry profoundly disturbed the faith of educated Christians and still trouble many today. The views arrived at about the dates of biblical writings, the authenticity of documents and what could be known about the historical Jesus were much more sceptical than the consensus now, but, more than that, the Liberal assertion that human knowledge could take precedence over biblical revelation was deeply troubling, especially to Protestants (Heimann 1999: 490). This intellectualization and rationalization of faith led to a separation between theologians and Christians in churches; causing the latter to look to other sources to sustain their daily Christian practice. Now that science began to take precedence over religion, Liberal theology became captive to its developments. Furthermore, some of the fervour once reserved for religion became transferred to science, which came to resemble a new religion and embody hopes for the future. The assertion of the pre-eminence of science over religion had a profound effect on European relationships with the rest of the world in the later nineteenth century. It formed part of the positivist philosophy that all knowledge passed through different stages of evolution before arriving at scientific knowledge. This supported the supposed superiority of European (or rational Christian) civilization and its colonization of other parts of the world that were perceived to be benighted by dark forces of irrational religion as Europe had once been.

Modern Europe: righteousness and justice

In the nineteenth century in Protestant countries, what is known in Britain as the Victorian era was one in which religion was the mark of respectability. Although the intellectual problems remained, religion was valued again as making an important moral contribution in maintaining civilized society. So it is not surprising that it was chiefly the morality of Christianity that came under attack in the late nineteenth and twentieth centuries. Karl Marx criticized religion for drugging people into quiescence and acceptance of the will of the powerful. The atheism of Bolshevism, which triumphed in Russia after the overthrow of the monarchy in 1917, and the spreading of Stalinism across eastern Europe after 1945, which caused so much suffering to Orthodox and other Christians there, tended to be used in western Europe by right-leaning governments to gain Christian support. However, many west European church people, remembering the communal sharing of the early church and the concern of Jesus for the dispossessed, were challenged by the Communist call for justice, and recognized its criticism of church complicity with oppression.

Established church leaders were also aware that the churches were barely present among the urban poor, especially in the newly industrialized cities of Europe. Evangelical missions and Catholic religious orders responded most quickly on the ground to the call for a 'home mission' to Europe, or into the heart of what William Booth of the Salvation Army called 'darkest England'. Social church historian Hugh McLeod shows how churches in different parts of western Europe were able to bring a sense of identity and moral support not only through their religious activities but also through initiatives such as workers' cooperatives. Religious revivals also helped to establish a moral order in the new working-class communities through the temperance movement, friendly societies and a rejection of violence, gambling, drunkenness and other forms of antisocial behaviour (cf. Gal. 5. 19–21). Churches also encouraged education and facilitated it through Sunday school movements, libraries and public institutes. People turned to the churches in times of crisis, such as epidemics and war, and churches were able to build solidarity in the face of adversity (McLeod 1997: 76–83).

This practical work, both at home and overseas, was justified among Protestants in the nineteenth and early twentieth centuries by two theologies: Evangelicalism in the first part of the nineteenth century, and the 'social gospel' of the liberal theologians dominant in the late nineteenth and early twentieth centuries. What was known as 'Christian Socialism' in Britain, 'religious socialism' in continental Europe and the 'social gospel' in North America was developed under the influence of Hegelian idealism (the progress of the human spirit), Darwinian theories of evolutionary progress, and comparative religion, and in reaction to the rise of individualism in religion and society. The Anglican theologian Frederick Maurice and those who followed him were more concerned with the historical Jesus than the doctrines about him, and saw the role of the church as ushering in, or even building, the Kingdom of God or the New Jerusalem on earth (Phillips 1996: 1–8). This resulted in movements of social compassion, because Jesus Christ came to give life in all its abundance (Jn 10.10), and efforts toward social and church unity, because Christ prayed 'that they might be one' (Jn 17.21). Christian Socialists saw a unity between sacred and secular, God and humanity, and church and state through their theology of the incarnation, and so they overrode any Christian misgivings about working with government at home or the colonial authorities abroad. Between 1880 and 1940 the movement developed from alms-giving and philanthropy to organizing trades unions and social democratic political parties, and advocating state intervention abroad to protect populations. It also led to movements of pacifism and reconciliation in the aftermath of the world wars. Their altruism and ethos of service led Social Christians willingly to transfer their projects to secular authorities and to work with groups which did not share their Christian belief. In this respect, they tended to secularize Christianity, but nevertheless this was a religious movement, which understood Christian faith as service in the fulfilment of human aspirations, and fused civilization with the purposes of God in Christ.

Friedrich Nietzsche made the opposite criticism to that of Marx: that Christianity protected the weak. Under the influence of Darwinian 'survival of the fittest', Christianity was described as a 'crutch' for those unable to walk, and therefore dispensable by a mature humanity. The Roman Catholic Church particularly became a scapegoat for those pushing forward liberal democracy. In Catholic Europe, the conservative reaction to the French Revolution was so strong that further revolutions occurred in France, Sicily, Poland and the Hapsburg Empire. Across Europe the Catholic Church was feared as reactionary, dogmatic and centrally controlled, and it began to be persecuted as the enemy of the nation-state and democracy. Anticlericalism persisted in France, Spain, Portugal and Italy, and these states insisted on wresting control of education and youth movements out of its hands. In the newly united

Germany, the chancellor Otto von Bismarck's *Kulturkampf* was intended to keep Catholics out of public life, and in early-twentieth-century France Catholic schools were secularized, monks and nuns expelled, the church disestablished and its property nationalized (O. Chadwick 2002: 370). This extreme situation did not last and during the twentieth century the situation of the Catholic Church improved, especially after the Italian Fascist dictator Benito Mussolini signed the Lateran Treaty (1929), which recognized the sovereign rights of the Church within the Vatican City. Now the pope was no longer imprisoned in the Vatican without recognized international status, the Holy See began to build diplomatic relations around the world, until today the Vatican state has links to more than 170 other states.

Adolf Hitler despised both Catholic priests and Protestant pastors because he believed they had Judaized the message of (an Aryan) Jesus and were therefore the enemies of nationalism. The Nazi party at first tried to co-opt the German churches; some liberal churchmen seriously tried to reconcile Christianity and National Socialism, and Pope Pius XI made a concordat with Hitler. However, in 1934 Protestant leaders of 'the Confessing Church' opposed Hitler with the 'Barmen Declaration'. This was inspired by the neo-orthodox theology of Swiss reformed theologian Karl Barth, which was a direct challenge to liberal theology, and particularly to Schleiermacher's religion of experience, which he accused of collusion with a sinful human society. Rereading the letter to the Romans, Barth denied that human beings could reach God by means of religion and asserted that knowledge of God was only possible through God's revelation in Jesus Christ. For him this, not nature or culture, was the only starting point for theology. Barth prophetically challenged modernity with what he believed was a plausible discourse from outside it: Christology through the lens of 'biblical realism' (cf. Jensen 1997: 27). His work is widely used by Evangelicals and others (including Catholics) who wish to construct theology on the basis of Christian sources rather than 'the world', and criticized by those, often following his fellow countryman Paul Tillich, who seek to engage cultures and religions more constructively. Many individuals suffered persecution and even martyrdom as a result of the Barmen Declaration. One of these, Dietrich Bonhöffer, greatly encouraged fellow Europeans struggling to profess Christian faith in modern secular society in the postwar years, through his emphasis that the grace exhibited on the cross is never 'cheap' and by his honest wrestling with faith in a world in which God is not a given.

For West European Protestants in the first half of the twentieth century, the main struggle was against Fascism; for Orthodox Christians in eastern Europe, it was against Communism; and the Roman Catholic Church struggled on both fronts. The Catholic struggle is demonstrated in the development of Catholic social teaching over the last century (Charles 1998; Curran 2002; Deberri and Hug 2003; Dorr 1992). It began from concern for the urban poor and conditions of labour, as expressed by Leo XIII (*Rerum Novarum* 1891), and grew as a result of the involvement of Catholic priests and laity in social work through Catholic Action and more recently in international development through organizations connected with Caritas. Catholic social teaching is addressed to 'all people of good will' on the basis (established by Aquinas) that there is a 'natural law', drawn from human reason. It sets forth what the church believes to be a universal framework for human societal behaviour and relations, beginning from the understanding that all human beings have a fundamental and equal dignity because they are made in the image of God and are social beings, who live in community with others as children of the same heavenly Father, and in relationship with the whole creation. It begins with economics and a concern for the poor, and proceeds on the basis that 'the goods of this world', given by God, 'are originally meant for all'. It does not oppose the present capitalist system as a whole but it encourages private property only as a way of safeguarding the earth's resources for all, and the individual accumulation of wealth only as part of human development. It opposes both economic collectivism and individualism, criticizing Socialism and Marxism for failing to recognize the sacredness of the human person, and liberalistic capitalism for neglecting the social aspects of the human person. The political implications of this approach are: to affirm the state which exists to bring about public well-being and private prosperity; to respect different levels of society in the principles of 'subsidiarity' and 'mediation' (as a bulwark against totalitarianism); and to uphold human rights (economic and social as well as political and civil) in so far as they uphold human dignity, are related to duties and are considered along with other values such as truth, justice and charity.

The new Europe: ecumenism and diversity

The different aspects of modernity challenged the churches of Europe profoundly and at many levels, although at a rate and in a way which varied considerably across Europe. In the postwar period, and especially in the new

Europe since 1989, Christians in Europe find themselves in a new position. First, although Europe is united to an extent it has never been before, it is no longer Christendom, and at the end of the twentieth century doubts would be raised as to whether European society was, or had ever been, a 'Christian continent' (Wessels 1994). In several countries in Europe – Norway, Sweden, Denmark and Greece are major examples – it is still the case that nation and membership of the national church are closely identified. And in southern Europe – Spain, Portugal, Italy and Greece – a large majority have a Catholic or Orthodox identity. A raft of social changes, including the breakdown of community, the loss of a common world-view, the rise of rationality, and the predictability of modern urban life compared with pre-industrial rural society, have made traditional Christianity an option, not a necessity, and often an irrelevance for most Europeans (Bruce 1995: 129–35). With one or two exceptions, European nations no longer assume their citizens are Christians by birth. In place of parish records, civil registers of births, marriages and deaths are kept and faith is a matter of personal choice. The disestablishment of churches signalled, in most countries, the end of the privileged relationship one particular Christian church had held with government in each territory. Church taxes are abolished or paid to the government, education, health and other services are mostly in government hands, and increasingly churches are treated like other non-governmental bodies, either charities or social service organizations. Although the former state churches usually remain the largest, most governments now recognize the legitimacy of many other churches and religions and adopt policies of religious toleration. The plurality of religions available and the possibility of making a choice, or not doing so, mean there is now a religious marketplace similar to that in the United States and there are now 'societies of Christians' rather than 'Christian societies' (Bruce 1995: 2). Second, the place of religion has shifted from the public to the private sphere of life. Governments no longer necessarily seek the church's blessing or advice, public ceremonies no longer always use Christian or even religious language, and religious broadcasting is limited. One aspect of this is that the presence of Christian theology in the academies is questioned, even though the most ancient and prestigious were founded for training clergy. Mathematics has replaced theology as 'queen of the sciences'. Other foundational assumptions in a Christian world-view such as the creation of the world by a loving God and God's exercise of justice over the world are no longer the basis for philosophical or legal thought. Departments of theology, where they have survived, have diversified into departments of religion using historical, sociological or philosophical tools, and the study of the self-understanding of the Christian religion and the systematic theology developed by the different European Christianities is neglected.

The confidence of Europe, built up from the Middle Ages, was shattered by the experience of the two major wars of the first half of the twentieth century. For Christians of central and eastern Europe, after the Second World War further horrors were in store, but western European Christians, who had more opportunity to reflect on the war itself, were stunned, with others, at the revelations about the Holocaust. Although Christians had actively helped Jews to hide or escape – often at great risk to themselves – the German churches had made no public protest at their treatment, and the realization that anti-Semitism might lie at the heart of Christianity caused a great deal of soul-searching, and prompted a rediscovery of the Jewishness of Christian faith and the theme of Jew–Gentile reconciliation in the letters of St Paul (Ochs 1997). Christian churches also committed themselves to the reconstruction and reconciliation of Europe. As well as the many aid and development activities of Christian organizations and the rebuilding of churches, religious initiatives aimed to bring people together, such as the International Centre for Reconciliation at Coventry in England and the lay religious community at Taizé in France which bridged the Catholic–Protestant divide through its worship life. Christians, especially Quakers, are prominent in the development of peace studies, and reconciliation has grown as a Christian ministry. Christian efforts toward resolving 'the Troubles' in Northern Ireland, perceived as a late-twentieth-century vestige of the Wars of Religion, involved the four mainstream churches – Methodist, Presbyterian, Catholic and Anglican – working together to stay the hand of the paramilitaries, comfort the victims, create safe places for dialogue (like the Corrymeela Community) and campaign for justice (Boyd 1988; Clegg 2004). The political solution based on the 1998 'Good Friday Agreement' recognized in its name the religious resources for a solution to the conflict, but in itself it 'is not reconciliation' (Porter 2004: 74, 77). The ongoing reconciliatory work is largely the job of the churches, whose temporal endeavours, writes Miroslav Volf out of his experience of the break-up of Yugoslavia, are 'based on a vision of [final] reconciliation that cannot be undone' (Volf 1996: 110).

Since the division of Europe into nation-states was closely related to the divisions between the churches, in the aftermath of the two wars the churches felt a great responsibility to work toward reconciliation among themselves. The initiative for ecumenism in Europe came originally from the Orthodox churches and, stimulated by the missionary conference of

1910, led to Protestant–Orthodox commissions for Life and Work, to look at ways the churches could work together in public life, and for Faith and Order, to discuss matters of doctrine and liturgy that divided the churches, as well as an ongoing International Missionary Council. The former two bodies, which included European-initiated churches across the world, agreed to form a World Council of Churches, but war intervened. Nevertheless, the WCC 'in process of formation' was active in postwar reconstruction in Europe (Visser 't Hooft 1993: 711–13) and also in the formation of the United Nations (Nolde 1993: 263). The organization was finally constituted in 1948, with its headquarters in Geneva. There were high expectations that historic divisions could be overcome and that visible unity could be achieved between the churches. Although some unions have taken place, and Anglicans and Lutherans in the Nordic and Baltic region are now in communion with one another (the Porvoo agreement), organic union is not expected and at present a commitment to continuing dialogue is perhaps the most that can be achieved (May 2004: 99). The Roman Catholic Church, seeing itself as unique, has never been able to join the World Council of Churches, but provision has been made for Catholic involvement in almost all its activities.

When John XXIII opened the Second Vatican Council (1962–5), which despite the presence of bishops from all around the world was mainly European in its concerns, other Christians were stunned by Catholic willingness to engage with the modern world after several centuries of resistance. They were even more surprised when they were invited to observe and were referred to in conciliatory terms as 'separated brethren'. This new approach owed much to the German Jesuit theologian Karl Rahner, who developed an inclusive model – seen by some as patronizing – of relations with the former heretics and infidels, because they might, without knowing it, be saved by Christ. The most fundamental development of the council was the redefinition of the church not as a hierarchy but as 'the people of God'. This apparently abrupt change of heart, the result of renewed interest in the Bible and Christian origins, had profound effects throughout the Catholic world. The relationship between faith and cultures was explicitly considered, and Pope Paul VI subsequently insisted on a 'synthesis between faith and culture' (see Shorter 1999: 57, 55). The term 'inculturation' became popular after its use in John Paul II's encyclical, *Redemptoris Missio* (1990, paras 52–4), where it is described as an act of incarnation. However, there are tensions within the church about the extent of inculturation (Burrows 1993) and about whether faith or culture should be the starting point for the process (Schreiter 1999: 68–75). Inculturation has been endorsed by the church not only for the mission *ad gentes* but also for liturgical renewal by the decision in the wake of Vatican II to translate the words of the Tridentine Mass, still said everywhere in Latin until that date, into vernacular languages. However, since the 1960s, Catholic attendance and vocations in western Europe have declined rapidly. Whether the two are connected or not, conservative sections of the church have welcomed the reinstatement of the Latin rite (as an option) by Pope Benedict XVI in 2007. The council ushered in a much warmer period of ecumenical relations in which it looked a real possibility that reunion of at least some Protestant churches with Rome might take place. The Anglican Church, which uniquely had broken with Rome but not with the Catholic faith (Küng 1995: 589–97), engaged in dialogue from 1970 through the Anglican Roman Catholic International Commission. However, although the unity of the churches remains a specific objective of the Catholic Church, it envisages this as the integration of all churches into the one Catholic church, and the papacy was not a subject for discussion in ecumenical dialogue (Vischer 2004: 29). The publication in 2000 of the letter from Cardinal Joseph Ratzinger – later Pope Benedict XVI – '*Dominus Iesus*: On the unicity and salvific universality of Jesus Christ and the Church', although heavily criticized within the Catholic Church, 'underlined the limits to ecumenism' (Vischer 2004: 30) and was regarded by many as a further retreat from the openness of Vatican II.

The aftermath of the Second World War also began a withdrawal from empire by west European countries and a need to rethink relations with former mission churches. Through a series of conferences from the late 1940s until the 1950s, churches and mission agencies connected with the WCC achieved considerable consensus about theology of mission and articulated what amounted to a new ecumenical paradigm, which was also in keeping in most respects with shifts in Roman Catholic theology and is profoundly affected by the Trinitarian theology of the Orthodox churches (Bosch 1991: 368–510; see also Bria 1986: 3–16; Karotemprel 1996: 37–49; Kirk 1999: 7–55; Newbigin 1995: 19–29). It began with a new understanding of church. In their new (for some) situation of displacement from political power and the knowledge of their complicity in Europe's problems, the churches understood themselves more humbly not as an authoritative institution representing God's will on earth but as a 'sign, sacrament and instrument' (Bosch 1991: 374) of God's will and in the service of others. Consequently, it could no longer be said that the church had 'missions' but that the church was privileged to join in one 'mission', that is the Triune God's mission to the world, as it participates in Christ, who is sent into the world (Jn 3.16) and receives the Holy Spirit who is at work in the world (Jn 20.22). This new paradigm, referred to as *missio Dei*, draws on John's gospel rather than Matthew's. It can also be understood as 'finding out where the Holy Spirit is at work and joining in' and so is widely accepted by Pentecostal and most Evangelical churches as well as Protestant, Catholic and Orthodox. Although there are differences in the way it is interpreted, depending on the scope allowed for the Spirit's work, it has proved to have huge ramifications in the theological and practical life of the mainstream churches of Europe. For example, mission could no longer be thought of as 'from the West to the rest' but must be 'from everywhere to everywhere' (Nazir-Ali 1991). Now Europe was seen to be as much a mission field as any other continent. Furthermore, since mission was no longer one-way, the relationship between the 'older churches' of Christendom and the 'younger churches' should now become one of equality, reciprocity and 'partnership in mission'. As former colonies became independent, this theology became the basis for the formulation of new relations. Although missionary paternalism has proved very difficult to overcome and continuing economic inequalities have made the implementation of partnership very difficult, most European churches now enjoy some sort of a conciliar relationship with former mission churches in other parts of the world. At its most radical this is expressed in the reconstitution of mission bodies as councils of churches with shared finance resources (for examples see Funkschmidt 2002). Others at least have programmes of exchange and mutual sending between national churches and joint programmes of mission activity. There are tensions in these relationships. While at a grassroots level most Christians are, naturally, grateful for the missionaries who brought the gospel to them, it is also true that missionaries have borne a considerable proportion of the blame for the colonial enterprise, and, understandably, European Christians face anger and resentment from some quarters.

In the post-colonial period, experience from overseas is being put to use in Europe. Theologies of religion developed in India (e.g. Dupuis 1997) and patterns of dialogue established on the 'mission field' have provided a resource for European Christians seeking to relate to their growing number of neighbours of other faiths in Europe. For example, Anglican missionaries in the context of Islam, with little hope of conversions, developed a theology of mission as Christian presence (Yates 1994: 141–2) and realized they needed to become learners of Islam before (if at all) they could expect a hearing (Cragg 2000); this led to the foundation of Christian schools of Islamic studies, often now incorporated into universities. Attempts at dialogue initiated by European Christians are bound to be met with suspicion that there are ulterior motives involved – if not for conversion then at least to establish human rights in Muslim countries (Siddiqui 1997: 194–200). As shown by the controversy over the Danish newspaper cartoons in 2006, Western Christians – even highly secularized ones – tend to emphasize freedom of expression over Muslim insistence on the proper respect for faith (S. Kim 2007a). Christians who have made the effort to live alongside Muslims and respect their faith, like the British Anglican Kenneth Cragg and the Dutch academic Antonie Wessels, are able to interpret Islam sympathetically to Europeans and suggest how Muslims and Christians can find ways to live together (Wessels 2006). They also suggest that the example of the Arab Christians has a great deal to teach European ones (Cragg 1992; Wessels 1995). As well as prompting European Christians to rethink their methods of evangelism, if not voluntarily then under pressure from governments anxious to preserve religious harmony, the increasing Muslim presence in Europe is already having other effects on western European Christianity. For example, Christians increasingly see themselves together with people of other faiths not only as Judaeo-Christian but as 'people of the book'. On the other hand, accommodation by the authorities to Muslim sensitivities has led to greater assertiveness by Christians of their right to profess faith publicly and of the contribution of Christianity to European heritage (Jenkins 2007: 260–5). Once again, awareness of Islam is increasing Christians' sense of identity and prompting a new discovery of the character of Christian faith.

Sociologists have devoted a great deal of time – perhaps too much (cf. Robertson 1992: 88) – to the question of whether religion in Europe is declining or not. Much has been made of the crisis of faith in western Europe, a crisis which, according to McLeod, has been talked about since the 1790s (1997: 83). But matters really came to a head in the 'cultural revolution' of the 1960s. Although, as Robin Gill has shown in the case of Britain, the perception of a crisis ignored the fact that most of the church buildings, built at times of revival and optimism, had never been full in any case (Gill 2003), there had been a gradual decline in church attendance over decades, and the demography of Christianity in Europe now changed drastically. This was partly due to the search for greater individual freedom, which led to rejection of moral and doctrinal codes and authority, but it was aggravated by social changes such as rapid decline in rural cultures, changes in work and leisure patterns, and loss of association of social identity with the church. As a result, 'religious community is ceasing to be a necessary source of identity and support' to the people of western Europe (McLeod 1997: 141–3). Callum Brown in a study of the situation in Britain, insists that though Christianity endured the challenge of the Enlightenment and modernity, the decisive decline in church attendance in the 1960s occurred because 'respectability' was supplanted by 'respect', the traditional moral code was replaced by toleration and greater individual freedom and, crucially, women stopped attending church and sending their children to Sunday school. Brown anticipates 'the death of Christian Britain', which 'took several centuries to convert' and 'less than forty years' to forsake Christianity (Brown 2001: 1). There is no shortage of those prophesying the doom of at least the traditional churches (e.g. Brown 2001; Jenkins 2007). The theory that modernization and secularization (in the sense of the decline of religion in public life) go together, which originated with the Enlightenment despisers of religion, has it seems been vindicated in western Europe.

However, in a worldwide perspective, the relationship between modernity and the decline of religion is much less obvious, and it even appears that western Europe is the 'exceptional case' (Davie 2002). The situation becomes even more complicated when we look further than church attendance and the decline of church membership and attempt to assess religiosity. Grace Davie has shown in the case of Britain (Davie 2002: 2–8; see also Davie 1994) that there is still a remarkably high percentage of people who are 'believing without belonging' (Davie 1994: title), and have a 'spirituality of the unchurched' (Hay 2002). Davie also maintains that even in Protestant Europe there is a vicarious sense of religion – associated with older patterns of priesthood – by which 'a relatively small number of people … "look after" the [Christian] memory on behalf of others' (2000: 177). The continued popularity of belief in the paranormal, séances, horoscopes and other supernatural forces shows that people are a lot less rational than might be expected three centuries after the Enlightenment. They continue to believe that the world is not as it seems (cf. Bruce 1995: 54–5). Considering the continued high levels of participation and belonging there, the real question in Europe is why, when people want to believe, they do not choose traditional Christianity. Many reasons have been suggested for this. As far as the exodus of women from the church is concerned, the opposition of the Roman Catholic Church to abortion and almost all methods of birth control, which, expressed bluntly by Paul VI in the encyclical *Humanae Vitae* in 1968, seemed to run counter to that decade of growing freedom for women, is often cited as a factor in women leaving the church (Brown 2001: 191), together with the slowness of the established churches to respond to growing demands for women's ordination. The conservative stance of most churches on divorce and sexuality has also compounded the perception, so deeply ingrained in Europe, that the churches are reactionary and anti-progress. A large number of scandals involving abuse of those in church institutions and sexual abuse by priests, centred especially on the Roman Catholic Church, has further undermined a clergy that is already stretched by acute lack of numbers (cf. Jenkins 2007: 26–54). The very physical presence of stone-built churches evokes the kind of rigid authority that the children of the 1960s rebelled against. As Vandana, one of the leaders of the Catholic ashram movement, observed in India, European young people looking for religious experience tend not to expect to find it in their home churches but in what is exotic to them (but traditional to most Asians): the eastern religions of Hinduism and Buddhism (Vandana 1991: 99–105). An extensive French study found many who turn away from traditional Christianity to find meaning in eastern religions have 'an axe to grind … with the institutional church', which they see as 'dogmatic', 'moralistic', 'having disdain for both physical and emotional life', 'too prescriptive' and hypocritical. In part, this is a rejection of the Enlightenment heritage in favour of Paganism and Gnosticism, but it is also influenced by a humanist anthropology (Ugeux 2006: 325).

The growth of 'New Age' movements – offering an alternative 'holistic', therapeutic religious experience – and other alternative forms of religion has been described by Paul Heelas and Linda Woodhead in terms of a shift from 'religion' to 'spirituality' (Heelas and Woodhead 2004: title). This they view as part of the wider 'turn' of modern culture from 'life lived in terms of external or "objective" roles, duties and obligations … towards life lived by reference to one's own subjective experiences' (Heelas and Woodhead 2004: 2). From their study of the shift from congregational modes of 'religion' to associational modes of 'spirituality' in the English town of Kendal, they predict a 'spiritual revolution' spelling the end for religion. But even if Heelas and Woodhead's prediction comes true, it does not spell the end of Christianity in western Europe, because many of the examples of the new spirituality which they include are Christian churches or groups which have adapted to the needs of the new generation by offering alternative forms of worship. Although Pentecostalism as a denomination has grown little in Europe, since the 1970s Charismatic movements have swept through the older churches (e.g. Kotila 2006). One result has been a huge growth industry in new liturgies and worship songs. There are also new Christian groups, such as 'house-churches', Pentecostal–charismatic groups which do not have a building, denominational affiliation or institutional presence but offer 'fellowship' and worship in an informal style with contemporary music. Churches have been encouraged to offer 'liquid' (as opposed to 'solid') forms of church which minimize the need for commitment and offer consumerist-style choice (Ward 2002). Nevertheless, there are people who are attracted to traditional worship or congregational forms and fear that a radical breaking with tradition for short-term gain will destroy the church's credibility and its unity and make it a hostage to fortune. In this respect, the Orthodox and Catholic Churches have much longer memories than Protestants.

Not all Europeans are so convinced that indigenous faith is dying out (Verstraelen 2007), and others point out that, even if it is, the lesson of history is that this means revival is just around the corner (Jenkins 2007: 288). Furthermore, the attention given to the decline in church attendance and membership of many of the older churches in western Europe masks the much larger reality of European Christianity in the twenty-first century. In almost every country of the former Soviet bloc, Christianity has undergone significant revival since the end of Communism. Inclusion of central and eastern Europe significantly improves the figures for Christian Europe (Jenkins 2007: 56–7). The populations of Russia, Ukraine, Belarus, Romania, Serbia, Macedonia and Montenegro are all more than 50 per cent Orthodox Christians. Poland, Croatia and Slovenia are largely Roman Catholic. The Baltic states, Hungary, Slovakia and the Czech Republic all have large Catholic and Protestant populations. Furthermore, the migration of huge numbers of these Christians to find work means they are now numerous in western Europe as well (Jackson 2005: 85; Jenkins 2007: 58) and are impacting the life of other European Christians.

In the countries of Europe that used to be Communist the churches find themselves coping not with decline but with growth. As well as struggling to baptize and instruct new Christians, the ancient churches have new competitors and all must adjust to a situation of religious pluralism. Relationships with the state and roles in the public sphere have to be negotiated anew. Instead of resisting modernity in the shape of Communism, the churches are invited to engage with it in the form of democracy and capitalism, but not all are equipped or willing to do so (Vassiliadou 2006). Since the collapse of Communism, the Russian Orthodox Church has reasserted itself, forming an alliance with the state. It is engaging in a mission aimed at conversion (Kozhuharov 2006) and preventing other churches proselytizing in its 'territory'. It is deeply involved in activities in Africa, Asia, Latin America and the West, which is of grave concern to some other Orthodox (e.g. Vassiliadis 1998: 46) who are worried about the perennial link between ethnicity, nationalism and religion (Clapsis 2004). Furthermore, the church has yet to find a constructive way of engaging with Islam – so long resisted – or Buddhism, which are dominant in parts of the Russian Federation (Cousins 2004). In Greece also, minority Christian groups, let alone Muslims, find it very difficult to establish a presence or find a voice (Jenkins 2007: 56–7).

The minority status of the West European churches and the new possibilities opened up in the East since 1989 have resulted in a renewed mission activity in Europe, both by local churches and also by foreign groups from North America, Latin America (especially in Spain and Portugal), Asia, Africa and the Caribbean. There is a trend toward 'mission in reverse' from countries that were evangelized by Europe in the last few centuries, but who are now shocked and dismayed by what they see as the decline of Christianity on the continent. A few of these come through church and mission exchange programmes; most find their own way. Migrants from 'the global South' are giving the church in Europe a more Southern, Pentecostal complexion and perhaps hold the possibility of reviving it (Jenkins 2007: 96–9). Of the local initiatives, some are clearly primarily directed at addressing declining numbers; they seek to inspire Christians with confidence to evangelize or proclaim their faith and bring others into the churches. In the Catholic Church the 'new evangelization', proclaimed by John Paul II at the outset of his pontificate, encourages public demonstrations of faith and popular religion such as pilgrimages. A famous example among Protestant churches is the Alpha courses originating at Holy Trinity Brompton in London and now a global phenomenon, designed to draw individuals into Christian faith in a low-key way (Brookes 2007). But there are equally desires to change lives by practical service and to address issues in the public sphere. Liberation Theology, developed in Latin America and mediated through the Catholic Church, resonates with Social Christianity. As a result, Christian churches may be associated with left-wing politics and are not so easily accused of political conservatism. Traditional churches have been looking at ways to make themselves 'mission-shaped' (Cray et al. 2004) by processes of restructuring and reorienting church life to those outside rather than to internal church concerns.

As Europe draws closer together, and modernity gives way to what is sometimes called 'post-modernity', the churches in East and West find themselves in a changing intellectual climate, and one which is in some ways less hostile to faith. While it is difficult to stake a truth claim in an age of suspicion of 'meta-narratives' (Kirk and Vanhoozer 1999), it is also more difficult to establish ground on which to deny Christian experience. The Christian story may play alongside many others, but it can be told much more straightforwardly than in the recent past and Christian worship can be made attractive in the marketplace of religious experience. The danger for Christianity is that, in an increasingly fragmented society, it will be tolerated but not engaged by those outside its network. The churches have no option of 'missionary war' or an authority that is not earned. As they seek to be 'all things to all men' and inculturate the gospel in Europe, they have to learn to use persuasion rather than fear and they have to live the gospel they proclaim.

Study Questions and Further Readings

- In what ways does Europe today reflect the long influence of the Roman Catholic Church and the Orthodox Church?
- Discuss the impact of the Reformation not only on Christianity but also on socio-political life in Europe.
- Discuss the relationship between colonialism, missionary endeavour and European churches in Africa, Asia and Latin America.
- How has Christian presence in public life in Europe changed since the onset of modernity, and what are the implications of this?
- What are the European factors which encouraged the Ecumenical movement in the twentieth century?
- Discuss the implications for the European churches of the expansion of the European Union and increasing migration.

Bosch, D. J. (1991), *Transforming Mission: Paradigm Shifts in Theology of Mission*. Maryknoll, NY: Orbis.

Clapsis, Emmanuel (ed.) (2004), *The Orthodox Churches in a Plural World: An Ecumenical Conversation*. Geneva: World Council of Churches.

Davie, Grace (2000), *Religion in Modern Europe: A Memory Mutates*. Oxford: Oxford University Press.

Küng, Hans (1995), *Christianity: Its Essence and History*. London: SCM Press.

McLeod, Hugh (1997), *Religion and the People of Western Europe, 1789–1989* (revised edn). Oxford: Oxford University Press.

Storrar, William F. and Andrew Morton (eds) (2004), *Public Theology for the 21st Century*. Edinburgh: T. and T. Clark.

African Christianity 3

In his foundational work on African religions and philosophy, John Mbiti comments that 'Christianity in Africa is so old that it can rightly be described as an indigenous, traditional, and African religion' (Mbiti 1969: 229). Furthermore, as Andrew Walls insists, Christianity in Africa cannot be treated merely as a 'colonial leftover', in view of the 'unbroken historical continuity of the churches of Egypt and Ethiopia of today and the ancient world'. Ethiopia has become an inspiration for African nationalism and a justification for black African churches. 'Ethiopian', continues Walls, 'stands for Africa indigenously Christian, Africa *primordially* Christian' so that 'African Christians today can assert their right to the *whole* history of Christianity in Africa, stretching back almost to the apostolic age' (Walls 2002: 90–1). The biblical world resonates with the people of Africa perhaps more than in any other continent, and inspires African Christian engagement with the age-old questions of spiritual power and the new questions of economic and political power raised by the encounter with the colonial and the globalized worlds.

Religions, empires and African traditions

Proudly independent, the Ethiopian Church has a unique musical tradition of great antiquity and other distinctive characteristics. Established by Frumentius, a Syrian, whose fourth-century mission was endorsed by Athanasius, bishop of Alexandria, Ethiopian Christianity pays special attention to the Old Testament, in which Ethiopia (Cush) is called to 'stretch out its hands to God' (Ps. 68.31). The Ark of the Covenant from Jerusalem is believed to be kept in the ancient Ethiopian city of Axum, and a replica of it is necessary to consecrate each local church. When these arks are paraded at festivals,

Ethiopian Christians dance to drumbeats in a way that is said to be how David danced before the Ark (2 Sam. 6.5, 12–16; Chaillot 2002: 139). The Ethiopian Old Testament has significant differences in content and order from other Orthodox churches; Christians follow dietary and purity rules laid down in it, and they observe a Saturday as well as a Sunday Sabbath. The church also reflects its African context in its attention to the spirit-world. Ethiopians give veneration not only to the Virgin and the saints but also to the angels, which have a special place in Ethiopian spirituality (Chaillot 2002: 136–7). Through centuries of relative isolation from other Christian centres, except for the 'umbilical' link (Walls 2002: 89) with Alexandria, the church kept faith with world Christianity until in 1959 the first Ethiopian patriarch was appointed. The church, which was closely bound up with a feudal society, fended off colonization attempts by Italy in 1941 and remained isolated from modernity until the Communist revolution of 1974 which overthrew emperor Haile Selassie. The church was deprived of its wealth and lands, which were not restored under the new democratic constitution, but about half the population remains Christian, mostly Orthodox, and now independent of Coptic rule the Ethiopian monastic tradition has renewed many aspects of church life (Persoon 2004).

The Coptic Church in Egypt treasures the story of how the child Jesus was brought to their country when his family fled from the terror of King Herod (Mt. 2.16–18), and they believe that the gospel was first preached to them by the Apostle Mark, who was martyred in Alexandria. The Copts, descendants of the ancient Egyptians, had been practising Christianity according to a non-Chalcedonian theology for several centuries when Muslim Arab invaders conquered Egypt in the seventh century. Christians were in a majority in Egypt until the tenth century, after which successive waves of Arab immigration, and persecution under the Mamluks in the thirteenth to sixteenth centuries, led to a greater decline in numbers until Copts now number only 6 per cent of the population. The Coptic Church is the largest Christian population in the Middle East and underwent a renewal in the late twentieth century, but in what is formally the *Arab* Republic of Egypt, the Copts are discriminated against and Coptic Christians have joined the exodus of Christians from the Middle East that has accelerated in recent years (O'Mahony 2004a).

Sudan came under Christian influence from the fourth century and the faith flourished until the fourteenth century when the country came under Islamic rule as Muslim Arabs moved south from Egypt. Today's Christians, mostly Roman Catholic, Anglican and Presbyterian, are the result of more recent missionary work among the black African tribespeople in the south of the country. Since independence from Britain in 1956, black Africans in the south, about half of whom are Christians, have resisted rule from the north and the country has been in a state of civil war. A ceasefire negotiated by the All Africa Council of Churches and the World Council of Churches in 1972 held for ten years, but, since the discovery of oil in the Dafur region, violence has been intense and Christian communities have suffered greatly.

In the first seven centuries of Christianity, north Africa was also strongly Christian and the issues then encountered about biblical interpretation and the role of the Holy Spirit resonate in African theology today. The theologians of Alexandria and Carthage, cities on the Mediterranean coast of Africa, are counted among the fathers of the church, and their work reflected the experience of Christians in these regions. Arab armies gradually conquered what they called the Maghreb, from present-day Libya to Morocco. One of the challenges for historians of African Christianity is to explain how, in a matter of five centuries, Christianity all but disappeared from there and became marginalized in Egypt, to be replaced by Islam. The usual explanation is that Christianity lacked indigenous roots, being largely confined to the towns. Added to this, as historian of the African church Elizabeth Isichei points out, there were economic incentives to convert (Isichei 1995: 44). Kevin Ward suggests many Christians from the Maghreb fled north to Spain and southern Italy and that the explanation for Christianity's disappearance was not a lack of indigenous roots 'but rather that world religions (as opposed to local "traditional" cults) were seen as being inextricably bound up with a universal civilization' that simply replaced the previous one (Ward 1999: 193–4). Over the centuries Islam has bonded with the local beliefs of the people and today these countries are almost entirely Muslim; the ancient churches have disappeared. Many of those converted to Christianity more recently, such as Catholics in Algeria, have left, and there is a background of bitter memories of 'Christian' conquests. Apart from some Christian development work, these countries generally resist or severely limit any form of Christian activity, and most Christians are expatriates.

The local religions of Africa, which existed before the coming of Christianity and other world religions, should probably not be considered one 'African traditional religion', but there are some 'recurring, though not universal' patterns of belief and practice in Africa (Isichei 1995: 96). Jesse Mugambi notes those which differ significantly from the traditions of Western Christendom and the Enlightenment (Mugambi 2002: 56–73). First, African cosmology does not separate a heaven or hell, and so salvation is a temporal rather than a spatial expectation and the dead can continue to influence the living for good or ill. Secondly, Africans did not expect progress or an end to the world but lived by the cyclical rhythm of their environment. Disturbances in the natural cycle were believed to be caused by someone offending the deity, ancestors or spirits, and so diviners were needed to investigate what had happened and prescribe remedies, including sacrifices and punishments, needed to restore harmony. Thirdly, African communities mostly knew of a deity – a male person or a spirit somewhat remote from them but contactable by certain special persons – whose power extended beyond their ethnic territory to the whole world. Although each group called this deity by a different name, they could understand one another religiously, although there were many different beliefs and cultural practices. There was no concept of Satan and no expectation of a judgment day because human beings were understood to be basically good. Fourthly, as well as ancestors and the high God there were spirits, although beliefs about these varied from community to community. In some parts of west Africa, there were pantheons of divinities and large numbers of spirits, and belief in spirit possession and the practice of exorcism were particularly strong. In addition, questions of individual liberty, plural marriage, clan initiation, attitudes to land and property, and what constituted appropriate religious behaviour were significantly different in most African societies than in Europe. It is also important to note that traditional morality was 'by customs rather than by reason' (Moyo 2003: 56), and so disruption of society and its traditions left individuals bereft of moral guidance.

The Africa the Portuguese encountered, as they searched for new routes to the riches of the East that avoided Muslim empires, was very diverse and composed of thousands of different states and groups, ranging from hunter-gatherer societies to structured clan groups, the Swahili city-states of the east coast, and some larger kingdoms or empires. The Portuguese only touched the fringes of the inland empires such as that of the Ashanti in what is now Ghana, but they were impressed by what they saw and heard of the African kingdoms. Although they heard there was a Christian king in Africa, they did not encounter Ethiopia until the seventeenth century. Portuguese activity in Africa was determined by 'the identification of national identity with Catholicism, and the hostility to Islam' (Isichei 1995: 53). In search of gold, the Portuguese took their first colony on the north African coast in 1415 and established bases for their exploration of Africa on the originally uninhabited Cape Verde islands, where mixed Portuguese–African communities grew up that provided many priests for missionary work. The alliances they formed in order to set up trading settlements around the coast en route to Asia were confirmed by the baptism of the local ruler, and the insistence on adherence to Roman Catholic Christianity, as a bulwark against Islam. The small Christian communities established by the Portuguese were 'fragile, exotic plants, which did not always survive well in African soil' (Isichei 1995: 52) and appear to have left little trace, with two significant exceptions, Angola and Mozambique. In 1482, the king of Kongo helped the Portuguese establish their colony. He was baptized Afonso, and his son Henrique became the first African Catholic bishop since the first centuries. They tried to establish Christianity in their kingdom but it was weakened by the Portuguese and the slave trade. Nineteenth-century visitors reported that a syncretistic version of Christianity was still practised, which had been sustained by lay leaders from the nobility. Down the Zambesi River from the impressive ruins of Great Zimbabwe, which had been abandoned in the previous century, the Portuguese took advantage of the relative weakness of the Mutapa state in the early sixteenth century to establish trading posts and large estates, which missionary priests, many of them Goans, attempted to Christianize, although slavery was used to run them. For the next four centuries, the Portuguese, who exported slaves from their colonies, were 'zealous in keeping out missionaries of other nations' (Ward 1999: 200), while their declining power meant they were unable to provide for the well-being of the church. The Portuguese government was forced to withdraw from both Angola and Mozambique in 1975, leaving chaos in its wake in both nations, an overwhelmingly Roman Catholic population in Angola and a much smaller Catholic minority in Mozambique. In both countries churches, along with other agencies, are heavily involved in humanitarian work.

Slavery, Islam and deliverance in west Africa

Much of the commercial interest in Africa centred on the trade in slaves, which saw between 9 and 15 million Africans imported to the Americas. Since for three and a half centuries the major contact between Europe and Africa was the slave trade (Ward 1999: 203), it is largely against this background that the spread of European Christianity there must be understood. The debilitating effect of slave trading on African society – which slid into endemic war to keep up the supply of slaves – and the suffering caused to Africans can hardly be exaggerated. A long-term effect of this activity was the creation of the 'black Atlantic' (Gilroy 1993), a diaspora of people of African descent spread through the Americas and Europe, with a particular concentration in the Caribbean Islands, which plays an especially significant part in African Christian history (Walls 2002: 94). At least 115 black Americans are known to have served as missionaries in Africa in the last quarter of the nineteenth century, supported from the limited resources of churches of recently freed slaves. Jamaican Christians founded a mission to Calabar (Nigeria) in 1846 and West Indian missionaries worked on the Gold Coast (Ghana) from the same year. Black churches also brought African students to study in America (Isichei 1995: 166–7).

There was some continuity of Catholic presence along the coast through the black priests of the Cape Verdes. Protestant missionary societies began work in Africa from the eighteenth century, beginning in the west, but their susceptibility to tropical diseases resulted in a high death toll. Europe proved as inhospitable to Africans as Africa was to Europeans, as the SPG discovered when they sent three Fante boys (from present-day Ghana) to study in England. Only one of the boys survived, but Philip Quaque returned to Africa in 1765 as the first African Anglican priest. The first Catholic orders to arrive in west Africa were the Sisters of St Joseph of Cluny, who worked in Senegal from 1819. The Basel mission began work on the Gold Coast in 1828 at the invitation of Africans and soon appointed local pastors. It is noteworthy that in this early period, mission agencies did not raise the same reservations about the suitability of Africans for mission and ministry as they were later to display; indeed they were only too glad to have African workers, who were often sent to the most difficult and disease-ridden areas, and who also saved the missions money since they were paid less.

Intimately related to the missionary movement, both in Africa and at home, was the anti-slavery campaign in Britain and the Caribbean. Abolitionist activities included the establishment of Freetown in the former Portuguese colony of Sierra Leone in 1787 as a home for freed slaves, or Creoles. A group of former slaves who had become Christians and had fought for the British in the American War of Independence founded the first church there. The Church Missionary Society and the Wesleyan Missionary Society, with the support of local community leaders such as Samuel Lewis (1843–1903; a lawyer, mayor of Freetown and the first west African to be knighted), were active in establishing a Christian society there after the pattern of Europe. Many freed slaves returned to Freetown for business or as missionaries, and it became a centre for training Africans, who then spread the Christian message and Western education throughout west Africa. Sierra Leonean missionaries were invited by rulers of Yoruba city states, who saw Christian connections as bringing trade and as a protection against rival groups and slave traders. Like Sierra Leone, Liberia was also founded for ex-slaves, but by an American abolitionist group. The first settlers arrived in 1822, many of the local people also embraced the Christian faith, and it too became a centre of Afro-American mission activity.

Whereas, earlier in the century, Europeans contented themselves with supporting African-American initiatives, in the latter part advances in medicines and growing numbers of missionary recruits led to greater missionary presence. Furthermore, as a result of Darwinian theories of race, and shifts in world-view due to the Enlightenment and technological advancement, Europeans adopted a more superior attitude to Africans. In 1881, for example, a white Baptist missionary in Yorubaland could write back to his headquarters that no more black American missionaries were required (Isichei 1995: 164). At the same time, European involvement in African affairs changed from trading to colonization. From about 1880, Britain, France, Germany, Belgium, Portugal, Italy and Spain engaged in a rush to take colonies and by 1910 the entire continent, with the exception of Ethiopia and Liberia, was divided between them. One effect of these changes was that Europeans became increasingly involved in church and mission affairs on the ground. Furthermore, whereas when their numbers were small, white missionaries were dependent on African hospitality, they now became part of a growing expatriate community and often cut off from African society. The African leaders in Sierra Leone suffered acutely from this changed state of affairs, as they experienced increasingly little respect and autonomy. The most famous example is the treatment of Samuel Ajayi Crowther (c.1807–91). He was a Yoruba captured and then rescued and released in Freetown, where he studied languages at Fourah Bay College, run by the Church Missionary Society. He went on to publish a grammar book and Book of Common Prayer in Yoruba and began translating the Bible into that language, a work finally completed in 1889 and which laid the foundation of Yoruba literature and ethnic identity. In 1864, he received an honorary doctorate from the University of Oxford in recognition of his language work and he was also ordained as the first African bishop of the Anglican Church, with responsibility for the whole of 'West Africa beyond the Queen's Dominions'. However, Crowther's two decades of work there were clouded by accusations against his leadership by CMS missionaries which reinforced theories that 'the African race' was not 'advanced' enough to hold high office. In 1890 Crowther was forced to resign and a European bishop was appointed as his successor. Europeans commentators agreed this was the best thing for the mission (e.g. Neill 1964: 377–8), but African leaders were upset by Crowther's treatment and this encouraged independence movements in the church and wider society. Recent historians of African Christianity have shown how Crowther was extremely highly regarded by his contemporaries, but ill-supported and put in an impossible position by CMS, and was a victim of commercial interests and the racism of the period (Ajayi 1999; Isichei 1995: 172; Sanneh 2000: 193–4; Walls 2002: 163–4; Ward 1999: 208–9). That missionaries are sometimes experienced as a hindrance rather than a help to the indigenous mission of local churches became apparent again in the late 1960s and early 1970s when there were calls for a 'moratorium' on the sending of missionaries and money, voiced most powerfully by John Gatu, chairman of the Presbyterian Church in Kenya, before the US National Council of Churches in 1971. This was taken up at the All Africa Council of Churches meeting in Lusaka in 1974, where it was said *a moratorium* would be 'the only potent means of becoming truly and authentically ourselves'. This suggestion was not seriously implemented across the churches, and in any case there were many indigenous churches without overseas support (Hastings 1976: 22–4), but the long-term result of the moratorium call was greater reciprocity between (some) churches in the West and in Africa (Anderson 1974: 138).

The growth of Christianity in west Africa has made the southern edge of the Sahara a flashpoint in Muslim–Christian relations. Countries on the west coast from Guinea northwards to Mauritania have mainly Muslims and very few Christian communities, and Mali and Niger have almost no Christians. However, Burkina Faso and Chad have substantial minorities and the coastal countries from Sierra Leone to Benin are more Christian than Muslim statistically. Nigeria has roughly equal numbers of Muslims and Christians: of the major tribal groups, the Hausa in the north are Muslim, the eastern Igbo are Christian and the Yoruba (in the west) are divided between the two faiths. This fact played a complex but significant role in the bloody Biafran war of 1967–70. The Igbo tended to see themselves as Christians, declaring independence from a government which was pro-Islamic, whom they blamed for massacring tens of thousands in 1966 (Hastings 1979: 197–200). Although

Nigeria recovered from Biafra, matters deteriorated again in the 1990s when the predominantly Muslim states along the northern border implemented *Shari'a* law. The city of Kano particularly, a Muslim stronghold, and other northern cities have seen periodic rioting, with hundreds killed and thousands displaced. The long-term result is the further diminishing of the Christian minority. The perception of west African history as a struggle between Christianity and Islam may reflect a Western missionary preoccupation (Sanneh 1983: 210), but it is one that many African Christians seem to have imbibed. Together with the growth of African-initiated churches, Islam is the major concern for Nigerian church leaders. But as Ken Okeke observes from within the Anglican church in Nigeria, there is confrontation but very little debate. In all the countries of western Africa there are substantial numbers who choose not to align themselves with either world religion, and who are consequently the target of evangelism by both (Okeke 1998: 322), but, as Sanneh suggests, their indigenous traditions may in the end be more enduring as they shape the two world faiths (Sanneh 1983: 211).

Apartheid, liberation and reconciliation in southern Africa

Whereas in west Africa Christianity was spread in the first part of the nineteenth century by Africans or Afro-Americans, in South Africa in the same period the chief Christian presence was white settler populations (cf. Ward 1999: 209). From 1652, the Dutch East India Company encouraged Dutch people, who were Reformed Protestants influenced by Pietism, to settle there to grow crops and raise cattle to supply their ships on the way to Asia. The company also imported slaves from India and east Asia to do the hard labour, and the Dutch used the struggling local tribespeople, Khoisan, as a source of labour. The British, who occupied the Cape from 1806, brought new settlers and encouraged 'Anglicization', although the presence of Scots among them later reinforced Calvinism with an evangelical fundamentalism which laid the foundations for the later system of apartheid. The Boers, who also included German settlers and Huguenots (French Calvinists), began to identify themselves as 'Afrikaner' from about 1800, and their experience of group preservation in the face of threats from local tribes and colonial authorities led them to forge a strong identity as a 'white tribe', which was bound up with Calvinistic Christianity and inspired by the exodus of the people of Israel from Egypt into the Promised Land. The Boers felt little sympathy for the black communities of Khoisan in the west and south and Nguni in the east and north, whom they deprived of their lands, but among new arrivals at the Cape were missionaries who aimed to reach the black populations, and this became the entry point for their work across the whole of southern Africa. The first to arrive were Moravians, who in 1792 established a community at Genadendal, where the Khoisan were encouraged to settle free from the depredations of the colonists to practise crafts, and which became a model for future mission stations. Criticism of Boer treatment of local people by missionaries of the London Missionary Society resulted in some measures by the British government to give black and 'coloured' people access to the courts, but this did not change the underlying inequalities of the colonial system. Naturally this action soured the relationship between British and Afrikaners, and it was one of the factors that provoked the Boer 'Great Trek' of the 1830s beyond the borders of even the enlarged colony to the 'Transvaal' to set up a new colony, displacing more black Africans.

As colonists spread eastwards they encountered the Nguni people, who were themselves in turmoil because of the expansion of one Nguni group, the Zulus. Among the first to respond to the missionaries' message were Mfengu refugees fleeing the fighting. The Xhosa also accepted Christianity on the advice of one of their number, Nitsikana, who claimed he was converted to Christianity before ever meeting a missionary, on the basis of what he already knew about God. He preached and wrote hymns that expressed the continuity between African tradition and the God of the Bible, although initially he could not read the Bible. Nitsikana advised the king to make peace, rather than follow the warlike traditions of the ancestors, and Xhosa Christians joined the LMS mission church. However, they maintained their allegiance to 'the God of Nitsikana', and later leaders of the African National Congress hailed Nitsikana as a forerunner of African nationalism (Saayman 1991: 56–7). Other outstanding Xhosa Christian leaders include Tiyo Soga, who became the first black South African to be ordained as a minister, a leader of his people, and whose belief that God had given Africa to black people led to his later being regarded as a pioneer of black consciousness (Saayman 1991: 62).

To the north, many Tswana became Christians following the reduction of their language to writing and the translation of the Bible in Tswana by Robert Moffat, an LMS missionary. The neighbouring Ngwato and Sotho peoples also became largely Christian in the nineteenth century. Many Africans turned to Christianity at a time when their traditional way of life was almost destroyed by displacement and warfare, and the discovery of gold and diamonds in southern Africa in the late nineteenth century only exacerbated the pressures. Christian missions offered protection and a new modern way of life which many accepted and, along with it, Christian faith. However, in this way the foundations were laid for the separate black reservations or 'homelands', which became part of the later system of apartheid in South Africa. Furthermore, even where they lived together, blacks and whites tended to be organized into separate congregations (Hofmeyr and Pillay 1994: 88). The 1910 constitution, agreed after the defeat of the Boers by the British in two wars, set up a 'caste-like' society, and the system of apartheid instituted in 1948 was accompanied by an ideology of separateness which amounted to a civil religion, for which the Afrikaner churches provided a theological basis. Furthermore, the Dutch Reformed missionary conference in 1950 advocated 'territorial apartheid' and prepared the ground for the notorious Group Areas Act and for policies of 'separate development' (de Gruchy 2004: 27, 32). However, leading English-speaking churches, Presbyterian, Congregational and Anglican, which, while not free of discrimination, had mixed race congregations, opposed apartheid from the start on the basis that God had created all human beings in His image. Spurred on by the Sharpeville massacre of 1960, the World Council of Churches took up the issue through its Programme to Combat Racism in 1970. In the aftermath of the Soweto uprising in 1976, the Reformed Church in the Netherlands broke with the Dutch Reformed Church of South Africa in 1978.

Influenced by James Cone and other black theologians in the United States and by African traditions, and encouraged by the Christian Institute of Beyers Naudé, a Dutch Reformed minister opposed to apartheid, Manas Buthelezi, Allan Boesak and others developed their own theologies of black consciousness and black power (Buthelezi 1976; Boesak 1977). In 1977, at the instigation of Buthelezi, a bishop, the Lutheran World Federation declared apartheid a heresy and the World Alliance of Reformed Churches followed suit. The appointment of an Anglican bishop, Desmond Tutu, as its president reinvigorated the South African Council of Churches, which now became a focus of government attention. As militant action and government repression increased, church leaders of all hues, including Catholics, and Baptist and Pentecostal churches that had tried to remain neutral, were brought together by Pentecostal leader Frank Chicane and Catholic theologian Albert Nolan who drafted the *Kairos Document* (1985). This was largely a black Christian response to the crisis and called on all the churches to face the 'moment of truth' and reject apartheid, and also any 'cheap reconciliation' as long as apartheid remained in place, urging direct Christian participation in the struggle. It was not long before the edifice of apartheid crumbled, and from 1990 the role of the churches changed from liberation to reconciliation and 'acting as a midwife' to the birth of democracy, in the words of the now Archbishop Tutu. The first act was reconciliation with the Dutch Reformed Church at a meeting in Rustenburg in 1991 where it is estimated that more than 90 per cent of South Africa's Christians and 70 per cent of its population were represented (de Gruchy 2004: 209).

As is well known, Christians played key leadership roles in the peace-making initiatives and in the Truth and Reconciliation Commission (TRC) which followed the end of apartheid. However, the international enthusiasm for the South African truth and reconciliation model is not entirely shared. The involvement of the churches had great advantages, such as access to grassroots networks and the possibility of greater support for victims, but it also changed what was initially a legal and political process into 'a morally and religiously sanctioned process of absolution' (Van der Merwe 2003: 274), a national 'baptism in tears' (Daye 2004: 2). In hindsight, this 'blurring of the line between politics and religion' may have taken place at the expense both of legal justice, on the one hand, and of the churches' specific gifts and ongoing work for reconciliation, on the other (van der Merwe 2003: 270; cf. Chapman 2003). From a black South African point of view, Tinyiko Sam Maluleke, professor of theology at the University of Natal, fears the work of the Commission was merely 'cosmetic'. Noting the absence or silence of black voices in the discourse of the 'New South Africa', he insists that true reconciliation presupposes liberation – a point which was made in the *Kairos Document* but not strongly enough for some. Furthermore, he finds that questions of justice, culpability and, most importantly, restitution are not being addressed. He reminds his readers that reconciliation 'is the sole prerogative of the victimized', who are overwhelmingly the black majority and, he believes, silenced by the TRC. He points out that the South African commission is one of many worldwide since the 1970s and regards them all as part of the 'Euro-American human rights campaign' by which the Third World becomes the victim of the 'new world order' (Maluleke 1999). The TRC can therefore only ever be part of the process of reconciliation and truth-telling; black theology, he suggests, will demand more: reconciliation to black cultures and world-view. In a continent where 70 per cent of the people depend on the land for their sustenance (Ndung'u 2003: 58) and where land is associated with wealth, the African world-view has a lot to do with distribution of land. The seizure of the land of Africa by Europeans had a devastating effect on the people, and land distribution is a burning issue for Africans today, as much in South Africa as it is in neighbouring Zimbabwe. Development in Africa cannot therefore be reduced to economics, while ignoring questions of justice and land ownership.

Domination, conversion and revival in east and central Africa

It was from southern Africa that the famous explorer David Livingstone, initially an LMS missionary, pushed into the interior of Africa in the 1850s to stop the Arab slave trade in the east, which was now spreading further and further inland – although part of the reason for the growth in slavery was to supply European plantations around the Indian Ocean (Ward 1999: 213). He succeeded in charting the river, but the Universities' Mission to Central Africa, which attempted to follow up his initiative, found the possibilities for commerce were overstated and soon withdrew to the coast. They later established missions in what are now southern Tanzania and Malawi. The coast being Muslim-dominated, missions there concentrated on freed slaves. Whereas in western and southern Africa, revived Roman Catholic missionary activity was about a generation behind that of Protestants, in the east which – being further from Europe until the opening of the Suez Canal in 1869 – was reached later, Catholic missions had a greater presence. The Holy Ghost Fathers established a settlement for slaves at Bagamoyo, now in Tanzania, in 1863, and in 1878 the Society of Missionaries in Africa, known as the 'White Fathers', was made responsible for the evangelization of the Great Lakes region (see Shorter 2006). The island of Madagascar was also an early focus of missionary attention. The LMS started work there in 1820, but after several years was forced to withdraw due to severe persecution from the government; although the church continued to grow. In 1868 a Protestant queen, Ranavalona, was crowned, and mission work recommenced, with Catholic and other groups joining. Christians are now a large minority in Madagascar, where the traditional religion is also particularly strong.

In east Africa, faced with growing Muslim influence and threats from slave-traders from Egypt in the 1870s, Mutesa, king of Buganda (north of Lake Victoria in modern Uganda), asked for Christian missionaries – apparently more in the hope of getting arms and balancing Muslim with Christian advice than out of any willingness to become a Christian. CMS missionaries arrived in 1877, and were soon followed by White Fathers. The king soon found the Christian presence as threatening as the Muslim one and had the first Anglican bishop killed en route together with his entourage. In 1885–6 Mwanga, Mutesa's son successor, blamed Christians for a series of misfortunes and martyred up to 200, including 31 men and boys – Catholic and Protestant – at Namugongo, which is now a shrine. After this Christians and Muslims united to overthrow king Mwanga but they could not agree on who should govern, the matter only being resolved – in favour of Protestants – when the British intervened and took over the country. In a remarkably short time, having taken root among the African leaders like chief Stanislaus Mugwanya (1849–1938), Christianity became an integral part of Ugandan society and had 'a profound effect on the moral, intellectual and cultural life, both nationally and locally' (Ward 1999: 215). Naturally this development did not satisfy Muslim leaders, and their resentment formed part of the background to the tyrannical rule of Idi Amin in the twentieth century, who created more Christian martyrs, including Archbishop Janani Luwum in 1977.

Although Western missionaries are prominent in the story of the growth of Christianity in east Africa especially, the day-to-day evangelization was largely the work of black evangelists, whose stories are only now being told – for example on the *Dictionary of African Christian Biographies* website. Louise Pirouet (1978) was the first to document the stories of Ganda church workers, many of them employed by Western missions but hitherto given little recognition. Reverend Apolo Kivebulaya, for example, worked for CMS as an evangelist in western Uganda and then moved on to work with another people group in Congo. He was paid a tiny salary, most of which he gave away, and is remembered for his radiating happiness. Pirouet showed how many of these 'evangelists' were as much 'foreign missionaries' as any of their white counterparts because they worked far from home in different cultural and linguistic settings. From experience in Nigeria, Andrew Walls points out that 'the terminal connection through which the Christian faith passes into African society' (Walls 1996: 87) is often not even an official church worker but lay Christians moving, individually or as a group, into a new area and practising their faith, or a returning member of the village who has become a

Christian elsewhere. Walls' research did not yield a single instance of a village congregation being founded by a missionary, white or black.

Many Africans embraced the Christianity brought by the nineteenth-century missions, but most were ignorant of it, indifferent to it, antagonized by its rejection of local customs or alienated because of Christian–Muslim tensions (Isichei 1995: 155). Among sociological studies of why Africans converted, Robin Horton's thesis (1971) remains very influential. Horton argued that Christianity and Islam were equally 'catalysts' in the process of transition from the 'microcosmic' world-view of village life to the 'macrocosmic' view required by modernity. The specific content of the religions was largely irrelevant because they were merely part of a process of change that was already underway. Horton's and other studies from sociological and anthropological perspectives are unsatisfactory because they fail to take into account the religious factors involved. Even if Horton's thesis is accepted, this is not to say that conversion took place for secular motives. The reasons that led Africans to convert arose out of their religious beliefs, especially their association of religion with power, so that, once they were convinced of the superior strength of the Christian or Muslim God, they redirected their religion towards this higher divinity (Walls 1996: 89). It may be argued that this response represents the teaching of traditional religion, not the teaching of Christianity in which 'power is made perfect in weakness' (2 Cor. 12.9). However, conversion is only an entry point to Christian faith; the influence of living in a Christian (or Muslim) community and religious education means that the reasons for retaining the new faith may be different from those for opting for it initially, so African Christians are not necessarily practising their traditional religion under a new guise (cf. Fisher 1973), although this is an accusation often made, especially against African initiated churches.

East Africa was the source of several significant movements within the mission churches. The best known, the Balokole ('saved people') revival of the 1930s, was led by a partnership of CMS missionary Dr Joe Church and a respected African leader Simeoni Nsibambi, and inspired a radical egalitarianism (see Church 1981). It began in Rwanda and Uganda but had a wide influence across east Africa. As Ward points out, at one level it was a typical Evangelical revival movement, emphasizing repentance from sin and dependence on the blood of Jesus for salvation. But at another level it was 'profoundly African' because members saw themselves as a 'new clan', and expressed this by looking after widows and arranging marriages (Ward 1999: 224). However, the movement distanced itself from African-led churches of the time by disallowing speaking in tongues, prophecy and healing ministries (Anderson 2001: 144). In Kenya the 'brethren' (and sisters) became famous for their courage in refusing to take the oath of the Mau Mau rebels in the 1950s. The movement left behind a traditional, conservative Church of Uganda, the second largest group after the Roman Catholic Church, which tends to see itself as 'the conscience of the state' (Kasibante 1998: 366). Although the mission churches in east Africa generally follow the pattern of male leadership brought from Europe, across all the churches women's groups are particularly strong and, being relatively free from clerical control, have provided church women with opportunities to express their faith in an African idiom (Isichei 1995: 277). New African religious orders in the Catholic Church include the Bannabikira (Daughters of the Virgin) and the Little Sisters of St Francis, both founded in Uganda. Women's organizations, wearing colourful costumes, are a prominent feature in all the churches in Africa. In 2007, according to its website, 1.3 million of the 3.6 million members of the (Anglican) Mothers' Union were in Africa, about half of them in Tanzania. The Mothers' Union offers women a place where their traditional role is supported and where, among other women, they can assert themselves and lead. It also provides a means of challenging the male hierarchies to listen to women's perspectives (Wild 1998).

African independence and African initiated churches

In the nineteenth century particularly, a gulf opened up in world-view between post-Enlightenment Europeans and most sub-Saharan Africans of the colonial period with respect to causality. Missionaries were shocked by witchcraft, invoking ancestors and belief in a spirit world, which evoked a pre-Christian 'dark' era in Europe and reminded them of practices condemned in the Old Testament. Many regarded traditional beliefs as a dangerous delusion; others gave credence to the beliefs but regarded them as devilish. Thus the traditional religion was either suppressed or demonized (Kirwen 1987), or discounted as a religion. Few missionaries were able to engage traditional religion in a constructive way, and so they tended to take a *tabula rasa* approach. African Christians were expected to reject their previous way of life and to exist in a culture vacuum, having abandoned their own cultural ways

of responding to problems, diseases, evil spirits and calamities on the instructions of the missionaries but discovering that the mission churches could not
provide alternative ways to deal with the problems (Adamo 2000: 339–40).
Furthermore, there were wide differences in the cultural customs of rural
Africa and those of the largely urbanized missionaries, but most missionaries
assumed that their customs were 'Christian'. Throughout the colonial period,
Europeans aimed to exercise a high level of control over church members'
lives, thus implicitly questioning the depth and genuineness of African faith.
This questioning was explicit in the common insistence on a long period
of preparation before baptism and the slowness of most missions to ordain
African leaders. Many missionaries were the products of movements in the
West that emphasized 'holiness' in the sense of detachment from the world and
moral purity, particularly sexual purity. The social issue that arguably caused
most misunderstanding was polygamy (or more accurately polygyny), which
was widely practised in Africa but anathema to Europeans, and associated in
their minds with Islam. Most missions had policies that male converts with
more than one wife 'put the others away' before baptism; men found to be
practising polygamy after baptism were excommunicated. Since these women
had no protection outside marriage, this caused great suffering, and it often
meant the most upstanding men of African society were denied baptism.

During the nineteenth century, there was a 'withdrawal upwards' of
missionaries into institutions and the creation of more of a social distance
between European clergy and 'natives' (Ward 1999: 221). African peoples
could even be described as 'child-races', although much missionary effort
was put into proving that they could become equivalent to Europeans (Walls
1996: 93). Until the colonial period this 'civilization' generally consisted
in creating Christian villages. Sometimes these involved the settlement of
nomadic groups, sometimes freed slaves; mostly they were places where
converts could live together untainted by the world around them; in east
Africa they became 'almost autonomous states' (Hinchliff 2002: 485). Later,
Christian boarding schools were seen as offering a similar opportunity to
mould Africans after a European model. Missionaries in charge of these
and other institutions were 'usually well-intentioned, sometimes harsh, even
brutal, but always autocratic' (Isichei 1995: 136). John William Colenso,
Anglican bishop of Natal in the mid-nineteenth century influenced by the
social Christianity of Frederick Maurice, was one of the first Europeans to
oppose the Darwinists and argue for the respect of African – in this case
Zulu – traditions, and for their rights. Furthermore, the questions of his

African students about the Pentateuch and the book of Joshua caused him to query their content and accuracy (O'Connor 2000: 82–3). Colenso's views on the Bible and on Africans dominated the first Lambeth Conference (of the worldwide Anglican Communion) in 1867, but what Victorians found most shocking was his defence of polygamy (Hinchliff 2002: 484). At the Lambeth Conference in 1988, African bishops were sympathetic to polygamy (which was the practice of the Old Testament patriarchs), but at the next conference (1998) they spoke out against homosexuality in a way that offended many whose forebears had slated polygamy (see below).

Missionary paternalism and other 'failures of love' (David B. Barrett quoted in Walls 1996: 112), coupled with increasing African knowledge of the Bible, led to dissatisfaction with missionary churches and their concepts of holiness. In the late nineteenth century, it became apparent that Europeans were less in control of the churches than sometimes appeared (Pirouet 1989: 149) when Africans began to form churches independent of missionary control, the so-called African initiated churches (AICs). The first stirrings took place in South Africa when, in 1872, 158 Sotho Christians left the Paris Evangelical Mission, only to return later (Isichei 1995: 125). In 1884 in Transkei, Nehemiah Tile (d. 1891), a talented African leader who clashed with his Methodist superintendent, founded an ethnic Thembu church with the king as its head. This was intended as a political statement of 'the ultimate supremacy of the Coloured races throughout South Africa' (quoted in Saayman 1991: 66). In 1892 Mangane Mokone and others founded the 'Ethiopian Church' in Johannesburg – the name 'Ethiopian' took on even greater connotations of African pride after Ethiopia's defeat of Italy in 1896 – in protest at blacks and whites meeting separately at a Methodist conference. They unsuccessfully tried to join the African Methodist Episcopal Church in America and then formed a rather ambiguous alliance with the (Anglican) Church of the Province of Southern Africa (see Goedhals 2000). In west Africa there were calls for secession because of the ill-treatment of Samuel Crowther. His staunch defender, and protester at racial discrimination in Sierra Leonean Anglicanism, James Johnson, resisted these, even when he was rudely dismissed as assistant bishop and 600 others formed the African Church Organisation in 1901 in protest. Lagos Baptists separated in 1888. Similar new churches to these were founded in other west African countries and are sometimes distinguished from the Ethiopian churches in South Africa by the label 'African'. The new Ethiopian/African churches were more a statement of independent governance than an attempt to be churches in an

African way. Most retained the worship and theology of the mission churches (Isichei 1995: 179–80) but they were (and are) a statement that Christianity is African. They were among the first independence movements.

A new wave of AICs arose in the period 1910–30 which, following professor of global Pentecostal studies Allan Anderson's classification, may be termed 'prophet-healing' or 'spiritual' (2001: 16–18). Like biblical prophets they arose in a time of crisis (Daneel 1987: 47); in this case from a feeling that 'the Western God was spiritually inadequate and irrelevant to deal with the reality of many aspects of our lives', and a concern about 'how deep the Christian faith really is when so many of its affiliates still continue to visit the caretakers of the African traditional religions' (Organisation of African Instituted Churches (OAIC) quoted in Pobee and Ositelu 1998: 68). African Christians turned to the Bible for their models because they 'did not want to imitate the practices of the mission Churches' (Ndung'u 2000: 241) but demanded 'spiritual independence from the religious imperialism of Western extra-biblical ideas' (Mbiti 1986: 29). What these churches have in common is that they represent a rediscovery of Christianity by Africans who, because of their African religious heritage, emphasize prophecy, healing and spiritual power (Anderson 2001: 16–18; Pobee and Ositelu 1998: 43, 34). They are led by a charismatic figure, a prophet; a few of them have women founders. Women are also perceived to 'get more possessed' ... are prone to give more testimonies '... are more operative in initiating songs, dancing, jumping and clapping, than men' (Ayegboyin and Ishola 1997: 30). The prophet is known as a preacher and as a healer, combining African practices with Christian patterns of exorcism. The priestly role of Christian leaders is not stressed and the celebration of Holy Communion is not prominent in the AICs (Walls 1996: 115). Most of the churches tolerate polygamy, and in their dress and activities they represent a turning away from modernity in favour of African culture. Especially in Congo and southern Africa, the new communities were formed by converts and often took on the features of a 'Christian tribe', often resistant to or uncooperative with colonial institutions (Daneel 1987: 48). However, it is difficult to generalize about what is a very diverse phenomenon, of which it is only possible to give a few of the most notable examples here, beginning with west Africa.

The Harrist churches in Ivory Coast and Ghana take their name from William Wadé Harris (1865–1929), a Grebo Liberian Methodist lay preacher, who began an itinerant ministry after he apparently received a call from the angel Gabriel, and later the gift of tongues, while in prison for political activities in Liberia. In many ways Harris is the classic example of the African prophet-leader. He walked barefoot from village to village with his companions. These included two women associates who led singing and dancing in traditional style. He wore a long white calico robe and white turban, with crossed black bands around his chest, carried a Bible, a rattle made from a gourd and a staff in the shape of a cross, which he used to perform miraculous acts of healing (although he destroyed it periodically so that people would worship the staff itself (Isichei 1995: 285)). Harris' activities attracted a mass following, an estimated 120,000 baptisms in one year, among the people of Ivory Coast and Ghana. He tolerated polygamy but urged people to renounce traditional religious practices, burn fetishes and believe in the God of the Bible. Like John the Baptist (and unlike the missionaries), he immediately baptized those who responded, as an act of purification and preservation before they received Christian teaching. Harris did not intend to form a church but directed people to existing churches, or to build prayer houses where there were no churches led by members of the village. Some joined the Catholic Church and others the Methodist Church, although groups later seceded from both. There are now several different Harrist churches, two of them founded by women. The French administration of Ivory Coast imprisoned Harris and he was deported to Liberia in 1914. His followers were persecuted and many of their prayer houses destroyed. The 'Aladura' churches of Nigeria are so named because of their emphasis on prayer and fasting, especially as a means of healing without medication – traditional or Western. By 1950 they were the most prominent Christian expression in Nigeria and very influential in society. They grew out of Anglican prayer meetings in Yorubaland during the 1918 flu pandemic, which were led by Joseph Shadare and Sophia Odunlami and were found unacceptable by the church authorities. Some of these churches have had contact with British and American Pentecostal groups, but only on their own terms. The movement is mostly urban and has several different branches. The Church of the Lord (Aladura) was founded by an Anglican schoolteacher Josiah Ositelu who had many visions, healed – sometimes by the use of 'holy names' and 'seals' – and exposed witchcraft by divine knowledge. His successor, Apostle Adeleke Adejobi, saw the church spread to Sierra Leone and Ghana. He laid a theological foundation for the church and took it into the World Council of Churches in 1975. Of later foundation, the Celestial Church of Christ, which may now be the largest Aladura church, has distinctive taboos and its members go barefoot. Founded in the 1930s as the result of a revival led by the prophet Joseph Ayo Babalola, the church is now very involved in education, and has good relations with government and the 'historic churches' (Anderson 2001: 81–7).

South Africa has more AICs than anywhere else – perhaps as many as six thousand – and more than half the Christian population belong to them; in other words, they are now the mainstream. They are usually known as 'Zionist' or 'apostolic' churches. They began in 1903 as a branch of a North American Pentecostal group, the Christian Catholic Apostolic Church in Zion, which claimed to liberate Africans and soon attracted several thousand Zulu followers. Like early Pentecostals, Zionists practise baptism by immersion, divine healing without medicine or doctors, encourage prophesying and speaking in tongues and do not take alcohol or smoke tobacco. However, African leaders soon split off from the American movement because of racism. The leaders are seen as 'Moses figures' who bring their people out of the slavery of sickness, oppression, poverty and evil spirits into the promised land, the 'city of Zion'. This new city is concretely expressed in the churches, which are called 'cities of Zion'. Baptism takes place in a river, as is common across Africa. The South African government encouraged the growth of AICs as part of its policy of apartheid, and the Zion Christian Church, the largest in South Africa, was accused of supporting the regime, although Anderson finds evidence that its members did not. Although smaller than in South Africa, Zionist churches were estimated to constitute 36 per cent of the population of Zimbabwe in 2000, substantially more than all the other Christian denominations combined (24 per cent; Anderson 2001: 93–120).

The most famous AIC in central Africa is the Kimbanguist Church founded by prophet Simon Kimbangu (c. 1887–1951) in the Belgian Congo in 1921. Kimbangu was denied the post of evangelist in the Baptist Mission Society because he could not read well enough, but later in the village of Nkamba he reputedly performed miracles of healing and even raising from the dead. Soon crowds flocked to hear him, believing that a new African Pentecost had come, and other prophets began to appear. The colonial authorities declared a state of emergency, and Kimbangu was sentenced to death but eventually held until he died in prison 30 years later. The authorities, often with the help of European missions, persecuted his followers, and many were deported, although this just encouraged the spread of the movement. Kimbangu's wife, Muile Marie, led the movement, which appealed to the United Nations for help, and was finally granted recognition in 1959. Kimbangu is regarded by the church as an African Jesus, and accorded a divine status as one who 'died and rose again and is with us in the spirit' (Anderson 2001: 128). Pilgrimages to Nkamba-Jerusalem are encouraged and the prison where Kimbangu was confined is also a shrine. However, the church has distanced itself from 'nguzi' movements, which regard Kimbangu as a black messiah who will restore the ancient Kongo empire. Officially Kimbangu is only a prophet, and the church, which has more than 7 million members – second only to the Catholic Church in Congo – is a member of the World Council of Churches.

In east Africa, Kenya is also home to the largest secession from the Roman Catholic Church, Maria Legio (the Legion of Mary), which is spread throughout east Africa. It was founded in 1963 by a layman, Simeon Mtakatifu Ondeto, and a laywoman, Gaudensia Aoko, who denounced witchcraft and began mass baptisms. The church retains much Catholic liturgy, and the leader is called 'Pope', but it also shares many of the common features of African churches. Within the Roman Catholic church, Emmanuel Milingo, Catholic archbishop of Lusaka from 1969 to 1983, practised a popular ministry of exorcism and healing, accepting the reality of the spirit world for the African (Isichei 1995: 6, 330). He was investigated by the authorities and removed from his see, but while in Rome he caught the attention of the Catholic charismatic movement and was allowed to continue his healing ministry in Italy. In general, the Roman Catholic Church has avoided schisms but has lost members to the new churches. AICs are most numerous in Kenya because of the 'Holy Spirit' movement, which began in a revival movement in the Anglican Church around the time of the First World War and spread among the Luo and Luyia people. In a study of the Holy Ghost Church of East Africa (HGCEA), one of largest and most orthodox of results of the movement in Kenya, Philomena Njeri Mwaura of Kenyatta University shows how the anti-colonial aspects of the movement now hinder the Kenyan government agenda for development, which focuses on overcoming poverty, disease and ignorance (Mwaura 2003). The church took root among poor people, originally peasants, who took the Bible as their sole authority and formed a 'church tribe'. The distinct community, distinguished by their turbans and long dresses or cassocks, are bound together by common worship and a shared millennialist and separatist theology, influenced by African traditions, which determines their social behaviour. Whereas at first they expected an imminent end, they now take a longer-term view and have bought land cooperatively and built permanent houses and churches. Their high moral standards, simple lifestyle and hard work make them popular with employers and they have seen some upward mobility. These days their children go to school, and some to university, although they still resist medical intervention. Sometimes their enthusiasm for 'spiritual' matters and excessive fasting affects productivity and detracts from social responsibilities, but the real reason that groups like these are seen as 'hindering development' is their lack of cooperation with government and their counter-cultural lifestyle. The value they place on community and concern for the weakest over commercial gain are under pressure from the neo-capitalist ethos of contemporary society, and AICs are generally declining. In their place have come the newer Pentecostal churches, which, with their emphasis on wealth, are more suited to late or post-modernity.

From the start, African initiatives in Christianity were heavily criticized by missionaries and leaders of mission-founded churches that lost members, and they were sometimes suppressed by the authorities. There is always a concern whether, in dealing with the spirit world, African churches are embracing African traditional beliefs or whether their intention is to confront the spirits with the power of the Holy Spirit (cf. Anderson 1991: 120–5). In the first Western study of the AICs, Bengt Sundkler damned AICs in the eyes of the West by describing them as 'the bridge over which Africans are brought back to heathenism', and calling them 'syncretistic' because they indiscriminately mixed Christian elements with those from African traditional religion. Others have viewed them as a 'witchcraft eradication movement', perceiving that they were preoccupied with overcoming the witchcraft which retains a powerful place in traditional African societies. Often AICs are labelled 'separatist' and seen as 'breaking away' from the churches founded by Western missions (Pobee and Ositelu 1998: 29–30). In fact, groups such as the Aladura churches in west Africa were pushed out, and others were the result of movements founded as alternatives to the existing churches rather than splits from them (Pobee and Ositelu 1998: 2). Some term the AICs 'nativistic', usually meaning 'primitive and barbarous' (page 32). Others make fun of them for claiming to be African while imitating Western churches (page 53). But Sundkler later revised his opinion of AICs, and nowadays churches of African origin are generally recognized by other Christians, although there are ongoing concerns about their doctrines and practices, especially since few have developed tertiary-level theological training. There are many legitimate criticisms of these churches: for example, they suffer from cults of personality, frequent schism and poor administration. There is evidence that some leaders 'have alliances with witches and wizards' and some abuse their positions to indulge in plural marriages and extramarital affairs (Ayegboyin and Ishola 1997: 156–7). But as John Pobee, an Anglican theologian from Ghana, and the late Gabriel Ositelu, primate of the Nigerian-based Church of the Lord

(Aladura), insist, they also make important contributions, which the OAIC themselves summarized in 1996 as the following: awareness of the wholeness of creation and the power of sacred symbols; an appreciation for the generation and sharing of life; a sense of family and community; relatedness to our predecessors in the communion of saints; rediscovery of the church as a life-giving organ to society; renewal in the Holy Spirit leading to freedom from fear of other spirits; an emphasis on healing by the Spirit (Pobee and Ositelu 1998: 70–1).

Health and wealth in African churches

Decolonization came relatively late to most of Africa. Expectations were high, but prospects for development were poor. There were the problems of drought, poor education and healthcare, rapid population growth and limited economic resources, and little preparation had been done to help Africans manage their own affairs (Meredith 2006: 141–2, 150–4). Furthermore, the nations of Africa were defined by territories drawn up by colonial map-makers with little regard for questions of ethnicity, language or African history. Nigeria, for example, 'had more linguistic, cultural, historical, and religious diversity than the whole of Europe put together' (Walls 2002: 105). Since independence, most African nations have followed a remarkably similar path: the independence leaders were authoritarian rulers, mostly at the head of one-party states; some survived there for two or three decades, others were overthrown by military coup. Twenty countries have experienced or continue to experience civil war, but most nations have held together and several have instituted democratic reform in recent years. But continued poverty, ongoing war, a refugee population comprising 40 per cent of the world's total, increasingly severe climates, and HIV/AIDS are just some of the problems facing African governments, and which concerned Christians try to address (e.g. Mugambi and Nasimiyu-Wasike 2003). Health and wealth are therefore a major concern for church leaders, but this is demonstrated in two different ways: the leaders of the former mission churches tend to work with governments on development programmes, whereas the leaders of more popular churches are inclined to help their congregations to better themselves by more 'spiritual' means.

The emphasis on healing in AICs is an important distinguishing characteristic and a major reason for their spread (Walls 1996: 97–100; Kyomo

2003: 151). Most of the prophets were regarded as healers, and many rejected medicine as a means of healing, thus heightening the power of God and the victory of Christ over the evil powers believed to be causing the sickness. Sickness is hardly less of an issue for Africans today than it was then. The scourge of AIDS, malaria and other pandemics is unabated, and disease due to lack of sanitation, unclean water and other preventable causes is rife, so healthcare is a major concern of Christian organizations in Africa. Although African governments now take the main responsibility, many churches in Africa continue to run hospitals, clinics and healthcare projects as they did in the colonial period, often supported by Christians in other wealthier countries, including South Korea and other new missionary-sending countries. Because AICs tend to reject medicine and professional healers, the question of whether (when they can afford it) Christians should use them is a live issue in African theology. Christians may need reassurance that 'it was God who gave doctors and scientists (including traditional medicine men) the skill and understanding of developing the many kinds of medicine that can cure sickness' (Kyomo 2003: 150). For those millions of Christians who cannot afford access to healthcare, or whose health practitioners are unscrupulous, the belief that healing comes from God gives at least a ray of hope.

Speaking in 1972, Manas Buthelezi declared, '[T]he African has a sense of the wholeness of life' in the sense that the living are in fellowship with the dead, the supernatural and natural interrelate and the sacred and secular are not separated (Buthelezi 1997: 85–6). Illness in African thought is disharmony in human and cosmic relations (Ela 1988: 50–1). Since God is master of all the cosmic powers, for African writers healing disease is only a specific example of the wider life-giving work of the God (Kyomo 2003: 148; Bula 1992: 247; cf. Stinton 2004) and healing is holistic – restoring life (Stinton 2004: 54–61). Healing in African traditional medicine and in the Bible is not a matter of treating the illness but of treating the person in their body and in all their relationships (Walls 1996: 98), including those with the 'natural world'. So there is no discontinuity between healing and reconciliation, or between healing and creation (Bula 1992: 247; Kyomo 2003: 149). African perceptions that illness is due to spiritual causes and that cure is wholeness offer challenges to Western theories and methods of health and healing and are reflected in international debate about church health services (Commission on World Mission and Evangelism 2005). Buthelezi also refused to separate health and wealth but went on to define poverty from the perspective of an African theology of creation as 'alienation from the wholeness of life' by being cut off from the life-sustaining gifts of God that we receive and share with others (Buthelezi 1997: 89). The perception of African traditional religion that 'a people are only definable in terms of their total environment' is borne out in studies of different people groups in east Africa, for whom 'the integrity of this environment is defined in terms of "peace, harmony and prosperity" and depends on people's cooperation with one another. Therefore, when their environment is destroyed, people lose their identity, and even their name' (Kinoti 2003: 10, 16). African theologians express a concern about the pursuit of wealth in Africa today in the context of late capitalism. That worry is not so much a fear of materialism – the material has not been separated from the spiritual in African faith – but that the ideal of what constitutes wealth is so far from the holistic vision of the ancestors (African and Christian) and that the demand to share wealth is undermined (Getui 2003; Moyo 2003).

Since about 1970, the concern of popular Christianity has shifted from health to wealth. Sub-Saharan Africa has seen a new wave of Christian-inspired movements, usually described as 'Pentecostal', which are more concerned with social success than healing. Western Pentecostal churches have been in existence in Africa for nearly a century. Some, such as the Assemblies of God, are large and widespread and many of the AICs also have Pentecostal–charismatic characteristics. But the initiative is now with the newer churches, which differ from the older AICs in that they are largely an urban phenomenon, they relate to modern Africa – a difference at once obvious in their dress and music styles (Walls 1996: 92–3) – and they respond to the needs of a new post-colonial and post-modern generation (Anderson 2001: 167, 170). They are partly the result of globalized communications systems, which make the broadcasts of Western 'televangelists' available to African audiences and enable these men to make regular visits to Africa. The most prominent of these is the German evangelist Reinhard Bonnke, who has been leading 'crusades' which attract hundreds of thousands since 1971. Some of the churches arose as a result of student groups or were founded by university academics. They share the general characteristics of worldwide Pentecostalism, practise some of the church growth methods of Yoido Full Gospel Church in South Korea, and use 'name and claim it' methods associated with some North American evangelists, but they have an African face, especially in their emphasis on deliverance from demonic forces associated with traditional religion. The most dramatic growth has been in west Africa, and some of the most prominent churches, which number their members in hundreds of thousands, are the Deeper Life Bible Church, the Redeemed Christian Church of God, Winner's Chapel, and Living

Faith World Outreach originating in Nigeria; Church of God International based in Benin; and Church of Pentecost in Ghana. These have spread in east Africa – especially Uganda – central Africa – particularly Zambia – and to a lesser extent in South Africa. These churches also have branches in Britain, the United States and where there are African diaspora. Within Africa too, Pentecostal churches are not just black but also white and Indian (Pillay 1994).

From a sociological point of view, the new churches have brought about a cultural shift: the emphasis on personal decision encourages individualism and the breakdown of the extended family; they reorder society for the benefit of youth and allow women leadership roles; and the gospel of faith legitimizes the accumulation of wealth, which might previously have been ascribed to witchcraft. They can also break down ethnic barriers, although equally they can demonize those outside (Gifford 1998: 347). Paul Gifford describes a visit to Winner's Chapel in Accra, Ghana, where the most commonly used word is 'breakthrough'. One way to achieve 'breakthrough' is for each member of the huge congregation to wave a white handkerchief, called a 'mantle' (in reference to the prophet Elisha, 2 Kgs 2.9), which is given a 'double anointing' by the 'man of God' or 'prophet' leading the service. The congregation then wave their mantles over 'their instruments of destiny' – objects associated with their desired success (a pen for scholarship, for instance). 'Breakthrough', writes Gifford, refers to God's intervention to prosper his chosen followers, for instance in the biblical cases of Abraham, whose faith was (apparently) rewarded with wealth, Joseph, who went 'from prison to palace', and David, who defeated Goliath. Winner's, which is part of a Nigerian multinational, and other large churches sponsor television and radio programmes, which are 'staple' fare for Ghanaian television and radio. They include many testimonies declaring what benefits people have received through their 'prophet', usually of a material kind, and sermons about achieving success. Gifford is highly critical of these new 'prophets' whose gospel is open to abuse and does not address the underlying problems of Ghanaian society. However, the most successful prophet of all, Mensa Otabil, preaches about success brought about by hard work, assuming responsibility and obtaining education. Otabil does not dismiss witches and spirits but rises above people's personal fears to address social ills and make calls for political reform. While others have been exposed as corrupt, Otabil's personal integrity and careful negotiation of politics, Gifford writes, has won him the admiration of younger pastors and had widespread influence for the good (Gifford 2005).

Most leaders of independence movements and the first generation of government leaders were products of mission schools, who had learnt there how to 'play the foreigners at their own game' (Walls 2002: 106). In some cases, their plans for development could be ascribed in part to these influences, such as Julius Nyerere of Tanzania's 'African socialism' (Parratt 1997: 109) and the 'humanism' of Kenneth Kaunda of Zambia (a Presbyterian) (Isichei 1995: 340; Parratt 1995: 143–8). On independence the mission churches became national institutions and 'seriously and self-consciously assumed for themselves a "nation-building role"' (Walls 2002: 106). However, after independence the roles became reversed. Governments stalled and weakened but the churches grew rapidly in numbers and strength. In times of crisis when government has all but broken down, there have been several instances where the churches have filled a vacuum until order was restored (cf. Walls 2002: 100): for example, in Uganda under Amin, in South Africa during apartheid and in Kenya under one-party rule. There are many examples of brave and costly leadership by Christians. In the political turmoil of 1980s Kenya, (Anglican) Archbishop David Gitari of Kenya drew on the prophets of the Old Testament to denounce injustice from the pulpit and, at great personal cost, helped to change the course of political affairs (Gitari 1996: 10). On the other hand, there have also been occasions when the churches have manifestly failed in their social responsibilities and have been complicit in injustices. The most horrifying example was the Rwandan genocide of 1994 which took place in a country more than 90 per cent Christian. Though there were many cases of heroism by individuals, many church leaders justified, orchestrated and took part in the killing, and betrayed their congregations, who were killed in their churches (McCullum 2004). Recently a number of African political leaders have openly declared their Evangelical faith, with varying effects. Frederick Chiluba, converted in prison and baptized in the Spirit at a Reinhard Bonnke crusade (Freston 2001: 155), introduced a new constitution when he was president of Zambia (1991–2002) that declared Zambia a 'Christian nation' but at the same time suppressed the opposition (Mwamba 2000). Olusegun Obasanjo, who stepped down as president of Nigeria in 2007, is a Baptist who openly uses Christian language despite the large Muslim community in his country – and probably commanded greater respect from Muslims than those using religious themes opportunistically (Freston 2001: 189). Good governance is a crucial concern for Africa, but leadership in the churches may be as autocratic and self-seeking as in the wider society (Gifford 1998: 343). In this sense, the advent of democracies in many former dictatorships is seen as a challenge to greater openness in church affairs (Kahindi 2003; Kanyandago 1999; Ndung'u 1999: 30; see also de Gruchy 1995).

Government development programmes ran into huge problems in the 1990s because of the structural adjustment policies imposed on many African countries, which severely constrained the ability of governments to offer education, healthcare and other services. In this context, churches and mission agencies were expected to take back many of the public roles which had been taken away from them at independence, and while most of the world passed Africa by, because of their development role Christian missions assumed even greater importance. The trans-national links of the churches were vital for sustaining development initiatives where local resources are so stretched (Gifford 1998: 308–35). The Roman Catholic Church is particularly well supported because it has many foreign missionaries on the ground (although the leadership is African). Compared to before, the 'mainline' Protestant churches whose links are with European churches have seen their funding dwindle. Some of the large independent Evangelical and Pentecostal churches are able to command much greater resources, mainly from North America and east Asia. Such is the attraction they exert that the other churches are drawn into their development initiatives, thus bridging the gap between the developmental and the spiritual approaches to health and wealth. These newer agencies usually include evangelistic activities and also offer clergy training. As they receive much appreciated theological education from the new churches, 'mainline' clergy also imbibe their ethos.

The development programmes that overseas churches and other agencies fund in Africa sometimes detract from the work of the local churches themselves, and are often able to attract their most talented staff. Governmental and non-governmental aid agencies have only recently become aware of the churches as agencies for development and sought to engage them constructively. In 2000 a conference on alleviating poverty in Africa was held in Nairobi between the World Bank and the Council of Anglican Provinces of Africa. In a joint statement, the World Bank and the churches 'recognized in mutual respect each other's role in addressing poverty issues' and both agreed that 'the spiritual dimension of life is an essential component of development', and the World Bank recognized the church's 'ability to influence constructively, based on its numbers, its position as the moral conscience of nations, its closeness to the poor, and its own accountability to God' (Belshaw, Calderisi and Sugden 2001: 8, 9). The World Bank wields great power over African governments at present, but through the trans-national or multinational churches it stands to gain even greater power to effect its development aims in Africa. The needs of Africa are so basic that there is a large measure of commonality between the development aims of government and international bodies and the vision of the kingdom of God: education, health, good governance, economic growth, conflict prevention and post-conflict reconstruction were the main points the Anglicans and the World Bank agreed on. Only in the area of the use of condoms is there any great tension between (some) Christian development agencies and their secular counterparts. However, even there, African Catholic theologians such as Laurenti Magesa are prepared to challenge the church's teaching and advocate the use of prophylactics to prevent the spread of HIV/AIDS (Magesa 2003).

Reading the Bible in Africa

Before European missionaries arrived, west African cultures were linguistically rich, politically sophisticated, artistically vibrant and musically distinctive. Many, like the Yoruba, had a substantial collection of oral literature but they did not have a system of writing, and it was this aspect of European culture that most impressed Africans. Africans who became Christians also became literate, and school teachers were synonymous with evangelists. The freed slaves who settled in Sierra Leone were so convinced of the importance of education that by the mid-nineteenth century they had a higher rate of literacy than most European countries (including Britain) and many were better educated than the Europeans among them (Walls 1996: 102–4). The most lasting legacies of the missionary period in west Africa were the schools and colleges founded, the spread of literacy, and the reduction of African languages to writing. As Lamin Sanneh explains, 'In their vernacular work, Christian missions helped nurse the sentiments for the national cause, which mother tongues crystallized and incited' (1989: 125). The education and literacy work both facilitated African access to modernity and also contributed to the formation of national identities. The long-term result of this was both national independence and also indigenous churches.

Not only did Africans emphasize the importance of reading, but they also laid claim to the Bible in particular, which they recognized as an African book, and which provided an 'indispensable guidance at a crucial period at which they would otherwise have been inarticulate' (Mbiti 1986: 29). It is noticeable in the descriptions above that the AICs have connected particularly with sections of the Old Testament – often with parts which make least sense in the cultures of the West, such as the food and purity laws of Leviticus. Reading the Old Testament, they discovered that polygamy was practised by the patriarchs; that the people of Israel approached God through their ancestors (Mafico 2000: 488); that the people of Israel danced and used a variety of percussion and musical instruments in their worship; and that dreams, visions, prophetic messages and miraculous signs are the means by which God communicated with his people. But the most interesting aspect of African reading of the Bible is the intense identification with the characters and events in the Bible, particularly in the Old Testament. This is especially so since many stories mention the people and places of Africa, which gives African Christians a sense of participation in biblical history (Holter 2000: 579). As the Ethiopians believed themselves to be the heirs of Judah, so the Akurinu Churches of Kenya understand that Mount Sinai, on which the law was given, is Mount Kenya (Ndung'u 2000: 241). African Christians seem to feel part of the biblical world and in continuity with its people; the two worlds 'interpenetrate' (Mbiti 1986: 228). The wisdom of the figures of the Bible has joined the wisdom of the ancestors (cf. Jenkins 2006: 35). For AICs the Bible 'functions primarily as a repository of narratives' which illustrate God's intervention on behalf of his followers (Gifford 2005: 86). This intervention is particularly needed because of the sense of living in a world of spiritual powers, in both the African and the biblical worlds (Parratt 1995: 59). The book of the Bible itself was a symbol of power over evil when brandished by William Harris and other prophet leaders, and the text may function as an incantation, as for example in the Church of the Lord (Aladura). In this church, certain of the Psalms are believed to be effective for specific purposes. For example, the imprecatory Psalms (particularly Ps. 55) are considered to protect from evil ones (Adamo 2000: 340). Other Psalms are regarded as therapeutic (for example, Pss. 6, 20 and 40) and are used in conjunction with traditional methods of healing. Some Psalms (such as Pss. 4; 119.9–16) are identified as efficacious for success in the passing of exams, getting jobs and so on. Careful instructions are given as to how these are to be used in a ritual setting to attain the desired results. AICs claim they 'sought to establish a Christianity of the Bible as we saw it, without Western additions and in harmony with our own cultural heritage '... to make the Christian faith come alive to our own thought and culture' (OAIC quoted in Pobee and Ositelu 1998: 68).

Since most of the members rely on oral rather than a literate understanding of the Bible, as Allan Anderson points out, it is 'meaningless to discuss the interpretation of the text by itself'. Instead African hermeneutics is the 'enlarging' of the meaning of the text being interpreted based on the belief that 'God is speaking' directly to them through the Bible and that the Bible relates to daily experience (Anderson 2000: 133–4). This approach is often referred to as 'fundamentalistic' and related to the attitudes of the colonial missionaries (e.g. Parratt 1995: 62). However, there are many other factors in African cultures that may have a bearing on attitudes to sacred texts, such as African oral traditions and Muslim use of the Qur'an. The controversies which produced Christian fundamentalism in the West have not taken place in Africa (cf. Gifford 1998: 333–4). As Philip Jenkins stresses, Africans are not being 'ultraconservative' in their reading of scripture because, on the whole, they are not taking a political or social stance against 'liberalism'. They may in fact be restoring (legitimate) traditions of interpretation long lost in Europe (Jenkins 2006: 17). R. S. Sugirtharajah's post-colonial approach to biblical interpretation shows the extent to which biblical interpretation and the methods of biblical interpretation serve the ends of the politically powerful – as the furious reaction to Colenso revealed – and equally how both may be powerfully appropriated by those at the margins, as in the case of independence leaders and South Africans under apartheid, who 'read the Bible back' to their oppressors (1995; 2001). Africans give the Bible authority because they choose to do so. They are not untouched by the Enlightenment – only resistant to its shortcomings (Bulangalire 2006).

It is important to bear in mind that most African Christians continue to belong to traditional denominations – Roman Catholic, Anglican, Methodist, and so on – or have dual identities (Ward 1999: 234), so there is considerable overlap between the AICs, Pentecostal and mission churches. The latter are far from being dead and formal, and are also shaped by their African context. Although initially resisted by the 'mainline' churches, Charismatic movements are now embraced by most as a necessary concession to popular demand, and Charismatic Christians are increasingly found in their leadership (Omenyo 2003: 19). The Charismatic movements cut across the different bodies (including the Catholic Church as well) and express the concerns for both health and wealth (Magesa 2003: 27). As this suggests, Africans do not divest themselves of their world-view when they enter the mission churches. A study of belief in witchcraft illustrated this when it was found that African Lutherans held a traditional world-view and understood Christian teaching within that, rather than within the context of anthropology and original sin in the Western Christian tradition. Even within the mission churches, which maintain relationships with churches from many different parts of the world, Christianity 'is already a uniquely African form' (Berg 2005: 49).

Anglicanism is stronger in Africa than in any other continent, and African reading of the Bible is currently at the centre of the controversy that is dividing the Anglican Communion. At the Lambeth Conference of 1998 a motion was passed by an overwhelming majority of the primates present that homosexuality was 'incompatible with Scripture'. The strongest defender of that statement has been Archbishop Peter Akinola of Nigeria, supported by Archbishop Drexel Gomez of the Province of the West Indies, other African, Asian and some European and American bishops. Akinola's pronouncements have been very strongly worded, and after the Episcopal Church in the USA (ECUSA) consecrated a practising homosexual as bishop, he declared the Church of Nigeria to be in a state of 'impaired communion' with ECUSA. The issue raises important questions about the nature of Christian communion and Christian attitudes to homosexuality, but here we will highlight the clash between what appear to be the dominant African approach to biblical inter-pretation and the Western one – at least in the Anglican Communion. The new *Africa Bible Commentary* (Adeyemo 2006), entirely authored by Evangelical African scholars, states that 'The Bible clearly defines homosexuality as a sin' (Turaki 2006: 1355). To appreciate the African position it is important to realize that homosexuality is against the law in most African states, a stance supported by Muslims as well as Christians, and that the responsibility to marry and have children is a very strong expectation, supported by traditional African and biblical world-views (Gen. 1.28; 9.7). It is also the case that there are passages in the New Testament, especially Rom. 1.24–7, which are most straightforwardly understood as condemnations of homosexual practice and orientation. For people who see themselves as inhabiting the world of the New Testament, the message of the Bible seems plain. Furthermore, ECUSA's actions seemed to be disrespectful both of the clear message of Scripture and also of African views. Although it is true that Akinola and others disregard scientific and cultural considerations, not to mention the experience of homosexual people – including many African Christians (Brown 2006) – if there is to be a reconciliation on the issue (and this is written in advance of the Lambeth Conference of 2008), one of the conditions must be that other Christians make a case on the basis of what is written in the Bible, not disregarding it or arguing that the text is superseded in the present context, as liberally minded interpreters tend to do. As leading African Anglican theologian Esther Mombo demonstrates, it is possible to argue that, taking the Bible as a whole, the conclusion that God condemns homosexual practice, and even homosexually oriented people, is unreasonable to draw (Mombo 2006). Christian communion, however, is about more than winning the argument, and biblical interpretation is a matter of spirit as well as letter (2 Cor. 3.6).

African Christian theology is usually described as having two strands: 'African theology', related to traditional African culture; and 'black theology', developed at first in South Africa, with respect to political concerns and relating to the black liberation theologies of North America. We referred to some of the major figures of the black theology in South Africa above: Manas Buthelesi, Alan Boesak and Desmond Tutu. In both cases, the approach to theology has paid close attention to the Bible. African theology as an engagement with traditional culture and religion arose in the independence period. In the face of criticism that this was a distraction from dealing with pressing social and political issues, Ghanaian theologian Kwame Bediako argues that African culture, more than any other, had been so vilified by missionaries and colonialists that it was a necessary first to recover it and affirm that it, like other religions, could be considered a *praeparatio evangelica* – an entry point for the Christian gospel (1997: 427–8). Missionaries produced the first studies of African religion and culture (Parrinder 1949; Taylor 1963; Tempels 1947) and the first modern generation of educated African Christians from the mission churches began their theology by considering – sometimes in a rather reactionary manner – its relationship to the Western Christianity they had received. British theologian John Parratt has helpfully collected and interpreted this work (1995; 1997). Here it is only possible to cite a few examples. Harry Sawyerr, a Protestant from Sierra Leone, was concerned that theology should function to give expression to the Christian gospel using, as far as possible, the religious ideals and rituals of African thought (1968). Charles Nyamiti, a Catholic from Tanzania, applied a similar intent to set the Christian gospel in an African context to the doctrine of God, where he saw that African concepts of the motherhood of God could complement Western emphasis on Fatherhood, and to Christology in a typology of 'Christ our Ancestor' (1973; 1984). Noting the relevance of the Old Testament in Africa, Kwesi Dickson, a Methodist from Ghana, showed how African traditions, such as the understanding that death 'binds up relationships in society', reinforce the Old Testament background to Christian concepts such as the atonement (Dickson 1983; 1997: 82). John Mbiti's thorough study of African religions and philosophy (1969), and his concern that Western theology was 'impotent' in dealing with the African spiritual powers (1976), informed his consideration of eschatology (1971). Mbiti, from Kenya, argued that African understanding of time was past- rather than future-oriented, which he argued made it difficult for Africans to appreciate Western expectations of a yet-to-be-realized kingdom but provided a strong basis for the sacramental in Christian thought. Theologians differed in the degree of continuity they saw between African culture and the Christian gospel. Opinions ranged from the Nigerian Methodist Bolaji Idowu (1965) at one end of the spectrum, who described African traditional religion as 'monotheistic' and used this to inspire pan-African cooperation, to Zairean Catholic Vincent Mulago (1965), writing in French, who saw African culture as merely an 'embellishment' to the Christian tradition (Parratt 1995: 30), and Zairean Evangelical Byang Kato (1975) at the other end, who rejected African traditional religion altogether (cf. Bediako 1997: 431).

Because the focus was on the validity of African traditional religion as a vehicle for theology, the early studies tended to highlight common concerns and not the distinctive aspects of the Christian message (cf. Stinton 2004: 6–9). Much of the initial discussion was on the nature of God, but once African theologians moved beyond missionary criticism and began to do theology on their own terms, African visions of Christ began to emerge. These were not in terms of biblical Christological titles, such as Messiah, Christ, Son of Man, Son of David, the Word, but more related to 'the deeds of Jesus in relation to the individual believer' (Parratt 1995: 78–81). The most prevalent image was of Christ as healer (Bediako 1997: 434; Stinton 2004: 54–61). Although African Christian theology is criticized as an 'elite academic theology' out of touch with grassroots Christianity (e.g. Gifford 1998: 333), Diane Stinton's work has shown that Christ as healer, or life-giver, is a common – if somewhat controversial – view of ordinary church members (Stinton 2004: 80–103). The reason for the ambiguity is that, though the traditional healer in east and west Africa is an educated herbalist, under the influence of Western mission-aries the term has acquired the negative meaning of 'sorcerer' (Stinton 2004: 80–103; cf. Schoffeleers 1994). Nevertheless, leaving aside the terminology, it can be said that Jesus is understood to fulfil the role of an African traditional healer. This is supported by the fact noted earlier that healing is also the chief concern of the AICs. In describing Jesus as healer, the African Christians Stinton interviewed understood Jesus as a life-giver, who recreates wholeness in all aspects of life and is supreme over every form of evil operating in the universe. Jesus as healer is related to other designations such as saviour, liberator and redeemer but is wider than these and overrides them (Stinton 2004: 101, 71–5).

Significantly, many of the church members Stinton interviewed were women, and in the next generation of African theology, women theologians came to the fore, especially through the 'Circle of Concerned African Women Theologians', inaugurated in 1989 by Ghanaian Methodist Mercy Amba Oduyoye. Parratt is right when he describes African feminist theology as 'concerned with women's role in the wholeness of a single humanity rather than in feminism as a revolutionary countermovement' (Parratt 1995: 51). Oduyoye endorses the concern for healing when she declares that 'the cry for salvation/liberation in Africa is primarily a cry for health and wholeness' and this is necessary because of the brokenness of life (Oduyoye 1986: 44). But she also explains that an African woman's commitment to Christ is to the one who countered the forces of evil and gave back her child to the widow of Nain; to the one who liberates from blood taboos and healed the haemor-rhaging woman; to the one who nurtures by feeding and breaking bread; to the one who served and washed the feet of others; to the one who sacrificed himself and approved the woman's sacrifice of oil; to the one who breaks down barriers and holds all things together – including body and soul; it is a commitment to the '"birthing", nurturing and maintenance of life' (Amoah and Oduyoye 1988: 43–5). Musimbi Kanyoro argues that, though the male theologians who started African Christian theology regarded African culture as lost and in need of recovery, from the point of view of African women the culture continues, only certain extra Western elements have been added on (Kanyoro 2001: 112). The reflections of the Circle on a wide range of topics demonstrate the truth of this in the way that they combine African women's wisdom with biblical texts and current issues in new and imaginative ways. In one publication Musa Dube tells the story of post-independence Africa in parallel with that of the bleeding woman who touched Jesus' robe for healing (Dube 2001a), and then she applies a method she likens to traditional divining to the book of Ruth to see the consequences for international relations (Dube 2001b).

Although the old ways persist, especially in women's lives, the rise of the newer Pentecostal–charismatic churches with their concern for success indicates the scale of the changes taking place in many parts of Africa, and questions of wealth and poverty are assuming a more prominent place in theological reflection. In the African context, these are inseparable from questions of land and also the growing environmental questions (Chepkwony

2002: 30). In this respect, the wisdom of the African ancestors has much to offer both in its own right and also in the insights it gives into biblical teaching. The danger is that, seeing it as strange or fundamentalistic, other Christians may fail to see the Christian-ness of African Christianity (Jenkins 2002: 161) and not take the trouble to appreciate its gifts.

Study Questions and Further Readings

- In what way does Christianity in Africa meet the questions Africans are asking?
- What is distinctive about the ways African Christians interpret and apply the Bible?
- How has Christianity hindered or helped African socio-political life?
- In what way is the rise of African initiated churches significant for the church in Africa?
- Discuss ways in which African Christians have responded to ethnic conflicts, political injustice and global economic problems.
- What are the main motifs and themes of African worship and theologies – and why?

Bediako, Kwame (1995), *Christianity in Africa: The Renewal of a Non-Western Religion.* Maryknoll, NY: Orbis.

Hastings, Adrian (1979), *A History of African Christianity, 1950–1975.* Cambridge: Cambridge University Press.

Isichei, Elizabeth (1995), *A History of Christianity in Africa, from Antiquity to the Present.* Grand Rapids, MI: Wm B. Eerdmans.

Pobee, John S. and Gabriel Ositelu II (1998), *African Initiatives in Christianity: The Growth, Gifts and Diversities of Indigenous African Churches.* Geneva: World Council of Churches.

Sanneh, L. (1989), *Translating the Message: The Missionary Impact on Culture.* Maryknoll, NY: Orbis.

Walls, A. F. (2002), *The Cross-cultural Process in Christian History: Studies in the Transmission and Appropriation of Faith.* Maryknoll, NY: Orbis.

4 North American Christianity

Despite the fact that the population of North America has migrated from many different parts of the world, Christianity in many varied forms is the shared religion of most of the people of the USA, Canada and the anglophone Caribbean, including those of non-European descent. In the USA particularly, Christianity has a high profile in public life, but US Christianity is not only what is projected by the 'Religious Right'. It is highly complex, with strong African American, Roman Catholic and liberal Protestant components, which are also linked to its neighbouring countries, as well as to the dominant Evangelicalism. Christianity in North America reflects North American enterprise and experience as well as drawing on the many traditions that have been introduced into the continent.

US Christianity: popular and plural

At the beginning of the twenty-first century, roughly nine out of ten US Americans believed in God, six out of ten belonged to a religious organization and four out of ten were at worship on Sunday (Marty 2002: 396). Classic secularization theories of religion which predicted the decline of religious adherence with modernization, on the basis that religion is a response to some form of deprivation or 'existential insecurity', have had to be revised (Cox 1996; Martin 2005), beginning with the US case (Berger 1970). The continued health of religion in the United States is explained in two main ways: first, in 'post-modern' US society the role of religion has changed from being a survival mechanism for people facing uncertainty to a means of self-expression (Norris and Inglehart 2004). This is evidenced by the growth of New Age or 'body, mind and spirit' in the United States, and also by the increasing use of therapies of 'inner healing' in Christian ministry. The second suggestion is that the growth of religious pluralism and freedom of religion in the United States lead to greater quality of religious supply and therefore higher demand for religious services (Stark and Finke 2000). There are also demographic reasons which may contribute to explaining why the religious picture in the United States is markedly different from that of western Europe and of most other developed nations. The USA has a growing population; it is a younger nation – the median age will probably remain at 35 until 2050 (Micklethwait and Wooldridge 2004: 299); and the proportion of (first-generation) immigrants was up to 11.5 per cent in 2002 (Huntington 2005: 199). Since the 1960s, relaxed immigration controls have led to the 'browning' of the US population and of its churches. According to US Census Bureau figures from 2005, black or African Americans are 12 per cent of the population, but they are now overtaken by Hispanics (of different races); the proportion of Asians (mainly East Asians) is increasing, but Nataive America are less than 1 per cent of the population. High levels of immigration do not necessarily mean an increase in religious diversity but, on the contrary, may be increasing America's levels of Christian adherence (Jenkins 2002: 103–5) because most immigrants to the United States are Christians before they arrive, or become so after arrival. The fact that the United States is perceived as a Christian nation may be a major pull factor for migrants, and being a Christian is an advantage for integration into American society. Being a Christian may also be a push factor from countries where Christians face discrimination or persecution (Phan 2003: 230). Therefore, Jenkins concludes, there is less religious plurality in the United States than its racial diversity might suggest: only 4–5 per cent of the population adhere to non-Christian religions, which is a smaller proportion than in France and in many African and Asian nations, and similar to the UK (Jenkins 2002: 104). Most US Americans are Christians and actively so.

But although there is relatively little religious plurality in the United States, Christian pluralism began there. The development of North America was led by Christian migrants from Europe, many fleeing the religious wars, who came to the 'New World' to create new societies where they expected to practise their faith. So in the eighteenth century there was a patchwork of religious enclaves across the continent like that established in Europe: the south-eastern and south-western parts of North America were Spanish Catholic; the centre of the continent from the Mississippi Delta to western Canada was French Catholic; Maryland was Roman Catholic; Virginia and Carolina were Anglican; the New England states mostly followed the Puritan model; and what was later to become the state of Alaska was being evangelized by the Russian Orthodox Church (Oleska 1989). However, Rhode Island and the 'middle colonies' of New York, New Jersey, Delaware and Pennsylvania welcomed various dissenting groups. In the creation of the United States, the toleration of a variety of Christian denominations and the separation of church and state were brought about of necessity, but the settlement was supported not only by the Enlightenment secular reasoning of Thomas Jefferson and other leaders of the time but also by the dominant religious group among the settlers, the Puritans, who separated the true church from the state and saw it as a community entered into by covenant rather than by birth. 'Church' referred primarily to one local congregation, whose life was free from state interference, and in which each adult male member was morally responsible. But by virtue of his church membership, he also had the right to vote for political leaders, so the church, though distinct from the state, was not separate from the society; nevertheless the respective roles of church and state were clearly demarcated.

When the 13 colonies rebelled against British rule and formed the United States of America in 1776, with a federal agreement, the establishment of any one national church was inconceivable and the de facto religious plurality of the new nation meant that the federal government was forced to be 'friendly but officially neutral' toward each (Williams 1990: 165). Furthermore, since for many Americans the War of Independence was a struggle for freedom from the Church of England as much as from the British crown, they fiercely defended their right to worship, or not worship, without state interference. So it was agreed in the First Amendment to the Constitution that federal government would 'make no law respecting an establishment of religion, or prohibiting the free exercise thereof', and in the Sixth Amendment that no religious tests should be applied for appointment to public office. Under this secular constitution, which makes no invocation of God at all, none of the new states retained established churches and the churches had to restructure themselves as voluntary bodies by instituting synods and other bodies for decision-making. Nevertheless, the USA was, and remains, overwhelmingly Christian, and the primary expression of this plurality was a variety of Protestant 'denominations'. The extent and meaning of religious freedom in the United States remain a subject of debate. Conservative Christians argue that the founding fathers did not envisage America as anything other than a Protestant republic (i.e. a Christian nation without an established church) and were not advocates of religious pluralism. Roman Catholics, and later Jews, challenged this perception, and in the twentieth century secularists and more liberal Christians have used the constitution to argue for full equality of treatment of all religious groups and total separation of the religions from political and civic life. The result is paradoxical. In the 1960s, corporate prayer and religious symbols were banned in public schools but they may be permissible in other public gatherings and places. On the other hand, the Christian religiosity of the overwhelming majority of Americans means that in the first decade of the twenty-first century politicians of both main parties are using biblical imagery and religious rhetoric to appeal for the popular vote.

Another aspect of the more or less level playing field created for Protestant churches in the United States is the possibility of 'both cooperation and competition' with one another (Mullin 1999: 431). 'Ecumenism' is not a term much used in American churches. Few of the large Evangelical denominations are members of the World Council of Churches, for example, partly because of its association in their minds with theological liberalism, which they oppose, but also because its desire for church unity is interpreted to mean the formation of a single world church, and the kind of ecclesiastical imperialism against which the first Americans fought. However, American churches have often worked together in evangelism, revival, social reform and world mission, and today there are hundreds of voluntary societies that cut across denominational lines. At the same time, disestablishment led to a free market of churches. While many denominations continue to draw most of their membership through their historic roots in different communities, others vie with one another for members. In a climate of religious freedom, where people are not necessarily bound to a particular faith by their birth family, community or upbringing, and which also encourages conversion, individuals are urged to make a choice about where they worship. Both in attitude and in law, churches and Christian organizations in the United States operate more as businesses than as associations or charities, and there is often a close relationship between business and religion, exemplified in organizations like the Full Gospel Businessmen's Fellowship. In this milieu, denominationalism is not seen as a failure of Christian unity, to be ashamed of, but as an opportunity for church growth. The 'supply-side' theory that competition increases demand is in evidence where church buildings of different denominations are found on opposite corners of street blocks with competing slogans and offers of enticing services. Advertising of churches in the media is common and the successful pastor is popularly perceived as one who has a large congregation. Church growth is a recognized area of the theological curriculum in many American seminaries, with material drawn from sales and advertising, and from group dynamics, being taught to clergy in training (e.g. Wagner 1986).

Martin Marty recognizes a common 'American religion', which is chiefly preoccupied by the question of 'the one and the many' (2002: 402, 397). On the one hand, the need for national unity has led, in the absence of an established religious tradition, to the creation of a single 'civil religion' or the evocation of a perceived shared Christian (or post-Second World War 'Judaeo-Christian') tradition (Marty 2002: 398, 435). On the other hand, the initial variety of denominations has continued to increase. The largest denominations are Roman Catholic, Baptist, Methodist, Lutheran and Mormon, although the latter are not generally accepted as Christians by the wider Christian community. Other large groupings are Congregational (Puritan), Church of Christ, Episcopal (Anglican), Presbyterian and Pentecostal. There are hundreds of other denominations and independent local congregations, and many of the large denominations are split into smaller groups. Although churches are linked through denominational structures, a further feature of the US church scene is an emphasis on the local congregation. This was the Puritan pattern and has also been emphasized by the Mennonites (Anabaptists) and especially the Baptists.

The Evangelical consensus

The first European settlers saw themselves as participating in a new exodus from oppression in Europe to a new life in the 'promised land'. The chief challenge they encountered was not the native American peoples, who were few and far between and easily pushed westward, but the forces of nature in what appeared to be a wild landscape. The first task of the settlers was to tame the land and construct 'the architecture of civilization' (Mullin 1999: 416). The Puritans proved to be the most successful and dynamic Christian force in the colonies, and they founded new towns on the 'plain and simple' New England model westwards across the northern US. The 'New England Way' was a congregational model in which the church was created 'not by legislative action from above but by contractual agreement from below' as people covenanted together to form a congregation (Gaustad and Schmidt 2002: 53). These ideas carried beyond the church into the society in the demands Americans would make for self-determination and democracy. The Bible was the Puritans' only basis of religious authority; its interpretation was the centre of worship and its study was the duty of all members not just the clergy. They considered every part of it as 'the Word of God', and relevant for instruction and guidance. From the reading of the Old Testament particularly they derived an emphasis on the sovereignty of God over all areas of life, and also a strong work ethic, which contributed to the growth of capitalism in the United States. Puritans regarded the Christian community as the new Israel of God, with a collective mission to be a 'city set on a hill' as witness of God's kingdom to all the surrounding people. The faith, solidarity and discipline of these 'commonwealths' contributed to the survival of Puritan communities in the hostile natural environment they called, with biblical resonance, the 'wilderness'. They themselves interpreted their survival as a sign of the providence of God who, they believed, had chosen them for this particular role and held them in his hands. Their custom of thanksgiving developed into the national tradition of Thanksgiving Day, an annual holiday, and the notion of being chosen by God for the sake of the world became part of the later rhetoric of American nationalism.

The Puritan concepts of religious conversion and revival resonate in American Christianity today. Church membership depended on conversion, which was a personal crisis, demanding an awareness of sin, then an intense period of introspection and repentance, which would be followed by 'new birth', an experience of personal transformation manifested in a changed and moral life. But this pattern of traumatic personal experience as the route to church membership, while meaningful for the first generation of settlers, proved unsustainable in the long term. Nevertheless, many hoped to revive the old way and saw a pattern in God's dealings with his people of the decline of piety followed by renewal. A 'massive religious revival' (Williams 1990: 127) did indeed break out in the 1730s and 40s that 'reshaped the religious topography of Protestant North America' (Mullin 1999: 423) when Puritan piety combined with Methodist enthusiasm in the 'Great Awakening'. The main catalyst for the revival was the British Methodist and associate of John Wesley, George Whitefield (1714–70), whose preaching stirred the emotions and reduced his huge congregations to tears. Whitefield has been seen as 'America's first celebrity' (Williams 1990: 130), and few of the colonists were unaware of or unaffected by his preaching. Jonathan Edwards, a Puritan who became the chief mover and theological interpreter of the Awakening, saw it as a 'surprising work of God' brought about by an outpouring of the Holy Spirit among his parishioners, which he suggested was a sign that America had a special place in God's plan as the place where God's millennial kingdom would come. Edwards reformulated Puritan doctrine to highlight conversion – now a more momentary experience – and bypass the process of church membership, focusing on the relationship of the individual with God. In his preaching he appealed to the emotions through sensual images, rather than to the mind, enabling the participation of a broad swathe of American society, including young people, women, and those who were less confident in the English language, in the revival. In the long term the revival may be said to have stirred anti-intellectualism (Mullin 1999: 423) which resurfaces many times in American religion (see Noll 1994), and its usurping of traditional society in the name of the Holy Spirit also struck at the heart of the colonial establishment (Stout 1983: 128–9).

The revival added Methodism to the Christian denominations in America and split the Puritans or Congregationalists, resulting in Unitarianism. Many moved so far from the old covenant theology toward individualism that they called for adult baptism and joined the American Baptists, a denomination founded by Roger Williams in Rhode Island. Baptist churches spread rapidly, especially in the colonial south, weakening the Anglicans. The Awakening unified different classes, colonies and languages in a common popular form of Christianity based on individual conversion and oriented toward mission, which broadened into a 'civil millennialism' (Mullin 1999: 425), an expectation of the establishment of liberty and freedom in North America. Those touched by the Awakening had an American identity with a sense of manifest destiny. They saw themselves as independent individuals accountable only to God and his Word for their behaviour, and so resisted institutional authority – whether of state or church – in which their views were not represented. In this way, the Great Awakening added a spiritual dimension to growing nationalism and led directly to the American War of Independence, to the extent that it is possible to see the Revolution as 'a continuation of the Revival' (Williams 1990: 162).

The pioneering spirit of the first settlers was continued after the War of Independence in the expansion of the United States across the North American continent as far as the Pacific Ocean, as land was purchased or ceded to the new nation. These acquisitions also introduced new populations into the United States, particularly Hispanic populations who were Roman Catholic. As European settlers spread out, the task of civilizing the landscape and gathering the population into churches continued in the nineteenth century, and the pattern of revival Christianity also continued. What is sometimes called the 'Second Great Awakening' (1800–40) had greatest effect in the south and west beyond the Appalachian Mountains. Settlers gathered at huge interdenominational camp meetings, where emotions ran very high. The ecstatic behaviour, such as fainting, 'jerking' and 'barking', was taken as evidence that God's Holy Spirit was at work. This seemed to 'fill a cultural and psychological void' (Mullin 1999: 429) and led to the precipitous growth of Methodist and Baptist churches, which rapidly overtook the Congregationalists and Anglicans as the largest US denominations. Their use of lay leadership, minimal requirements for worship and loose ecclesiology made them 'perfectly suited' to the needs of the expanding nation (Gaustad and Schmidt 2002: 166). The pre-eminent figure of the Second Awakening was Charles Finney. Instead of seeing revivals as dependent on unpredictable intervention from above, he believed that they were the result of individual decision and that people could be induced to convert by using the right techniques. Finney popularized an activist style of religious leadership which measured success in terms of numbers and employed the latest communication techniques to achieve it. His pragmatic approach to evangelistic ministry, informed by sociological and psychological method and making full use of available technology, is very widespread today.

Evangelical belief in a direct and contractual relationship between the individual and his/her Maker, through the atoning sacrifice of Jesus Christ, tended to separate the material and moral/spiritual worlds: the material world, including the market economy, was seen to operate according to natural laws put in place by God, whereas the moral or spiritual realm was understood to be where God intervenes for the redemption of humankind (Hilton 1988: 8, 16–17). Between 1785 and 1865, mainstream Evangelicalism supported the free-market individualism which was the basis of American economic growth, and which was linked to their own ethos of independence and sense of responsibility to increase and multiply in the land God had given them. The Second Awakening had a number of important effects. It heightened the sense of the potential of converted humanity to do good and the optimistic outlook that individuals and society could be transformed. As in Europe, Evangelicals were concerned to effect moral change in society by engaging in new religious, social and mission movements. These were so numerous and wide-ranging they became known as 'the benevolent empire'. The first American overseas missionary organizations, including the American Board of Commissioners for Foreign Missions (1810) and the American Baptist Foreign Mission Society (1814), also derive from this period. The Awakening also spawned new movements based on a plain reading of the Bible. The expectation of the imminent return of Jesus Christ, and a desire to be found to be obedient to his law, led to the founding of the Seventh-Day Adventists, the Jehovah's Witnesses (who are not usually counted Christian by others) and other millennialist groups. 'Restorationism', which attempted to recreate the primitive perfection and unity of the early church and rejected any religious practice that could not be found in the New Testament, resulted in the Churches of Christ and Disciples of Christ and other groups. Most significantly, the Second Awakening created a broad coalition of churches which shared the Evangelical characteristics of the 'Bebbington quadrilateral': conversionism, activism, Biblicism and crucicentrism (1989: 2–17). This 'evangelical centre' effectively 'functioned as the hegemonic religious vision of the young republic' (Mullin 1999: 432).

Slave religion, black churches and the Civil War

The greatest Evangelical campaign was against slavery. Finney himself supported this, though it was not a straightforward choice for all Evangelicals. By the late eighteenth century most northern Evangelicals did the same, but white Christians in the South tended to see abolition as a threat to their way of life. Northerners found it difficult to mount a convincing case that slavery was against biblical teaching, and the Southerners could find scriptural texts to support it. The main Evangelical churches – Presbyterian, Methodist and Baptist – eventually divided before the Civil War along North–South lines, and the Southern Baptist denomination remains separated from its Northern counterpart. African American churches, of course, were not divided by the issue, which was a particular problem for white Americans, especially because slavery was 'never merely a system of labour' but also 'a system of race control' (Mullin 1999: 436). Even those who opposed slavery were rarely ready to admit people of African descent to equal status in their society; that is why many white Christians favoured the founding of colonies in Africa for freed slaves to 'return' to as a solution to the problem. White Christians who were implicated in the system of slavery tended to assuage their guilt by arguing that they could save the souls of Africans, otherwise destined to hell, by converting them to Christianity. At the same time, the conversion of slaves was contested because baptism into the Christian community might imply emancipation. So those who evangelized slaves faced the delicate 'task of ensuring that the egalitarian tendencies of Christian instruction would remain safely within the boundaries of slave management'. Slaves were disadvantaged in the white churches not only by their colour but by the literary culture and behaviour requirements of the churches; however, the new religiosity of the 'Great' and subsequent 'Awakenings' was much more accessible to African Americans because it did not require literacy or make moral demands for church membership (such as marriage) which under the conditions of slavery they could not fulfil. Many blacks were among those who responded to the preaching of Edwards, and by the late nineteenth century, perhaps a quarter of the swelling ranks of Baptists and Methodists were black. Furthermore, the revival setting, especially in the camp meetings of the Second Great Awakening, which slaves attended with their owners, was an egalitarian one in which all were sinners before God. The emotion of the meeting appealed to black as to white, and the ecstatic behaviour and congregational involvement 'were amenable to the African religious heritage of the slaves' (Raboteau 2004: 171, 131, 149).

It emerged after emancipation that slaves had developed their own expression of Christian church, termed by Albert Raboteau 2004 'the invisible institution'. Although slave religion included some African traditional religion and Islam brought from Africa, most African Americans retained little knowledge of this because they had been disconnected from their heritage by transportation, separated from their families and, for the bulk of the North American slave population, born in North America. Having no other religious framework, many slaves adopted the Christian religion of their masters. Because many masters forbade them from learning or practising it, slaves had to 'steal away' (the title of a popular slave song) to hold secret meetings far from the house. There they invested Christianity with a distinctive content and expressed it with 'shouting', which reflected in a general way the African heritage of singing, dancing, spirit possession and magic. Raboteau describes slave religion as necessarily clandestine, led by preachers, based on the slaves' interpretation of the Bible, expressed in African-influenced music of the 'spirituals', characterized by the theology and practice of conversion, and often integrated with use of 'conjure' to deal with the spirit world. 'By the eve of the Civil War, Christianity had pervaded the slave community' (Raboteau 2004: 212) and it had taken on a distinctively African American form.

In addition to being members of white-founded denominations, most of which were segregated into black and white at a local and even national level, freed slaves had been founding their own churches since the 1750s, when black Baptist churches were started on plantations in Virginia and South Carolina. The African Methodist Episcopal (AME) Church was founded by Richard Allen who, with others, walked out of his white-dominated church in 1816 when it was decided that African Christians should be relegated to the gallery. To achieve better treatment for blacks, the church laid considerable emphasis on what was considered proper conduct and appearance, and it stressed literacy and education. African American Baptists eventually came together nationwide to form the National Baptist Convention, the largest of several Baptist conventions, in 1895 with the goal of 'uplifting African Americans ... independently of white involvement'. In order to bring African Americans into the mainstream of American life, some of the leaders tried to downplay the more emotional elements of worship, but this was strongly resisted by local congregations. Both the Methodists and Baptists began extensive overseas missions and founded institutions of higher education. Most blacks are members of seven denominations, which have together between 20 and 25 million members (Pinn and Pinn 2002: 77, 17).

When they were freed after the end of the Civil War, African Americans flocked to join the existing churches, and hundreds of black congregations – mostly of Baptist and Methodist affiliation or type – sprang up in rural areas of the South, where 90 per cent of black Americans still lived in 1900. Emancipation did not bring inclusion in mainstream society, and in the Southern states, particularly, the 'Jim Crow' systems of segregation were soon in place, together with more sinister forms of harassment. Hans Baer and Merrill Singer (2002) have described the life of rural black churches in the mid-twentieth century, which they regard as little changed today, even after the civil rights movement of the 1950s and 60s. In the absence of many trained ministers, lay (usually male) leaders maintain and operate the churches in the countryside. At the main Sunday service, the prayers, hymn-singing and testimony all lead up to the sermon, an emotional delivery which may last over an hour, during which the congregation responds with noises of approval or conviction. Baer and Singer comment that 'In contrast to the grim puritanical tone of many white evangelical churches, black churchgoers unabashedly see no contradiction between their search for spirituality and having 'fun' or a 'good time'. African American Christianity does not stress messages of judgment, as white Evangelicals tend to do, but is more inclined to celebrate God's mercy. The churches continue to be a 'center of sociability' and 'repository of the black cultural ethos', and during the 'caste-like system' of segregation, and the continuing discrimination today, black churches have provided a 'cathartic mechanism' for coping with a hostile world (Baer and Singer 2002: 30–40).

The Civil War was a traumatic event for the new nation and had contradictory effects on white American Christians. In the places of longer-established European settlement, and among the educated middle classes, the growing stability lessened the sense of crisis that characterized the earlier conversionist faith, and evolutionary views crept in to form what became known as the 'post-millennial' view of history. In this scenario, God's kingdom is slowly but inevitably being established on earth through human activity to improve society, until the earth becomes a fit place for Christ's millennial reign. Leading theologian and Congregational minister Horace Bushnell (1802–76), influenced by Frederick Maurice in Britain, downplayed conversion as the way of entry into Christian life and emphasized nurture in a Christian society. His followers were concerned to Christianize American culture; victory in the fight for emancipation and the Civil War gave them the confidence to think it could be achieved. However, those who had experienced the destruction of the Civil War, and those, particularly in the South, whose social order had been overturned by the emancipation of the slaves, were among those for whom the world seemed to be getting worse rather than better. They did not share the optimism of Bushnell but felt themselves and their way of life under threat in the late nineteenth century. There were many who saw the world as a battleground between the forces of good and evil. Other concerns were waves of new immigrants (the population of the United States increased by nearly a third between 1860 and 1890), the growth of Roman Catholicism due to migration and annexation of territory, rapid technological changes and urbanization due to the industrial revolution, and social instability caused by labour disputes.

The Social Gospel and Christian Fundamentalism

From the mid-nineteenth century, the Protestant coalition in the USA began to diverge into two different groupings often referred to as 'Liberals' and 'Fundamentalists'. This was due partly to the differential effects of the Civil War and also due to the impact of modernity, which had been held back by the strength of the Evangelical consensus in the antebellum period and the urgent necessities of establishing and evangelizing the nation and now struck with greater force. The divide between these two groups and its effects on present-day US Christianity has been the object of major studies in an effort to understand contemporary religious fundamentalism (Marsden 2006) and distinguish it from broader American Evangelicalism (Marsden 1991; Noll 2001).

In the more liberal society of New England and the old middle colonies, which was more developed and urban, there were world-class institutions of higher learning in close contact with European scholarship, where theologians engaged with German methods of biblical criticism and with the questions raised by scientific advances, especially Darwin's theory of evolution. But these new ideas threatened the Evangelical orthodoxy: Darwin's theory of evolution implicitly questioned the sovereignty of God and the need for life-changing conversion, and the methods and findings of historical criticism seemed to undermine biblical authority, another central tenet of Evangelicalism. However, the greatest crisis for the American churches in the nineteenth century came not in the realms of intellectual discussion but in pragmatic terms as questions of salvation and mission. Around the turn of the nineteenth century, and building on Bushnell's optimistic anthropology, Walter Rauschenbusch expounded Jesus' preaching of the kingdom of God, which he was sure would transcend the kingdom of evil. His 'Social Gospel' was based more on the Sermon on the Mount and other teachings of the historical Jesus than on doctrines of salvation and judgment, which were questioned by modernity and the Universalist views encouraged by Unitarianism. By glossing over problems of human sinfulness, Rauschenbusch was confident that unity, peace and goodwill and the 'brotherhood of man' would be the corollary of the loving 'fatherhood of God'. The discovery of the suffering caused by urbanization and industrial strife led to Christian criticism of capitalist society and a wave of new initiatives for social reform. In 1908, the newly inaugurated Federal Council of Churches adopted a 'social creed' to inject 'conscience and justice and love into a Christian civilization' (quoted in Gaustad and Schmidt 2002: 244).

Those who did not share this confidence in the future were more attracted by the revivals led by Dwight L. Moody and the hymn-writer Ira D. Sankey in the last quarter of the nineteenth century, which were enormously popular. Although he himself initiated many charitable activities, Moody placed primary emphasis on bringing about a change of heart in human individuals. He preached that the greatest thing Christians could do in the world was to pull drowning souls out of the sea and into the lifeboat. Moody's approach reflected a shift in popular Evangelical piety toward 'pre-millennialism', the belief that the world could not be improved until Jesus Christ came again in judgment. Since until then it was a matter of clinging to the lifeboat, Moody did not promote long-term causes. Like the Student Volunteer Movement, which was founded as a response to one of his conferences, he aimed for 'the evangelization of the world in this generation'. Moody's style was not sensationalist but restrained and businesslike. He focused on the 'Three R's': Ruin by sin, Redemption by Christ, and Regeneration by the Holy Ghost. The third 'R' is an indication of the key to Moody's success: he was able to combine an appeal to the Reformed or Calvinist emphasis on repentance from sin with the Wesleyan or Methodist expectation of renewal and perfection by the work of the Holy Spirit (Williams 1990: 253).

Moody's preaching encouraged the growth of 'Holiness' movements and churches, which amplified Wesley's teaching of a 'second blessing' after baptism by which the believer became free of sinful impulses. Those who believed they had received 'entire sanctification' were impatient of the level of spirituality in the existing churches and soon formed their own denominations, including the Church of the Nazarene, the Wesleyan Church, the Church of God, the Christian Missionary Alliance and other denominations. But the Holiness movement was influential across the churches. In the United States one of its leaders was Phoebe Palmer; she and other influential women like the hymn-writer Fanny Crosby encouraged a more gentle vision of Christ as the Good Shepherd. In keeping with this is the characteristic Holiness belief in 'divine healing'; that is, healing of infirmity, sickness or disease through prayer, laying on of hands or anointing by the elders of the church (Jas 5.14–15). The affliction is believed to be due to sin or Satan (and not due to incorrect thinking as in the Church of Christ, Scientist, founded in the same period), and belief in divine healing is often combined with a rejection of modern medicine and other remedies on the grounds that Jesus is the 'Great Physician'. There were many people looking for alternative treatments in nineteenth-century America, where medical practices were unreliable and expensive and the health of the population was poor, and divine healing flourished at camp meetings and conferences (Hardesty 2003: 1–4). One of the most famous practitioners, A. B. Simpson, working closely with his wife Margaret, founded the Christian and Missionary Alliance, one of the main Holiness denominations. The reliance 'on faith alone' was also expressed in the new wave of missionary movements in the late nineteenth century, the 'faith missions', following the pattern developed by James Hudson Taylor's China Inland Mission (see Chapter 2; Fiedler 1994).

A difference of eschatology, and therefore in mission imperative, lay at the heart of the growing divide between modernist and conservative Evangelicals in America. Conservatives were worried that evangelism, in the narrow sense of calling for conversion, was missing from the agenda of the Social Gospel. Furthermore, the Social Gospel itself was a threat since the values of the kingdom it propounded posed a socialist challenge to the existing political and economic order, which unsettled many conservatives. It also suggested a radically different reading of the Bible from the Evangelical norm, which prioritized the incarnation of Jesus Christ and his social teaching over the cross and doctrines of salvation, and played down sin and judgment in the light of the love of God. Conservatives suspected that this was because Rauschenbusch and others were succumbing to biblical criticism, and labelled them 'Liberal' as a term of abuse. Conservative Evangelicals who had lost hope for society began to displace their millennial expectations from earth onto heaven. The Moody Bible Institute popularized the Scofield Study Bible (first published in 1909), which promoted 'Dispensationalism', a doctrine based on apocalyptic passages of the Bible which added to pre-millennialism the belief that on Jesus' return, true believers would be 'raptured', that is taken up from the earth to be with Christ while the tribulations of the end times are played out. After the cleansing of the earth, the believers would return with Christ to restore the nation of Israel and set up the kingdom in Jerusalem. These beliefs persist today in US Protestantism and have been revived by popular writers such as Hal Lindsay and Tim LaHaye. Pragmatist millennialist Christians have been reluctant to sit back and let the end happen but have found ways in which they believe the end can be precipitated. Quoting Matthew 24.14, 'And this gospel of the kingdom will be preached in all the world as a witness to all the nations, and then the end will come', some argue that world evangelization will hasten the fulfilment of prophecies of the last days (e.g. Ladd 1981: 66).

In reaction to the Social Gospel, conservative Evangelicals underwent a 'great reversal' (Marsden 1980) and gradually withdrew from social and political involvement. While many focused their energies instead on reviving the faith of their churches by holiness, others concentrated on defending traditional Evangelical doctrine against biblical criticism. In 1909 two wealthy businessmen financed a series of 12 books written by leading conservative theologians from Britain as well as North America, defending what were considered to be 'the Fundamentals' of Christian faith. The writings condemned higher criticism of the Bible, along with liberal theology, Romanism, socialism and spiritualism. They argued not only for the 'infallibility' of the Bible in matters of faith and conduct but for its 'inerrancy' – that is, its historical and scientific accuracy – as well. According to this theory, the first three chapters of Genesis must be a historically and scientifically accurate record of the beginning of the world. The term 'Fundamentalist' was coined in 1920 as a self-designation for anti-modern Protestants in general. The perspective became dominant in many Southern denominations and looked set to take over many Northern ones as well. The test of true faith increasingly became belief in right doctrine, rather than moral uprightness or social work. In an attempt to defend 'true doctrine', those who joined Evangelical churches and para-church groups were expected to sign 'statements of faith', creedal statements that began by affirming the inerrancy, or at least the infallibility, of the Bible, on which the rest of the edifice of Christian belief was seen to depend.

Those for whom Fundamentalism posed the greatest threat were intellectuals and scientists because the movement challenged freedom of thought and speech, which were staunchly defended by groups such as the American Civil Liberties Union. The 'monkey trial' in 1925 of a schoolteacher charged with teaching Darwinism in school, contrary to the (recently passed) law in the state of Tennessee, easily demolished the Fundamentalist case. The press represented the trial as 'a clash of two worlds': rural and urban: 'on the one side the small town, the backwoods, half-educated yokels, obscurantism, crackpot hawkers of religion, fundamentalism, the South ... Opposed to these were the city, the clique of New York–Chicago lawyers, intellectuals, journalists, wits, sophisticates, modernists' (Marsden 2006: 185). This compelling image of conservative religionists retarding national progress also had echoes of the Civil War, which would resound down the rest of the twentieth century. Fundamentalist Christians felt their beliefs were ridiculed by the establishment, and Evangelicalism as a whole did not emerge again into the public domain until after the Second World War. Fundamentalists did not give up, however. Still today the threat of the teaching of evolution encourages conservative Evangelicals to home-school their children or set up Christian schools, which teach 'creationism' or 'intelligent design'; the latter seeking to redefine science to accept supernatural causation.

It is important to distinguish Fundamentalism from Evangelicalism as a whole, of which it is best regarded as a militant subgroup: 'a fundamentalist is an evangelical who is angry about something' (Marsden 2006: 235). Few denominations describe themselves as 'Fundamentalist' today, but many are 'fundamentalistic', displaying traits of the movement because of pressure groups within them. The largest single Protestant denomination, claiming more than 16 million members, is the Southern Baptist Convention, which since the 1980s has become more fundamentalist. The statement of faith on its website (which is not binding on its member churches) begins with a declaration of belief in biblical inerrancy, and the description of 'the last things' takes a pre-millennialist line. This stance is out of step with other Baptists worldwide, and in 2004 it withdrew from the World Baptist Alliance because of worries about 'liberalism' and 'anti-Americanism'. The Southern Baptist Convention affirms the equality of men and women but, along with theologians such as Andreas Kostenberger (2005), excludes women from leadership, arguing that God-ordained gender roles are 'distinct' and 'complementary'. Evangelical feminists such as Catherine Clark Kroeger (1992) argue on the basis of the biblical text that the 'difficult passages', such as 1 Timothy 2.11–15 which apparently forbids women from having authority over men, have been wrongly translated or interpreted, and that the New Testament as a whole recognizes and affirms the partnership of women in ministry. Positions on this issue are one way of distinguishing Fundamentalist churches from the more broadly Evangelical. Fundamentalists originally distanced themselves from Holiness groups by strongly rejecting divine healing and other modern miracles, because they argued miracles were confined to biblical times as the authentification of Jesus Christ and the apostles only. However, the influence of Pentecostal spirituality (see below) has confused this divide. The most popular 'televangelists', who offer healing and prosperity as well as eternal salvation, have included Fundamentalists Jerry Falwell (d. 2007) and Pat Robertson. They and most other televangelists are Southerners – an indication of the way in which the Christianity of the South, despised at the 'monkey trial', has now become mainstream (Marsden 2006: 237).

The conservatism of Fundamentalism attracts those with anti-modern tendencies, including some immigrant groups (Marsden 2006: 194); this has led to the co-option of Fundamentalists and other Evangelicals into right-wing politics. In the 1950s, Evangelical preachers joined in the rhetoric against Communism both because it was socialist and because it was atheist or 'Godless'. But the liberalism of the 1960s, which included assaults on traditional standards of family and sexuality and aggressive attempts to secularize American culture, together with the fallout of the battle over black civil rights, especially in the South, incensed conservative Christians and reignited

'Puritanical' moral tendencies. 'It seemed that America was a Christian nation that had forsaken its heritage' and that it was time to bring Christianity back to centre stage. The major focus of concern for Evangelicals was not now the 'Liberalism' of their fellow Christians but the 'secular humanism' of the wider society, especially with regard to family, sexuality and religion in public life. The 'custodial' control (Marsden 2006: 238–40) exercised over local culture by Fundamentalists in the South during the first half of the twentieth century began to be applied to the whole nation in organized political movements. Psychiatrist James Dobson's broadcasting on childcare is one example of a new genre which attempted to develop 'Christian values' and apply them to everyday life. Writer and film-maker Francis Schaeffer played an important role in convincing Fundamentalists that secular humanism had replaced Christianity as the American cultural framework. Tim LaHaye convinced them that it was also a government agenda (Marsden 2006: 246), and played into fears of government intrusion into people's lives that went back to the experience of the first European settlers in their search for freedom from earthly and spiritual powers.

Paradoxically, while seeking to reconstruct American society, many of the same people preach a pre-millennialist message that the earth will soon be destroyed (Marsden 2006: 247–50). Christian Fundamentalists have formed an alliance with Jewish Zionists to encourage the rebuilding of the temple in Jerusalem which, based on dispensationalist theories of New Testament interpretation, they believe will trigger the return of Christ, the 'rapture' and the battle of Armageddon, in which most of the rest of the world's population will die (Chapman 2002: 274–6; see also Sizer 2005). It is claimed that as many as one in ten Americans shares these beliefs (Halsell 2003: 5), which are no longer limited to Fundamentalists but pervade Evangelicalism. Christian Zionists include all the 'televangelists', Billy Graham and presidents Jimmy Carter and Ronald Reagan, and they have a significant impact on American policy toward Israel (Chapman 2002: 276; see also Marsden 2006: 249–50). Christian Zionists make no attempt to understand the present conflict in the Middle East in its own terms and do not represent the views of Christians in the Middle East. Yet they take a one-sided political stance in favour of the state of Israel, and this without showing any real concern for the fate of the Jewish people (Chapman 2002: 284–7).

Conservative Roman Catholic Christians, who had also been largely apolitical up to the 1970s, shared Evangelical concerns to a large extent, and also had another grievance: 1973 permissive legislation on abortion.

Influenced by films produced by Francis Schaeffer and C. Everett Koop in 1979 which argued that abortion was the culmination of secular humanist disregard for God's law, most Evangelicals were persuaded to adopt the anti-abortion agenda as part of their support for traditional family life and more traditional roles for women. In 1979 Jerry Falwell founded the 'Moral Majority' with the support of Catholic leaders, which supported Ronald Reagan's conservative Republican campaign. It was dissolved in 1989 and succeeded by the 'Christian Coalition' supporting Pat Robertson's (unsuccessful) campaign for the Republican nomination in 1988. A looser coalition termed by others the 'Religious Right' or 'Christian Right' was a major factor in the election of George W. Bush to president in 2000 and 2004, to the extent that 'The best predictor of whether a white American votes Republican is not his or her income but how often he or she goes to church' (Micklethwait and Wooldridge 2004: 12). It is remarkable, considering how implacably opposed to the Roman Catholic Church Protestants have been in American history, that now the deepest divide among US Christians is no longer the old Catholic–Protestant one but the one between conservative Christians and those of a liberal or secular persuasion (Mullin 1999: 456).

Many American Christians are dissatisfied with, and even embarrassed by, the antics of the Religious Right. 'How did the faith of Jesus come to be known as pro-rich, pro-war, and only pro-American?' asks Jim Wallis (2005: 3), a preacher and political activist of more left-wing persuasion. Wallis, who also has Evangelical credentials, leads Sojourners, a 'nationwide network of progressive Christians working for justice and peace'. He advocates a kind of North American liberation theology, using biblical arguments to persuade Evangelicals to be more socialist in outlook, but is also critical of 'secular fundamentalism' that has an 'allergy to spirituality' because it makes the mistake of 'throwing all people of faith into the category of right-wing conservative religion' (Wallis 2005: 346). Mennonite Evangelicals, heirs of the radical Reformation, also offer a different perspective from the prosperity preachers and the Religious Right. Ron Sider and Jon Bonk have looked at the problems of Christian affluence and advocated simplicity (Bonk 1991; Sider 1984). Mennonites are known for their pacifism and peace-making, as expressed by John Howard Yoder in his influential book *The Politics of Jesus* (1972). He argued that the Constantinian settlement and subsequent close church–state relationships are dangerous to Christian faith and urged that the church witness to an alternative society, not based on violence or the threat of it.

Evangelism, church and theology

The Great Depression of the 1930s dented faith in American progress, and the atrocities of the Second World War and Cold War fear brought home the depth of the evil of which human beings are capable. These provided a climate in which some of the Puritan doctrines of human sinfulness and need of grace could be reaffirmed. Among the heirs of theological liberalism and the Social Gospel, the brothers Reinhold and H. Richard Niebuhr, who grew up in the German Evangelical tradition, were most influential and stimulated the development of theological ethics and post-liberal theology, respectively. Reinhold Niebuhr dominated Christian social thought for the first half of the twentieth century and was influential in shaping US foreign policy after the Second World War. Influenced by the biblical realism of Karl Barth, Niebuhr was highly critical of what he saw as the idealism of social Christianity and the sentimentality of its compassion, though not of its desire to restrain market forces and establish social and political democracy (Werpehowski 1997: 15). Niebuhr rejected moralism, but in view of God's forgiveness he encouraged 'proximate justice', involving pragmatic solutions and necessary compromise – including 'just war' – for addressing the political issues of the age (Grenz and Olson 1992: 102). Stanley Hauerwas, one of the most prominent of the many theologians who continued Niebuhr's style of theological ethics, rejects liberalism as a social strategy and instead emphasizes the role of the church to demonstrate a new society (Hauerwas 1999). H. Richard Niebuhr, professor at Yale University, was famous for his typologies of the relationship between Christ and culture, in which he stressed the work of Christ in transforming culture. He and his colleague Hans Frei laid the foundations for a post-liberal approach which shifted biblical interpretation and theological method from an Enlightenment scientific approach to a literary approach more in keeping with the narrative tradition of Scripture. George Lindbeck added an appreciation of different forms of discourse which he thought suggested that Christians should develop their own culture and language of faith which could not be gainsaid from within a different discourse (see Placher 1997). Post-liberal theology is opposed by those who see it as withdrawal from, rather than an engagement with, the world. Other theological movements have been more concerned for the credibility of Christian faith, particularly in view of developments in philosophy and in science. Of these, 'process theology' is perhaps the best known. Developed from the philosophy of Alfred North Whitehead by John B. Cobb, Charles Hartshorne and others, process theology lays God open to scientific investigation by understanding God as a dynamic within evolutionary processes (see Grenz and Olson 1992: 130–44). Such apparent speculation, which has difficulty accommodating traditional Christian doctrines such as the Trinity, has limited appeal to the majority of North American Christians who are of an Evangelical faith.

The same awareness of evil encouraged the reinvigoration of the central Evangelical programme of evangelism. The National Association of Evangelicals, formed in 1942, signalled the rebuilding of an Evangelical coalition which, while sometimes displaying fundamentalistic tendencies, remained distinct from hardline fundamentalist organizations. The rise of Evangelicalism has been accompanied by a sharp decline in those denominations which maintained a Social Gospel: including Episcopal, United Methodist, American (Northern) Baptist and Presbyterian. Today Evangelicalism can be understood as a broad coalition of diverse Protestant subgroups with a broadly similar statement of faith (Noll 2001: 56–66). The single most important figure in maintaining Evangelical unity in the second half of the twentieth century was the next great revivalist, Billy Graham (Noll 2001: 44–55). Graham came from a Southern Fundamentalist background and preached a typical Evangelical message of the sinfulness of human beings, the necessity of conversion, and the salvation offered by faith in Christ – a message which has been heard in person, as well as through the media, by millions of people. Graham's revival meetings had a unifying effect because they were organized at the invitation of a coalition of local churches, usually including a very broad range of denominations. His organization, college at Wheaton, Illinois, and his magazine *Christianity Today* gradually became more moderate, closer to other Protestants and more academically credible. Graham was a key figure in bringing Evangelicals back into the public sphere, both on a worldwide stage through the Lausanne Movement for World Evangelization and also in American political life. Graham has personally known every US president since Harry Truman in 1950 and been an unofficial pastor to many. Although he was outspoken against Communism in the 1950s, Graham also publicly opposed segregation in the 1960s and has been careful not to side unilaterally with the Religious Right.

Evangelical re-engagement with society was led by the theologian Carl Henry, who tried to affirm the 'Protestant orthodoxy linked with American revivalism' of Evangelicalism and at the same time reject Fundamentalism (Anderson 1997: 490) by a method of 'biblical theism', which aimed to make the revelation of God, verified by the Bible, both credible and socially constructive. He did not produce a systematic theology but a critique of liberal theology and rational arguments for biblical authority (Grenz and Olson 1992: 296). His contemporary and fellow Baptist, Bernard Ramm, preferred to make his starting point the 'biblical realism' of Karl Barth, in whose 'neo-orthodox' Calvinist theology he found a biblical framework for an Evangelical theology (in its North American sense). Leading Evangelical theologians today, Stanley Grenz and Roger E. Olson, see twentieth-century theology as a dialogue between theology of transcendence and theology of immanence and optimistically regard Evangelicalism, which earlier stressed the former in the face of the latter, as having now achieved a healthy balance between the two, between the God of revelation, who breaks in from outside our world, and the God of experience, who moves within it (Grenz and Olson 1992).

Having an activist mentality, Evangelicals tend to be less concerned with developing theology than with discovering or devising strategies to bring about conversion and the growth of the church. To the denominational missions and Faith Missions were added 'parachurch organizations', which are intended to support the work of the church but often take on a life of their own. These include evangelistic associations like the Billy Graham Evangelistic Association, and youth movements including Campus Crusade for Christ, Operation Mobilization and the charismatic YWAM (Youth With A Mission). These specialize in 'personal evangelism', or one-to-one attempts to persuade another of the truth of the Christian faith (Bright 1989). This pattern, which uses techniques similar to sales and advertising, is unquestioned in the North American context, and at the heart of Evangelical mission activity, so that it is often referred to simply as 'evangelism'. On the other hand, as a result of 'the great reversal', 'social action' continues to be questioned. However, in 1974 an initiative of Billy Graham and the British Anglican Evangelical John Stott, stimulated by Third World Evangelicals such as the Peruvian Samuel Escobar, led to the signing of the 'Lausanne Covenant' (available online) by leading figures, which affirmed that 'evangelism and socio-political involvement' are both 'necessary expressions of our doctrines of God and man, our love for our neighbour and our obedience to Jesus Christ'. The international Lausanne Movement now works closely with the World Evangelical Alliance, which probably represents most Evangelicals. As a result of this shift, many new Evangelical mission agencies specializing in relief, humanitarian and development work have emerged, among the most influential of which are Samaritan's Purse (headed by Billy Graham's son, Franklin) and World

Vision. However, Evangelicals remain suspicious of agencies that appear to compromise traditional Christian doctrines (cf. Glasser 1993).

On the whole, Evangelical theologians have not been comfortable dealing with political questions of justice or with questions arising from religious pluralism, but they have engaged with the concept of culture in order to communicate the gospel message more effectively. The Willowbank Report of a consultation sponsored by the Lausanne Movement developed an appreciation of the role of culture in gospel communication, church life and also in the writing and reading of the Bible, that has been widely appreciated by other Christian bodies (available from the Lausanne Movement website). However, two more controversial North American initiatives in evangelistic method since the 1970s, which were based on the study of culture, have also been extremely influential in missions worldwide. Donald McGavran and Peter Wagner believed that 'People like to become Christians without crossing racial, linguistic, or class barriers' (McGavran and Wagner 1990: 163), and so argued, on biblical and sociological grounds, that the most effective way to achieve church growth was to create 'homogeneous units' within which the gospel message can therefore spread more easily and become a movement of a whole 'people group'. This 'people-group' orientation is maintained in world mission by initiatives such as the Joshua Project. Research into the distribution of unevangelized groups worldwide led evangelist Luis Bush to encourage Christians to target the '10/40 window', the region of the world between latitudes 10 and 40 degrees North, where most such groups are found (and which also includes most of the Islamic world). Other Evangelicals have strongly criticized this approach for its apparent denial of the impulses of the Christian gospel to break down barriers and unite different peoples (e.g. Bosch 1991: 466), and because of its obsession with numbers, targets and goal-setting (Newbigin 1995: 124–32), but it has been very popular in a context in which Christian missions are also business corporations.

The second initiative is the method of 'power encounter' which was developed by some returned missionaries, Paul Hiebert, Alan Tippett and Charles Kraft, all of whom had backgrounds in anthropology. They had all witnessed exorcism and deliverance on the 'mission field' in India, the Pacific and west Africa respectively and recognized it as part of the biblical ministry of Jesus. Instead of dismissing it as earlier generations of missionaries had done, they argued missionaries should practise such a ministry of confrontational prayer as a missionary method (Kraft 1992), and furthermore that this 'spiritual warfare' was applicable also in North America to deal with supernatural demonic powers and 'territorial spirits' (Wagner 1989). John Wimber, a California pastor, became the best-known practitioner of such 'power evangelism' (Wimber 1985). Despite criticism from both within (Lowe 1998) and outside (Percy 1996) the Evangelical movement, 'power encounter' was much in evidence at the second Lausanne Conference in Manila in 1989 (see Douglas 1990). The more politically correct 'spiritual conflict' is now preferred in moderate circles (World Evangelical Alliance 2000: 20). A similar language of spiritual conflict was developed independently by Liberal theologian Walter Wink, who applied the biblical terminology of spirits, demons and angels to liberation theological concern with social and political powers and systems (Wink 1984; 1986; 1992). However Wink emphasizes that the struggle against the powers is by non-violent resistance and deplores the 'myth of redemptive violence' which he sees as underlying cartoons and movies and many other aspects of American life (Wink 1998). A more therapeutic method of dealing with questions of power and conflict is in evidence in the use of psychological methods in what is known as Christian or pastoral counselling, which applies the insights of psychology and the methods of psychotherapy to Christian ministry (Collins 2007). Most North American churches offer this kind of ministry, and the practitioners are usually women.

In the 1990s particularly, Evangelical theologians began to study post-modernity and to develop apologetics and methods of evangelism for a new age in which many of the old certainties against which neo-Evangelicalism defined itself seem to be breaking down and in which there is suspicion toward all 'metanarratives'. Drawing on some of the insights of the post-liberals, Richard Middleton and Brian Walsh (1995) are hopeful that Christians will rediscover resources within the biblical story which, like contemporary society, is plural and diverse. The call for a mission to Western culture and the context of post-modernity also demand new models of church, which tends in North America to refer to the local congregation. Two ideas have emerged most clearly: 'missional church' and 'emerging church'. 'Missional church' is a call for the 'continuing conversion of the church' from a static institution into an instrument of mission in its broadest sense (Guder 2000). Rather than sending missionaries elsewhere, local churches are urged to become witnesses for Christ in their own culture primarily by their attractive community life (Guder 1998; cf. Van Engen 1991). 'Emerging church' encourages the creation of new types of Christian community appropriate to post-modern cultures (Gibbs and Bolger 2006). Some pastors of large churches have developed their own distinctive models. To give two prominent examples: Bill Hybels of

Willow Creek Community Church, Chicago, stresses that the biblical model of church is a mixed community and focuses on the importance of relationships within the church and with the wider community. Rick Warren of Saddleback Church, Lake Forest, California, is probably the most 'successful' American pastor today. In his book, *The Purpose Driven Church* (1995) he focuses on making disciples as the primary purpose of the church and agent of growth.

Pentecostalism and civil rights

African Americans responded positively to the post-Civil War Holiness movement, to which many of them were introduced by the preaching of black woman evangelist Amanda Berry Smith, a follower of Phoebe Palmer, who exercised a national preaching ministry. The first black Holiness congregations developed in the late nineteenth century in the rural South. From the description in the book of Acts of the outpouring of the Holy Spirit on the disciples, they concluded that sanctification would be followed by such a 'baptism in the Spirit' or 'filling with the Spirit', and that the 'initial evidence' of this should be 'speaking in tongues' or 'the gift of tongues' (*glossolalia*) (Acts 2.4; 1 Cor. 12.10). A white former Methodist, Charles Fox Parham, became the chief proponent of this doctrine and led a revival at Topeka, Kansas, in 1900, which led to the formation of 'Pentecostal' churches. However, most scholars of Pentecostalism today, following Walter Hollenweger, regard the revival at Azusa Street, Los Angeles, in 1906 – not Topeka – as at the heart of the movement (Hollenweger 1997: 20–4). The former was led by African American William Seymour, who had been excluded from Parham's classroom because of his race. Seymour's revival meetings were focused around speaking in tongues but also included testimony, song (unaccompanied) and intercessory prayer and healing. The services were multiracial, including not only black and white but also the Latino and Asian residents of Los Angeles, and soon many foreign visitors. Seymour preached a clear message that, as through Pentecost Jew and Gentile were reconciled in Christ, there should be no 'color line'. The ministry of women was also prominent, including the woman who later became Seymour's wife and who led the mission after his death, Jennie Moore. Both the intimacy between the genders and the interracial nature of the meetings created scandal at the time (Hollenweger 1972: 23).

The Church of God in Christ (CoGiC), founded by Charles Harrison

Mason, an African American, is the largest offshoot of the Azusa Street revival. Mason introduced elements of African religiosity, which resonated with Old Testament sacrificial traditions, into worship (see Pinn and Pinn 2002: 112–19). There are now numerous other black Pentecostal denominations in the United States, such as the Pentecostal Assemblies of the World, one of the first 'Oneness' Pentecostal churches (which do not accept the doctrine of the Trinity), and countless independent congregations. In the South, virtually all Holiness churches became Pentecostal (Hardesty 2003: 114). The Pentecostal churches arising out of Azusa Street were not for long able to maintain the racial and gender equality of the initial revival. White members withdrew from the CoGiC in 1914 and joined others who had split from the Christian and Missionary Alliance to form The Assemblies of God (AG). The AG, which now has affiliated churches across the world, finally renounced its segrega-tionist tendencies only in 1991, and in 1994 the 'miracle of Memphis' occurred when the all-white Pentecostal Fellowship of North America was dissolved to form the Pentecostal/Charismatic Churches of North America. Women were very active in early Pentecostalism, and when the earliest Pentecostal denom-inations were formed they constituted a third of the ministers, but their status was always questioned and soon legally restricted (Wacker 2001: 158–76). However Aimee Semple McPherson, who had a nationwide healing ministry in the 1920s and 30s, founded a Pentecostal denomination, the Church of the Foursquare Gospel. McPherson was one of the first of the 'televangelists', who have always been controversial. Oral Roberts is the best-known Pentecostal televangelist today, after Jimmy Swaggert and Jim Bakker were exposed for sexual transgressions and financial misconduct.

It was 'through religion ... that African Americans found a voice', and so black religion and politics have gone very closely together in the United States (Baer and Singer 2002: xvii; Pinn and Pinn 2002: 125–6). Although the black Pentecostal churches provided an alternative experience, they largely adopted a conservative Evangelical theology which did not provide tools for social critique (Yong 2005: 78). However, leaders of the older black churches espoused the 'Social Gospel' and saw that the 'fatherhood of God' and the 'brotherhood of man' should mean that 'the destiny of our [African] race is bound up with the destiny of the world' (Ransom 2002 [1905]: 158). That the Social Gospel would lead to black civil rights was not obvious to the leaders of the original movement, but in his commitment to the Social Gospel in 1905, AME church leader Reverdy Ransom predicted that 'an individual life, a race or national life' which does not see its duty and destiny in terms of 'solidarity' 'will become more and more a thing to be despised' (Ransom 2002 [1905]: 158). Black gospel-motivated social concern issued in the civil rights movement of the 1950s and 60s in which leading figures Martin Luther King, Jr and Ralph Abernathy were ministers of urban black churches in the South. King's theology was rooted in the biblical belief of his childhood formation that God was active in history to bring about justice through the suffering of his servants, the prophets. He was also convinced that since Jesus loved his enemies and died for them, justice could only be achieved by non-violence (Harding 1996: 55). His was a social gospel influenced by reading of Rauschenbusch but tempered and shaped by his encounter with the theology of Reinhold Niebuhr, which purged him of political naïveté, helped him to distinguish between personal and institutional racism (Ling 2002: 234) and also suggested the direction his leadership would take by highlighting Gandhi's *satyagraha* strategy (Branch 1988: 73, 84–87).

Not all black Christians were satisfied with the theology of King, who worked toward consensus and assimilation without satisfying the anger felt by the black community at the humiliations and violence they continued to suffer despite the civil rights movement. A combination of the context of slave religion, the biblical stories of the God who liberates, the civil rights and black power movements, and the 'rhythm' of the liberation spirituality of poor African Americans gave rise in 1970 to 'black theology of liberation' (Hopkins 1999: 15–48). James H. Cone, the AME minister who first gave voice to this new approach, argued that King's Jesus was not black enough (1990: 37–8), and sought to introduce into black theology the black power ideology of Malcolm X, which affirmed black identity and the right to self-determination. Unaware of the development of liberation theology in Latin America, Cone similarly refused to accept any religion which did not offer liberation (Cone 1990: xii). Unlike King, and like X, he was prepared to alienate white theologians (Cone 1990: 199). He called Christianity 'black power' because the liberation of the black poor is at the heart of the gospel, and called white religion 'satanic' because 'God is black' (Cone 1990: 63, 64). Other theologians, black as well as white, found Cone's insistence that the gospel is about power dangerous and unchristian and rejected black theology as racism in reverse. A second generation of black theologians in the 1980s and 90s developed black theology by dialoguing through the Ecumenical Association of Third World Theologians (EATWOT) with other Third World theologians (Roberts 1987); by introducing the role of capitalism and class in black oppression (West 1979); and by relating black theology more to the music of slave religion, the language of the black poor and the traditions of Africa (see, e.g., Hopkins 1993). Black Christian women like Rosa Parks and Fannie Lou Hamer stood at the forefront of the civil rights movement. Womanist, as distinguished from feminist, theology affirms black women and questions the claim of black theology that the gospel brings liberation. Delores S. Williams examines the story, embedded in African American traditions, of Hagar, the black (Egyptian) wife who bore Abraham his son Ishmael and then was cast out in favour of Sarah and her son Isaac, wondering whether quality of life or mere belief in survival should be the central theme of black theology (Chopp 1997a: 399). Jacquelyn Grant compared the 'white women's Christ' unfavourably with Jesus as black women understood him, as the Anointed One who suffers with them (Grant 1989).

In the dialogue with other liberation theologians, black theologians from the United States built particularly close relationships with the political theologians of South Africa, who had been inspired by Cone's work but found it harder to relate to African theologians using indigenous culture (Hopkins 1999: 161–6; Maimela and Hopkins 1989). When black theology and Latin American liberation theology encountered one another, the Latin Americans, who were mainly white, were challenged to take race into account in their theologizing, and black theologians began to consider economic issues and employ Marxist analysis (Hopkins 1999: 167–72). However, Alistair Kee points out that black, and womanist, theology continues to pay very little attention to issues of black poverty, or to showing solidarity with Africans in Africa or other parts of the world (2006: 195, 198). As the second generation of black theology has become detached from any people's movement, there are complaints that it shows even less relationship to the life of the black churches (Kee 2006: 200; Pinn and Pinn 2002: 145), especially the Pentecostal churches, which tend to be suspicious of academic theology, particularly if it is not straightforwardly concerned with changing lives. Vincent Harding urges black Christians to recover the memory of the later Martin Luther King, who came increasingly under fire because in his concern for the poor he moved from civil rights to human rights, challenging US government policy in Vietnam and Central America and highlighting poverty at home (Harding 1996).

African American religion is increasingly diversified, especially in urban areas. Between the world wars, 'storefront churches' proliferated, catering to displaced migrants to the cities, and these sprouted new movements. Recent migrants from Africa and the Caribbean look for other forms of religious experience. Baer and Singer identify four types of African American religious sects (in a sociological sense) according to different responses by blacks to their minority status. The established black denominations cater for those wishing to accept the cultural patterns of mainstream society. They do not have a major political role but carry out a great deal of social service. Paradoxically, perhaps, those blacks who affiliate to white-controlled denominations (except Roman Catholicism), who are overwhelmingly middle-class, tend to do more to bring about social change. Messianic-nationalist groups, many of them Islamic or Judaic rather than Christian in inspiration, founded by individuals who are regarded by their followers as messiahs or 'messengers of God', protest against mainstream society and seek to create a new ethnic identity. Conversionist sects, mainly Holiness or Pentecostal, are apolitical and mainly focused on worship. Finally, thaumaturgical groups hope to achieve the ends desired by mainstream society, such as prosperity or health, but believe they can do so by magical rituals and esoteric knowledge. Their use of the occult puts 'spiritual' (or spiritualist) churches outside the category of 'Christian', although some churches that promise healing and prosperity on the basis of Christian faith have similar patterns of worship. Some groups, such as Father Divine's Peace Mission, combine elements of all four types (Baer and Singer 2002: 273–6).

It is very difficult to establish any specific characteristics of black churches in the United States that can be ascribed only to the African heritage of their members. However, it is possible to argue that African spiritual traditions of black Christians reinforced similar elements in European religion and that therefore there has been an Africanization of Christianity in North America. Raboteau points specifically to ecstatic behaviour and magical folk-belief (2004: 59–86). He suggests that the motor behaviour of jerking, shouting, clapping, antiphonal singing, hyperventilation and dancing exhibited at the camp meetings reflected the influence of slave religion on white religiosity. Similarly, African belief in the supernatural may have reinforced that dimension of white religion. A lively belief in a spirit world was (and is) prevalent across US Pentecostal churches (Wacker 2001: 91–3). Walter Hollenweger described this influence as the 'black root' (among others) of Pentecostalism. He believes this explains what he sees as the distinctive behavioural characteristics of Pentecostalism and is also the reason for its growth (Hollenweger 1997: 18–141; 1999: 36). The adoption of Christianity by African Americans should not be seen as passive reception but as a two-way interaction in which white Americans were challenged by the Christian faith of their slaves, and later their compatriots.

Christianity in the Anglophone Caribbean

Taken as a whole, the Caribbean has the third largest African diaspora population in the world, after Brazil and the United States. Nearly 90 per cent of the people of the Caribbean are of African descent, although the balance of population may vary greatly in specific countries. Compared to the United States, in the Caribbean and Latin America African Americans have had much greater ongoing contact with Africa and have mixed more with other races. Consequently, there is a much greater African influence on the culture in the Caribbean, and, from the point of view of religion, the retention of distinctive African traditions and institutions is much greater in the rest of the Americas. In contrast to the United States, there are many examples of African religious forms and meanings persisting in religions with a Roman Catholic component, such as Santería in Cuba and Vodu in Haiti, and with a Protestant component such as Baptist Shouters (Trinidad) and Kuminia (Jamaica) (Vernooij 2007: 148; see also Bisnauth 1996).

Jamaica is in many ways central to the Christian culture of the Anglophone Caribbean, or former British West Indies. More than 90 per cent of the people of Jamaica, which was seized by Britain in 1655 and finally declared itself independent in 1962, are of west African descent. The island could be described as having three types of Christian church: colonial, Zion revivalist and Pentecostal (Austin-Broos 2001), each representing a different period of reception. The colonial period resulted in Catholic, Baptist, Anglican, Methodist and Seventh Day Adventist churches. The Baptist church originated from the work begun in 1783 by George Lisle, a freed slave from the US state of Virginia, and had its own overseas missionary society from 1842. Today the former mission churches tend to have an Anglo-American identity, especially as they have become more middle class (Newman 1998). The Great Revival in 1860–1, which stemmed from American and British revivals of the period, led to the formation of independent and indigenous churches emphasizing spirit possession and healing, such as Revival Zion. By the 1950s, however, the dominant popular religion in Jamaica was Pentecostalism. The main denominations were all US-based: the New Testament Church of God, the Church of God of Prophecy and the United Pentecostal Church (see Austin-Broos 1997). These all now have a strong presence among the Caribbean diaspora in other parts of the world. In the case of the Church of God of Prophecy, at least, it was Jamaicans who were the primary missionaries in the expansion to Britain (Austin-Broos 2001: 151–2). After Pentecostal missionaries from the United States began arriving in Jamaica in the second decade of the twentieth century, Diane Austin-Broos argues that Jamaicans used this new form of religion to 'circumvent the colonial religious order' in three main ways: they used missionary resources to distribute religious texts over which the colonial authority had no control; US Pentecostalism legitimated the existing focus on healing that was integral to Jamaican popular religion; and the connections with the United States allowed an alternative accreditation for Jamaican pastors (Austin-Broos 2001: 157–8). The US connections did not make these churches any less Jamaican, Austin-Broos argues, because Pentecostalism's 'values and symbols are used by Jamaicans in ways that are specifically responsive to their history and cultural environment' (page 156). Jamaicans 'did not need "Americans" to tell them about a spirit-filled world' (page 149); they have their own experience of the Spirit and may be critical of aspects of the North American Pentecostal denominations to which they belong (page 50).

The Caribbean is not only subject to African influence but is also a meeting place for North American, Latin American and also Asian influences through substantial Indian and Chinese communities whose presence goes back to colonial times. In this religiously plural society, there are many examples of the overlapping of religious practice: for example in Trinidad, where the churches worship alongside a quarter of the population who are mostly Hindu. These 'East Indians' and the (approximately 30 per cent) Roman Catholic population, which includes a wide range of ethnicities, venerate the same shrine in Siparia. The Holy Shepherdess (La Divina Pastora), or Suparee Ke Mai (an expression of Mother Kali), is understood by both groups to grant favours, guide and protect (Boodoo 2000a). Hemchand Gossai and Nathaniel Samuel Murrell (2000) see Caribbean inter-religious relations from the point of view of interpretation of the Bible which, they point out, does not belong to any one community. Rastafarians in particular have 'made the Bible an instrument for black dignity, pride, and hope in the God of the future' (Murrell 2000: 304).

Post-independence there was as experiment in 'decolonizing theology' (Erskine 1981) to create a 'Caribbean theology' (Williams 1994), encouraged by EATWOT and engaged in across the former mission churches (Protestant and Catholic). As part of the development of post-colonial theory, the Bible, which had been used by the colonizers to justify their oppression, was subjected to a rereading by the newly emancipated. Kortright Davis argues that this was an 'emancipation from below' to complement the 'emancipation from above' which freed slaves at different periods in the nineteenth century but kept populations still bound into the cultural, racial and economic systems with the former powers (Davis 1990: 135–9). New sources for theological method from shared musical cultures were suggested, such as calypso (Mulrain 1995) and reggae. The method that has come to the fore in Caribbean theology is not the inculturation method inspired by Garveyite pan-Africanism (there are too many cultures for coherent theological development) or liberation theologies of Latin America (the Caribbean is more closely integrated with North America) but using the common denominator of Caribbean history, in the sense that the Caribbean reality of 'peoples and spaces', created by slavery, colonization and forced migrations, is taken as the material and place for theological reflection (Boodoo 2000b; Williams 1994: 62–5).

The Canadian contrast and First Nations Christians

The people of Canada are on the whole less religious than their counterparts south of the US border, but still more religious than most western European countries. Their Christian experience provides an interesting counterfoil to that of their southern neighbours. Canadian religion has tended to be a matter of Protestant–Catholic relations. French explorers entered North America from the 1530s and Jesuit missionaries began work among the American Indians. In the seventeenth century a young Native American girl, Kateri Tekakwitha, showed such exemplary faith that her grave site in Quebec became the object of pilgrimage and in 1980 she became the first Native American to be beatified. The French government established the colony of New France (1655–1763) which eventually cut a vast swathe through the heart of the continent, from what is now north-eastern Canada through the Great Lakes to the Gulf of Mexico. Evidence of French settlement is retained in the names of cities from Quebec to Detroit and down the Mississippi to St Louis and New Orleans; Jesuits, Sulpicians, Ursulines and Grey Nuns established churches, schools, hospitals and Indian missions there.

As the British began to acquire territory in Nova Scotia, they pursued a policy of Anglicanization; however, the preservation of Roman Catholicism under British rule was assured by the Quebec Act of 1774, which created a francophone-Catholic enclave. The Catholic Church adopted a policy of '*survivance*' or maintaining the religion and the conservative ways of pre-revolutionary rural France in the face of Protestant dominance. After the War of Independence, in which the Québecois fought on the British side, Canada became a separate territory under the British crown. Among the Protestants, many of the same forces were at work as south of the border. However, the first revival only reached Canada, through the preaching of Henry Alline, after the Revolution, and was interpreted as vindication of Canadian loyalty to the British crown (cf. Mullin 1999: 427), rather than as an encouragement to revolution. It was the Methodist Church which grew rapidly as a result of revival, and not Baptist churches as in the United States, which put greater stress on independency. The Canadian Methodist Church became particularly close to the British Methodist Church, and so 'functioned as a culturally centripetal force', in contrast to the US pattern (Mullin 1999: 433), although that did not result in Canadian civil institutions being invested with religious meaning as they are in the United States (Marty 2002: 419). Even though the Anglican Church came to represent a smaller proportion of Canadian Protestants, it kept its special status until 1854. The impulse of the Protestant churches to unity rather than competition bore fruit when in 1925 Methodists, Presbyterians and Congregationalists joined together to form the United Church of Canada. The churches in Canada were less easily split by the modernist controversies over biblical criticism and Darwinism, and did not develop extreme Fundamentalism, but they were morally conservative, supporting a Lord's Day Act (1906) and prohibition (of alcohol) laws in the 1920s. In 1940, Canadians were more likely than Americans to attend church, but by 1980 this statistic was reversed as Canada became a more secular society (Mullin 1999). Even in Quebec, where in the 1950s 93 per cent attended Sunday Mass, since the 1960s the Catholic hold over society has been strongly challenged and has diminished dramatically. Canada has seen a strong charismatic revival movement within the older churches, including the highly controversial 'Toronto blessing', and there are many new churches due to immigration, especially of Chinese.

Canadian churches have done more than their US counterparts to address the injustices done to the people of the 'First Nations', the native American population. The older churches supported the government policy of assimilation by running schools to which children were forcibly removed from their parents and where they were forbidden to use their native tongue. The United Church of Canada has already issued two apologies for its role in suppressing

Native American culture and complicity with the system, and is committed to 'concrete acts that demonstrate that the church is committed to living in a new way in its relations with First Nations peoples' (see church website). In practical terms, this means looking for alternatives to litigation such as 'truth telling', compensation or reparation, and memorials. The churches are also seeking to recognize the gifts and spirituality of First Nations people in their liturgical life (e.g. Carlson 1998). Christian Native Americans themselves have articulated a distinctive perspective on Christian faith. Robert Allen Warrior complains that the use of the exodus story in theologies of liberation casts his people in the role of the unfortunate Canaanites. He urges Christians to read the whole Bible and encourages his people to look to their own resources for theologizing (Warrior 1995). George Tinker suspects that 'the way immigrants pray and how they understand creation and their relationship to creation' lies at the root of the oppression his people have experienced, and argues that Western Christians reread the Bible to see how God's kingship is expressed in God's relationship to creation (Tinker 1994).

US Roman Catholicism and migration

The focus of this chapter has been on the dominant form of religion in the United States, which is Protestantism, but a quarter of US citizens are Roman Catholics and this proportion is growing. The oldest European settlement in what is now the United States is reputedly a Spanish colony at St Augustine, Florida, established in 1565. Settlements among the native peoples of New Mexico (such as Santa Fe, the state capital founded in 1610) and in Texas and Arizona were more lasting. In the eighteenth century, the Spanish began to colonize California, and under Junípero Serra (1713–84) a chain of missions was established up the coast from the tip of lower California (now part of Mexico) northwards as far as San Francisco. Like San Francisco, many Californian cities take their names from these missions, including San Diego, Santa Barbara, Santa Monica and Los Angeles itself. Under Mexican government from 1821, the mission lands were confiscated, but when California was ceded to the United States in 1848 the properties were returned to the church. Later settlers moving across from the east, Catholics and Protestants alike, were shocked to find a late-medieval Spanish Catholic presence already in the west. They denounced its 'barbarities' (such as self-mortification) and took over its structures but the western and south-western states remain predominantly

Roman Catholic today, and due to immigration are becoming more so. People of Hispanic descent are so prevalent that major cities like Los Angeles have a majority Hispanic population and society is becoming bilingual.

As a result of French colonization, the Great Lakes region and southern Louisiana remain predominantly Catholic today. Hardship in Quebec in the nineteenth and twentieth centuries led to large migration into New England, once the Puritan stronghold, which is now predominantly Catholic. Clergy and religious orders exiled during and after the French Revolution strengthened the Catholic community in North America. The Sulpician order supported the clergy by offering training, and new orders of mystical devotion, many of them founded by women, encouraged a popular Catholic spirituality that emphasized the visionary, which could hardly have contrasted more with the Puritan emphasis on the word. While at the level of popular religion Catholicism and Protestantism seemed worlds apart, at the level of leadership Roman Catholics were very much part of the American enterprise. The colony of Maryland was established by English Catholics. Although it later became Anglican, wealthy English Catholic families and Jesuit missionaries were landowners (and slave-holders) in the South. The first Catholic bishop in the United States, John Carroll (1736–1815), descendant of a Maryland family, was an enthusiastic supporter of democracy and of church–state separation. The first religious order founded in North America was the Sisters of Charity (1809), and their founder Elizabeth Bayley Seton was canonized as the first American-born saint.

The complexion of US Catholicism changed drastically between 1815 and 1860, when 2 million Irish Catholics arrived in the United States, fleeing the potato famine and British oppression. From Boston and other north-eastern ports they soon spread out across the country, aided by being English-speaking. In 1850, the Roman Catholic Church became the single largest denomination in the United States (Gaustad and Schmidt 2002: 170). The threat the new immigrants posed to the American-born poor led to widespread antagonism and anti-Catholic feeling from among the Protestant majority (Williams 1990: 276–7). The inventor Samuel F. B. Morse, for example, saw massive Catholic immigration as evidence for 'a papal takeover of the American republic' (Mullin 1999: 435). Catholics often set up their own community schools for reasons of language and also religious instruction. Demand for public support for these schools sparked anti-Catholic riots in the 1840s, and in the 1850s a secret organization known as the 'Know Nothing' party was set up to oppose the election of Catholics to public office.

By the end of the nineteenth century, priests of Irish descent were in a majority and dominated the leadership of the US Catholic Church. Large numbers of German Catholics also entered the United States in the same period, and many of them were wealthy enough to buy farmland, mainly in the 'German triangle' bounded by Milwaukee, St Louis and Cincinnati in the central United States, where they tried to maintain German language and religion. They and other minority Catholics, who also included Poles, Italians, Spanish and Portuguese, were dismayed when the priest appointed by the hierarchy did not speak their language or was unfamiliar with their particular saints and customs (Williams 1990: 277–82). Polish Catholics, who began to arrive from the 1870s, felt so strongly that they even founded a breakaway Polish National Catholic Church from 1897, which still exists. Some churches formed committees of lay trustees (as Protestant churches did) and tried to employ their own preferred clergy. But the Irish Americans who dominated the hierarchy until the mid-twentieth century argued for a centralized church, using English as its language medium, as the best way of maintaining a strong church which could defend Catholic interests. 'Liberals' wished to cooperate with American government and society as closely as possible, especially in public education, ecumenical activity, and support of labour unions, but an apostolic letter in 1899 from Pope Leo XIII, who shared liberal concern for social issues, nevertheless warned against 'Americanism', by which he referred mainly to 'individualism'. As a bulwark against this, and as an attractive alternative to 'culture-bound Protestantism' (Mullin 1999: 450), American theologians revived medieval Scholasticism.

In 1908 the Roman Catholic Church in North America ceased to be regarded as a 'mission field' by the hierarchy in Rome (Marty 2002: 422) and started to send missionaries. The first American missionary orders were the Maryknoll Priests and Brothers in 1911 and the Maryknoll Sisters in 1912. Before Vatican II, the Catholic Church rarely intervened in the public sphere, except to call for the protection of Catholic interests at home and overseas; popular Catholic anti-Communism was mediated by the activities of Senator Joseph McCarthy in the 1950s (Williams 1990: 375). However, the church took a progressive stance on economic issues, and American Catholics have been leaders in developing Catholic social theory. For example, Catholics worked with President Franklin D. Roosevelt to improve labour relations and social programmes for the urban poor, where the vast majority of Catholics were found (Mullin 1999: 435). John A. Ryan's (1869–1945) long campaign for a 'living wage' resulted in 1938 in the passing of minimum wage legislation, and the Catholic Worker movement, founded by Dorothy Day (1897–1980), pioneered Catholic social action. From the 1960s, many individual Catholics were involved in political activism for civil rights, against war and on behalf of the poor. One of the best known is the Jesuit priest Daniel Berrigan, a radical theologian and activist, who has campaigned against US foreign intervention from Vietnam to Iraq, against nuclear armaments and against abortion.

In the second half of the twentieth century, more Catholics began to enter the mainstream of American life. In part this was due to their increasing social mobility, symbolized in 1960 when John F. Kennedy was elected to the presidency, despite anti-Catholic attempts to derail his campaign. The opening up of the Roman Catholic Church as a whole to the modern world through the Second Vatican Council (1962–5) had a profound effect in the United States as elsewhere. Americans particularly welcomed the Declaration on Religious Liberty, which owed much to an American Jesuit, John Courtney Murray (Mullin 1999: 454). However, the same people were horrified by the promulgation just a few years later by Pope Paul VI of the encyclical *Humanae Vitae* (1968), which prohibited almost any form of birth control. The moral theologian Charles E. Curran has been an outspoken critic of Vatican teaching on birth control and issues of sexuality generally (Curran 2006) and was removed from his post at the Catholic University of America in 1986. Other American Catholics, however, accepted the Pope's ruling, and those who supported traditional Catholic ideals of family life also campaigned with Phyllis Schafly against the 'equal rights amendment' to the Constitution passed in 1972 to end discrimination against women. Attempts to legislate on family life and sexuality were seen by many Catholics, as by their Evangelical counterparts, as unwarranted interference by government in the private sphere. In the Catholic case this went against the principle of 'subsidiarity' established in Catholic social teaching (see Chapter 2).

One result of the emphasis on the laity given by Vatican II was increased numbers of women students at Catholic seminaries and the emergence of a strong feminist movement. Some developed a radical feminist position: Mary Daly renounced the faith altogether as irredeemably patriarchal – and therefore in her view misogynist – in favour of a 'cosmic covenant' based on pre-Christian traditions (Daly 1973); Rosemary Radford Ruether argued that the language of theology and Christian liturgy needed to be revised for women to be able to share in it, and advocated the formation of 'feminist base communities' (Ruether 1983). Others attempted to remain true to the teaching of the church, while rethinking its traditions and authority. Elisabeth

Schüssler Fiorenza re-examined the early church of the New Testament to uncover the 'memory of her' and show the extent of women's participation in the early Christian mission (Fiorenza 1983). Elizabeth A. Johnson exposed the feminine images of God in the Bible, which she argued amounted to an alternative vision of 'She Who Is' (Johnson 1992). These and others support the calls for women's ordination in the Roman Catholic Church, which have been made since 1975 when the first Women's Ordination Conference was convened in Detroit. Other key issues for the Catholic Church at large in the last decade or so have revolved around issues of sexuality. Revelations of the sexual abuse of children, especially boys, in Catholic institutions by priests have provoked shock within the church and caused some dioceses to file for bankruptcy because of the size of compensation payouts. Although it is claimed that the incidence of abuse is no higher than in the general population (Jenkins 1996), these cases have raised the issue of homosexual practice among priests, which is condemned by the church, and caused many to question the rule of priestly celibacy. These problems are not unique to the Catholic Church in the USA but they have received greatest attention there because of the thoroughness with which they have been investigated and the size of the claims against the church.

Since 1900, the largest migration into the Catholic Church in the United States has been Hispanic. In the main these have come from Puerto Rico, since it became American territory in 1898, from Cuba after Fidel Castro took power in 1959, and from Mexico and other parts of Central America. The instability and poverty of the region has meant that many entered illegally, and some Catholic activists have been involved in sheltering them. The extent to which Hispanics keep their own culture and language and resist integration with the wider society worries some political commentators (e.g. Huntington 2005: 18) and challenges Anglo-American society, although it should not be forgotten that many Latinos are Protestants (cf. Jenkins 1996: 101). Catholic Hispanics bring with them a spirituality heavily influenced by their folk religion, which tends to put a distance between them and other American Catholics (Williams 1990: 378–9). However, Pope John Paul II gave encouragement to such popular religiosity, and now that the Mexican Virgin of Guadalupe is recognized as the patron saint of all the Americas, celebration of her saint-day is required in all Catholic churches. Churches which seek to help migrants take different approaches to their problems: in one Latino-dominated town a Lutheran church operating in a Spanish medium encourages assimilation with 'multicultural America', while a neighbouring Catholic mission, dedicated to the Virgin of Guadalupe, helps immigrants connect with their roots and critically engages US society, challenging the identification of the United States with 'America' as a whole (Vásquez and Marquardt 2003: 145–70).

Roman Catholicism is also well represented among Asians in the United States, who number more than 10 million in 2000 and are mainly Chinese, Filipino, Indian, Vietnamese and Korean. Estimates of numbers of Catholics include 19 per cent of the Chinese community, 65 per cent of Filipinos, 30 per cent of Vietnamese and 8 per cent of Koreans (Phan 2003: 6–7). Their presence further diversifies American Catholicism, and now Vietnamese Catholics, for example, have several of their own parishes where their populations are most concentrated. Elsewhere they often worship together using the local parish facilities. In 2003 there were approximately 500 Vietnamese priests, working both in the Vietnamese and in the wider community (Phan 2003: 230–1). The presence of migrant groups poses many questions of organization for the church, but Peter Phan, a leading Catholic theologian of Vietnamese descent, argues that it also presents theological opportunities for '*mutual* criticism and enrichment between cultures' (2003: 238). In addition to the culture the Vietnamese bring with them, Phan also argues that the experience of Vietnamese immigrants in the United States is a resource to critique the dominant culture, for example its individualism, and suggest constructive alternatives (page 243). Phan hopes not just for an intercultural Vietnamese–American theology but also for an 'inter-multicultural theology' resulting from the encounter 'not *between* but *among*' the many different cultures represented in North America (page 10).

Study Questions and Further Readings

- Discuss some differences between North American Christianity and European Christianity.
- How did the series of revivals starting from the eighteenth century shape Evangelicalism in the United States?
- Discuss the differences between Evangelicals, Fundamentalists, Conservatives and Pentecostals in North American Christianity.
- In what way have Afro-American forms of Christianity influenced the churches in North America?
- What are some of the characteristics of Caribbean Christian experience, and how does Christianity there relate to churches in North America and in Europe?
- How do you assess the contribution of Roman Catholicism to North American Christianity?

Anderson, Allan (2004), *An Introduction to Pentecostalism*. Cambridge: Cambridge University Press.

Gaustad, Edwin S. and Leigh E. Schmidt (2002), *The Religious History of America* (revised edn). New York: HarperCollins.

Marsden, George M. (2006), *Fundamentalism and American Culture* (2nd edn). Oxford: Oxford University Press.

Noll, Mark A. (2001), *American Evangelical Christianity*. Oxford: Blackwell.

Phan, Peter C. (2003), *Christianity with an Asian Face: Asian American Theology in the Making*. Maryknoll, NY: Orbis.

Pinn, Anne H. and Anthony B. Pinn (2002), *Introduction to Black Church History*. Minneapolis, MN: Fortress Press.

5 Latin American Christianity

We have chosen to define this part of America by its 'Latin-ness' because many of its common features in the present day are traceable to its colonization by the rulers of Spain and Portugal. The label 'Latin' also expresses a contrast with North America, which has been shaped more by the cultures of the Reformation and the Enlightenment. In many ways, to cross the border between the United States and Mexico is to 'change civilizations'. However, the colonial title 'Latin' disguises many other influences, such as the cultures of the indigenous peoples and of the millions imported from Africa as slaves, as well as of later migrations of people from northern as well as southern Europe. Global processes in religion as well as economics, politics and technology also shape contemporary 'Latin' America and have resulted in new religious movements. Nevertheless, we will take Latinness as an important key to understanding this part of the world, because it also refers to the dominant form of Christianity. Not only do nearly 90 per cent of its population belong to the Catholic Church, but all areas of Latin American life are 'infused with Catholic-Christian beliefs' (Wiarda 2001: 9, 351).

The Christianization of the Americas

The first inhabitants of the Americas arrived there across a land bridge from Asia perhaps as much as 40,000 years ago. Whereas in North America it is estimated there were only about 3 million Indians, who were only loosely organized into tribal groups, in Latin America there were probably ten times as many, and several large-scale societies (Wiarda 2001: 104). The Mexica or Aztec civilization in Central America was a loose association of city-states, some of them among the largest in the world at the time, paying tribute to the ruler in the capital city of Tenochtitlan, where Mexico City is today. Their lingua franca, Nahuatl, is still spoken by some 1.5 million people. The even larger empire of the Incas to the south had its capital at Cuzco, modern Cusco in Peru, and included large parts of modern Ecuador, Peru, Bolivia, northern Argentina and Chile, and Colombia. Its official language, Quechua, continues to be spoken by about 10 million people in South America. Both civilizations were highly structured and organized, but outside them were large numbers of independent or semi-independent groups. Except perhaps for some Viking explorers around 1000 CE, it seems the peoples of the Americas had had no contact with people from other parts of the world before the end of the fifteenth century. When they did meet others – Europeans – it was Spanish noblemen excited by their recent victory over the Moors, who were confident that God was granting them new lands for the exaltation both of the Christian faith and the glory of Spain. In their eyes, the destiny of the nation and the destiny of the church were united: Spain was a temporal messiah, and the purpose of the Spanish crown was 'essentially missionary' (Dussel 1981: 38–9). The arrival of Europeans took the indigenous people by surprise and they were ill-prepared to resist.

The Taíno, who found Columbus in 1492 and helped him and his men when he first made landfall, were spread across the Caribbean islands and northern South America. A papal bull the following year made clear the obligation on Spain to bring these and other peoples of the newly discovered lands to Christian faith. Although the Portuguese were eventually given jurisdiction over what is now Brazil, they were occupied in Asia and did not develop their transatlantic lands at first. Spanish *conquistadores* were able to seize lands in the Caribbean, Central and South America rapidly because the centralized empires collapsed, but groups of Indians outside the empires held out for longer, and isolated groups remain in the rainforests of the Amazon even into the twenty-first century. The *conquistadores* carried over into the conquest of the Americas the 'energy, crusading spirit, militarism, missionary fervor, and social and political institutions that had carried [them] to victory over the Moors' (Wiarda 2001: 77) in Iberia. The social vision they brought with them was essentially feudal but also militarized as a result of the period of 'reconquest', and centralized as a consequence of the policies of the unification of the many Iberian kingdoms into two (Wiarda 2001: 98). The conquest was justified by Scholastic philosophy, but its execution was in the hands of the monarchs of Spain and Portugal. In feudal society the acquisition of land carried with it the labour of its inhabitants, and so on each *encomienda* the people were settled in villages. Missionary religious orders, mainly Franciscans and Dominicans, and later Jesuits, baptized, instructed and disciplined the Indians until the church was established. The missionaries themselves desired to build a new, pure Indian church, free from the worldliness of the church in Europe (Elizondo 1997: xiii); however, the reality was very different. The peoples of the Americas were humiliated by their political defeat, the rape of women, by neglect in the New America, and deprivation of their language and customs – a situation that could be said to continue today – and were then exploited and enslaved (Beozzo 1990). The effect of the conquest on the local population was catastrophic population decline. Estimates of the number who died vary hugely, but the figure of 20–25 million given by Bartholomé de las Casas in the sixteenth century is probably not far from the mark (Gutiérrez 1993: 461–4). Warfare, brutal treatment, dislocation, malnutrition and dietary changes are among the causes, but perhaps the greatest factor was that the people had no resistance to imported diseases. Furthermore, the destruction of their way of life, disruption of society and forced separation of men and women led to despair, death wishes and suicide. As well as the military conquest, there was a 'deeper violence' against their culture and religion (Elizondo 1997: xiv). As Aztec survivors said in the aftermath of the conquest, 'Well let us die, let us perish, since our gods are already dead' (quoted in Beozzo 1990: 84).

The secular priests generally supported the system and were supported by it; missionaries either worked within the system to ameliorate its effects or outside it. There were often clashes between the two groups (Klaiber 1998: 4). Among the missionary friars and (few) bishops who tried hard to protect the people from the predations of the colonists and traders, and protested the treatment of the indigenous people, Bartholomé de las Casas particularly has been held up as the first theologian of liberation (Gutiérrez 1993: 57). As a result of his efforts, some justice for the Indians was obtained in the papal bull of 1537 and the promulgation in 1542 of laws to combat the main abuses and dangers of the *encomienda* system. But by then millions of the indigenous people had perished and the system had descended into slavery. In the early seventeenth century Jesuits, who were influenced by Renaissance humanism toward a more positive appreciation of human culture and nature, followed up the dream of Las Casas and persuaded the Spanish crown to allow them to use a huge region in central South America covering parts of present-day Argentina, Paraguay, southern Brazil and Uruguay for an alternative to the *encomienda*, the *reducción*. These were 'Christian villages' run by missionaries to protect the people from the predations of Europeans, which were greatly admired by subsequent generations. They were highly paternalistic and aimed

only at assimilation to European culture, but they did allow for Indian participation. When the Jesuit order was suppressed worldwide in the 1760s, the
reducciónes were also 'grabbed by the colonists' (Dussel 1981: 60).

In Brazil and most of the Caribbean Islands, the indigenous population was
virtually wiped out, and large numbers of Africans were imported as slaves to
fill the labour shortage. But Guatemala, Bolivia, Peru and Ecuador, and large
areas of Mexico and Colombia retain substantial indigenous populations,
and in most other countries a large proportion of the population has some
indigenous blood. The lives of the ancient peoples also live on in the landscape,
the diet, local languages and customs, and in some aspects of Latin American
Christianity. Although some missionaries, especially from the second generation, learnt Indian languages and provided almost the only documentation of
local customs, few found value in these, or in the traditional religions, which
they demonized. The collapse of indigenous culture, the imposition of the
Spanish world-view and the lack of mediating figures between the old and
new worlds left no opportunity for dialogue between the two (Dussel 1981: 43;
Elizondo 1997: xv). So the Indians were taught to worship a new god in a new
way, with many church leaders believing that all who lived before the Spanish
conquest were 'children of Satan' (Hastings 1999b: 342). Despite the imperious
and condescending approach, Mexicans showed great enthusiasm for the new
faith. Many were prepared for the priesthood, but none were ever ordained.
At the other extreme, the Incas, were much less responsive. However, the
pre-Columban past did not just disappear from the minds and hearts of the
people. For example, the Q'eqchi' of Guatemala understand the cross to be
symbolic of Christ but to this day a cross erected in a field when maize is being
planted symbolizes the spirit of a good harvest (Siebers 1999: 268). The record
of Gauman Poma de Ayala, an elderly man from what is now Peru, penned
in the early seventeenth century, shows how the indigenous people tried to
make sense of what had happened by fusing the past with biblical history and
Christian belief. He viewed 'the Indians of old' as 'Christian' because 'although
they were pagans, they observed God's commandments and the good works
of compassion', while at the same time being bewildered that there seemed to
be no God in Peru anymore, but only in 'Rome and Castile', and bemoaning
the fact that the 'priests and rulers of every sort' persecuted 'the poor of Jesus
Christ' (quoted in Hastings 1999b: 338). However, the conquest was not
entirely one way because aspects of Indian faith influenced the colonizers
and they are retained to this day in popular religiosity. Ahead of the five
hundredth anniversary of the conquest in 1992, Latin American liberation

theologians and Indian leaders called for redress of these injustices, in the form of resistance to the imposition of Latin culture as the definer of 'Latin' America, restitution of Indian lands and recognition of indigenous languages and customs (e.g. Beozzo 1990: 88–9; Wagua 1990: 54–5).

Male and female in Iberian Catholicism and indigenous religion

Although the imperial religions of both Aztecs and Incas centred on the Sun, other gods were probably more significant in the lives of most of the people, especially the goddesses, who were associated with the earth and fertility. Among them, the Aztecs worshipped the goddess Tonantzín and the Incas worshipped Pacha Mama. When, in 1531 at dawn on the day after the feast of the Immaculate Conception (of Mary, mother of Jesus), a native American, Cuauhtlatoatzin, baptized Juan Diego, saw a vision of 'a lady from heaven' on the hill near what is now Mexico City where the shrine of Tonantzín once stood, he understood he had seen the Virgin Mary. But he saw Mary from within his own world, with darker skin and speaking in his native tongue (Elizondo 1997: xviii) and the story of his encounter is described in a later poem in the Nahuatl language, the Nican Mopohua (see Elizondo 1997: 5–22) in which Mary is described as the one who would hear the laments of the nations and 'cure all their miseries, misfortunes, and sorrows' (translation in Elizondo 1997: 8). The miraculous imprint of the image of a dark-skinned virgin on Cuauhtlatoatzin's skirt convinced the Spanish bishop. He built a church on the site dedicated to the Virgin Mary, who in this appearance has become known as the Virgin of Guadalupe. In Juan Diego's vision, there was a fusion of the old and new worlds and the faint dawn of reconciliation between them. It provided a way for the Indians to reach their heaven through the new religion, which hitherto had seemed to offer little but hardship and suffering. The vision was followed by mass conversions of Indians to Christianity, and a festival in honour of this Indian Mary, and from the seventeenth century Creoles also identified with the vision.

The Spanish church, fresh from its struggle against Islam, did not promote syncretism (Dussel 1981: 65–6); it preferred to see the veneration of the Virgin of Guadalupe as an indigenous response to the Christian gospel. Whether this was respect or manipulation is a difficult question. From the indigenous peoples' perspective, to some extent it allowed them to worship Tonantzín disguised as Mary, and so preserve their indigenous cultures (cf. Wagua 1990: 53) and it was instrumental in developing Mexican national consciousness (Lafaye 1976). From the point of view of Latin American Christianity, the event has been seen as 'revolutionary, profound, lasting, far-reaching, healing, and liberating' and comparable to Pentecost because it was the birth of an indigenous church (Elizondo 1997: xi). Its celebration has become Mexico's most popular religious event and there are many other such celebrations of the Virgin-Mother across Latin America, which include Our Lady of Copacabana (Bolivia), the Virgin of Luján (Argentina) and La Virgen de la Caridad del Cobre (Cuba). Latin America is not the only part of the world where the veneration of Mary is prominent, but it has been significant in a revival of the cult in contemporary Catholicism, especially under John Paul II, who published an encyclical *Redemptoris Mater* 'On the Blessed Virgin Mary in the life of the Pilgrim Church'. In this (1987: para. 28), Guadalupe is the first-listed example of a centre where pilgrims seek to meet 'the one who is blessed because she believed', and in 1999 John Paul II declared Our Lady of Guadalupe the patron saint of all the Americas.

The high profile of the Virgin of Guadalupe is an example of what Frederick Pike has called the 'matriarchal' nature of popular Catholicism in Latin America, which results from a fusion of both the pre-Columbian goddess traditions and the Iberian Catholicism which was exported there (2002: 450–1). The first canonized saint of the new world was a woman, St Rose of Lima (1586–1617), a Creole whose extreme penance and acts of charity were very much in keeping with the intense spirituality of sixteenth-century Spain, and not distinctively American (Hastings 1999b: 337), and Latin America has produced many other such women saints, who are understood, like the Virgin Mary, to play a mediatory role, interceding for sinners before the judgment throne of God (Pike 2002: 450). Pike argues that the veneration of Mary, the mother of Jesus, in Latin America has assumed such magnitude that 'she came, always unofficially, to be seen as a member of a "quaternity" that challenged the Trinity stipulated by orthodox theology'. Furthermore, he regards this 'cult of the female in the supernatural order' as having a huge effect on Latin American Christianity and society both in promoting the self-sacrificing mother-virgin and also in encouraging its opposite, the warrior-saint of special significance to upper-sector males (2002: 450).

The Virgin Mary, portrayed as a manifestation of the feminine principle, requires a complementary masculine symbol (Warner 1985: xxiv, 335–6).

Popular male saints in sixteenth-century Spain were warrior figures, especially St James (Santiago) of Compostela, who helped defeat the Moors. Their aggressive and assertive manliness was a role model for the *conquistadores* and this may partly explain the cult of *machismo* in Latin America today, especially among the *mestizo* community. This 'cult of exaggerated masculinity' (Chant 2003: 14), which involves the assertion of masculine power and control over women (and other men), manifesting virility, and the repudiation of anything feminine (Chant 2003: 15–17), is related to alienation of men from the household, and is therefore not to be identified with patriarchy (Brusco 1995: 82). This behaviour may also be related to cultural norms in the empires of pre-conquest America (Chant 2003: 15). *Machismo* is a compensation for a lack of masculine confidence to attain to the ideal of *macho* (or strength, courage, endurance and self-control), which results from the humiliation of Indian manliness in the conquest and subjugation of Latin America and the behaviour of Iberian males toward their Amerindian womenfolk. It is perpetuated by the class/caste culture (Brusco 1995: 77–91). *Machismo* is coupled with idealization of women and the exaggeration of femininity, which demands *marianismo* behaviour in women of self-abnegation and submission, and an emphasis on the specifically feminine roles of motherhood and nurturance (Chant 2003: 9–10). Although *marianismo* is not a religious practice, the portrayal of Mary, the mother of Jesus, in Roman Catholic Marianism provided it with religious legitimation and a role model (Chant 2003: 9). In this context where the woman is revered as a virgin, as a mother and as a heavenly intercessor, the real woman is deemed a failure for not having lived up to the impossible ideal of being at the same time virgin and mother (Warner 1985: 337).

Many problems of Latin America are blamed on *machismo*. The emphasis on male virility is blamed for the reluctance of Latin American males to offer for the (celibate) priesthood, which threatens indigenization and limits the control the church is able to exercise over local Catholic communities (e.g. Pike 2002: 466; Hastings 1999b: 335). The promiscuity of men and their power over women is a contributing factor in the large numbers of 'street children' (Pike 2002: 466), although the violence of poverty is an even more important cause (Hecht 1998: 192). Although population growth is now slowing down, continued opposition to most birth control methods and to abortion by the Catholic Church (ignored by many) and *marianismo* are often blamed for child and female mortality and poverty (e.g. Chant 2003: 73–4, 78). On the one hand, contemporary Christian feminists bemoan the culture of *machismo* and try to transform society, or at least work at a local level to free women from male control (e.g. Caipora Women's Group 1993: 21–3). Julia Esquivel from Guatemala compares the suffering of Indian women at the hands of the *conquistadores* with those who were raped and abused by soldiers in 1980s Guatemala, and complains that the 'spirit of he conquest' is still alive today and has not yet given way to the 'discovery' of the other (1990: 75). Expatriate Cuban Ada María Isasi-Díaz developed a *Mujerista* theology – a women's liberation theology (Isasi-Díaz 1996). And others try to rescue the biblical figure of Mary from gender stereotyping, pointing out, for example, that the exaltation of Mary is the exaltation of a poor woman (Lk. 1.48; Gebara and Bingemer 1994). On the other hand, where motherhood is both privately and publicly venerated, it can be embraced and used to subvert male power (Chant 2003: 9–13). In popular portrayals of the Virgin, the mother is one who submits to God's will and suffers, thus gaining a sense of spiritual superiority. An individual example of this phenomenon of the *supermadre* ('supermother'; Pike 2002: 459) is Eva Duarte de Perón (1919–52), the second wife of Juan Domingo Perón, who was president of Argentina in 1946–55. The highly popular Evita promoted and publicly revered her husband. She was seen to sacrifice herself in social work, like the female saints, acted as a mediator between the poor and her husband, and behaved as mother of the nation. She founded a women's political party and ran for vice-president. Idolized by the masses, her name was even put forward for canonization (Fraser and Navarro 1996). Another example of women using the sanctity of motherhood in Argentina is the group known as the 'mothers of the disappeared' or the Mothers of the Plaza de Mayo, a square in Buenos Aires where the women first gathered in 1977 in defiance of a ban on demonstrations to campaign silently for justice for their children who were taken away during the military dictatorship and never seen again. Their motherhood did not guarantee complete immunity, and one of their leaders, Azucena Villaflor, herself became one of the 'disappeared', but other mothers were able to maintain almost the only visible political protest throughout the remaining years of the 'dirty war'.

Latin society and Roman church

Latin America today is a 'homogeneity without unity' (Ribeiro 1990: 26). It is the result of five centuries of mixing of the indigenous peoples with others from Europe, Africa and, more recently, Asia. The violence of the conquest and the later military suppression of any resistance have led to a remarkable uniformity of language and culture across 20 countries, although the unity of purpose toward a democratic society envisaged by the revolutionary leader Simón Bolívar (1783–1830) has not been achieved. However, the divide, as many Latin American theologians have seen it, is not into the many ethnic groups but a single fissure between the conquerors – or at least today's landowning elites – and 'the poor' (e.g. Ribeiro 1990: 27–9).

In the immediate aftermath of the conquest, the European population grew rapidly and a network of Spanish towns grew up, together with structures of governance and social organization on the centralized feudal and militarized model of Iberia. Unlike the settlers in North America, the *conquistadores* did not bring their wives and families with them (Wiarda 2001: 100), and so the European, Amerindian and African races were very soon mixed. Although there was initially some doubt as to whether the peoples of the Americas and the imported Africans were indeed human, the medieval European social hierarchy was soon modified for the new conditions, with class structure being based on a system of caste. At the top were Europeans or *creoles* (American-born Europeans), followed by *mestizo* (white and Indian), *mulatto* (white and African), *castizo* (white and *mestizo*), and so on – more than 100 different categories in all (Wiarda 2001: 100). At the bottom were the slaves and the Indians (cf. Ribeiro 1990: 20–2). The whites together formed the ruling class and lived in the cities, where the *mestizo* formed urban masses. The Indians formed the rural poor, and the blacks were enslaved on the great estates.

Especially in the Spanish colonies, the political structure under the monarchy was authoritarian and imperious. Furthermore, unlike at home, the colonies had no representative body. The social and economic order was exploitative and mercantile. Everything belonged to the crown and was expected to produce revenue for it; and on the estates the rule of the landowner was absolute (Wiarda 2001: 98–9). The institutions imported to Latin America included the church, which served as an arm of royal authority, and was just as absolutist (2001: 99). The Catholicism of Spain was under the monarchy – with papal power almost excluded – which, when unified under Ferdinand and Isabella, exercised very tight control through the Inquisition. Spanish church leaders played a very active role in the counter-Reformation and encouraged Christian scholarship, especially the revival of the theology of Thomas Aquinas, bringing to the fore his juridical method and emphasis on the natural order with its God-ordained hierarchy. This led to a tendency toward legalism at the expense of justice, or what the Latin American church historian Enrique Dussel has described as 'a "perfect legalism" in theory, and a shameful illegality and inadequate application of the laws in fact' (1981: 39). Huge numbers of Creoles joined the secular clergy, and 'the splendour of the baroque churches of seventeenth-century Mexico and Peru testifies to a religious culture anxious to outdo that of its mother country' (Hastings 1999b: 344). Since all appointments were made from Madrid, Creoles were not appointed to the highest posts, but '*peninsulares*', Spanish and Portuguese who were brought over from Europe. Indians were not ordained in any numbers until the late eighteenth century and were sometimes even excluded from the Eucharist.

The colonial grip of Spain over most of Latin America lasted three centuries, and the authoritarian institutions exported from Europe lasted virtually unchanged and unchallenged until the turn of the nineteenth century (Wiarda 2001: 76–8). The hold of Portugal on its American territories was looser, however, and the Portuguese were less strict about social relations. Brazilian society developed most rapidly in the eighteenth century, when the slave trade was at its height. The number of slaves imported into Brazil is estimated at more than 3 million, making the slave community larger than the European one. As a consequence, the culture of slavery permeated the country to a much greater extent than in Spanish territories. Despite the very large slave population in Brazil, the religious orders concentrated, as elsewhere, on evangelizing the remaining Indians. The black population was never systematically evangelized at all (Hastings 1999b: 348) but largely left to develop its own religious expressions from its mixed African traditions, elements of Catholicism and Amerindian religion, and later influences.

Spanish American independence was marked by a series of local wars from 1810 against what was a declining power. The Mexican war began that year with an uprising of mainly Indians and *mestizos*, carrying the banner of the Virgin of Guadalupe and led by a Creole priest, Miguel Hidalgo y Costilla. By 1824 the whole of Spanish America achieved its independence, and a string of new republics was created. Brazil eventually became a republic in 1889. All the new regimes were basically socially conservative. There was some commitment to modernization, but the Creole upper class kept power for themselves. Independence caused a crisis for the church, which had been under control of the crown, not the papacy. There was no obvious reason why any of the people of Latin America should defend the institutional church. The church was also a landowner, and so it was both 'an instrument and beneficiary of colonialism' (Wiarda 2001: 99). Furthermore, it seemed to serve few. White males regarded themselves as Christians but 'without any existential linking of conduct and gospel' (Dussel 1981: 69). They relied on the Virgin Mary and other intercessors to plead their cause but felt they had little need of bishops and other church officials (Pike 2002: 438). The remainder of the population, whether devout or not, were 'second-class Catholics' (Pike 2002: 437), denied ordination to the priesthood for reasons of gender, race or illegitimacy. In all cases, following independence, states immediately abolished the Inquisition, the bishops appointed by Spain and Portugal had to return home, and, since many new governments suppressed the religious orders as well, this led to a crisis of manpower. In the period 1820–50 the church faced a wave of anticlericalism and assaults on its privileges, led by the new 'liberals' in Latin society, who looked to emulate the United States in material progress and in the separation of church and state. For them it was 'either Catholicism or democracy' (quoted in Bonino 1975: 9) so they argued for state control even over the internal workings of the church, and anticlericalism became the centrepiece of their reform programmes. As a result, the clergy became more conservative, looking to Rome for support in the crisis. They, and many other members of society, also tended to see the church as the only bastion of tradition that could stabilize their nations in the precarious political conditions post-independence (Pike 2002: 442, 444). The result was that the Latin American church gradually embraced Ultramontanism. Its numbers were reinforced by clergy from Europe, and its Latinization contributed to the increasing isolation of the hierarchy from the people, which is a recurrent theme in Latin American theology. The Church gradually worked out new relationships with different states; in several cases this was by means of civil war; for example in Mexico in 1857–60. In contrast, in Peru a settlement was relatively easily achieved. As world church historian Adrian Hastings laments, in general the church appeared more concerned for its rights than those of the people (Hastings 1999b: 352).

The status of the church was changed by independence but the status of the aristocracy was not. By 1850 the liberals had achieved the goals of their anticlerical programme but had abandoned most of their economic and social goals. The continuing two-class nature of Latin American society provoked many uprisings and much unrest by Indians and *mestizos*, expressing complaints about taxation and ill-treatment. Some of these included a religious motivation. On the one hand, the church sided with the state in condemning these actions of the 'ignorant, superstitious, impertinent and fanatic' (quoted in Hastings 1999b: 357). Despite their differences, the elites of church and society found mutual support in maintaining their status. The clericalism of the church helped maintain the social order by reinforcing the dependent status of the other classes and of Creole women and children, and the focus on the suffering of Christ and the Virgin reminded the masses that they could expect no less in this life (cf. Pike 2002: 438–9). On the other hand, the religious motivation of the poor in these struggles showed that Catholicism was not merely a colonial survival but an indigenous force and the church was forced to recognize that, but for the support of the masses, it could be 'cut out' of modern Latin America (Hastings 1999b: 357).

The Catholic Church worldwide began to revive in the late nineteenth and into the twentieth century, and in 1899, realizing the importance of the continent, Pope Leo XIII convoked a plenary council of Latin American bishops in Rome. The development of Catholic social teaching from this period helped alleviate the conditions of the poor; the church also worked to stabilize society by founding labour unions, and later in the 1950s it encouraged the establishment of Christian Democratic parties. In Latin America these parties demanded state intervention and a communitarian society. Alberto Hurtado Cruchaga (1901–52), a Chilean priest, was beatified by Pope Benedict XVI in 2005 for his work for social justice (becoming the second Chilean saint). Hurtado was director of Catholic Action, a youth movement, and went on to found the Chilean Trade Union Association in 1947. Renewal of the church, aided by an influx of priests from Europe to alleviate the perennial shortage in Latin America, took place gradually over the twentieth century until in 1960 the continent could boast 35 per cent of the world's Catholics – more than in Europe (Hastings 1999b: 358). In 1955 a general conference of Latin American bishops was held in Rio de Janeiro to build the capacity of the church to respond to its own problems. The first Latin American Episcopal Conference (CELAM I) was the first continental gathering of its kind and a model for others around the world.

Liberation theology and base communities

In the first part of the twentieth century, Latin American leaders reacted against the liberal positivism of the late nineteenth century and returned to the idealism which Pike sees as their more natural state (Pike 2002: 453–4, 463). Some espoused an almost mystical form of Marxism that encouraged secularized versions of Christ's death and resurrection (Pike 2002: 455–6), of which the figure of Ernesto 'Che' Guevara, the Argentinian-born Marxist guerrilla leader, was a late manifestation. Others, such as Víctor Raúl Haya de la Torre of Peru, constructed their own unorthodox religio-political movements to support their messianic status. In many cases, it was the colonial warrior-saint model that was invoked to solve the problems of society. As the century wore on, more and more nations were in the grip of an alliance between the right-wing church and military dictators. The relative prosperity that many Latin American countries had enjoyed until the mid-twentieth century ebbed away and development aspirations did not materialize.

Disillusioned with Christian democracy, a new generation of Latin American priests sought answers to the profound socio-economic problems of their continent by studying economics, sociology and political science in the Marxist-influenced atmosphere of 1960s universities. They did not have strong indigenous traditions to draw on as in Asia and Africa, nor could they engage in anti-Western polemic since Latin America is culturally much akin to Europe (Freston 2001: 192), but Marxist analysis encouraged them to see the continent's problems in terms of unjust structures rather than individual failings and to view economic underdevelopment as the consequence of the inequity of the global capitalist system, which rendered the Third World dependent on the developed world. In short, Latin American underdevelopment is the dark side of Northern development (Bonino 1975: 26–7). At a national level they also identified vested interests that kept the poor in poverty, and theologically they began to redefine sin as a matter of the collective failure of society and not only of personal guilt (Gutiérrez 1988: 102). As a result, they came to regard revolutionary change in society as necessary. In the mid-1960s, bishops from the continent attended the Second Vatican Council. Because of the numbers of Catholics in Latin America, they constituted more than 22 per cent of the total there, although this still left Latin American Christians underrepresented. At the Council it became clear that many of their concerns differed from those of the European bishops (Dussel 1981: 139–40) and, as Hastings points out, the teaching of the Second Vatican Council with regard to social justice, empowering the laity, use of vernacular languages, encouragement of pluralism, and concern for the poor offered a greater challenge to the church of Latin America than perhaps anywhere else. The combined reflections of bishops and priests led to a unique response to

Vatican II, which was to have worldwide influence. This came in three main ways: at the second meeting of CELAM, in liberation theology and through the 'base communities' (Hastings 1999b: 359–60).

CELAM II in Medellín, Colombia, in 1968 was a momentous event in the history of the Latin American church in two ways: first it was visited by Pope Paul VI, the first time a pope had ever set foot in the 'New World'; secondly, the bishops took the extraordinary step of declaring the church to be a 'poor church', against injustice and for the liberation of the poor as part of evangelization, and so rejected the socio-political order that had existed in Latin America since the sixteenth century (Hastings 1999b: 360; for documents see Hennelly 1990: 89–119; for details see Dussel 1981: 141–7). The conclusions of Medellín were endorsed by all the episcopacies, and in the turbulent years of the 1960s and 70s national churches took stances on behalf of the poor and against military regimes and other injustices in several different countries (Dussel 1981: 148–84). Eleven years later, the 'preferential option for the poor' was reaffirmed at CELAM III in Puebla, Mexico, despite conservative attempts to 'bury Medellín' (Dussel 1981: 239). The situation of the indigenous peoples and African Americans was described as abject poverty, which represented 'institutionalized injustice' (Hennelly 1990: 225–58; Dussel 1981: 229–39). For many Latin American Christians, like Enrique Dussel, these momentous events signalled a break of the Latin American church with the model of Christendom, and the shift to a missionary stance (Dussel 1981: 255). The 'option for the poor' eventually became enshrined in Catholic social teaching in the encyclical of John Paul II, *Centesimus Annus* (1991: para. 11), making clear the church's position of solidarity with the poor in their struggles for justice, but not before it had caused major upheavals in theology in the region and worldwide.

The reverberations of the second response, 'theology of liberation', are still being felt around the world today. Pike sees in its emergence a number of currents in the Latin American society and church: 'mystical Marxism, dependency analysis, an apocalyptic world-view extending back to pre-Columbian times, and utopianism, often verging on post-millennialism, of twentieth-century populist movements steeped in religious mythology' (2002: 463). Peruvian priest Gustavo Gutiérrez was the first to clearly articulate 'a theology of liberation' (1973) which he defined as 'a critical reflection on Christian praxis in light of the word of God'. Reading the story of the exodus from Egypt, for example, he concluded that this liberation of Israel was 'a political action' and that this is foundational to the Judaeo-Christian faith (1988: xxix, 88). This led him first to interpret Christian faith out of the suffering, struggle and hope of the poor, and second to criticize society and the ideologies sustaining it, and also the activity and theology of the church from the angle of the poor. Gutiérrez put 'orthopraxis' alongside 'orthodoxy' (right practice as well as right doctrine) as the test of faith (1988: 8). This revolutionary movement demanded not only a theology of liberation but also 'the liberation of theology' from being 'the erudite theology of textbooks' to 'a theology arising out of the urgent problems of real life' (Segundo 1976: 4–5).

Constructively, liberation theology called for the reinvention and realignment of the church from an institution which supported and mirrored the unjust structures of society to communities with charismatic ministries appropriate to the context (Boff 1986). The creation of 'base (ecclesial) communities' was a way of involving the laity in ministry, as instructed by the Vatican Council, and utilized the encouragement given by the Council for lay people to read and interpret the Bible. Unlike celebration of the Mass, reading the Bible was something they could do without a priest and so the communities can also be seen as a pastoral strategy to deal with the shortage of priests, and also a response to the challenge of a growing Protestant movement. But in Recife in north-east Brazil, base communities took a new turn when, with the support of Archbishop Hélder Câmara, leader of the 'Movement for Moral and Liberating Influence', they were combined with the educational method developed by Paulo Freire. This involved 'conscientization' among the poor, raising their awareness of the causes of their condition and of the ideologies used to perpetuate it, to empower them to change their situation (Freire 1970). Groups of lay people were encouraged to read the Bible together (with priests participating only on an occasional basis), to reflect on it in the light of their social condition, to use it as the basis for community action, and then to read the Bible again in the light of their experience, following the 'hermeneutic circle' explained by Juan Luis Segundo (1976: 7–38). Perhaps as many as 3 million people were involved in the early 1980s, two-thirds of them in Brazil (Pike 2002: 467). From this movement emerged a new way of understanding the Bible, which saw a message of social justice that could be applied directly to community life to bring about social change. Inspired by 'the crucified God', liberation theology turned attention to 'the crucified people' (Sobrino 1990: 120). And as it developed, liberation theology drew also on the resources of popular Latin American religiosity to develop a spirituality of liberation (e.g. Gutiérrez 1984).

Liberation theology encouraged a hermeneutics of suspicion that raised questions of power and vested interest in theology. Since it challenged church and state, liberation theology inevitably faced resistance from the authorities in Latin America and in Rome. Because of their work on behalf of the poor and action to reduce the power of the landowning elite, Catholic priests, nuns and church workers suffered violent attack and persecution in the militarized societies of 1970s and 80s Latin America. El Salvador had perhaps the most highly charged atmosphere. Marxists opposed a military junta (backed by the US), and in 1980 Archbishop Óscar Romero (1917–80), an advocate of the poor, was gunned down while celebrating Mass in his cathedral. Even at his funeral, attended by mourners from all over the world, a bomb went off and shots were fired. The violence continued to the end of the Cold War, and in 1989 six Jesuits were murdered in one incident in the same country.

As well as attack from political forces, liberation theologians also had to face the weight of the church hierarchy, which came to be represented by Bishop López Trujillo of Colombia, secretary of CELAM from 1972 to 1984 and now a cardinal in Rome. The Magisterium condemned aspects of the new theology, censuring some theologians and appointing conservative bishops in Latin America. Under the prefecture of Cardinal Joseph Ratzinger, now Pope Benedict XVI, the Congregation for the Doctrine of the Faith issued two 'instructions' regarding liberation theology. The first in 1984 was highly critical; however, the second in 1986 was more conciliatory, and accompanied by a letter to the bishops of Brazil, which described liberation theology as 'not only timely but useful and necessary' (quoted in Gutiérrez 1988: xliv). The main criticism given was the 'use, in an insufficiently critical manner, [of] concepts borrowed from various currents of Marxist thought' which made liberation theology 'a perversion of the Christian message as God entrusted it to His Church' (Congregation for the Doctrine of the Faith 1984: introduction and chapter IX, para. 1; see Vatican website). But although Marxist social theory was used in the analysis of the question of poverty, the construction of liberation theology was mainly based on Conciliar documents (especially *Gaudium et Spes*, the 'Constitution on the church in the modern world') and papal encyclicals on the themes of human dignity and development: *Mater et Magistra* (John XXIII 1961) and *Populorum Progressio* (Paul VI 1967). Those censured included Leonardo Boff, a Brazilian priest who was a strong critic of church power structures and advocate of base communities. He responded in 1984 by accusing his critics of having 'a European mind-set', which deals in the abstract essence of liberation rather than its concrete reality (Boff 1990b). It is likely that the root cause of Rome's unease was the undermining of clerical control by the 'new way of being church' in the base communities (Hastings 1999b: 360–2), which led in early 1980s Nicaragua under Sandinista rule to a partial schism by the formation of the 'Church of the People' (Klaiber 1998: 193–215). Therefore conservative bishops were appointed to counter liberation theology. Other critics have expressed concerns about liberation theology's equation of liberation with redemption, its reduction of human life to the political sphere, and about how it relates theological concepts to social theory (Chopp 1997b: 419).

Despite, and because of, its censure by the Vatican, liberation theology rapidly spread worldwide, first among 'Third World theologians' through EATWOT (Ecumenical Association of Third World Theologians) and then into the wider theological community. Some Latin American Protestants also took up liberation theology. José Miguez Bonino, an Argentinian Methodist prominent in the WCC, has emphasized that history is the arena in which theology must be done (e.g. Bonino 1975; see also Chopp 1997b: 418–19). Elsa Tamez from Costa Rica has re-examined the doctrine of justification to show that it means God's affirmation of life for all human beings (Tamez 1993). Because of its foundations in a simple reading of the Bible, Evangelical Protestants have also affirmed many of liberation theology's tenets and have disseminated it worldwide through their networks. Puerto Rican Baptist theologian Orlando Costas challenged Evangelicals to 'mission outside the [city] gate', on the periphery of society (Costas 1982). And Peruvian Samuel Escobar worked through the Lausanne movement to justify social action and bring issues of justice to the attention of Evangelical thought (Escobar 1976).

There is no doubt that liberation theology has changed the theological landscape worldwide by attempting to bring the poor and poverty – rightly seen as central to Jesus' ministry – back into the centre of Christian concern. It raises critical questions about who has the right to do Christian theology – the powerful or the powerless? It questions the ideological standpoint of any theology: does it support the status quo or does it represent the interests of the poor? And it encourages Christians not to stop at charity but to raise structural questions and engage in advocacy to change the structures of society for the better. As Las Casas had understood from reflecting on the book of Ecclesiasticus, 'It is of no use ... to pretend that one believes in the God of the Bible when one "lives ... on the blood of the Indians"' (Gutiérrez 1993: 61). Within Latin America, although the church gained credibility in the public eye, the structures of the church were not radically changed by liberation theology. And as far as the indigenous people are concerned, even liberation theology is 'conceived *from outside the indigenous community*' (Wagua 1990: 51; italics original) and does not recognize indigenous regions or churches as such. At its height in the early 1980s, liberation theology and the base communities resembled a revival movement and some of the other messianic movements in Latin American politics, but it did not quite translate into a popular movement. One of the reasons for this was the tightened control by the hierarchy (Pike 2002: 467). Many base communities continue, but their involvement may be more at the level of community projects than political action (Theije 1999: 116). Another reason was that the poor themselves were more interested in gaining wealth than in fighting poverty and were being attracted away from Catholicism to newer religious movements (see below).

The Catholic Church in the restoration of democracy

Although the structures of the church remained in place, liberation theology did change the church from being the supporter of military regimes into a force for democracy and human rights (Klaiber 1998: 5). The single most important factor in the installation of more democratic and centrist governments which took place across Latin America in the late 1980s and 1990s was the ending of the Cold War, but Jeffrey Klaiber (1998) has charted the highly important role the Catholic Church played long before 1989 and afterwards in challenging the military and promoting democracy. The church both gave the new popular democracy religious legitimation but also 'in turn received a new legitimacy from the popular classes'. The role of the church varied in each country. In some cases, the church itself was divided between a more conservative hierarchy and liberation activists. This division was particularly acute in Nicaragua, where perhaps the most that can be said is that Christians 'braked the extremists in both camps' (Klaiber 1998: 6, 264). In other places in Central America the church was more constructive. Throughout the conflict in El Salvador the church acted as mediator between the two factions under the guidance of Romero's successor, Arturo Rivera y Damas. In both El Salvador and Guatemala, the church sponsored 'national dialogue' to widen participation and strengthen democracy, forcing governments and guerrillas to move more quickly toward agreement. In the Andean nations of Bolivia and Peru the church once again became an advocate of the rights of the Indians when grassroots Christians, along with peace and human-rights groups, helped to break though the passivity and fear which gripped the population. In the Southern Cone, the church censured the dictatorship in Paraguay; in Brazil it became the principal voice of opposition and supported the organizations of civil society to overthrow the regime; and in Chile the church intervened directly in the political process to support the main opposition party. But in Argentina and Uruguay the principal voices of protest in the church were from below. Although Mexico did not experience military dictatorship, during the 1990s there was sustained oppression of the indigenous population in Chiapas. The latter was Las Casas' old diocese, yet more than 400 years later the bishop, Samuel Ruiz, was again struggling for the rights of the Indians there (Hastings 1999b: 362–3). However, Ruiz's partiality led to his resignation as a mediator, and a volatile situation continues in the predominantly Indian lands. As Klaiber recounts the story, in most of these cases, liberal and anticlerical forces in government wished to exclude church participation but in the end the church was the only body with enough support to break the deadlock between opposing forces.

Now that there is greater democracy in Latin America, the role of the church has changed again. Mass mobilization in the streets is not so necessary and church efforts for a more just society are being pursued through less high-profile means. In Peru for example, grassroots Catholic action among the poor has shifted its attention to business and the marketplace through new modes such as partnership with business corporations and encouraging micro-enterprise (Brooks 1999). In many cases, the public stance of the church is now more conservative. This is not only because of the appointment by Rome of more conservative bishops but also because current political issues relating to women's rights, the family and sexuality are ones on which the hierarchy has a strongly counter-cultural stance. So the church in Chile, for example, which stood firmly against the right-wing dictatorship of Augusto Pinochet, is now aligned with conservative political forces (Haas 1999). Another reason for the drop in political involvement is the move under John Paul II to affirm and incorporate much popular religiosity into the life of the church through the worldwide 'new evangelization'. Although liberation theologians could argue that the 'new evangelization' was continuous with liberation theology (Boff 1990a), it shifted attention from the directly socio-political to the religio-cultural. In Latin America this is seen as a strategy to stem the flow of people out of the church into new religious movements (Gill 1999; Norget 1999), of which the most threatening is seen to be Pentecostalism.

The rise of the *Evangelicos*

The European Reformation bypassed Latin America, so Protestantism represents an external tradition recently introduced. Trade with Britain in the nineteenth century necessitated freedom for Protestant worship, initially Anglican, and Protestantism became attractive to some of the upper classes, who admired Britain and America and who disliked the clericalism of the Catholic Church (Martin 1990: 11, 50). European immigrants also brought their own forms of Protestantism with them in the nineteenth and twentieth centuries. These were mainly British and North American but also included Lithuanian Baptists to Brazil, Russian Mennonites to Paraguay. Germans, Scandinavians and Scots set up their own churches in Brazil, Chile, Argentina and Guatemala (Prokopy and Smith 1999: 3). More recently Korean Protestants, AICs and many others are included in the mix. All kinds of Protestant missionary activity has been directed at Latin America from Europe, and especially North America, but churches and missions that are ecumenically minded have tended not to send personnel – not at least for evangelistic purposes – out of respect for the presence of the Catholic Church there. Missionaries working in the subcontinent are therefore generally conservative Evangelicals or Pentecostals who do not regard the Catholic Church as true to the biblical faith.

David Martin's detailed historical work (1990) reveals that different countries show varying patterns of Protestant growth to the mid-twentieth century according to patterns of immigration, mission activity, and political, social and religious conditions. Three examples will suffice: Protestantism gained some popularity in Brazil in the mid-nineteenth century as an ideological alternative. Presbyterians grew rapidly and became independent of their US mission in 1888 but they were overtaken in the early twentieth century by Baptists, mainly evangelized from the southern United States (Martin 1990: 62–4). In Argentina Protestantism has tended to run along ethnic lines, with people of different European nations having their own churches. Methodist churches were influential in the nineteenth century but since then there has been successful mission work by Plymouth Brethren, Baptists and Adventists. In Chile, by contrast, there has been much less migration and a more indigenous growth of Protestantism by conversion, at first among Methodists and Baptists (Martin 1990: 74–9). However, since 1960, across Latin America, it is Pentecostalism (of various sorts) which has become the main non-Catholic Christian movement.

In the 1980s, exaggerated claims were made that Latin America was 'turning Evangelical', and from the early 1990s a rash of books was devoted to studying the growth of Protestantism and Pentecostalism there (e.g. Martin 1990; Stoll 1990). In 1940, there were still probably no more than 1 million Protestants in the whole of Latin America. Figures vary widely, but Jenkins suggests that in 2002 there were 50 million Protestants, a little less than one-tenth of the total population of the continent (2002: 57). In the still overwhelmingly Catholic context of Latin America, all non-Catholic Christians may tend to be labelled 'Protestant' or *Evangelicos*, but as we have indicated, Pentecostalism represents a rather different form of spirituality which, while it may be included under 'Protestant', is best treated separately. Furthermore, as Jenkins points out in the Latin American context, Protestants and Pentecostals are by and large two different communities: Protestants tend to be middle-class (although they may have started poor (Martin 1990: 53)) and Pentecostal churches are found among the poor, indeed the very poor. It is the Pentecostal churches that have been responsible for most of the 'Protestant' growth (Jenkins 2002: 63).

The first Pentecostal revival in Latin America was in Chile in 1909 in a Methodist church in Valparaiso, encouraged by a North American Methodist missionary who had heard of the revivals in India and Europe, and it led to the founding the Methodist Pentecostal Church (Iglesia Metodista Pentecostal). Allan Anderson estimates that there are at least 1,000 Protestant denominations in Chile. More than 30 of these are Pentecostal churches that have come out of the Methodist Pentecostal Church, and these make up 95 per cent of all the Protestants in Chile (2004: 67). Although there was a North American connection, the Methodist Pentecostal Church has never been connected with North American Pentecostalism and maintains Methodist doctrine, practice and structure (Sepúlveda 1999). Estimates of the proportion of Protestants in each country of Latin America vary hugely, depending on what is measured: compare for example the figure of 25 per cent given for Chile by Anderson (2004: 68) with the figure of 11 per cent in 2005 given by the Religion in Latin America website maintained by the University of Texas, Austin. It is not possible to discuss each country in detail but only to note some prominent developments (for more information Anderson (2004) is an excellent source). The country with the highest proportion of Protestants is Guatemala, which may now have up to 40 per cent. In Central America, Panama, Costa Rica and Nicaragua also have high proportions of Protestants (15, 16 and 17 per cent respectively), particularly in the Assemblies of God. In the Caribbean, Haiti also has about 16 per cent. Pentecostal growth in

Argentina (about 10 per cent) started rather later than elsewhere, when in the 1980s the evangelistic ministry of Carlos Annacondia 'converted the [existing] Evangelical community to charismatic practices' (Marostica 1999: 147; Míguez 1999). Other evangelists introduced prosperity teaching, and the 'Argentine Revival' soon spread beyond Argentina itself, especially in the USA and Canada (Jenkins 2002: 208; Marostica 1999: 162–5). Perhaps 15 per cent of the population of Brazil are Protestant, mostly Pentecostal. And since Brazil has such a huge population, this means it has one of the largest populations of Pentecostals in the world. Because they are mostly practising, there are probably more Pentecostals at worship on a Sunday than there are Catholics (Anderson 2004: 69). The largest denomination in Brazil is the Assemblies of God (Assembléias de Deus), with at least 4 million members – at least four times as large as the Assemblies of God in the US (Jenkins 2002: 64). Many Pentecostal churches have been started by Brazilians. The Universal Church of the Kingdom of God (Igreja Universal do Reino de Deus) is the largest and most controversial of these. Bishop Edir Macedo, a former lottery official, rejects Christian morality and theology and encourages a cash-for-blessings approach (Anderson 2004: 73–4). Brazil is reckoned as one of the largest missionary-sending countries in the world (Johnstone and Mandryk 2001: 123), especially to Spain and Portugal.

Various explanations have been put forward to explain the rapid growth of the *Evangelicos* in Latin America in general. David Martin sees it as part of a four-century-long struggle for supremacy between Anglo and Latin civilizations, dating back to the attack of the Spanish Armada on England but played out largely in the Americas, which has come in three 'waves': Puritan, Methodist and Pentecostal. This struggle is usually portrayed in the global North, and by Southern liberals, as a clash of 'freedom against authority, equality against hierarchy, individual conscience against organicism, progress against reaction, and peaceability and commerce against unproductive militarism' (Martin 1990: 5–26) – although Latin Americans would be some of the first to raise questions about the 'peaceable' nature of British or North American imperialism, and the negative value assumed to attach to authority structures and 'corporatism' could be strongly debated (cf. Wiarda 2001: 345). Evangelical faith, Martin argues, is just one aspect of a general North Americanization of Latin America. While Martin's view undoubtedly carries some truth and links in with theories of contemporary globalization, in which North America is the strongest force, from the point of view of the growth of world Christianity, Latin America is another example of the spectacular growth of worldwide Pentecostalism, which has a significant African as well as Anglo component, and which may also be seen as part of a wider resurgence of 'primal spirituality' (Cox 1996: 161–84), or a globalization from below. Latin American Pentecostals object to the commonly held view (also implied in a surface reading of Martin) that Pentecostalism originated in North America. While it is now indisputable that leading figures in most, if not all, of the earliest revivals knew of one another (Robeck 1993: 170), Chilean Pentecostal Juan Sepúlveda argues strongly that earlier Pentecostal movements in other parts of the world were simultaneous with North American Pentecostalism but not dependent upon it. He objects to white North American Pentecostals defining Pentecostal identity as 'a western attempt at domestication of the liberating power of Pentecost' (Sepúlveda 1999: 113, 134) and shows that the Chilean Pentecostal church is the result of an independent development that represents indigenous Chilean experience. Martin himself also insists that Latin American Protestantism has become an indigenous movement through the rise of Latino-led Pentecostalism (2002: 71–82).

In addition to Martin's global culture-clash theory, political reasons have been advanced for the growth of the *Evangelicos*. In the 1980s, it was suggested that Protestant evangelism in Latin America was in conspiracy with the CIA because converts were likely to be conservative and politically quiescent, supporting the governments backed by the US and inclined toward American culture (see Jenkins 2002: 157; Martin 1990: 54). The huge growth of the *Evangelicos* in Guatemala has received particular attention. Hastings, a Catholic, sees this as the result of 'a huge and concerted campaign to eradicate both traditional Maya culture and Catholic influence … and replace both by the religious culture of the American Bible Belt'. This 'missionary offensive', in which Catholic priests and nuns were harassed and killed by government forces, was funded by US televangelists and supported by 'born-again' president Rios Montt (1982–3), a member of the highly authoritarian Pentecostal Church of the Word (*El Verbo*), who was simultaneously violently suppressing the Indian population (Hastings 1999b: 366, 365). US citizens' support of evangelism in Latin America was certainly increased by the perceived threat of Communism there (Pike 2002: 470), US televangelism was very effective in Central America (Brouwer, Gifford and Rose 1996: 59–60), and the agenda of president Ronald Reagan to expand US influence did attract right-wing activists to join the missionary movement (Stoll 1990: xv). Paul Freston, a Protestant, rejects this view by arguing that most of the circumstances were coincidental (Freston 2001: 272). However, David Stoll, who recounts the story of Guatemala in detail, argues that the *Evangelicos* did not uncritically endorse American foreign policy; indeed many were critical of it and were using Evangelical religion for their own ends of raising themselves out of poverty. In the end, the need for survival pushed many of the people into the hands of those churches (Evangelical/Pentecostal) which supported the government (Stoll 1990: 180–217, xv–xvi, xix; Brouwer, Gifford and Rose 1996: 47–73; Vásquez and Marquardt 2003: 203). Catholic and left-wing accusations about American missionaries disguised the fact that Catholicism in Latin America is more 'foreign' in terms of both personnel and funding (Freston 2001: 283), and whatever the initial motives, Hastings recognizes that the resulting Pentecostal churches are self-generating, and suggests that they result from very similar religious motives on the part of contemporary Guatemalans to those which brought their Indian ancestors into the Catholic Church three centuries before (Hastings 1999b: 366). In Chile, Pentecostals were found both supporting and actively opposing General Augusto Pinochet's regime in the 1970s and 80s (Kamsteeg 1999). As the prominent Argentinian Methodist theologian José Míguez Bonino has said, the growth of the *Evangelicos* has more to do with 'internal political and social struggles on the continent' than with external 'imperialist' forces (Bonino 1997: 3).

Many structural explanations have been advanced for the growth of Pentecostal churches in Latin America. Both the democratic tendencies and the dominating tendencies of Pentecostal polity have also been suggested as reasons for its attractiveness (see Gooren 2007: 163). Other reasons include the need for fellowship among people displaced by industrialization and urbanization (e.g. Jenkins 2002: 72–3; Martin 2002: 49). The success of Pentecostalism in Latin America has been largely among the very poor (which in Latin American 'pigmentocracy' implies Indian, black and mixed heritage), and, as Martin has shown, from a phenomenological point of view there are striking parallels with the beginnings of Methodism among the poor in Europe and processes of capitalistic development (1990: 31–42). In the context of the integration of Latin America into the global economy, Evangelicalism contributes a work ethic; it teaches and reinforces discipline in a supportive community environment and gives people strength to resist the street (Martin 2002: 74). Martin also sees the growth of the *Evangelicos* in the context of women's resistance to Latin American *machismo* culture. In its conservative morality, it reforms the errant male and eliminates the double standard of morality for the two genders, leading to improvements in health, work, family life and the well-being of children (Brusco 1995). The openness of women, particularly, to try this new form of religion may be in part because 'women prefer peaceable, stable homes to itinerant male violence' (Martin 2002: 50). Ironically, therefore, conservative Evangelicalism, which has a strong patriarchal rhetoric, may actually be contributing to the undermining of *machismo* in Latin America (Steigenga and Smilde 1999).

But structural explanations alone do not adequately explain why, amid all the many Evangelical Protestant mission endeavours in Latin America, it is Pentecostalism that has grown (Gooren 2007: 163). To understand this requires a knowledge of Pentecostalism as it 'is in itself' (Sepúlveda 1999: 128, 111). Theories which take an insider view stress that Pentecostal churches helped people find ways of coping with their various problems, but even these rarely discuss the particular features of Pentecostalism that attracted them (cf. Gooren 2007: 163). Henri Gooren finds a huge variety of reasons for conversion and disaffiliation. The few common factors to emerge were a sense of crisis that precipitated conversion and a religious approach to life that led to a search for a religious solution to the problem. Social and contingency factors then determined whether the individual joined Pentecostalism or some other religion or pseudo-religion (2007: 170). Important though his study is, Gooren's approach still does not explain the specific growth of Pentecostalism – other than that it is widely available. While cultural, political, structural and individual reasons are significant, the growth must also have to do with Pentecostal characteristics.

Writing from the perspective of people of the Caribbean, Laënnec Hurbon combines cultural, political and structural arguments and sees the turn from Catholicism to US Pentecostalism as a protest against, and rejection of, 'the symbolic cultural system that is the heritage of slavery and conquest' in which converts re-found their life on the written word, 'placing it in radical opposition to the image'. At the same time he sees Pentecostalism as offering a bodily experience of the Holy Spirit which mirrors many aspects of African-derived religions of the Caribbean, so that Pentecostalism subsumes the Voodoo gods (2001: 131–4). Commentators agree that the particular strength of Pentecostalism in Brazil is related to interest in the world of spirits, which is in turn related to the large proportion of the population with African ancestry, and the strong presence of African-derived religions there (Anderson 2004: 70; Jenkins 2002: 126; Martin 1990: 68). Once suppressed by the authorities, the African-derived religions of Candomblé and Umbanda are now legal and attractive in a climate of black consciousness and where whites seek alternatives to Western rationalism (Jensen 1999). The religious culture of Brazil is such that they coexist with the others, and people who count themselves as Christians will also consult mediums and join in festivals (Prokopy and Smith 1999: 11). So, one of the relevant characteristics of Pentecostalism itself is its theology of the Holy Spirit that takes seriously the world of demons and spirits which trouble the poor, whatever their ethnic background, and offers ways of dealing with their problems which they can understand within this cosmology (cf. Martin 1990: 69). Taking into consideration the wider social and cultural context, David Martin argues that Pentecostalism is well shaped to help people be successful in post-modernity because it energizes – through the power of the Spirit in worship, imbues confidence – because God is on your side in 'spiritual warfare', and gives hope – because God does not fail (Martin 2002: 79–80). This is also the view of Juan Sepúlveda, from Chile, who argues strongly that the reason Pentecostalism grew was that it had a particular appeal to the poor, in a way that Protestantism in general did not, and was able to 'translate the Protestant message into the forms of expression of the local popular culture'. Its healing ministry 'could be seen as a "point of contact" between primitive Christianity, revivalist Protestantism, popular Catholicism and Amerindian religiosity' (1999: 128–9).

Catholics and *Evangelicos* in plural society

The current popularity of Pentecostalism may not be permanent. Many of the converts to Pentecostalism are only in their teens and disaffiliation may be very high – up to 68 per cent in one study in Mexico (Gooren 2007: 170). Furthermore, there has been a 'transformation of the religious field' in Latin America (Míguez 1999: 222): Pentecostalism is far from the only alternative to Catholicism on offer to Latin Americans these days. Prokopy and Smith make the point that 'Latin America is experiencing a genuine and profound pluralisation of faith' more complex than the rise and fall of liberation theology and the growth of Protestantism and Pentecostalism. Although Catholic leaders imply that before the arrival of Protestants Latin America was Roman Catholic, there were always other religious alternatives among the indigenous people (1999: 2), and today some of these are being revived: traditional Mayan ceremonies are performed in Guatemala, for example (Siebers 1999: 267). In addition, there are the religions of African origin, especially in Brazil and Cuba. Migrants from South Asia brought Islam and Hinduism with them to Guyana and Surinam. Japanese immigrants to Peru and Brazil introduced Buddhism there, and this now has several million adherents not of Japanese descent (Prokopy and Smith 1999: 12). Add to this mix other Christian-derived groups such as Mormons and Jehovah's Witnesses, and Prokopy and Smith paint a picture of religious variety quite different from what is often assumed in discussion of what is often described as the only 'Catholic continent'.

Since the work of David Martin (1990) and others, attention to religion in Latin America has made a rather sudden shift from Catholic liberation theology to the growth of evangelical Protestantism and Pentecostalism. This tends to ignore several other important developments. First, it fails to explore the significant interface between Catholicism and Pentecostalism. Second, it neglects the bigger picture of the general pluralization of society we mentioned above. And, third, it ignores the Catholic response to this pluralization in general and Protestantism in particular. The overlap between Catholicism and Pentecostalism in Latin America occurs in three main areas: first, in the charismatic spirituality that is also found within Catholicism; second, in the common practical concern of the base communities and Pentecostal churches for the poor; and third, in the shared theological interest in the Holy Spirit. Since the 1970s, the worldwide Catholic Charismatic Renewal – which offers many of the same benefits as Pentecostalism, such as prayer for healing, exorcism and warm fellowship – has been an established part of life in many parishes as well as the base communities of liberation theology. Individuals may be members of both a base community and a charismatic group within one Catholic parish, each satisfying different spiritual needs and offering avenues of service (Theije 1999), but in most cases individual priests tend to favour one or the other for their parish; in which case, charismatically minded Catholic lay people in a liberation theology parish may join a Pentecostal church as well as, or instead of, attending Mass.

Practically, as is often pointed out (e.g. Hastings 1999b: 367; Martin 1990: 70), both liberation theology and Pentecostal concern centre around the poor and poverty, although on the surface they offer very different solutions. At the surface level, liberation theology encourages the church to take 'the option for the poor' by working with the poor in the base communities it organizes to bring about structural change in society. In Pentecostal churches, on the other hand, the poor themselves are encouraged to pursue healing and wealth by means of prayer and personal transformation. In the last 40 years the quip seems to be true that 'the Catholic Church opts for the poor but the poor opt for the Pentecostals'. But digging a little deeper, the base community and Pentecostal approaches to poverty are not so very far apart. The base communities' struggle to change social structures also results in personal transformation and spiritual growth. On the other hand, joining a Pentecostal church is generally linked to upward social mobility, and many Latin American Pentecostal churches are deeply involved in community care and even political action. Hastings fears that by undermining the base community movement, the Catholic Church in Latin America may have been 'throwing away the only instrument with which ... it could hold the Protestant advance at bay' (1999b: 367).

Theologically, both liberation theology and Pentecostalism understand themselves as movements of the Holy Spirit. Pike comments that the Holy Spirit only surfaces as a member of the Latin American 'quaternity' in 'periods of popular millennialist frenzy' (2002: 451, 463; cf. Martin 2002: 50), of which liberation was one and Pentecostal revivals could be considered another. Although much liberation theology has been done in a Christological framework – the work of Jon Sobrino (1978, 1993) is the pre-eminent example – theology of the Holy Spirit is foundational to liberation theology's expectation of the liberating transformation of the earth because God is encountered in the world through the Spirit (Comblin 1989: xii). In the key biblical verse of liberation theology, Jesus declares, 'the Spirit of the Lord [Holy Spirit] is upon me because he has anointed me to proclaim good news to the poor' (Lk. 4.18). The outpouring of the Holy Spirit on the disciples at Pentecost led directly to personal and community transformation (Acts 2.41–7). Pentecostalism and liberation theology may therefore be regarded as 'two manifestations of the work of the Holy Spirit for the renewal of the church' (Sepúlveda 1993). Liberation theology also has a – largely unrealized – potential to tap into the popular religiosity of the Latin American poor (Hastings 1999b: 367). In Brazil, for example, Pentecostalism appears as 'a form of base community plus the therapeutic recourse to the Spirit found in Umbanda' (Martin 1990: 60).

The Catholic Church has been alarmed by its decline in membership and it has struggled to redefine its role now that 'Latin American Christians no longer recognise only one church as the font of charisma' (Pike 2002: 472), and the Catholic Church is becoming one denomination among others (Martin 2002: 21). The Church sees the rise of the *Evangelicos* as a regional threat. Since 1955, popes have warned about the 'mortal danger' of the advance of 'sects' – a term for all non-Catholic religious groups – in Latin America, comparing them to sheep-stealing predators (Gill 1999: 19). In his exhortation to the bishops of America following the Special Assembly for America of the Synod of Bishops held in the Vatican in 1997, John Paul II urged a 'thorough study to ascertain why many Catholics leave the Church' and join 'sects' (*Ecclesia in America* 1999: para. 73). Comparing the Catholic Church to a commercial company that has lost its monopoly of the market, Anthony Gill argues that the Catholic Church has responded to its new situation in two main ways: first by seeking government assistance in dealing with the 'competition', and secondly by 'institutional restructuring to become more efficient at maintaining parishioners and converting nominal Catholics into active participants in the faith' (Gill 1999: 17–18). The government assistance sought by the church includes restricting the entry of foreign missionaries, limiting registration for religious groups and properties and banning groups deemed to be aggressive (Freston 2001: 193–4). The church has used its historic privileges to pressure governments and lobby for financial concessions. However, with the increased numbers, the rise of democracy and therefore the political power of the 'sects', the room for tactical manoeuvre is now very limited (Gill 1999: 24–9). The institutional restructuring has resulted in increased numbers of parishes and dioceses. The Church has developed its personnel by continuing to encourage lay participation and utilize congregational gifts, and it has had considerable success at increasing clergy recruitment. Re-establishing hierarchical control over the base communities can also be seen as part of this restructuring, and alongside this the 'product' has also been diversified by the inclusion of charismatic groups, popular religiosity and other variations to offer diversity under one institutional umbrella (Gill 1999: 30–5).

From the point of view of the church, what has been going on is a revision of pastoral policy so that each particular local church 'can offer the faithful more personalized religious care', a strengthening of the 'structures of communion and mission', and attempts to 'make the most of the evangelizing possibilities of a purified popular religiosity'. As part of the 'new evangelization', the church is aware of the potential of small groups of different sorts for building 'interpersonal bonds of mutual support' and of the need to move people from 'a faith of habit' to 'a faith which is conscious and personally lived' (John Paul II, *Ecclesia in America* 1999: para. 73; Gill 1999: 29). The growth in the continent of Opus Dei, founded in 1928 in Spain to strengthen the faith of believers and its application to their everyday life, has also attracted the attention of commentators. Many of the prelates brought in as conservatives to counter liberation theology are also members of this international organization, which emphasizes personal piety and submission to the hierarchy in matters of faith. However, as Pike suggests, Opus Dei is also part of the Catholic answer to prosperity teaching. Traditional Catholicism has focused on poverty as the context for faith, but Opus Dei appeals to the successful and to the entrepreneur; it operates mainly through courses and retreats for personal development: it replaces the 'Christian knight' with the 'godly businessman' (2002: 471). Cultivating a living and personal faith in terms of both personal holiness and social action was the opening theme of *Ecclesia in America*, which emphasized a spiritual life of conversion and guidance by the Holy Spirit alongside the traditional sacraments of Catholicism (John Paul II 1999).

The *Evangelicos*, who are now mostly Pentecostal, are taking an increasing role in the public life of Latin American nations, to the dismay of journalists and political commentators who habitually portrayed them as other-worldly and quiescent (Cleary 1998: 12). Edward Cleary and Hannah Stewart-Gambino (1998) have produced a detailed study of *Evangelicos* in politics, and so has Paul Freston (2001); here we just mention a few points. First, Pentecostals, unlike US-style Evangelicals, are generally undogmatic. They have entered politics because experience suggests practical advantages to this course, and they may withdraw again for pragmatic reasons (Cleary 1998: 13). Second, unlike US Evangelicals, the *Evangelicos* do not represent a tradition which they are trying to reinstate, so their political alignments vary considerably (Freston 2001: 288); nevertheless, Brazil is the only country in Latin America with an Evangelical left wing (Freston 2001: 33). Third, compared to Evangelical and Pentecostal Christians in other parts of the Third World, in Latin America *Evangelicos* have been more inclined to form national political parties, which are particularly prominent in Colombia, Nicaragua and Venezuela. Many of these represent concerns for human rights and democracy but some merely seek to enlist state resources for their church (Freston 2001: 285). Fourth, in some countries the *Evangelicos* represent a distinct voting bloc, which has been decisive in some elections, such as the election of Alberto Fujimori in Peru in 1990. But their enthusiasm is being tempered by experience (Cleary 1998: 12). Evangelicals have been portrayed, especially by liberation theologians and other left-leaning commentators, as showing little concern for social justice. This impression is reinforced by the Evangelical tendency to blame the social ills of Latin America not on foreign dependency or the caste structure but on Latin Catholic social mores (Stoll 1990: 180). Evangelicalism emphasizes personal moral transformation as a prerequisite for social change and expects a gradual leavening of society by conversion, and, as Martin and others have shown, this does lead to improvement in the social condition of believers within existing social structures. However, Pentecostalism has a greater orientation toward power, which encourages mass movements and public demonstrations of solidarity. Pentecostal theologians, such as Steven Land (1993), argue that Pentecostalism necessarily incorporates a practical concern and a missionary intent. Land sees Pentecostal spirituality (rather idealistically) as essentially 'a passion for the kingdom', which combines 'orthodoxy (right praise/belief), orthopraxy (right practice) and orthopathy (right affections)' (1993: 13) because the Holy Spirit is the Spirit of love (1993: 131–6; Rom. 5.5; 1 Cor. 13).

But despite growing involvement by *Evangelicos* in politics and society, it is the Catholic Church which has by far the greatest social reach. CELAM V, which took place in May 2007 at Aparecida in Brazil, expressed a series of hopes for church and society that indicate the social agenda of the church in contemporary Latin America (CELAM website). Many of these were on the agenda of all churches worldwide at the time, such as commitments to dialogue with other churches and religions, to reconciliation and to stewardship of creation. More particular to the Latin American context were commitments to 'value and respect our Indigenous and Afro-American peoples', and to the integration of the peoples of Latin America and the Caribbean. The plenary session on Latin America at the ninth WCC Assembly at Puerto Alegre, Brazil, in 2006 (transcript available online) also laid great stress on the legacy of colonial domination in the continuing injustice done to Amerindians and Afro-Africans. Equally prominent among the resolutions of CELAM V were the intention 'to impel the active participation of women in society and in the Church' and 'to strengthen with audacity' the church's ministries in support of the family and respect of life (CELAM website). The juxtaposition of these last two 'hopes', which are often seen to work against one another, shows where the main controversy in the Catholic Church lies. This tension also reflects the political as well as practical importance of issues of gender, sexuality and morality in Latin America in the first decade of the twenty-first century. Many Catholics and *Evangelicos* take a similar stand against abortion and for traditional gender roles and family structures but they differ on divorce; the unacceptability of divorce for women in traditional society could explain why there is a disproportionate number of divorced women in Pentecostal churches (Mariz and Mafra 1999: 207). In general, the strength of feeling aroused by these issues is because they raise fundamental questions about *machismo*, which despises homosexuality and enforces women's submission to male will.

CELAM V placed a strong emphasis on the church's mission to proclaim Jesus Christ as 'the Way, the Truth and the Life' with vigour and enthusiasm, with Mary the mother of Jesus as the model because she 'gives birth to Jesus Christ' (CELAM V 2007: para. 362). Despite the rise of Protestantism and other religions, there are over 400 million baptized Catholics in Latin America, which is 40 per cent of the global total, and more than in all of Europe and North America – and furthermore, many of the Catholics in North America are also Latinos (Jenkins 2002: 58). The renewed Catholic Church is likely to continue to be very significant for all the Americas, and it may be that 'the religiosity of the masses' will turn back to it (Hastings 1999b: 367).

Study Questions and Further Readings

- Discuss the relationship of indigenous spirituality with Roman Catholicism in Latin America with special reference to the cults of *machismo* and *marianismo*.
- Discuss the relationship between church and the state in Latin America and the rise of the liberation theology.
- Identify contributions of liberation theology to traditional theologies and also its weaknesses.
- How have Christians been involved in the revolutionary movements in Latin America?
- What ways has the hierarchy of the Roman Catholic Church used to relate to grassroots Latin American Christians?
- Discuss the reason for the rapid growth of *Evangelicos* and its implications for the Roman Catholic Church in Latin America.

Brusco, Elisabeth (1995), *The Reformation of Machismo: Evangelical Conversion and Gender in Columbia*. Austin, TX: University of Texas Press.

Dussel, Enrique (1981), *A History of the Church in Latin America* (trans. Alan Neely). Grand Rapids, MI: Wm B. Eerdmans.

Freston, Paul (2001), *Evangelicals and Politics in Asia, Africa and Latin America*. Cambridge: Cambridge University Press.

Gutiérrez, Gustavo (1973), *A Theology of Liberation* (trans. Caridad Inda and John Eagleson; first published in Spanish in 1971). Maryknoll, NY: Orbis.

Klaiber, Jeffrey (1998), *The Church, Dictatorships, and Democracy in Latin America*. Maryknoll, NY: Orbis.

Martin, David (2002), *Pentecostalism: The World Their Parish*. Oxford: Blackwell.

6 Asian Christianity

The name 'Asia' refers to nearly one-third of the world's land from Suez and the Ural Mountains in the west to the Pacific in the east. The adjective 'Asian' defines nearly two-thirds of the world's people from Palestinian to Japanese, from Siberian to Sri Lankan. 'Asian' does not refer to a shared cultural or historical identity. Even the Mongol empire of the thirteenth century, the largest contiguous empire ever, still did not embrace more than half of what is called Asia; South and South East Asia were never included. The incredible diversity of the continent is illustrated by the fact that all the 'world religions' originated in Asia, including Christianity. Nevertheless the peoples of Asia have interacted with one another for centuries, and many aspects of culture have been shared across boundaries, not least religious culture. Christianity and Islam are established right across the continent; Hinduism and Buddhism from India eastwards; Confucianism and Taoism are influential across East Asian cultures, and Zoroastrianism similarly in West Asia. Although the proportion of Christians, less than 10 per cent, is much lower than on any other continent, in absolute numbers there are more Christians in Asia than in North America; relatively small changes in calculation of the proportion of Christians in China and India, as the world's most populous nations, can affect the figures considerably, though. The point is, however, that most Asian Christians live as minorities among people of other faiths. It is the religious context which most affects the shape of Christianity in each country, so it is this that we shall use as the entry point for our analysis. Nonetheless, the concern of many Asian Christian leaders is also for the poor of the continent, and it is the dual reality of 'religions and poverty' (Abraham 1990: 3–27; Pieris 1988b: 45) which is reflected in Christian thought and action.

Martyrdom and blessing in North East Asia

The nations of north-east Asia share a Confucian and Theravada Buddhist heritage. In the Confucian way of thinking, China is the 'elder brother' to the other nations of north-east Asia, namely Korea and Japan, which look westwards for their classical art and literature, and the Chinese Confucian model of a strong centralized state has determined the pattern of reception of the gospel in all three countries. Ever since the experience of the East Syrian or 'Nestorian' Christians in East Asia in the seventh to ninth centuries (see Moffett 1998: 287–323), it has been clear that religious belief and practice is subject to the favour of the rulers and closely regulated. The Catholic missionaries to the Mongol court and Ming Dynasty, including the great Matteo Ricci, also understood this and won the emperor's favour. A Chinese church was established, supported by the three 'pillars', the scholars Paul Hsu, Michael Yang and Leon Li, who also introduced Western science and philosophy to the nation. But after the pope ended the Rites Controversy (Moffett 2005: 120–32) in 1715 by asserting the authority of Rome over the Chinese Christians and Jesuit inculturation, there were episodes of severe persecution against Chinese Christians. In the mid-nineteenth century, British and French missionaries took advantage of the establishment of 'treaty ports' and other privileges won for foreigners by the Opium Wars, but their efforts to establish Protestantism were naturally hampered by their political affiliations. Christians were seen as a subversive force – especially because the Taiping Rebellion (1851–64) had a 'syncretic Christian veneer' (Tiedemann 1999: 392) and converts were labelled 'rice Christians'. After 1860, China became the largest mission field in the world, with missions of the older denominations, related to Western governments, prioritizing programmes of social work of various sorts and courting the elite. But, except through the Roman Catholic Church and Hudson Taylor's China Inland Mission, the mass of Chinese in the interior, not to mention minority groups in China, had little encounter with Christianity. Converts, both Catholic – now protected by France – and Protestant, lived in Christian villages isolated from other Chinese and were frequently in danger from anti-Christian violence. The worst was the Boxer Rebellion of 1900 when over 30,000 Chinese Christians were killed. During the unstable years of the early twentieth century, Christian fortunes fluctuated: they were either favoured as 'anti-traditional' or persecuted as 'cultural imperialists'.

From a Chinese point of view, the net result of both the Social Gospellers of the big denominations and the independent Faith Missions was the same: the first Westernized and then Christianized, and the second Christianized and then Westernized (Leung 2001: 142). The first type of mission established institutional churches closely related to Western structures, although after the conversion of the Nationalist leader Chiang Kai-shek to Christianity in the 1930s, a more indigenous church emerged, following the 'three-self' paradigm (known in East Asia as the 'Nevius method'). The second type resulted in local fellowships on a book of Acts, house-church pattern. When, around the 1920s, Chinese Christians founded their own churches, they tended to follow the latter model, but since these were active in evangelism, networks of independent churches soon emerged. These included the 'Little Flock', led by Watchman Nee who emphasized spiritual life as the key to bodily holiness (e.g. Nee 1989); the 'Jesus Family' of Jing Dianying who, with his wife, set up a cooperative or commune, which was then replicated across northern and north-western China; the 'True Jesus Church', a Pentecostal group; and the 'Christian Church in Christ' of Wong Ming-Dao, who exercised a strict and prophetic ministry (Wong 1981) and was imprisoned for 23 years for his criticism of the later patriotic church. Wong was regarded by many as the unofficial leader of the underground churches. At the grassroots in all the churches were women attracted particularly by the more femininized, compassionate Jesus of nineteenth-century holiness movements (Kwok 1996). At the same time they learned to read, experienced liberation from foot-binding and other oppressive customs and engaged in movements for social change (Kwok 1994; see also Kwok 1992).

The War of Resistance against Japan (1937–45), followed by the Civil War (1947–9), was a time of turmoil for all Chinese, and the churches especially came under tight control (Brook 1996). After the Chinese Communist Party won the power struggle with the nationalists in 1949, the government of the new People's Republic of China demanded that all Christian churches, Catholic and Protestant, should be Chinese-run without any foreign links. In 1954 all Protestant churches were required to join the Three-Self Patriotic Movement (TSPM), led by government-appointed patriotic Christians. The Chinese Catholic Patriotic Association (CCPA) established in 1956 was the result of considerable struggle because for Catholic Christians the formation of the CCPA meant rejecting the authority of the pope and any further teaching from the Vatican. At the outbreak of the Cultural Revolution in 1966, all religious activity – except the quasi-religious Maoism – was regarded as superstitious and anti-revolutionary. Bibles were burned and priests and pastors were imprisoned and often tortured. From 1966 until Deng Xiaoping's open-door policy in 1979, Christianity survived in only a deinstitutionalized and declericalized form in 'underground' or 'house churches', the style to which many were already accustomed. In the rural areas they grew strongly despite the rigours of Communist oppression (Lambert 1991).

Since 1979, the permission given to religious activity and recognition of the legitimacy of Protestantism and (Chinese) Catholicism has led to what even the authorities have called 'Christian fever'. Thousands of churches have (re) opened, and new groups are encouraged to join the China Christian Council, controlled by the TSPM. Under the leadership of (former Anglican) Bishop K. H. (Kuang-hsun) Ting from 1980, the TSPM has maintained good relations with government, which has fostered Christian freedoms, but at the same time it has limited those by keeping a tight rein on church activities. Ting, who has also held government posts, has a social gospel, promoting 'reconciliation between church and society, Christian and non-Christian, China and the world' (Wickeri and Wickeri 2002: vii–viii). The Vatican is making efforts to regularize the status of the Chinese Catholic Patriotic Association, which it has never declared heretical, and with which it was able to maintain almost continuous links. Although the distinction between official and underground churches is now breaking down, accounts of the church from these different situations can yield widely varying views (compare the reports of McCullum and MacArthur (2006) with those of Johnstone and Mandryk (2001)). The house churches tend to regard the official churches with suspicion, and many have chosen not to register; consequently estimates of the numbers of Christians vary widely but are reported to be huge (Lambert 2006). An official government website (www.china.org) gives figures of 4 million Catholics and 10 million Protestants. Using figures from churches themselves, registered and unregistered, the *World Christian Encyclopedia* gives a figure of more than 7 per cent of China's huge population in 2001 (Barrett 2001: 191).

Not only has Christian belief and practice become widespread in China, but centres for the study of Christianity have opened in university departments of religion, which not only introduce Western theology to China but also engage in Sino-theology (Choong 2008). This is stimulating the emergence of an intellectual Christianity with a distinctive theology of modernization (Sørensen 2003), motivated by social concern (He 2003a). Religion is seen not only as a matter of individual belief, but also as a 'political existence' (Gao 2003a: 54). According to Gao Shining of the Chinese Academy of Social Sciences,

Christians still face a considerable amount of ridicule in society, although they are also respected for their high moral standards (Gao 2003b: 69–70). Christian faith is officially incompatible with membership of the Chinese Communist Party, and therefore with social advancement, but there are party members willing to declare themselves Christian. In 2005 new regulations on religious affairs were produced by the government in an attempt to further centralize control, but it may be that events on the ground are running far ahead of government measures (Fielder 2007). As He Guanghu points out, the upsurge in religion is having a constructive effect politically in encouraging Chinese trans-nationalism, against a background of rampant nationalism (He 2003b). The long-term impact on Chinese society of the Christian revival is too early to call, but an extensive North American project suggests that 'it may be in the latter stages of a process of inculturation that will make it as much a part of the Chinese scene as Buddhism became over a thousand years ago' (Bays 1996). Whatever happens, this revival is certain to have a huge effect on world Christianity.

The Chinese Communist Party could not halt the spread of Christianity in the huge Chinese diaspora, or in the territories of Macao, Hong Kong and Taiwan. Not only are Western denominations represented there but so are many of the indigenous churches, including some groups which diverge far from Christian norms (Tang 2005: 476–9). By the terms under which it was returned to China in 1999, the Roman Catholic Church is permitted to maintain its strong presence (about 5 per cent of the population) in the small former Portuguese territory of Macao. In the former British colony of Hong Kong, Christians, about equal numbers of Protestants and Catholics, form about 10 per cent of the population despite the relatively high emigration of Christians before the handover to China in 1997. Large numbers of these Christians are now found in Canada, Australia and the US. Despite the fears of those who left, there is continued religious freedom, and Hong Kong is a hub for ministry in China and in the Chinese diaspora. Christian leaders who chose to remain in Hong Kong after 1997 feel a responsibility to work for reconciliation with China. At the political level this means overcoming the suspicion that exists between the Hong Kong Chinese brought up in the Western system and the Chinese Communist Party. Evangelical Lutheran theologian Lap Yan Kung suggests that trust between the two depends on a revision of the Confucian filial piety analogy, in which the relationship is often couched. While traditional Confucianism expects unconditional love of child for parent, the Christian gospel highlights the love of the parent for the child (Jn 3.16) (Kung 2005: 185). In Taiwan, claimed by China and occupied by Japan from 1895 to 1945, leaders of the Presbyterian Church, which draws its main support from among the majority population who lived in Taiwan before 1949, campaigned vigorously, and at the cost of imprisonment, for their rights against the Nationalist-Chinese government, who ruled Taiwan as a one-party state from 1949 to 2000. Taiwanese Presbyterians have been leaders in the discussion as to how theology should be done in Asia. C. S. (Choan-seng) Song, former president of Tainan Theological Seminary (Presbyterian in foundation), developed an influential 'theology from the womb of Asia' through telling the histories of peoples as a continuation of God's creation. Theology, he claims as he weaves together biblical and Asian stories, is 'God's story in the parables and folktales of our brothers and sisters' (Song 1988: 227).

Some of the Mongolian people live inside modern China, and others in the separate nation of Mongolia along China's northern border, the world's most sparsely populated country. Nestorian Christianity was present in the country in the seventh century but disappeared by the tenth; at the height of the Mongol empire in the thirteenth and fourteenth centuries, Roman Catholics made representation at the Mongol court; Russian Orthodox Christians have also been present more recently. A handful of attempts by Protestants to evangelize the people in the eighteenth and nineteenth centuries resulted in the translation of the Bible but few if any converts. The modern Mongolian Protestant church has only officially existed since 1991, following a bloodless transition to democracy which brought an influx of aid workers, including Christians.

The mountainous and tightly controlled Korean peninsula was difficult for foreign missionaries to penetrate, and not high on their agenda, but in both the Protestant and the Catholic case, Koreans took the initiative to bring Christianity to their homeland. In 1784 Yi Seung-Hun, a Korean student in Beijing, was baptized by a Catholic priest and returned home to start a church himself. Being after the end of the Rites Controversy, Korean converts were instructed to stop their traditions of ancestor worship. This set them at odds with their rulers, and Catholics were subjected to several waves of perse-cution, culminating in 1866 in the deaths of at least a quarter of the Catholic population (Yu 1996). In 1984 eight thousand Korean martyrs were canonized en masse, giving Korea the fourth largest number of martyrs of any country in the world. Almost 100 years after Yi's baptism, a Protestant convert Suh Sang-Yun risked his life to carry copies of a translation of Luke's gospel into

Korea. In this highly Confucian culture, the new book was read avidly and the first Protestant church began. A year or so later in 1885, under pressure from foreign powers, the government permitted the first foreign missionaries to enter. The three-self missionary policy shared by all the main missions from 1893 was taken equally seriously by Korean Christians, who started local congregations, schools and hospitals across the country. Much of the pioneer work was done by women's fellowships and by 'Bible women' – lay women evangelists. In a transitional period they represented the forces of modernization, and as the rapid rise of Japan threatened Korean independence this offered a sign of hope. In 1907 a revival broke out in Pyongyang, now capital of North Korea, and an indigenous Christianity was born. The chief characteristic of Korean Christianity was its unquestioning approach to the biblical text, employing Confucian methods of repeated reading and memorization to study it. Reading the Bible, Christian converts saw parallels between their situation of subjection to Japan and the experience of the Israelites (Kim 1981a), and revival leader Kil Son-Ju and other Christians initiated the independence movement of 1 March 1919. The movement failed but it sealed the Protestant churches' association with nationalism (Wells 1990; Yi 2004). During the period of Japanese occupation (1910–45) the churches kept the millennial hope of liberation alive (Min 2004: 134), especially through another revival movement led by Lee Yong-Do from 1928 to 1933 (Park 1998: 61, 64–72). Some Christians resisted the imposition of Shinto shrine worship, believing it contravened the first commandment; at least 50 were killed and other imprisoned (Kim, Yang-sŏn, 2004).

In the aftermath of the Second World War, atheistic communism took hold in the North, although the revolutionary leader Kim Il-Sung had come from a Christian family. All religious activity was prohibited and today little is known for certain about the state of Christianity in North Korea, which remains a closed state. Many Christian men fled south and founded new churches among the displaced there, but reconstruction of church and nation was halted by the outbreak of North–South hostilities in 1950. After the war, the mainline Evangelical churches committed themselves to evangelistic and social work, under leaders such as Presbyterian pastor Han Kyung-Chik, one of the refugees from the North, who was awarded the Templeton Prize for his work in 1992 (Rev. Kyung-Chik Han Memorial Foundation 2005). Because they shared the government's fear of Communism and looked favourably on the United States, pastors encouraged their congregations to support governments in their drives for modernization. Remembering the suffering of Jesus

Christ on the cross, which they believed lifted the burden from their back, Christians were willing to work hard and make sacrifices for the national good (Kim 1981b). However, their uncritical support for military governments was denounced by radical Christians, influenced by theologies of humanization and liberation, and looking back to the Christian role in the independence movement. Although imprisoned and tortured for their political activities, Suh Nam Dong and other first-generation 'minjung theologians' took the side of poor people and oppressed workers (minjung) (Commission on Theological Concerns of the Christian Conference of Asia 1981; Suh 1991). Roman Catholics were also active in the minjung movement, and Protestant theologians were inspired by the writings of the Catholic activist Kim Chi Ha. During the 1970s and 80s these Christians made a significant contribution to workers' and human rights and to the eventual achievement of democratic government in South Korea in 1988.

As, from the 1970s, South Korea built up its industrial base to become by 1997 the eleventh largest economy in the world. The churches also grew rapidly. Most of the growth in the peak period took place in the mainstream Presbyterian and Methodist churches. In urban areas particularly, the churches offered networks for pastoral support and for business purposes, together with opportunities to develop skills in English, for example, and leadership. Those who put themselves under the discipline of the church testified to its benefits and spread the message of salvation (and judgment) spontaneously and also in systematic evangelistic campaigns. Korea became famous for its 'megachurches', the most famous of which is the Full Gospel Church of Cho Yonggi which now claims more than three-quarters of a million members. Based on 3 Jn 2, Cho developed techniques of prayer and evangelism which would guarantee a 'three-fold blessing' of health, well-being and prosperity (Cho 1989), which outwardly resemble some of the practices of the ancient shamanistic religion of the Korean people (Cox 1996: 226; Martin 2002: 161) and the 'positive thinking' of late capitalism (Cho 1999). Although Cho's church is neo-Pentecostal, all the mainstream churches look back to the Korean revivals, which they seek to reproduce through annual revival meetings, and therefore have a strongly charismatic stream, especially among the women. However, this is under the control of the (overwhelmingly) male leadership and their preferred Confucian style of operating, which is ordered and disciplined. Korean churches thus combine two complementary faces which meet both elite and popular religious needs. This is comprehensible in the context of the yin–yang balance between female and male principles, but *yin–yang* is experienced by many women as oppressive, so Korean feminists have sought an alternative framework of traditional religion for their theologizing (e.g. Chung 1991).

In the 2005 census, nearly 30 per cent of the population of South Korea professed to be Christian. These Christians tend to be urban and middle-class. Post-War Korean churches are built in modern styles and make use of the latest technology to convey a future-oriented message of good news. Christians regard the growth of the church and the economic miracle of twentieth-century Korea as blessing from God – and understand a close connection between the two (Ro 1995). This confidence has led to a huge overseas missionary movement from South Korea. Through the widespread Korean diaspora – there are particularly large Korean communities in the United States, China, Russia and parts of Central Asia, Japan and Brazil – and through the sending of missionary families and single women for long-term work, and groups for 'mission trips', the Korean gospel is exported across the globe. Missionaries, who like all Koreans are very well educated, not only bring their religious practices but also business and practical skills, especially medical skills, both Western and acupuncture. As Korea moves rapidly from modernity into post-modernity, the mainstream Protestant churches have been losing ground, but numbers of Christians have remained high because of the growth in the number of Roman Catholics, now 40 per cent of all Christians. Because Catholicism became perceived as anti-national, Catholics had something of a 'ghetto mentality' until the 1970s, but since then they have grown for several possible reasons. First, tastes in spirituality seem to be moving toward more traditional forms of both Christianity (Anglo-Catholics are also growing) and other religions. Secondly, under Cardinal Stephen Kim, the Catholic Church took a strong stand on human rights. Thirdly, the Catholic Church has remained above the allegations of corruption and scandal which have damaged some Protestant leaders. Since the 2002 football World Cup was played in Korea, a Korean or 'Hallyu' wave of cultural influence has spread across Asia, and particularly China, and in this low-key way Christian influence is also being spread.

The first Japanese to respond to the message of Jesus Christ was a fugitive named Anjiro, who searched South East Asia to find the great Jesuit missionary Francis Xavier and persuaded him to come to Japan. The Christian message was well received at the court of Daimyo Ouchi Yoshitaka, who traded with the Portuguese through the port of Nagasaki. During the following 'Christian century', a faith adapted to Japan was spread to the capital city Kyoto, and by

1614 there was probably a larger proportion of Christians in Japan than the 1 to 3 per cent there are estimated to be now. However, subsequent rulers persecuted Christians: all churches were closed, all Christian practice, in public or in secret, was prohibited, and Christians were tortured to produce apostasy, often by treading on an image of Christ. The suffering of the period has been captured by Shusako Endo in his novel *Silence*, which has been very widely read in Japan and around the world. According to one estimate, about half of the Catholics in Japan today are descendants of those who hid their faith for the next two centuries (Moffett 2005: 93).

When Catholic missionaries re-entered the country in 1859, now led by the Paris Missionary Society, they made contact with the 'hidden Christians', especially around Nagasaki. While many rejoined the Roman Catholic Church, a much larger proportion, mainly islanders, chose to keep attending the Buddhist temples and to maintain the practices they had evolved while keeping their faith secret; about 30,000 remain today. There are now more than three times as many Protestants as Catholics in Japan. Protestant churches were planted after Japan opened selected ports to foreign settlement, at first by American missionaries: Episcopalians, Presbyterians, (Dutch) Reformed, Methodists and some independent Baptists. Most Japanese continued to be suspicious of foreigners, and anti-Christian edicts were still in place, so very few converted. A Russian Orthodox mission begun in 1861 made better progress; by 1875 there were already two Japanese priests. Protestant educational work attracted more and helped to produce some outstanding leaders, who were formed in the Student Christian Bands. Progressive thinkers understood Christianity to be the secret of the West's success, but the enthusiasm for Christianity soon cooled with the rise of Japanese nationalism. During the next 55 years, as Japan built up its military power and expanded its empire across East Asia, Christians sometimes resisted but more often accommodated the growing militarization and imperial conquest. Churches sent missionaries to help Christians in occupied countries. Catholics and virtually all Protestants also complied with the requirements for Shinto shrine worship and observance of the emperor cult, even making theological justification for the practice (Mullins 1998: 20). From as early as 1877, some of the mission churches had united in an ecumenical spirit, but it was the threat of organizational extinction by the government, as war threatened and the regulations on denominations tightened, that resulted in almost all the Protestant churches joining together in 1941 to make a single United Church of Christ in Japan (*Nihon Kirisuto Kyodan*). The church retains the core of the union – Reformed,

Methodist and Congregational – and remains the largest single denomination today. After the end of the Pacific War, several thousand foreign missionaries entered the country, leading to a proliferation of smaller churches, but not to significant long-term increases in the proportion of Christians. The Protestant churches in Japan have spawned many indigenous groups (Mullins 1998). The earliest, the Nonchurch Movement founded by Uchimura Kanzo in 1901, was primarily a prophetic reaction against the foisting of foreign denominational divisions and extra-biblical practices on Japanese Christians. The founders of The Way (1907) and Christ Heart Church (1927) rebelled against the institutionalism of Western religion and its exclusivism, insisting that the scriptures of various Asian religions were also vehicles of revelation and adopting traditional Japanese religious practices. Later indigenous churches are more oriented to popular religiosity and more Pentecostal or charismatic in nature, such as the Restorationist-style Spirit of Jesus Church (1941). This church and some others have evolved ways of relating to the world of the dead, which was the function of traditional ancestor veneration. Japan has its share of neo-Pentecostal movements; some of these come from among the substantial Korean minority and from South Korea itself.

Although Japanese Christians are numerically in a small minority, their contribution to the modernization of Japan is commonly acknowledged. Disproportionate numbers of Christians have contributed to education and social welfare (Phillips 1981). Tetsu Katayama became Japan's first socialist (and Christian) prime minister in 1947. As a Christian pacifist he effectively put a stop to the remilitarization desired by the Americans and some other Japanese (Phillips 1981: 21). Christians have also campaigned for the rights of minorities such as the indigenous Ainu people in Hokkaido. In the aftermath of Japan's defeat and the dropping of the atom bombs, theologian Kazoh Kitamori wrote his groundbreaking work *Theology of the Pain of God*, which was published in Japan in 1946. Kitamori used the words of Jer. 31.20 to encourage the Japanese people that the 'transcendent pain of God is immanent in the painful reality of the world' (England et al. 2003: 397; Kitamori 1965). The book reached a worldwide audience and influenced German theologians particularly, including Jürgen Moltmann. However, Kitamori did not address the issue of Japanese complicity in their suffering and the suffering they caused other Asian nations during their imperial rule. Although in 1967 the Kyodan and other churches began to admit their wartime collaboration, they have yet to succeed in persuading the wider society to deal with it to the satisfaction of neighbouring countries (Miyahira 2008).

Diversity and struggle in South East Asia

Each of the countries of South East Asia has evolved its own patterns of Christian life and worship. The Vietnamese, like their neighbours further north, have also had to contend with Confucian centralized state control of religion. Nevertheless the Catholic Church has been well established in parts of the country since the seventeenth century, due to French initiatives and early indigenous movements (Tiedemann 1999: 384–7). As in other parts of Confucian Asia, the church experienced periodic persecution, repeated again more recently under Communism. After the end of the Vietnam War in 1975, the huge exodus of Vietnamese included relatively more Catholics, many of whom are settled today in the United States. Religion continues to be strictly controlled in the socialist republic, but an indigenous Christian, mainly Catholic, minority of about 8 per cent of the population remains. Despite Communism, Vietnamese Catholic theologian Peter Phan argues that Confucian norms dominate Vietnamese lives today and influence the way Jesus Christ is understood. Jesus, Phan points out, was the epitome of filial piety: he upheld the commandment to honour father and mother (Mt. 19.18) and honoured his parents (Lk. 2.51–2). What is more, he was the first-born Son of the heavenly Father (Jn 1.14) and offered the perfect sacrifice (of his death) to the Father (Heb. 10.12). Phan goes on to show that the biblical traditions can be interpreted to mean that Jesus has become the pre-eminent ancestor in a way analogous to Vietnamese tradition (2003: 126–43). So Phan believes that Matteo Ricci was wrong to regard ancestor veneration as only a civil and social, not a religious, act. On the other hand, the Franciscans and Dominicans who opposed him were also wrong in seeing it as a threat to Christian orthodoxy. Instead he sees in the image of Jesus as the eldest son offering sacrifices to the ancestors the Ancestor par excellence.

In the Theravada Buddhist-dominated contexts of South East Asia – Cambodia, Laos, Burma/Myanmar and Thailand – Christians are part of a much smaller minority, although Nestorian Christianity was present in this region in the seventh and eighth centuries. Despite centuries of efforts by Roman Catholics from France (who kept Protestants out), and more recent efforts by Vietnamese, Catholics in Cambodia number fewer now than in 1900. Christians (and Buddhists) were almost annihilated by the Khmer Rouge in the 1970s. More recent efforts by American missionaries and diaspora Christians have resulted in the growth of independent churches, the largest of which is a Pentecostal body, the New Apostolic Church. In Burma/ Myanmar, Christians – mainly Evangelicals, especially Baptists – are concentrated among three tribal groups, the Kayin (Karen), Chin and Kachin, who do not identify with the majority Burmese and are discriminated against. Similarly, in Thailand most of the Christians (who form less than 2 per cent of the population) are not of Thai descent but are Chinese, Vietnamese or from tribal minorities. In a nation defined by ethnic identity, and which has the distinction of being the only nation in southern Asia which has never submitted to colonial rule, Christians in Thailand are perceived as foreign. In none of these countries has Christianity ever been associated with nationalism (cf. Tiedemann 1999: 408). Nevertheless, as Thailand becomes more urban and more cosmopolitan, Christianity is growing and Korean missionaries have been particularly influential on Thai Christianity (Pongudom, Swanson and Chumsriphan 2001: 834).

In Malaysia and Indonesia, Christians live mainly in the context of Islam. In Malaysia, the constitution was set up to favour the majority Malay community, who are identified by it as Muslim. There is increasing Islamization, including *Shari'a* law, and proselytization of Malays is forbidden. Christians are from the other major communities: Chinese, who are financially powerful; Indians, mostly among the Tamils who came (or were brought) there to work for the British when it was colonial Malaya; Eurasians; and indigenous peoples, a tiny minority in Peninsular (West) Malaysia but a much larger proportion in East Malaysia, a separate territory on the island formerly known as Borneo. Together Christians form about 9 per cent of the total population. Although denominations fall along ethnic and language lines, all come together in the Christian Federation for political purposes, especially to oppose more radical Islamic reforms. Roman Catholic missionaries including Francis Xavier were active from the Portuguese base in Malacca from the early sixteenth century. The Dutch did not evangelize the locals, so the earliest Protestant church is Presbyterian, begun by the London Missionary Society in the early nineteenth century, and mainly Chinese. Methodists – Chinese and Tamil – are the largest group among the Protestants in peninsular Malaysia, and there are also many Anglicans. In East Malaysia the Evangelical Church of Borneo, started by Australian missionaries in the 1960s, which saw mass conversions of tribal people and rapid growth, is the largest single denomination. Since the end of the Second World War many more Evangelical and Pentecostal groups have grown up in different parts of the nation. These have been introduced by missionaries from the West, from other parts of Asia, including immigrants from mainland China who brought the True Jesus Church, and by Malaysians themselves, especially Chinese. Despite vibrant church activity, Anglican bishop Hwa Yung memorably complained that Malaysian theology was dominated by issues from the West. He wrote that it was more like a banana – yellow on the outside but white inside – than a juicy mango (Yung 1997: 240–1). Christians have found moves toward Islamization 'frightening' (Walters 2000: 134), but theologians like Albert Sundararaj Walters caution against reactionism and advocate a proactive approach of deep engagement with Islamic thought by theologians and lay people (Walters 2000, 2002). As Anglican archdeacon Eddie Ong puts it, Christians may be prevented from persuading Muslims toward Christianity but they 'are not prohibited from reflecting afresh on their understanding of Islam' and working with Muslims for the good of Malaysia (Ong 1998: 176).

Singapore, which separated from the rest of the Malay peninsula in 1965, is dominated by the Chinese community. Among Chinese across South East Asia, Evangelicalism and Roman Catholicism were strengthened by their anti-Communist stance (Tiedemann 1999: 408). The government of Singapore has been strongly anti-Communist and also very conservative. About 15 per cent of Singaporeans are Christians (including some from the Tamil and other communities) and there are many new churches, of which the most prominent example is City Harvest Church. These use English (not Chinese) and attract the young (Ma 2005: 61–2). Singaporean culture and politics discourage Christian involvement in social matters and theological reflection, but Evangelical and Pentecostal practice flourish (cf. England et al. 2003: 266). In this small but wealthy and globally connected nation, there is a strong emphasis on overseas mission.

Indonesia incorporates former Hindu and Buddhist kingdoms but today is overwhelmingly Muslim. The fourth most populous country in the world, spread across thousands of islands, and home to many different people groups, Indonesia resisted Islamization when it gained independence from the Japanese in 1945. The constitution is based on five principles (*Pancasila*), which begin with belief in one God but guarantee equal rights. The decision in the mid-1960s to require everyone to belong to one of five different religions – Islam, Protestantism, Catholicism, Hinduism or Buddhism – resulted in rapid growth in the number of Christians. Partly as a reaction against Islamization, tribal peoples, nominal Hindus and Muslims – among them Communist sympathizers – and also members of the economically powerful Chinese minority flocked to join the churches in some parts of the country. However, there is pressure on Christians from Islamists, with some discrimination and, since the 1990s in some parts of the country, outbreaks of Muslim–Christian violence. These have been most severe in Posso (Central Sulawesi) in 1998 and in Ambon (Maluku) in 1999, but there have been many other examples (e.g. Farhadian 2005: 1–2). In these situations Christians naturally turn to foreign Christian support (Titaley 2008).

Christianity entered the Indonesian archipelago first with Persian (Nestorian) traders and later with Portuguese traders in the fifteenth century. When the Dutch East India Company took over in 1695, it expelled the foreign Catholics and restricted missionary activities until the Dutch government established Indonesia as a colony in 1800. After that, until the Japanese occupation in 1942, a variety of Dutch, German, other European and later American mission agencies worked in different parts of the islands. Few Indonesians were ordained until the twentieth century, and lay people were largely responsible for reaching others with the gospel (see van den End 2001: 377). During the Second World War, all foreign missionaries were expelled or interned, so the churches had to govern themselves anyway. However, after its end the Dutch tried to reassert their rule in Indonesia, and in the ensuing revolutionary war Christians were caught in a very difficult position. During 1944–8, Indonesian Christians in the Dutch Reformed Church took great risks to negotiate with the Dutch church, while at the same time supporting the nationalist cause (van Ufford 2007).

Since all religious bodies are required to accept the *Pancasila* as the basis of national life, Indonesian theologians are challenged to theologize on the basis of it. Indonesian theologian John A. Titaley laments the slowness of its indigenous theological development but suggests the greatest contribution of Christianity has been, and is, 'a sense of human equity regardless of one's religious or racial background' (Titaley 2008). Catholic theologians particularly have sought to recognize and celebrate the diverse cultures of Indonesia in the church (England et al. 2003: 126). As in many other countries in Asia, the number of Christians is a politically sensitive issue, and figures are offered both considerably below and above 10 per cent. The Catholic Church may number 13 million; the Communion of Churches in Indonesia, founded in 1950, has more than 60 member (Protestant) denominations, some of which themselves number a million or more members. There are also many independent churches, often sparked by more recent evangelization initiatives by American and other Asian missionaries, and many indigenous churches, usually of a Pentecostal variety.

As elsewhere in South East Asia, those who converted to Christianity were mainly from groups not incorporated into the major religious systems. In states of largely tribal population, generally in the eastern parts of the country, there are large numbers of Christians. The Karo Batak Church in Northern Sumatra, with perhaps 3 million affiliates, is one of the largest in Asia. The indigenous people living in the eastern half of the small island of Timor, which lies very close to Australia and was a Portuguese colony until 1975, were 30 per cent Catholic until the Indonesians annexed their land. Under the Indonesian system of compulsory religious affiliation, 90 per cent opted for Catholicism, and the Catholic Church supported them in their resistance to Indonesia. Since their economy was in the hands of Indonesians, the people were exceedingly poor, and they endured huge suffering and death at the hands of forces loyal to Indonesia. But due in part to the advocacy of Timorese bishop Carlos Filipe Ximenes Belo, who was jointly awarded the 1996 Nobel Peace Prize, East Timor was eventually internationally recognized as an independent state in 2002.

Moving even further east, the people of the Philippines, apart from some Muslim communities in Mindanao, followed local religions until the arrival of Christianity. Unlike the rest of East Asia, the first Catholic missionaries there were not Portuguese, but Spanish priests coming across the Pacific Ocean from Latin America in the sixteenth century. They applied the same *encomienda* methods as they had done in the Americas, although somewhat less oppressively, and as in Latin America a distinctive folk Catholicism emerged. Today the islands are about 90 per cent Christian and more than 80 per cent Roman Catholic. The institutional church was firmly in Spanish hands – and Protestantism was forbidden – until the revolution in 1896, despite local unrest from 1800 onwards, some of it Christian-led. After the Spanish–American War the country became an American colony, although with continued resistance, and Spanish bishops were replaced with American ones. In 1902, nationalist fervour led to at least a quarter of all Catholics at the time forming the *Iglesia Filipina Independiente* (Philippine Independent Church) led by a Filipino priest Gregario Aglipay, who had earlier been excommunicated for condemning foreign domination of the church. The large Iglesia Filipina Independiente is now in communion with the Philippine Episcopal Church. Nationalist feelings have also led to the emergence of breakaway Protestant groups such as the Evangelical Methodist Church in 1909, and indigenous churches, such as the Iglesia ni Christo (Church of Christ), founded in 1913 by Felix Manalo.

The Philippines finally became independent in 1946, after occupation by the Japanese from 1942, but a close relationship with the United States was resumed. Many Filipinos have been attracted to US-style Protestantism, but at least two-thirds of the population remain Catholic. Rather than the growth of independent Pentecostal churches, there is a strong charismatic movement, which has cut across the Catholic and Protestant churches and blurred denominational boundaries. There continues to be a great deal of missionary activity in the Philippines; South Korean missions are particularly numerous, working with the poor and more remote mountain tribes (Ma 2001). However, the international links and knowledge of English has also made the Philippines a major missionary-sending country. Millions of Filipinos find work abroad, especially in domestic service, and these migrants are often active in spreading their faith, after the fashion of the servant girl who directed her master Naaman the Syrian to seek healing from God's prophet in Israel (2 Kgs 5.1–8). The Roman Catholic Church was deeply involved in the 'people power' movement which in 1986 overthrew the military dictator Ferdinand Marcos and his wife Imelda. Nevertheless, most Filipinos continue to live in poverty, and considering the Catholics in the Philippines are more than half of the Catholics in Asia, this means the Catholic Church in Asia is still the church of the poor. Eleazar Fernandes has characterized Philippine theology not as a theology of liberation – for that is yet to be achieved – but as a 'theology of struggle'. The story of Jesus' struggle is popularly retold in verse form in the *pasyon* (passion), in which parallels are drawn between political figures and those who opposed him; and the fact that Jesus' followers were poor and illiterate and yet changed the world is not lost on Filipinos. During the struggle against the Marcos regime, the image of the crucified Christ so prominent in the movement was not, for Filipinos, one of passive endurance, but an image of ongoing struggle (Fernandes 1994: 103).

Religions and poverty in South Asia

Christianity in Assyrian or Syrian form has been part of the religious tapestry of the Indian subcontinent for nearly two thousand years. Not only has the Indian Orthodox church maintained the ancient faith in South India, but Syrian Christians, who consider themselves among the high castes, have held privileged positions in society over many centuries. The greatest problem for the Orthodox church has not been its minority status among the Hindus and Muslims, but the actions of other Christians. Roman Catholic Christians arrived in South India in the shape of the Portuguese, who established and maintained the coastal territory of Goa as their chief colony on the subcontinent from 1510 until 1961. Local fishing castes, including the Paravas, turned to Christianity and laid the foundation of an Indian Catholic church. The growing Latinizing power of the Roman Catholic Church in India itself caused the St Thomas Christians to experience what some describe as 'suppression and disfigurement' (quoted in Moffett 2005: 12) and 'slavery and persecution' (Jacob 2001). Using the power of the Portuguese state and the Inquisition, at the Synod of Diamper in 1599, Catholic church leaders sought to force the allegiance of all Christians in India to St Peter, not St Thomas. Most of the St Thomas Christians were brought under Rome but allowed to keep their Syriac liturgy. However, in 1653 a large number gathered at Coonen Cross near Cochin to reject Catholicism. The Indian Orthodox church (also known by the adjectives 'Jacobite', 'Syrian', 'Malankara' and 'of the East') gained recognition from the patriarchate of Antioch (not Baghdad), becoming monophysite, rather than Nestorian, in Christology. The Syrian Orthodox split again in the mid-nineteenth century as a result of a reform movement that began under the influence of missionaries of the (Anglican) Church Missionary Society (CMS) who translated the Bible into the vernacular language, Malayalam. Under Abraham Malpan, those affected by the movement established the Mar Thoma Syrian Church of Malabar, which is Evangelical Protestant in doctrine, while retaining traditional St Thomas vestments, church structures and liturgical features. The two churches are in dialogue with one another. The Syrian Orthodox Church maintains many social and evangelistic activities and supports smaller denominations; leaders such as Geevarghese Mar Osthathios have been active in the World Council of Churches (WCC). There are about 3 million Syrian Orthodox in India today.

Since the partition of British India in 1947, Christians in Pakistan and Bangladesh have been separated from their fellow believers in India, where the strength of the church lay, and living among overwhelming Muslim majorities. Although there were ancient churches in both regions, most Christians – Catholics and Protestants – in both countries are drawn from among the lowest castes, who converted en masse in the colonial period. In Pakistan most Christians are street cleaners or toilet cleaners. The most popular Psalms sung in the (Protestant) Church of Pakistan in Punjabi, the language of most of the Christian population, are those which deal with suffering and patience (Nazir-Ali 1987: 91). Increasing Islamization, especially the introduction of the death penalty for blasphemy against the prophet Muhammad, has been used to stir up hatred against Christians (Ramalshah 1998: 264) and also to inhibit the economic development of religious minorities (Berner 2001: 630). In Bangladesh, however, Christians are relatively free to practise their faith. The largest churches are Roman Catholic and Baptist, and the majority of Christians are in tribal communities along the border with India. Though Christians form less than 1 per cent of the population, they have a relatively high profile since local and overseas churches run many social development programmes for the wider community. To the south of India, Christians were a powerful minority in Sri Lanka in the sixth and seventh centuries, but today's Christians are more recent: Catholics since the sixteenth century and Protestants since the Dutch period. Since they belong in equal numbers to both the Tamil and Sinhalese communities, between which there has been such tension in recent years, Christians have acted as peacemakers (Peiris 1998). In the Roman Catholic Church, Sri Lanka has been a centre for Christian–Buddhist dialogue, especially through the work of Jesuit priest Aloysius Pieris (1988a). To the north of India, Christianity was forbidden in the isolated Hindu kingdom of Nepal until 1960; Christians suffered severe persecution in the 1990s, in what is a very unstable situation, but Pentecostal churches have grown rapidly, evangelized by Indians as well as foreigners, and Christians are estimated to number about 2 per cent today.

In the nation of India itself, Roman Catholics now make up more than two-thirds of Indian Christians. The Catholic population remains concentrated in the modern Indian states of Goa and Kerala, and in the city of Mumbai, which were most influenced by the Portuguese, and among the Malayalam-speaking community. The colonial Protestant churches were established from the beginning of the eighteenth century by missionaries from Britain (Baptist, Anglican, Methodist), Germany (Lutheran and Reformed), other European countries and, later, North America. Today most of India's Christians live in the South Indian states of Kerala, Tamil Nadu and Andhra Pradesh, and where there are Christian villages there are parts of those states where Christians form a local majority. The other major centre of Christian population is in the hill country of north-east India, the pocket between Bangladesh and Burma/Myanmar, where the tribal people, who had migrated there from the direction of China, were evangelized by English Baptists from Serampore, American Baptists and Welsh Presbyterians from the late nineteenth century. As a result of Holiness revival movements, in these relatively small states up to 90 per cent of the population are Christians. North-east Indian Christianity is in keeping with the customs of the people, some of whom were head-hunters within the last 100 years. For example, Mizo Christians celebrate Christmas in large church groups by roasting wild pigs and singing throughout the night. The annual Baptist convention in Meghalaya attracts tens of thousands of people in family and church groups to a huge tent meeting. Evangelists from north-east India work with their kinsfolk across the relatively porous borders into Burma/Myanmar, in the isolated Buddhist Kingdom of Bhutan and in Bangladesh. Others work cross-culturally among the majority communities of India through indigenous mission organizations.

Because of the highly stratified caste structure of Hindu India, and because in the Indian context the colonial presence allowed them relative freedom, from the start both Catholic and Protestant missionaries were faced with the dilemma of whether to aim to win the high castes in the hope of changing society from the top down or whether to preach to the lowest castes, who were most obviously in need of salvation. Of the early Jesuit missionaries, Robert de Nobili chose the former and Francis Xavier the latter group. A great deal of effort was put into evangelizing the upper castes, especially through education, and some outstanding Indian leaders became Christians in the nineteenth century, including Brahmabandab Upadhyay, a Bengali *brahmin* who became a Roman Catholic, and laid the foundations of Indian Christian theology on Vedantic Hinduism rather than Greek philosophy (Lipner 1999), and Narayan Vaman Tilak, who was known as the poet-saint of Maharashtra and established a tradition of hymnody in Marathi (Jacob 1979). The attempt to reach the high castes required a deep engagement with Hindu culture, but since the ending of the Rites Controversy the Catholic Church had kept a distinctively Latin identity, despite the many affinities between Catholic and Hindu devotional practices (Ballhatchet and Ballhatchet 2002: 520), until after Vatican II. When Upadhyay suggested the formation of a religious order of Indian Christian *sannyasis* (holy men) based around an *ashram* (hermitage), he was refused permission, but this model was pioneered from the 1970s by Vandana, formerly leader of the Sisters of the Sacred Heart of Jesus in India, as 'an open community' of *guru* and disciples in which Hindus and Christians could together pursue *Brahmavidya* (knowledge of God) (Vandana 1982: 3–4). Raymond Panikkar followed this through in the realms of systematic theology, comparing the perfect union of Jesus Christ with God the Father, with the Hindu aspiration to self-transcendence in the realization of the oneness of the Divine (*Brahman*) and the human spirit or self (*atman*). Indian reflection significantly influenced the positive approach of *Nostra Aetate*, the declaration produced by the Second Vatican Council on the relation of the church to non-Christian religions (Gispert-Sauch 1997: 458). Other pioneers of Indian Christian theology, such as A. J. Appasamy, an Anglican bishop, preferred to use the *bhakti* tradition of Hindu mysticism, which finds its inspiration in the *Bhagavadgita*, for their theologizing. Inspired particularly by Sundar Singh, a Sikh convert who took up the wandering life of a *sadhu* (wandering holy man) and offered Indians 'the Water of Life in an Indian cup', and using John's gospel, which has a particular appeal to Hindus, Appasamy compared *bhakti* with the love of God – ethical as well as emotional – and also reflected on salvation (*moksa*) as life. Contemporary theologian Sebastian Painadath suggests that inculturation of the gospel needs to be with respect to all the different Hindu *margas* (paths): knowledge, devotion and action (Painadath 1993).

Despite the efforts to reach the elite, in the late nineteenth and early twentieth centuries all the churches grew rapidly by 'mass conversions' of communities of outcaste and tribal groups, and these make up the overwhelming majority of Indian Christians today. Many of these poor Christians, formerly known as 'untouchables' but who now choose to designate themselves '*dalit*', used conversion as a protest against Hindu caste practices and also as a means of improving their socio-economic status. In keeping with the socialist model of national development, Protestant lay theologian M. M. Thomas, Jesuit activist and theologian Samuel Rayan and others developed theologies of revolution and humanization. To support these they looked to the pre-Aryan *shakti* tradition of the creative force, which subverts Vedic Hinduism. Rayan was one of the first to welcome Latin American liberation theology and the Christian option for the poor and oppressed. While acknowledging a debt to Marxist analysis, Indian liberation theologians soon recognized its limitations in dealing with the caste system. They also challenged the historical and rational framework of Latin American liberation theology and led the way among Third World theologians in developing a spirituality of liberation which draws on indigenous cultural traditions and experience (Amaladoss 1981; Rayan 1983). There are now a number of paths of liberation theology in India. Not only does each provide different resources, it also offers a different method, enabling Indian theology to break out of the rigidity of Western academic method and embrace new creative forms (Selvanayagam 2002; Wilfred 1998).

Alongside expressions of solidarity, Indian theologies of liberation also include the voices of the oppressed themselves: *dalits*, tribals and women.

Although caste distinctions are being broken down by urbanization, a market-oriented society and positive discrimination by government, especially in rural areas *dalit* communities still face harassment, exclusion from water supplies, and exploitation by the higher castes (for examples, see Aruldoss 1998). But caste practices were by no means eradicated in the churches. Despite the reputation of Jesus Christ for eating with outcastes and sinners, in all the churches, Orthodox, Catholic and Protestant, there are many instances of outcastes not being invited to share the same loaf or communion cup (Forrester 1980; Robinson 2003: 70–92). Christian *dalits* suffer doubly, being discriminated against in the church and also socially, in that they do not qualify for government benefits intended to counter discrimination, on the grounds that Christianity does not (officially) acknowledge caste (Parratt 1994). Thus the *dalit* Christian struggle is both with Hindu society but also with the Christian community. Using the tools of liberation theology but applying them to caste rather than class, theologians of outcaste groups have developed a theology from below, of the *dalits* rather than for them (Prabhakar 1988), to counter what V. Devasahayam (1997) has described as their 'pollution, poverty and powerlessness'. A. P. Nirmal began *dalit* theology when he described Jesus Christ as a *dalit*, because as the Suffering Servant he was scorned and rejected, and he came from a people who were slaves in Egypt (Nirmal 1988). Tribal identities are generally stronger than those of *dalit* communities because of their distinct languages, religions and identifiable homeland, which provide a framework for their theologizing in a way similar to other indigenous or First Nations communities (Thanzauva 1997). India is one of the few countries in the world where the number of females is less than the number of males, due to selective abortion, female infanticide, deprivation and abuse. Faced with problems such as the dowry system, lack of education, discrimination, ill-treatment and lack of representation (despite government quota systems), Indian feminist theologians have condemned this situation as sinful and drawn inspiration from the 'alternative' society of Jesus (e.g. Gnanadason 1988: 74). *Dalit* women are 'the *dalits* of the *dalits*', thrice alienated by class, caste and gender (Manorama 1992). Since '*shakti*' is feminine, there is a natural connection between feminism and ecological concern in India (Gajiwala 1998; Gnanadason 1993).

As well as the alternative development represented by those who campaign for the rights of the poor, Christian churches run large numbers of institutions, mainly schools and hospitals. Standards are known to be high and they attract the elite, although in many cases they have a specific mission to the poor. In practice, holding together the dialogue with the high caste and the low, with religions and poverty, with traditional culture and with modernizing forces, has proved very difficult. The debate between inculturation and liberation, which is rooted in Hinduism, goes on in the Catholic Church (Knitter 1995: 163–6), Protestant churches (Boyd 2002) and the Syrian Orthodox (Osthathios 1979), between those loyal to Vedantic traditions and *dalit* causes. In the 1990s climate of rising Hindu nationalism, both approaches came under attack. Attempts to present the Christian gospel in a Hindu way, particularly the ashram movement, arouse the suspicions of Hindus that they are a duplicitous attempt to win more converts. Liberation theologians have also been criticized as the contemporary successors of missionaries who encouraged 'rice Christians', because of their justification of motives of social advancement for Christian conversion. In this debate Indian Christians who are the products of mass conversion movements see the motives of their ancestors impugned by both Hindus and Christians (S. Kim 2003: 130), and the stories of their search for liberation and identity which led to their conversions remain untold (Hrangkhuma 1998).

Indian Christian theology is not only concerned with inculturation and liberation but also dialogue with other faiths and ideologies (Chandran 1993; Kim 2004; Thomas 1997). In the religiously plural situation of India, the form and theology of the church is a difficult question for Protestants and Catholics (Kunnumpuram, D'Lima and Parapally 1997). In order to present a united witness, in 1947, the year of independence, a merger of Congregational, Presbyterian, Methodist and Anglican churches formed the Church of South India, and provided the basis for similar schemes of union of episcopal and non-episcopal churches in North India (1970), Pakistan (1970) and Bangladesh (after 1971). In 1978 a joint council was established by the Church of South India, Church of North India and the Mar Thoma Church, exhibiting a high degree of union: intercommunion, doctrinal unity, episcopal polity, mutual recognition of one another's ministry, and some joint activities. After independence, Christian leaders like P. D. Devanandan, first director of the (Protestant Ecumenical) Christian Institute for the Study of Religion and Society in Bangalore, redefined Christian mission as actively participating in the struggle for a new society in dialogue with neo-Hindus and secularists. Proponents of dialogue, such as leading ecumenist Stanley Samartha, have advocated 'commitment with openness', and see the church as integrated with the wider community (Samartha: 1981: 32–4; cf. Kavunkal 1995). But Evangelical theologians stress the distinctiveness of the Christian community (e.g. Sumithra 1992: 79–97) and the Christian responsibility to evangelize and the mission of conversion (Ramachandra 1996). Others urge Christians to be both 'evangelical and dialogical' (Selvanayagam 2000: 338–53).

Conversion has been the most contentious issue between Christian and Hindu communities. The traditional understanding of conversion as leaving the former religion and joining the Christian community is not only offensive to Hindus and misunderstood; it is also a politicized act. Hindu objections to conversion have been concretized in three main ways: by the introduction of Hindu 'personal laws', which were disadvantageous for caste Hindus who converted to another religion (1955–6); by the limitation of social benefits for converts from Scheduled Caste backgrounds (1950s); and by the passing of the 'freedom of religion acts' in various states (1960s and 70s). Where they operate, these measures effectively block individuals or groups from changing their community allegiance, except by 'home-coming' (*shuddhi*) to Hinduism (Kim 2003). The rise of militant Hinduism with its ideology of *Hindutva*, or Hinduization, reached a peak in 1998 when a Hindu party was elected to central government, but since the victory of the Congress Party in 2003 there has been a relaxation of tensions. While insisting on the need for conversion, many of today's Indian Evangelical missionaries, often working cross-culturally within the subcontinent, are deeply committed to social projects and even advocacy for the poor. As well as international agencies such as Operation Mobilisation and InterServe, there are many indigenous Indian missions, including the Indian Missionary Society and the Friends Missionary Prayer Band.

Indian Protestants have not often rebelled en masse against the mission churches. One example where they did so was a caste group called the Shanars or Nadars in the Tirunelveli district of South India who in 1857 founded the Hindu-Christian Church of the Lord Jesus (Kumaradas 2004). Among the new churches that have emerged as a result of revival movements and the work of indigenous mission organizations, a well-known example is the Bakht Singh movement, a network of autonomous 'assemblies' founded on the teaching of Bakht Singh a British-educated engineer, and now found mainly in Madras, Hyderabad, Kalimpong (West Bengal) and Mumbai. The assemblies did away with membership registers and elected officials, emphasizing instead commitment to Christ, the authority of the Bible and the leading of the Holy Spirit (Premanandham 2004). Pentecostal churches were first established in South India around 1911. One of the best known today is the Indian Pentecostal Church of God, founded by Syrian Christians in Kerala in the

1930s. In 2001 it was estimated that 20 per cent of South Indian Protestants are Pentecostals, participating in an indigenous version of Christianity with strong parallels with traditional Indian popular religion in the areas of miracle healing and exorcism. The most influential charismatic evangelist today is probably D. G. S. Dhinakaran, a member of the Church of South India, whose Jesus Calls Ministry, which has a lot in common with that of Oral Roberts in the US, offers healing and whose followers have helped establish a Christian University (Bergunder 2001; 2004; 2005).

The Sri Lanka Catholic theologian Aloysius Pieris has called for a 'double baptism' of Christianity in both the Jordan of Asian religions and the Calvary of Asian poverty (Pieris 1988b: 45–8). First, Asia remains deeply religious. Even M. M. Thomas, who emphasizes the need for Christianity to appeal to the secular, does so with the Asian understanding of secularism in mind: the equal respect of all religions. India has been the laboratory in which ecumenical theology of inter-religious dialogue has been developed, led by Stanley Samartha at the WCC (Samartha 1979); however, this model of religious pluralism and inter-religious dialogue is not replicated in all the different multi-religious contexts of Asia. For example, Christians in Korea think differently about inter-religious relations: Korean Christians do not feel any colonial guilt about their treatment of other religions; the Confucian cultural context values loyalty to a particular religious discipline (Lee 1999); and because Korean identity is firmly grounded on an ethnic basis, religious conversion is not a political issue. In Korea, therefore, though the context is multi-religious, the contours of debate about conversion and church are very different. Second, even where Asians are rapidly joining the world's elite, poverty remains an issue because both Hinduism and Buddhism promote the ascetic life. Across Asia, Jesus Christ is attractive and respected as a religious figure. Although Asian portraits of Jesus show wide variation, depending, for example, on whether Jesus is set alongside Buddha, Krishna, Confucius or Muhammad (Sugirtharajah 1993: x), there is some common agreement that Jesus' significance lies in his suffering. From Japan's Kitamori to *dalit* theologian Nirmal, Christ as the suffering servant of God speaks powerfully to the people of Asia. But they are divided on whether this suffering is an example to follow by self-denial or a once for all sacrifice which means his followers need not suffer. Asian feminist theology was sparked by the work of Marianne Katoppo, a Catholic theologian from Indonesia, who suggested that Asian feminist theology would not draw on the male-dominated major religions of Asia but on the folk spirituality of feminine power (1979: 65–77).

In keeping with this, feminist theologians have no hesitation in seeing Jesus above all as life-giving, the 'many-breasted mother' who does everything to sustain the life of her child (Orevillo-Montenegro: 156; cf. Chung 1990; Kwok 2000: 125). This dilemma about suffering is another aspect of the inculturation–liberation debate because it is about whether Christianity should be ascetic, as the elite religious traditions of Asia are, or life-affirming like the local religions of the poor.

Gods and goods in Australasia and Oceania

The Aboriginal peoples of Australia, who had been there for at least 50,000 years, probably first encountered Christianity in the form of Spanish Roman Catholic friars accompanying early explorers in the sixteenth century. The first colonists, transported from British gaols to the furthest 'corner' of the earth from 1788, were attended by small numbers of Anglican chaplains, although the many Irish Catholics transported often, resented this. Catholic priests were permitted as chaplains only after the Napoleonic wars (Hilliard 1999: 509–10). From the nineteenth century Sydney became a base for evangelical missions to the indigenous peoples of Australia and then New Zealand and other islands of the Pacific, by the (Anglican) CMS and later the Wesleyan Methodists. The Aborigines, who had been devastated by dispossession and disease, were first encouraged to assimilate and then to settle in separate reservations where they were taught English, Christianity and what was regarded as 'civilization'. Despite this beginning, a large proportion of Aborigines profess some form of Christianity today. The Maori in New Zealand are Polynesians who had been there for about a thousand years before they were visited by Dutch and British explorers and later traders from Britain and North America. The Maori were receptive to the Christian message brought by the first settlers, who were CMS missionaries, and rapidly spread it among themselves. Through the initiative and mediation of the missionaries, in 1840 the Maori leaders concluded the ambiguous treaty of Waitangi with the British government. *Pakeha*, or European settlers, soon started arriving from Britain and Australia, accompanied by clergy, mainly Anglican and Church of Scotland (Presbyterian). French Marist missionary priests ministered to the Catholics among them. When settlers occupied land they regarded as their own according to the treaty, many Maori, led by Christian converts inspired by the Old Testament stories of Israel, defended it against British troops (and some other Maori) in the New Zealand Wars. When the missionaries supported the government's use of troops against Maori, there was a breakdown of trust between them. Maori turned to their own prophets who claimed to receive visions from Jehovah. Their indigenous movements, such as Pai Marire, Ringatu and Ratana, syncretized the biblical language of prophecy with traditional Maori beliefs. However, today neo-Pentecostal churches are growing among the Maori, such as 'Destiny' which is theologically conservative Evangelical and has its own political party to defend Maori rights according to their interpretation of the treaty of Waitangi (Ross 2005: 154–7).

Settler Christianity in both Australia and New Zealand stayed very closely bound to Britain and Ireland until the late nineteenth century, especially as most of the clergy were supplied from there. In the twentieth century, Christian influences from North America became relatively stronger (Hilliard 1999: 518–19) and new denominations such as the Churches of Christ, Seventh Day Adventists, Assemblies of God and Mormons entered from across the Pacific. Until the mid-twentieth century, four denominations, autonomously constituted by the twentieth century, were fairly evenly balanced in numbers: Anglican, Methodist, Presbyterian and Catholic. As a result of pressure from non-conformists, the Anglican Church was disestablished in both countries in the mid-nineteenth century. In the new context, and especially in the 'bush' or the 'backblocks', Christians were few and far between, and the need to minister to remote communities led to new mission initiatives of travelling clergy: on horseback, by bike and even plane. Partly as a consequence of this, denominational differences between Protestants became less strongly felt. Methodists and then Presbyterian groups buried their differences in the early twentieth century. In Australia the Uniting Church was formed in Australia by Methodists, Congregationalists and most Presbyterians in 1977. However, partly due to the influence of tensions from the Irish conflicts, the Catholic community has remained quite separate, with most Catholics attending separate schools, for which new indigenous religious congregations were formed. Since the 1960s, secularization has increased and the older denominations have declined – but not as drastically as in Europe – and there are many new churches. Many of these are the result of new migrations. Owing to immigration from southern and eastern Europe, the Catholic Church is now the largest denomination, and various Orthodox churches are also represented. In New Zealand, major Protestant denominations now recognize Maori churches within them with their own structures of government (for the Anglican case see Davidson 2000), and the Pakeha Christians in those churches, who increasingly refer to their country as Aotearoa-New Zealand, have tried to incorporate aspects of Maori spirituality and language into their liturgical life. Pacific Islanders from Samoa, Tonga and the Cook Islands especially have also brought new forms of worship with them. In Australia, where a lower proportion of the indigenous population has survived, attempts have also been made to build continuity between Aboriginal and Christian spirituality (e.g. Porter 1990). Both Australia and New Zealand have been forging greater links with East Asia, and mission activity has been stimulated, for example the Greek Orthodox mission from New Zealand (Tambras 1989). That region was the source of the greatest immigration in the last quarter of the twentieth century, bringing many young Vietnamese, Korean and Chinese churches into urban areas in Australasia. David Tacey, who describes himself as a 'mystical Christian', has suggested that increasingly secular populations are exploring these spiritualities and constructing their own private forms of religion influenced by both: 'The East is teaching us how to transcend the ego, and indigenous people are showing us how to overcome our otherworldliness' (Tacey 2004: 6).

Some of the tribal peoples of the Pacific Islands first heard the Christian message from Catholic missionaries in the seventeenth century, and Protestants in the eighteenth. Unlike most of Asia, here generally 'the Bible came before the flag – the islands being of relatively little interest to traders – and Protestants preceded Catholics' (Davidson 2004: 142). From 1795 several Protestant missions began work in the region, agreeing among themselves to concentrate on different island groups, with the result that today the islands still reflect a patchwork of denominations: British Congregationalists in eastern Polynesia, the Cook Islands and Samoa, English Methodists in Tonga and Fiji, New England Congregationalists in Hawai'i, Kiribati and Micronesia, Anglicans in the smaller Melanesian islands. After the Napoleonic Wars, there was competition from French Catholics – Picpus Fathers and Marists; the latter were particularly anti-Protestant. However, in most cases the impetus for new mission work was the initiative of the islanders themselves, who took it upon themselves to share their 'happiness in Jesus' and explain the story of creation, the advent of sin and forgiveness because of the sacrifice of God's son, and how they were liberated from Satan's power. Tahitians passed on the Christian story to the Cook Islands, Hawai'i, Fiji and Samoa; Cook Islanders and Samoans shared the good news in New Caledonia and Vanuato; Tongans evangelized Fiji (Hilliard 1999: 514–15; Swain and Trompf

1995: 198–205). One outstanding example of the islanders' mission activity is the Melanesian Brotherhood, the largest male religious community in the Anglican Communion, which was founded by Ini Kopuria, a Solomon Islander, in 1900 to win converts in a Melanesian way. In a pattern which is also reminiscent of Jesus' disciples (Lk.10), the lay brothers went out to the communities, accepting their hospitality and offering practical help with fishing, house-building and other tasks, as well as sharing Christian teaching. Many responded to the message when they saw that the brothers were unafraid of devils and ancestral spirits (Carter 1998).

Reasons for conversion vary widely among these very diverse and widespread people, with many different local religions. Many of the concepts of Christianity were very new to the islanders: it was a case of the missionaries having 'to introduce their evangelical world view in order to save Pacific people from the consequences of it' (Davidson 2004: 139). But they were generally impressed by the personal possessions, goods and technology of Europeans; so impressed that some of them believed the goods were the product of divine spirits and they developed 'cargo cults' (later replaced by money cults), especially in Melanesia, and millenarian sects (Swain and Trompf 1995: 167–78, 180–1). In many cases, the islanders decided to burn their traditional religious artefacts and adopt the missionaries' faith. What resulted, at least in rural areas, were many indigenized versions of Christian faith, depending both on the islanders' previous religion and the particular theology of the missionaries. In areas evangelized by the LMS, for example, traditional chants with a 'hymnic quality' are used in worship and called 'prophet songs' (Swain and Trompf 1995: 206). Where Finnish Pentecostals have worked in Papua New Guinea, wailing and shaking characteristic of the traditional religion are part of the worship (1995: 207). Church buildings are often built with local materials in a variety of styles. The lifestyles of most islanders have been transformed by the encounter with Christianity in its European form. In most cases, tribal warfare has stopped – although sorcery has not – and the people are settled in modern villages. The traditional role of the chief has been replaced, at least in the public sphere, with democratic processes. But during the Pacific War many islanders suffered greatly as a result of Japanese invasions and American and Australian counter-acts and atomic testing. In most cases, Protestant churches became self-governing before Western Samoa became the first nation to gain independence in 1962, and Christians were active in independence movements.

Patterns of church life across the Pacific have become much more complex in the last few decades, as many have turned to newer Pentecostal churches – partly because the mission churches, in their faithfulness to the received tradition, had become inflexible, and also because of the modern and prosperous image of the new churches and their affinity with traditional religiosity. In the Pacific as in South East Asia, churches are involved in ethnic movements, for example in Fiji, an island which the indigenous, mainly Christian, Fijians share with Indians encouraged to settle there by the British, who are mostly Hindus. The mountainous island of Papua, the largest land mass of Melanesia, which is divided into Indonesian (West) Papua and the independent nation of Papua New Guinea, has a combined population of about 8 million divided into thousands of different tribal groups, with more than a thousand mutually unintelligible languages. Over the last 130 years, as well as indigenous Pacific Islanders, a wide range of overseas agencies have worked on the island. There continue to be hundreds of specialists in Bible translation – indigenous and foreign – working to translate the Bible into the viable languages. These are also among the poorest people in Asia, and many of the social services of Papua New Guinea are run by Christian agencies.

Doing theology in this 'liquid continent' poses a unique challenge (Forman 1994: 106). The first step is to see Oceania as a whole, with the ocean in the centre as the source of its life (Davidson 2004: 136, paraphrasing Epeli Hau' ofa). The 'father' of Pacific theology, Tongan theologian Sione 'Amanaki Havea, first chairman of the Pacific Council of Churches, coined the term 'coconut theology' (Havea 1987: 14–15). However, modernity has changed island life so much that 'A tin of cola replaces a coconut' (Fepai Kolia quoted in Davidson 2004: 151) and there is now a need to connect theologically the traditions with modern developments. Human activity and natural catastrophe, very often related, have wreaked havoc on the natural environment of the Pacific in many places and are a major concern of the churches. The Pacific Conference of Churches and the Catholic Bishops' Conference of the Pacific have been raising the issues of mining, prospecting, weapons-testing and global warming in the international forums, since the end of the Second World War. The WCC has taken up these concerns, encouraging Christians to be co-creators and co-stewards in God's economy (WCC (Pacific) 1991; cf. Boseto 1995: 183). In the 2004 Otin Taai (Sunrise) declaration, Pacific churches together committed themselves 'to care for the earth as our response to God's love for creation'. They affirmed an affinity between biblical teaching on creation and traditional Pacific Island stories of the interrelatedness of the whole earth. Reflecting on the story of Noah, they concluded that God's rainbow promise was not a guarantee against flooding in the future but an invitation to respond by reducing the human causes of climate change (available on WCC website).

Minority and migration in West and Central Asia

Philip Jenkins draws attention to the fact that the 'Pacific rim', from South Korea to New Zealand and Chile to Alaska, increasingly looks like a 'Christian Arc' (2002: 102) – and he omits to mention the overwhelmingly Christian populations of the islands in the middle (cf. Davidson 2004: 136). Considering Asia, there could also be said to be a 'Muslim band' right across Asia from Turkey through the Middle East and the Gulf to Pakistan and Bangladesh, then across the Bay of Bengal to southern Thailand, Malaysia, Indonesia and the south-western part of the Philippines. It stretches northwards also into Central Asia and north-west China. In most of these countries Christians are few. Most of them were occupied by Muslim powers by the fifteenth century. The effect on Christians within conquered areas of the change of ruler was varied. Christians were encouraged to convert to Islam but otherwise allowed to practise their faith as long as they surrendered their arms, paid a poll tax, refrained from criticizing Muhammad and the Qur'an, and made no public display of their religion. Muslims who converted to Christianity risked being killed. While the system of *dhimmi* offered protection for Christian (and Jewish) minorities, it was a 'marginalizing protection' (El-Zahlaoui 1989: 99), but when European treatment of minorities in the Middle Ages is considered, the verdict is that 'it was generally better to be a Christian or a Jew in an Islamic society than a Jew or Muslim in a Christian society' (Armour 2002: 29). Gradually, however, over the next few centuries the pressures on Christians increased, and the majority of Christians under Islamic rule converted or were absorbed by marriage. Nevertheless, substantial Christian communities remain in Muslim lands to this day, the churches being the main way in which the different identities and heritages of the various peoples were preserved.

The new Central Asian republics of Kazakhstan, Kyrgyzstan, Tajikistan, Turkmenistan and Uzbekistan all have significant Christian minorities, mostly Russian Orthodox with some Ukrainian. The freedom of religion since the end of Soviet domination has seen the revival of Orthodox Christianity and a great rise in practice of Islam in all these countries. There have been some attempts at Islamization, especially in Kyrgyzstan, but in most cases the Orthodox Church has a good relationship with Muslim leaders, born of centuries of coexistence. The same cannot be said for many of the Evangelical and Pentecostal churches which have sprung up since 1991, as a result of missions from Asia and the West as well as local initiative. The Orthodox Christians are generally united with Muslims in opposing these. Among the newer missions, South Koreans are particularly active, especially as there are substantial Korean minorities in Uzbekistan and Kazakhstan, some of whom are Christians. In some places Roman Catholic, Lutheran and other churches serve minority groups originally from Poland, Germany and other parts of Europe. The extent of religious freedom for Christians varies greatly from country to country.

There are no known Christians in Afghanistan and have hardly been any witnessing communities in the seven centuries since Nestorian Christianity was expelled by Timur (Tamarlane). Since then it has been a capital offence for any Afghan to convert to Christianity. The Persian Church of the first millennium spread the Christian gospel across Asia but today there are hardly any ethnic Persian Christians in Iran, although there are many in diaspora in the United States and Europe. During the Iranian Revolution of 1978–9 and after it, Christians suffered badly. For example, the Anglican bishop Hassan Dehqani-Tafti escaped with his life but his son was shot and killed (Dehqani-Tafti 1981). Most churches had some or all of their properties and institutions (hospitals and schools) confiscated. The Islamic Law instituted after the Revolution protects Christians, and allows for their representation in the legislature, but cases of conversion of Muslims to Christianity have led to martyrdom of the convert and those who baptized him or her. After centuries of Christianity and different influences, Christians in Iran and most other Middle Eastern countries are of many different kinds. In Iran, among the less than 1 per cent of the population who are Christian, the Orthodox are Armenian, Assyrian, Russian and Greek; the Roman Catholics worship according to three different rites: Chaldean (Assyrian Christians in communion with Rome), Latin, and Armenian Uniate; Protestants are Anglican, Presbyterian, and various independent groups, some of them worshipping clandestinely. Christians have been in Iraq virtually since the inception of Christianity, and several groups of Christians today still use an ancient Syriac liturgy that was indigenous to Mesopotamia: Chaldean Catholics, Assyrians (Nestorians), Syrian Catholics and Syrian Orthodox (Jacobites). The first two of these are now in communion with one another following a landmark declaration by John Paul II in 1994 (O'Mahony 2004a). There are other Orthodox – Armenian and Greek – small minority communities of Catholics following other rites, and several Protestant groups. Under former president Saddam Hussein, the Ba'athist regime protected Christians – 3 per cent of the population – from Islamizers and they had their own community law and schools. Saddam's deputy prime minister, Tariq Aziz, was from the Christian community. But among its other devastating effects, the US-led invasion which toppled Saddam's government also unleashed violence against Christians, causing tens or hundreds of thousands of them to flee, mostly to Syria.

The Arabian peninsula is the homeland of Islam, from which all Christians were expelled in the seventh century. The seven countries currently occupying it do not permit conversion to Christianity or allow clergy into the country, except perhaps to minister to foreign nationals on an occasional basis, so Christian activities there have been restricted to social service. Since most of these countries are now exceedingly rich with oil wealth, few Christian charities are now working anywhere except in Yemen. Many Christians live in Arabia – they form 10 per cent or more of the population in Kuwait, Bahrain, Qatar and the United Arab Emirates – but most are expatriates. The majority are Catholics; many of them are domestic workers or work in the oil industry; they include Westerners and Asians. While there they usually have to rely on lay leadership, if it is possible for them to meet at all. In Saudi Arabia particularly, Christian meetings, particularly of Asians, may be broken up and their leaders expelled or even executed (Johnstone and Mandryk 2001: 557). Bahrain is the most relaxed country for Christians; it has an American Mission Hospital and an Arab Christian community. Some Christian agencies encourage Christian evangelists with a mission to Muslims to enter these countries as 'tent-makers' (Acts 18.3); that is, to take secular employment and make use of opportunities to witness. To do so is exceedingly difficult and dangerous – not least to those local people who may respond to the message. As Muslim communities grow in the West, and demand increasing freedom to practise their religion, and even live by their own law, Christians feel entitled to ask why Christian minorities in the Middle East are denied these rights.

The three nations between the Black and Caspian Seas – Azerbaijan,

Armenia and Georgia – have some of the most ancient churches in the world. The Udin Christians of Azerbaijan, who first believed in the third century, were left largely undisturbed by Muslim invaders in a remote part of the country. A few thousand still remain today in a context of Islamic resurgence since the end of the Soviet era. Azerbaijan is in conflict with its neighbour Armenia over the enclave of Nagorno-Karabakh, home of a large community of Armenian Orthodox Christians. The first nation to declare itself Christian, Armenia has changed hands between several empires. In the late nineteenth century the Armenians sought independence from the Ottoman empire with the encouragement of wealthy Armenians in Russia, with the result that they were persecuted by the Turks from the mid-1890s, culminating in what many Western nations have called genocide in 1915–17. By the end of the First World War, the Armenians in Turkish territory had been completely annihilated. As a result of the genocide, most Armenians live outside the state, many of them in the West. Today the Catholicos of All Armenians, in Etchmiadzin, Armenia, exercises responsibility not only over the 3 million Orthodox in Armenia but also over an estimated diaspora of twice that number. Under Catherine the Great in the late eighteenth century, the Russians helped revive the church in neighbouring Georgia, founded in 330 and distinguished for its literature and church architecture in the eleventh and twelfth centuries but fragmented by Mongol invasion. In the nineteenth century it underwent a process of Russification, including the submission of its leadership to the Russian patriarch. National resistance was led by the church, but although autocephaly was restored in 1943, under Soviet rule the church had little freedom until the 1980s. The church grew rapidly in the post-Soviet era when the president and former Communist leader Eduard Shevardnadze was baptized. Christians form more than half of the population of this still unstable country, in which there is a substantial Muslim community as well. In all three nations, there are growing Protestant and Pentecostal minorities: mainly Baptists in Georgia and Armenia and independent charismatic fellow-ships in Azerbaijan.

The Christian history of the Holy Land, where the central figure of Christianity and the Christian faith were born, is very long and complex. The region of Syria, Lebanon, Jordan and Israel and the Occupied Territories is home to many different Christian groups, from the most ancient churches in the world to very new groups. Even before the heightened tension caused by the Iraq War, the decline of the ancient Christian population in the Holy Land – a continuous process over 1,400 years since Muslim armies first moved out of Arabia – had been noticeably accelerating (Dalrymple 1998: 453–4; Jenkins 2002: 169–70). Today that situation is catastrophic, with every country in the region reporting an exodus of Christians, usually the best educated, mainly to the West. Christian leaders are worried that Christianity in the Middle East could soon be extinct (e.g. El-Assal 1998: 88; Williams 2006). Those that remain include more than 1 million Christians in Syria, where the largest church is the Greek Orthodox Church. This is an Arab community worshipping in Arabic but led by Greeks, a fact that causes not inconsiderable tension. There are also Syrian and Armenian Orthodox churches. Catholics are the next largest group but they follow six different rites. The same six rites are celebrated in Lebanon, which has the largest Christian minority of any country in the Middle East (about 40 per cent). There the Maronite Catholics, a group which originally seceded from the Greek Orthodox Church in the seventh century, predominate. Despite the fact that the Maronite population is barely the largest any more, the community holds a privileged political position, a situation resented by other groups. There are many different Orthodox groups in Lebanon, plus a significant Anglican community, and Evangelical churches founded by nineteenth-century American missions. Christians in Jordan are mainly Greek Orthodox congregations of Palestinian Arabs. Many other churches are present working among Palestinian refugees.

Many Christians were among those Palestinians displaced by the creation of the state of Israel in Palestine in 1948, and again in the 1967 war by the Israeli annexation of East Jerusalem, Gaza and the West Bank. Hundreds of thousands are still living with 4 million other Palestinians in the refugee camps. Within Israel-Palestine, Christians – mainly Arab – are concentrated in Galilee and the Occupied Territories. Better-educated Palestinian Christians have emigrated and are now no more than 2 per cent of the whole population. Nevertheless most of the ancient churches maintain a presence in Israel-Palestine: Catholics are the majority following seven different rites; the Greek Orthodox, which claims precedence as the direct successor of James, leader of the very first church, is now, due to emigration, reduced to being the second largest church; the Russian and Armenian Orthodox churches and all the Oriental (monophysite) Orthodox Churches – Armenian, Coptic, Ethiopian and Syrian – are represented. Several Protestant churches have a long-standing missionary presence: the Church of Scotland dates back to 1939; the Christian and Missionary Alliance goes back to 1890; the Anglican church (present since 1820) was strengthened during the period of the British mandate but is now the Episcopal Church in Jerusalem and the Middle East; Lutherans (present since 1860) work in the West Bank, the Church of the Nazarene (since 1921) in East Jerusalem; but the Southern Baptists (present since 1911) form the largest church, and there are also other Baptist churches not related to the Southern Baptist Convention. There are other missionary groups, mostly from the United States, some of which promote a Zionist position, and there are Messianic Jewish congregations as well (Feher 1998: 165).

The Palestinian question and the status of the city of Jerusalem are central to the politics of the whole West Asian region, if not the world, but Christians are divided on these issues. The holy places in Jerusalem and Bethlehem are managed internationally by centuries-old agreements between various Orthodox churches and the Roman Catholic Church. Arab Christians often feel hurt that the Christian tourists who visit the holy places rarely encounter the local Christian communities, most of whom are imprisoned by Israeli occupation. In political discussion about a solution to the crisis, the presence of Palestinian Christians is often ignored and all Arabs are (wrongly) assumed to be Muslim. On the other hand, there are Christians in many parts of the world actively campaigning for the rights of Palestinian Christians. Although the WCC (in process of formation) supported the establishment of the state of Israel and helped Jews to emigrate there, it now has a special programme of 'accompaniment' to highlight the plight of the Palestinians and in 2006 launched a new Palestine Israel Ecumenical Forum. However, many Evangelical Christians are influenced by US-based Christian Zionism to support the security of the state of Israel over the Palestinian cause. These Protestant Christians tend to ignore the views of the ancient churches, believing that they are not 'bible-based' or living churches. According to its website, the International Christian Embassy Jerusalem, for example, 'offers relevant information to help Christians and others gain greater appreciation of the Biblical credentials behind the modern-day Jewish restoration to the land of their forefathers and its unique role in world redemption'. The suffering of the Palestinians is keenly felt around the Muslim world and a focus of Muslim anger directed at the West (Chapman 2004), which to many Muslims is indistinguishable from the old Christendom (Armour 2002: 166). Eastern Orthodox Christianity has had no political links to the West, yet it is these Christians – some of them Palestinians themselves, who have been present among Muslim majorities for centuries – who are suffering as a result of this. Many have left but some will remain. When asked how they had endured after being forced from their homes in Turkey after the massacre of Syrian Orthodox there in 1915, an elderly man in Aleppo replied, 'To remain faithful we must be conscious of ourselves; love and help each other; encourage the youth to obey and serve the church; and study the tradition. In this way we can keep our identity' (quoted in Chaillot 1998: 149).

The Eastern Orthodox churches share much in common with their Muslim neighbours: the same land, history and destiny; indeed the churches have been shaped by their experience of living among Muslims (Keshishian 1992: 104). There has been a long dialogue with Islam going back to John of Damascus, whose defence of icons also served to distinguish Christianity from Islam, and Gregory Palamas, whose Christian Hesychasm is remarkably similar to Muslim *dhikr* (El-Zahlaoui 1989: 99; Peters 2003: 304–5). Christians played an important role in the first renaissance of the Arab world and this leads Syrian Orthodox priest Joseph El-Zahlaoui from Damascus to believe that, despite the difficulties of today, Christian witness 'lies in the ability of Christians to remain an essential qualitative dimension in the life and development of the Islamic community'. In particular he sees the Christian contribution as lying in the theology of the incarnation, which by resolving the tension between God and man is able to help maintain a balance between the humanism of the West, which tends to 'kill God', and the theocracy of Islam, which in its extreme form 'even kills the human being' (1989: 96, 98). But, as Alexander Malik from Pakistan complains, Islam leaves very little room for manoeuvre because Muslims must give precedence to their own Qur'anic Christology, which 'corrects' Christian Christology, and furthermore, they have their own 'Christ' in the person of the Prophet (Malik 1993: 79). Nevertheless, he insists the Christian must confess Christ, but advises that this should be Christ as revealed in the Bible and stripped of any other offence. The mission of the Eastern Orthodox churches is not aimed at the conversion of Muslims who, as Aram Keshishian, leader of the Armenian Apostolic Church in Lebanon, puts it, 'are different in many respects and intend to remain different'. But neither does it mean compromising the Christian gospel. In this very difficult situation, Orthodox leaders stress the importance of the witness of life before the witness of the word. Keshishian stresses that dialogue is 'not a conceptual notion but an existential reality', 'a way of life' (1992: 103–5). Doing Christian deeds and having a clear conscience is a prerequisite for authentic testimony (1 Pet. 3.15; El-Zahlaoui 1989: 102–4). So the churches are urged to continue to serve the wider society, through medical, social and educational means, as they have done for centuries (El-Zahlaoui 1989: 100; Keshishian 1992: 101) but through the local resources of the churches themselves because Western aid is divisive and raises Muslim suspicions. The threat to the survival of the ancient churches makes their unity of the utmost importance (Keshishian 1992: 101, 105; El-Zahlaoui 1989: 102). Furthermore, unity is not only a practical necessity but integral to the Christian message in the Middle East because what distinguishes the Christian God from Allah is that God is one in three and three in one (El-Zahlaoui 1989: 103). For Orthodox Christians the Eucharist, communion in the Triune God, is the primary expression of both unity and mission because it is both an ingathering of the people (representatives of the world) and also the outgoing of the church into the world as the bread is shared among all and for all (cf. Keshishian 1992: 100).

Study Questions and Further Readings

- Why has Christianity been attractive to Chinese in China and elsewhere in the last 50 years?
- In what ways have Indian Christians related to caste in India?
- Why is Christian conversion such an important issue in so many Asian contexts?
- How would you explain the variations in response to Christianity across Asia?
- What are the causes of the difficulties Christians face in the Middle East?
- Discuss some of the indigenous forms of church in Asian contexts.

Kim, Sebastian C. H. (ed.) (in press), *Christian Theology in Asia*. Cambridge: Cambridge University Press.

Moffett, Samuel Hugh (1998, 2005), *A History of Christianity in Asia: Vols I & II*. Maryknoll, NY: Orbis.

O'Mahony, Anthony (ed.) (2004), *Eastern Christianity: Studies in Modern History, Religion and Politics*. London: Melisende.

Sugirtharajah, R. S. (ed.) (1995), *Voices from the Margin: Interpreting the Bible in the Third World* (2nd edn). London: SPCK.

Sunquist, Scott W. (ed.) (2001), *A Dictionary of Asian Christianity*. Grand Rapids, MI: Wm B. Eerdmans.

7 World Christianity

The coming of world Christianity

Our survey of Christianity continent by continent has demonstrated that Christianity is a world religion because it is present across the globe in countless local expressions which are linked by criss-crossing networks. We can identify some emerging features of world Christianity. First, Christianity is now represented in some shape or form in virtually every country in the world. The major exception to this widening spread is the Middle East and some other Muslim countries. Furthermore, it is increasingly also the case that every major expression of Christian faith is present in each country, as the faith spreads and migration leads to societies becoming less homogeneous. Politically, this means that Christians speak with many voices. At grassroots level, many Christians relate only to their local church and may not be aware of much beyond that. Where different churches coexist within the same locality, as they do increasingly, they may not be much aware of one another. The local ecumenism of parts of western Europe is something of an exception worldwide. Thus it seems that, unless some common threat brings them together or governments take initiatives to unify Christians (as in China), Christians in any one country rarely form a single bloc, still less across regions or worldwide. In discussing 'African Christianity' for example, we do not mean to suggest that Christianity in that continent is uniform or united but that it is indigenous. Since Christianity is essentially polycentric and multi-traditional, the greater the indigeneity the more diversity we would expect to see. There are many trans-national and even global organizations and networks that bring Christian leaders of a common persuasion together, but the prospect of a single 'world church' or another Christendom seems remote.

Second, Christian faith is present in society in many different levels. It is both a personal faith and a public confession. It is practised in homes and in public buildings. It is the faith of both poor and wealthy. The profile(s) of a church in any particular society depends on its particular theology and also the attitude of the state: churches may be established institutions in Europe or underground groups in China, mutually supportive communities in Africa or protest groups in Latin America, businesses in North America or caste groups in India. Given the opportunity and an interest, any kind of church can participate in public life, including those often thought to be apolitical, such as Evangelical and Pentecostal churches.

Third, Christianity is spread primarily by local believers and developed by them in local ways. Attention to the activities of foreign missionaries has tended to obscure this fact, and the present diversity of world Christianity is testimony to it. Within the denominations that resulted from foreign mission activity, local believers such as black evangelists and Bible women have built up the church, although those who brought the gospel were often reluctant to transfer leadership. Nowadays it is rare to find foreigners in the leadership of former colonial churches. Although there are usually ongoing links with the founding church, these may now be mutual and, in a globalized world, churches anywhere in the world may have multiple international links. Countless new churches and denominations have been founded in parts of the world once considered by Europeans 'mission fields', which are entirely locally staffed and funded.

Fourthly, there are strong global flows of Christian influence across the world. Some of these appear to follow political and economic globalization. Roman Catholicism, Protestantism and Ecumenism arose in Europe, Evangelicalism and Fundamentalism arose in North America and these forms of Christianity are embraced in other continents; however, the strength of all of these movements arguably now lies outside their continents of origin because of the numbers involved. For example, 45 per cent of all Catholics live in Latin America, so the policies of the Catholic Church cannot simply be dictated according to European concerns (Jenkins 2002: 118). Within the Anglican Communion, majority African opposition to homosexuality is now putting pressure on North Americans and European Anglicans not only on this issue but also in much wider matters of biblical interpretation and the meaning of Christian Communion. Furthermore, even economic and political flows are not always from North America or Europe. A strong South Korean vision for world evangelization has developed alongside Korean economic power, and large Christian communities in other increasingly powerful countries have overseas missionary movements, such as Brazil and Nigeria; it is not impossible that China could become another. Most importantly, and arguably more characteristically of Christianity,

Christian influence flows worldwide along many other currents that arise from below rather than above. The contemporary Pentecostal–charismatic movement demonstrates this most clearly. Its growth could be regarded as Americanization (Martin 1990: 280), but it could equally be seen as an Africanization, a Latinization, or even a Shamanization from Asia of world Christianity. Pentecostalism is essentially missionary (Anderson 2007), yet it is a movement with virtually no 'visible means of support' such as 'the force of a great leader', 'a captivating theology', a 'national or social class impatient for expression' (Wilson 1999: 105), political ideology (Martin 2002: 167) or the sponsorship of wealthy individuals. Yet it is among the largest and most widespread movements on the planet (Wilson 1999: 105). The spread of Christian faith from below occurs because Christianity is primarily a people-movement. Although non-personal forms of communication are used in evangelism, the development of world Christianity as described here is largely the result of personal contact, the formation of communities and migration. Christians today move around the world as the first Christians moved around the Roman empire – for employment, as slaves or domestic servants or due to persecution. As they do so, they share their faith. One of the unforeseen consequences of contemporary globalization may be the further spread of Christianity from below.

Fifthly, it is increasingly difficult to identify a geographical centre of Christian faith. Jerusalem and Bethlehem continue to have special meaning because of their associations with the historical Jesus, but they do not function as organizational centres, and most Christians never visit them. The Roman Catholic Church has a clear centre in Rome, but this allegiance is not shared by other Christians. The Orthodox churches have always been multi-centric, and each of the various Protestant denominations has its own headquarters. The most recent movement is the most difficult of all to place; even its origins are in dispute. US Pentecostals tend to maintain that Pentecostalism originated in the USA (e.g. Robeck 1993: 170), but they remain divided as to where: Topeka (1900) or Azusa Street (1906). Some maintain a theory of multiple origins, on the grounds that there were many outbreaks of revival in different parts of the world with similar characteristics in that period, including Wales, India, Korea and Chile, resulting in a global movement (Sepúlveda 1999; Wilson 1999). Other churches, particularly indigenous churches in Africa but also some in Asia, are co-opted by some scholars under the umbrella of 'Pentecostalism' because of phenomenological similarities only. They do not have any historical or contemporary affiliation with Pentecostal denominations. It is a case of 'categories originating from the North being used to explain and somehow take credit for what is going on in the South' (Robert 2000: 57). Historically and functionally, Pentecostalism is a multi-centred movement (cf. Anderson 2004: 170–1; Cox 1996: 64–5).

Lastly, looking at Christianity continent by continent shows that it is not a monolithic extension of Western power but a lively meeting-place of many different expressions of faith, which do not have a common political, economic or cultural agenda but only a shared allegiance to Jesus Christ. This allegiance is informed by the Bible (in many languages and forms) and by knowledge of Christian tradition that has been passed on in some way, either through casual contact with other Christians or through intentional mission activities. The message has been received in ways often very different from the transmitted version and, primarily through the efforts of local people, has become part of different societies. The spread and fragmentation of Christianity over two thousand years makes it impossible to trace a single historical tradition. There are different confessions of faith, each arising from the response to the Christian gospel in a particular historical context. However, these now exist within very different social and cultural settings from the ones that gave them birth and are taking on local features, so that it is now possible to talk about 'African' and 'Asian' Christianity as well as about Roman Catholicism, Lutheranism and the Baptists. A regional approach, which has long been the pattern in the Orthodox churches, has been adopted by the Roman Catholic Church, which has bishops' conferences for different continents and, in the decade before the year 2000, held consultations in each continent. The WCC also encourages regional ecumenism, especially for theological and advocacy purposes (Tsetsis 2004). Christianity must now be understood geographically as well as historically, ethnically as well as confessionally, locally as well as globally.

Regional expressions of Christianity

Christianity in Europe has had a rather different history from elsewhere because, following the pattern of the Roman empire, it was favoured by rulers and governments and grew alongside the ruling powers. The Roman Catholic Church and the Orthodox Church developed systematic theologies in European contexts. With the encouragement of monarchs and rulers, the peoples of Europe were evangelized through the work of apostles or mission-aries: 'the patron saints', monastics, friars, priests, preachers and revivalists. The Protestant churches arising after the Reformation became, after the wars of religion, linked with particular ethnic groups and nation-states. There were occasions when the churches were deprived of temporal power under the Moors, the Mongols or the French Revolution, and there were some Christian communities who dissented from the established confession, but generally speaking it was only in the twentieth century that churches of Europe underwent what has been the experience of most Christians down the centuries: a climate indifferent or hostile to Christian faith, and marginalization from political power. When the nations of Europe gained global ascendancy, in their position of shared power, the churches of Europe carried the gospel to other parts of the world using several different models: 'missionary war', 'radical inculturation', colonial 'civilizing' and church planting, the 'Social Gospel' and 'proclamation'. This resulted in the extension of European churches to most other parts of the globe, largely without regard to the ancient churches already present in Asia and Africa or other pre-existing traditions and beliefs. However, modernity, in the form of secular science and secularist or atheistic philosophies, challenged European Christian confi-dence and resulted in changed circumstances: privatized religion in the west and suppression under atheistic Communism in the east. Movements toward church unity and the rise of the Ecumenical movement were a major Christian response to Europe's fractured political experience. In the post-War, postcolonial period, the churches in western Europe are still coming to terms with their decreasing numbers overall, a new relationship with churches in other parts of the world and the resurgence of other religions. Since 1989, in central and eastern Europe, the churches no longer face persecution and are popular, but face new challenges in democratic and capitalist societies. Christians long separated from one another are brought together in the new Europe, along with an increasing variety of Christians from other parts of the globe, and challenged to live out their faith in a pluralist society.

Since the time of the ancient Ethiopians, whose descendants still practise an ancient Hebraic form of Christianity today, Africans have claimed Christianity as African and understood it as the answer to the questions they were asking, questions about spiritual power, deliverance, liberation and life. Since the Bible was reintroduced to Africa, sub-Saharan Africans have recognized themselves and their societies particularly in the narratives, genealogies and wisdom of the Hebrew Bible and found in Jesus Christ one who revealed the God they already knew, became part of that history as an ancestor and at the same time confronted its demons. Christianity has grown less in areas already reached by Islam, some of which are flashpoints of religio-ethnic tensions; and in the countries of north Africa, which were Christian in the first seven centuries, there is almost no Christian witness except for the Coptic community in Egypt. African encounters with Christianity in European forms were seldom affirming to African identity; on the contrary, they were often experiences of aggression and domination. Nevertheless, a majority of black Africans appropriated what was useful in the message translated into their context, celebrated the freedom it brought and some made it into a tool of liberation from oppressors and of social transformation. Most did this from within the framework of the colonial churches, which they now lead, but others exercised a prophetic ministry from outside in African initiated churches. In South Africa different kinds of churches (though not all of them) worked together to overthrow the system of apartheid and participated in the process of truth and reconciliation. Although traditional African spirituality was mostly condemned by the churches, aspects of it were used in the new churches and have found their way into the older ones, giving African Christianity a unique aspect, particularly in terms of music, bodily participation in worship, and expectation of God's involvement in the whole of life. Sometimes described as 'Pentecostalism', in most cases this is a development independent of Western Pentecostal denominations. Particularly as developed in west Africa, these new churches are growing worldwide. The legacy of the slave trade and colonial exploitation, an unequal global economic system, disease and climate change pose huge social problems, within which overseas missions and local churches are working to bring relief and improvement. In the context of corrupt leadership within the churches and in government, some African Christians have taken risks to speak out for justice and others have sought to exercise political power in the name of Christ. In the context of late capitalism there has been a shift in the concern of popular Christianity from health to wealth; many African church leaders and theologians struggle to balance this preoccupation with emphasis on education and ethical behaviour. With confidence in their faith, African Christians increasingly question the descendants of those who brought the gospel in the colonial period, rethinking the gospel for themselves and raising difficult questions about biblical interpretation, sexuality, and reparation for past injustice.

Christians – mostly Protestant – came to North America from Europe looking for freedom to practise their religion, and a place to establish a godly society. Believing God had led them to this 'promised land', they spread across the vast continent, displacing the Native Americans. The presence of groups of Christians from different ethnic groups and church traditions led to a situation of Christian pluralism, known as denominationalism. Among the majority Protestants, this pluralism and resistance to colonial authority encouraged the growth of independent local churches as the primary expression of the body of Christ. These were only loosely connected to the traditions of the older churches and under the influence of the Puritans, but invested authority in the Bible as the Word of God. In Canada, where there are relatively more Catholics and a different political context, Christians across the country valued their connections more. In both countries the traditional European relationship of church and state was severed and replaced with voluntary religion into which people 'converted' from a state of sin and, increasingly, with a market of religious options in competition with one another. From the eighteenth century a series of revival movements further developed the independent, pragmatic faith of the settlers into the form of Christianity known there as Evangelicalism, which is conversionist, activist, biblicist and crucicentric. Evangelicals resist aspects of modernity they see as threatening to Christian faith, and the Fundamentalist movement represents an extreme form of protest at the perceived loss of the authority of the Bible and moral underpinnings for society. Despite predictions of secularization, most North Americans practise a form of faith in Jesus Christ. This is private and personal but they expect it will be respected in the public sphere and resist legislation that impinges on areas they consider matters of religious freedom. Africans brought as slaves to North America and the Caribbean adapted European Christianity to their own needs in the 'invisible institution' of slave religion which developed, after emancipation, into black churches and denominations. It was from within this context of black Christianity that the civil rights movement was born in the United States, which was also challenged to develop its African identity further through the black theology movement. African identity also expressed itself in the most influential Pentecostal revival, at Azusa Street, which widely influenced other churches worldwide through the Pentecostal–charismatic movement. In the Caribbean, black churches are at the crossroads of 'the black Atlantic' and combine African, European, North American, Latin American and even Asian influences in a unique historic situation. Many of the more recent migrants to the continent from Asia and Latin America are also Christians and have introduced still greater variety into the North American church scene, while also increasing the size of the single largest denomination, the Roman Catholic Church.

The Iberian *conquistadores* and the priests who supported them were mandated both to exploit and to Christianize the land and native peoples of Central and South America, Latinizing them according to the feudal, militarized pattern of churches in Spain and Portugal. While realizing their goals of wealth and faith, they crushed those of the Indians, decimated their populations and destroyed their societies; only a few defended them. Nevertheless aspects of the spirituality of the indigenous people live on in the practices of Latin American Catholicism. The Virgin of Guadalupe became a powerful symbol of indigenous faith, and in the veneration of Mary an aspect of the traditional reverence for the feminine was retained, which can be used to subvert the cult of *machismo. Machismo* is blamed for many of the social ills of Latin America, encourages an attitude of *marianismo* (which feminists challenge by rereading the biblical stories of Mary) and is also blamed for some aspects of Latin American Catholicism such as the perennial shortage of priests. In the new society in which peoples of European descent were ranked above native Americans, and in which Africans were enslaved, the Latin Church established a close relationship with the elite. The power of the church was contested in different countries after independence in the nineteenth century, but in the mid-twentieth century it was still the case that the church tended to support the powerful. This was challenged by the advent of liberation theology in the 1970s, which declared God to be on the side of the poor and held up the ideal of justice. Brought about by a combination of the bishops' attendance at Vatican II and the priests' conscientization along with many grassroots Christians in 'base communities', liberation theology changed the church (although not structurally) and spread worldwide. Christians campaigned for human rights, and in most cases the church supported the people against military dictatorships. The rise during the twentieth century of the *Evangelicos* eroded the near religious monopoly of the Catholic Church. *Evangelicos* are mainly Pentecostals, whose popularity is variously explained as due to gradual Anglicization, political interference from North America or a protest against Catholicism, but it is also due to the Pentecostal experience of power over evil and the hope of a new life. The Vatican hierarchy was unsettled by the power of the base communities, the use of Marxist analysis and other aspects of the new theology, and the growth of Pentecostalism. The more conservative bishops it appointed, who now operate in a situation that is more religiously plural and democratic, have defended the traditional status of the church, opposed abortion and supported traditional feminine roles. There has also been some restructuring to be closer to the people and meet some of the needs indicated by the turn to Pentecostalism by encouraging popular religion under the church's umbrella.

Asia is very diverse and the presence of churches is very patchy. In general, the response to Christianity has been among populations following local religions and not the other world religions, which all originated in that continent. The major exception to this is South Korea. Many Chinese also, both within and outside China itself, have converted to Christianity, and the Chinese church is destined to have a big influence worldwide. Two concerns are characteristic of Asian Christianity: religions and poverty; and Christians are divided about whether Christian mission should address itself to the religious leaders (inculturation) or the needs of the masses (liberation). Asia is a highly religious continent, and Christians also are inclined to be religious but in a distinctive way. In the Confucian context of north-east Asia, they have made great sacrifices for their faith and struggled for justice and human rights; at a popular level the churches help people deal with domestic problems through a life-affirming spirituality which relates to popular Buddhism, Taoism and Shamanism. In South East Asia, Christians are an overwhelming, but poor, majority in the Philippines, East Timor and parts of Indonesia. In Indochina they are a small minority (not so small in Vietnam) in predominantly Buddhist contexts. In Malaysia and Indonesia, Christians are concerned about increasing Islamization. In south Asia, Christianity has a history stretching back to the first centuries, and a deep theological engagement has taken place with philosophical Hinduism. More recently the churches, the majority of whose members converted from low- or outcaste groups have been vocal in their opposition to caste and practical in their support for liberation movements. Hindu nationalism has caused Christians to reflect on their complicity with colonialism and also brought political restrictions on further conversions to Christianity. Many of the peoples of the Pacific Islands embraced the Christian gospel with enthusiasm, partly because it seemed to offer the material benefits sought through indigenous religious means. Churches were an integral part of the reconfiguration of Pacific society in the twentieth century and today try to raise the concerns of the Pacific nations, particularly about the environmental degradation of the ocean and its habitats. The – originally European – Christian populations of Australia and New Zealand are influenced both by the asceticism of East Asian religions and also by the holistic spirituality of the Pacific Islanders – which is mediated also through the spirituality of their migrant churches. This, combined with North American cultural influence, has led to experimentation with new and alternative forms of religion. West Asia is the birthplace of Christianity and home of some of the most ancient churches. For centuries Christian communities lived under the protective but marginalizing rule of Islam, for the most part in peace. However, the last two centuries have seen increasing discrimination against Christians along with a resurgence of militant Islam. In country after country, the numbers of Christians are decreasing, partly by emigration, and the future of Christian presence in the region is altogether uncertain.

Global meeting points: Communion, Bible, spirituality, mission

In view of the tendency for Christianity to exhibit regional differences, its polycentric nature, and the different trans-national movements we have been looking at, we might ask what makes world Christianity one, and if there is anything that draws Christians across the world together.

The Eucharist, Holy Communion or the Lord's Supper was one of the signs, and for most Christians the chief sign, of unity in Christ. And this round-table model led to the conciliar model of relationships by which, recognizing the ethnic and geographical diversity of Christianity, the ancient churches met together, representing the whole household of God (*oikoumene*). But although they recognize one another as Christian, the Roman Catholic and Orthodox churches are not in communion with one another today (in the sense of being able to celebrate the Eucharist together and recognizing one another's rites) or with Protestant churches, and many of the latter do not 'communicate' either (although for many Protestants of newer or independent churches Communion is less significant as a sign of unity). One of the hopes which inspired the creation of the WCC was the desire to overcome ancient divisions, which are now expressed doctrinally, and celebrate Communion together. Theologically the church is the body of Christ and it is unthinkable that Christ can be divided (1 Cor. 1.13). The aim of visible church unity is pursued by the Faith and Order movement within the WCC. Its most impressive achievement has been the *Baptism, Eucharist and Ministry* document (1982 – available at www.oikoumene.org), for which, in an unprecedented way, Orthodox, Protestant and Roman Catholic leaders worked together. 'Once unthinkable consensus' was reached on justification by faith, the two natures of Christ and other key areas of doctrinal debate (Kinnamon 2004: 51). An unofficial liturgy (the 'Lima liturgy') was developed from these discussions which has been widely distributed and used, and areas for further discussion were identified. These theological matters are discussed in academic forums and doctrine commissions; however, these tend to be dominated by Christians from the (modern) West. Since 1982, progress toward common Baptism, Eucharist and Ministry has stalled, and one of the main sticking points is the question of ministry: the ordination of women in many of the historic Protestant churches has driven a wedge between them and the Roman Catholic and Orthodox churches. So there continue to be separate Orthodox and Roman Catholic Churches, and there are also 'world communions' of Protestant Christians: the Anglican Communion, the Lutheran World Federation, the World Methodist Council, the World Alliance of Reformed Churches, and several others. The latter meet and work together at different levels and in different areas of church life but they are consultative rather than formulating doctrine and policy.

Many Christians wish to celebrate Communion together and are prevented; others, especially in many newer churches, do not put any limitations on participation in the Eucharist and do not understand what the problem is about. But, whether they share Communion together or not, all Christians read the Bible (in various languages and with minor differences). The Orthodox churches are accustomed to quoting the Church Fathers in their discussions, and Roman Catholics the Scholastic theologians, but when it comes to interaction with Protestants and others the lowest common denominator is the biblical narrative. Christians study and interpret the Bible trans-nationally in their churches, denominations and communions and in a number of other ways. Biblical studies and hermeneutics are studied inter-nationally in universities and seminaries and widely published in books and journals. The academic discourse is in English, Spanish, French, German, Greek, Russian and increasingly in Korean, Tamil and other languages, and Bible commentaries are being developed in different languages and regions. Among church leaders, especially in Ecumenical circles, there is a growth in cross-cultural or inter-cultural reading of the Bible and theologizing. This takes place through world communions and across them through organizations like EATWOT, which brings together Third World theologians. There is a growing literature bringing together readings from different cultural perspectives (e.g. Oduyoye and Vroom 2003; Sugirtharajah 1995).

However, a major rediscovery of the twentieth century (as in the Protestant Reformation) is that the Bible need not be read only at an academic level. Liberation theology and the Pentecostal–charismatic movement particularly have opened up new approaches for lay readers: socio-political readings and narrative readings respectively. The Christians who put most emphasis on Bible study are Evangelicals, for many of whom it is a daily discipline. All Evangelical networks, such as the World Evangelical Alliance, the Lausanne movement and the International Fellowship of Evangelical Students, include biblical studies as a central activity. However, being suspicious of any method which questions the historical truth or teaching of any particular passage, Evangelicals, and Fundamentalists especially, tend to find it hard to appreciate other methods of interpretation. There are widely differing methods of biblical interpretation: whereas Evangelicals insist on the authority of Scripture, liberation theologians make justice the hermeneutical key, feminists cannot countenance any reading which undermines the equality of men and women, liberal theologians emphasize inclusivity (e.g. of homosexuals), and so on. Differences in biblical hermeneutic are a major source of tension not only between Christians in North and South (Jenkins 2006) but between churches in the same region and within churches of the same confession.

Pentecostals, charismatics, many indigenous churches, and mystics from other branches of Christianity point to an experience of the Spirit of God which Christians share because the Holy Spirit is also the Spirit of Christ. However, most groups that emphasize the Holy Spirit have particular ideas about what form authentic spiritual experience should take (K. Kim 2007). For many Pentecostals this involves speaking in tongues; members of African initiated churches look for a particular vitality in worship which they often find lacking in more traditional churches; and mystics tend to emphasize techniques of meditation. Pentecostals and charismatics are connected globally through several different bodies such as the Pentecostal World Fellowship and International Catholic Charismatic Renewal Services. Christians with a particular concern for spirituality meet in international communities, such as Taizé in France or Shantivanam Ashram in India. Openness to the work of the Spirit can cut across traditional church lines. Educated Pentecostals, for example, find much in common theologically with the Orthodox churches, which have a more developed pneumatology than the Western churches. However, Harvey Cox's suggestion (1996) that Pentecostals, charismatics and indigenous churches all participate in a 'primordial spirituality' does not translate into a mutual recognition. Pentecostal–charismatic Christians distinguish themselves clearly from the indigenous religions from which their members may have come. Christians differ also in the scope they allow for the Spirit's work. Some limit the Spirit to their own church; others are more generous to other Christians (e.g. Pinnock 1996) and some allow for the Spirit's work beyond the boundaries of Christian confession and discern the Spirit in people of other faiths or in movements for liberation in a wider ecumenism (e.g. Yong 2003).

The final major area in which Christians relate to one another globally is in mission. The sense of a common purpose and the obvious desirability, especially in non-Christian environments, of working together drew colonial Protestant missionaries together from 1860 in international gatherings to share insights and consider cooperative work. The great missionary conference in Edinburgh in 1910 was continued by the International Missionary Council. This was formally integrated into the WCC in 1961 and is represented within the Council by the Commission on World Mission and Evangelism. Within the WCC, mission was redefined as 'common witness'. In 1966 many Evangelical missions which did not wish to be part of the Council met together for a conference in Berlin in 1966 to discuss evangelism. The World Evangelical Alliance now has a Mission Commission and there is also the Lausanne movement which links mission leaders. Roman Catholic missionary orders are connected through special interest groups; for example, those with an interest in liberation interact more informally through the SEDOS, the Service of Documentation and Study on Global Mission. Most overseas mission agencies are themselves international and work cross-culturally, but they come together for practical reasons both on the 'mission field' and also in the country (countries) of their home base. They also relate to one another through academic networks for the study of mission, such as the International Association of Catholic Missiologists and the International Association for Mission Studies (which also has Catholic members). Mission is also a point of conflict between Christian churches, especially where one church is perceived as 'stealing sheep' from another.

The WCC is at present the only body trying to link *all* Christians worldwide together. Recognizing that growing numbers of Pentecostal–charismatic, indigenous and independent churches are not members of the WCC, since the 1980s the emphasis has shifted towards 'fellowship' (*koinonia*) as a way of bringing together a wider constituency, and also to encouraging bilateral dialogues, for example between Pentecostals and Roman Catholics, Anglicans and Orthodox. From the fourth-century council of Nicaea until the twentieth century, Chalcedonian and non-Chalcedonian Orthodox and Roman Catholics (and later Protestants) grew out of touch with one another or developed antagonistic relationships with one another. This was largely to their detriment since each developed itself as the true church and ceased to be inwardly reforming. With the increasing diversification in Christian faith, there is a need for creating more open spaces in which Christians of all kinds can come together. The most recent initiative is WCC the Global Christian Forum which met in Nairobi in 2007. From within the Roman Catholic Church, Robert Schreiter argues for a 'new catholicity', not in the sense of the Catholic Church to which only part of the Christian community belongs, but in the sense of the 'Church catholic' (1997: 122) which 'is marked by a wholeness of inclusion and fullness of faith in a pattern of intercultural exchange and communication' (1997: 132). Such catholicity would not be expressed by a single global institution but in terms of conversation – perhaps leading to communion – between and among both global and local expressions of Christian faith.

The world future of Christianity

In just over 100 years, the map of world Christianity has changed almost out of all recognition. In 1900, it is estimated that 70 per cent of all Christians were to be found in Europe (Barrett 2001: 4, 14), whereas now, as we have seen, Christians are much more evenly distributed around the globe, and, if present church growth and population trends continue, by 2025 Africa and Latin America will be vying with one another to claim the most Christians, having about a quarter each of the world's Christian population. Europe will be in third place, with Asia coming up fast behind (Jenkins 2002: 3). In spite of this, Christianity is still misrepresented as a European religion (Tiénu 2006: 40). When Protestant mission and church leaders from Europe and North America met at the watershed World Missionary Conference in Edinburgh nearly 100 years ago to discuss the state of the project of world evangelization, they rejoiced at the growth of churches around the world but they did not foresee the effect that the growth of Christianity in Asia and Africa was to have later in the century (Stanley 2004: 77). Although the eventual independence of the churches there was envisaged, the few 'native Christians' invited, including V.S. Azariah from India and Yun Chi Ho from Korea, were regarded as members of the 'younger churches' whose relationship to the 'older churches' of Europe was forever expected to be one of child to parent. In Edinburgh in 2010, there will be a centenary gathering in Edinburgh but it may well be completely eclipsed by much larger meetings planned in Africa and Asia to commemorate the same event. In the light of this dramatic turn of events, it is a little risky to make predictions for the next century or even the next decade; nevertheless we will venture some cautious observations.

The first observation concerns the relations of Christians globally North and South. In *The Next Christendom*, Philip Jenkins has presented a future scenario of North–South confrontation between two Christianities: the one liberal, rational and socially concerned, and the other traditional on social issues, conservative in beliefs and moral issues, and interested in the supernatural and in personal salvation rather than radical politics (2002: 161–2). But despite their differences, he sees the missionary efforts of the South toward the North being instrumental in the sustenance or even revitalization of the churches in the North. Although in many ways she shares Jenkins' thesis, Grace Davie, in her survey of the shift of the Christian presence to the South, arrives at a different conclusion. In *Europe: The Exceptional Case* (2002), she argues that modernization and secularization are closely related in Europe but not necessarily in the rest of the world. Therefore she sees European Christianity as following a course separate from the rest of world Christianity (including the United States) (see also Kim 2007b). Our study suggests that the destinies of the Christianities of North and South are linked in very many respects: through historical and institutional ties, through mission activity and migration, and through common Christian interest, especially in view of the global rise of militant Islam, aggressive secularism and other challenges to the Christian world-view. We agree with Jenkins in so far as there is a sector of traditional Western Christianity that finds it very difficult to engage with the Christianity of the 'South'; these are the Christians who have been most influenced by the Reformed rejection of supernatural power and the Enlightenment preference for rationality rather than emotion. But we do not see this estrangement as a problem for the whole of Northern Christianity since it has strong Pentecostal–charismatic movements which share a similar form of spirituality with others across the globe, and Evangelical movements in which the Bible is handled in a way that is recognizable to Christians in other continents. Although there are strong conservative voices in what Jenkins calls the global South, such attitudes are found in the North also, and both parts of the world have many other voices. Finally, it is easy from the perspective of the North to overplay the importance of the North–South axis. Global Christian interaction is much more complex and multi-directional, as we have seen. The future shape of the church will not be a series of confrontational encounters or clashes of different forms of Christianity, as some have predicted, nor will it be the situation that the North and South will exhibit such divergent characteristics that there is little in common between the two. We do not regard these two notions as a reflection of the nature of Christianity or an accurate assessment of ground reality. Rather, the different traditions and expressions of faith will form a mosaic of Christianity as a whole, as each contributes its own distinctive colour to the wider community. The future of Christianity can be imagined as a mosaic within a mosaic, with an ever greater variety of colours being added into the whole.

The second point is about the notion of Christendom. Even in 1910 the church and mission leaders in Edinburgh had difficulty distinguishing the Christian from the 'non-Christian' world (see Stanley 2006). These days, such an exercise has been rendered impossible not only by the spread of the churches worldwide but also by the spread of all sorts of other ideas and organizations which contribute to increasingly plural societies in most parts of the world. Furthermore the increasing voluntarism of religion means that few churches have a local monopoly. Not only are national churches challenged by this new situation, but the traditional European pattern of parish ministry is also under serious threat. Where there are different ethnic communities sharing Christian faith but differing in language and customs, it is increasingly common in the Episcopal churches to appoint bishops for those communities, wherever they are located, rather than to expect them to all come under the jurisdiction of the bishop of a particular region. As has recently been brought home to the (worldwide) Anglican Communion, this pattern can also be used in the case where communities differ theologically; so that in 2005 Archbishop Akinola established a 'Convocation of Anglicans in North America' comprising churches that have disaffiliated from the Episcopal Church of the USA. It is difficult to foresee a situation in which Christendom in a territorial sense could reassert itself. Moreover, even if Southern Christianity is taken together, it is also difficult to conceive of it as a world-dominating group. Despite the 'success' stories of church growth in Africa, Latin America and some countries in Asia, there are vast numbers of small and struggling churches that can hardly be described as constituting 'the next Christendom'. It is these weak groups which exhibit a more accurate picture of Southern Christianity, and are more true to the nature of the faith of Jesus Christ. Of course, Christendom was never a geographical fact or a political reality in any case – only an ideological construct. In this sense of mind-set, Christendom will persist unless challenged by constructive encounter with the other. Like Jenkins, we encourage Christians in the West to get to know their Christian brothers and sisters in other continents. More than 30 years ago, Kenyan theologian John Mbiti challenged Western Christians when he asked how there can be mutuality and reciprocity 'if only one side knows the other fairly well, while the other side either does not know or does not want to know the first side' (1976: 17). At a church level, twinning, mutual exchange visits and joint projects will help to foster mutual understanding, although an openness to different cultures and world-views needs to be created before these can be successful. Achieving this is not just a problem for churches but for Western society in general. It requires an educational approach that helps people enter one another's world-views, see through another's eyes (cf. Pobee and Ositelu 1998: 2–3) and see themselves from outside (cf. Griffiths 1990: 4, 10–11).

Thirdly, the church's relation to the society and the state has always been problematic and will probably remain so. From the point of view of churches, we have seen a number of different patterns of relationship: at one extreme, the church dominates the state, as in the case of medieval western Europe, or at the other extreme, the church withdraws from involvement in political life, as Evangelicals did in the 'great reversal'. The church may be oppressed by the state, as under Communism in eastern Europe, or it may collude with the state as the Dutch Reformed Church did in South Africa in the apartheid years. The church may become part of the state power, as in many countries of Latin America under dictators, or it may form the main opposition to state power, as in Uganda under Idi Amin. Whatever the context, followers of the one who preached the kingdom of God will be involved socially, at least at the level of helping the needy, or challenging injustice like the liberation, *minjung* and *dalit* theologians. But there are many more constructive ways in which the church (or churches) can engage in public life in democratic society. As the world becomes more democratic, we predict that churches will play an active role in national affairs, not limited to the religious domain but, for example, dealing with issues of ecology, economic justice and social equality. We have given many examples of Christian contributions to public life in different parts of the world, not only to protect Christian interests but for the public good. One further example that could be highlighted is the broad coalition of Christian, other religious and humanitarian groups brought together in Britain in 2005 to campaign to 'Make Poverty History'. Although initiated by Christians, it was not claimed by them, and so was able to draw a quarter of a million people to Edinburgh to put peaceful pressure on the leaders of the G8 to cancel Third World debt, promote fair trade and give more aid.

The fourth and final observation about the world future of Christianity concerns the structures and movements within it. Over time, and as Christianity moves into new contexts, old divisions break down and new distinctions emerge. One example of the breakdown of divisions is the denominations. The major denominational structures of Catholicism and Orthodoxy remain intact, but, from a global perspective, other distinctions have become very confused. For example, organizationally, Methodists in Korea follow the Presbyterian pattern of church leaders with 'elders'; Pentecostal churches in Africa adopt Anglican models of hierarchy; Catholic and Orthodox congregations in the USA have to fit their organizations within the same legal structures as Protestants, which means the adoption of some form of democratic decision-making. Structurally, in many places churches which are – or were – divided in their places of origin have come together. Congregational, Presbyterian and other Reformed are the most frequent examples, but much wider unions have also taken place, for example in Japan and India. At the level of theology, Protestant students in India read Catholic theology books because they are most widely available; and in terms of activities, Roman Catholic and Orthodox Christians in the USA may join in Evangelical mission events; just as Protestants in Europe enjoy Catholic and Orthodox retreats. Another example of these shifts is in the Liberal/ Evangelical divide, which was so pronounced in the mid-twentieth century. We have seen that the usage of the term 'Evangelical' differs in Europe, North America and Latin America, and the same could be said of 'Liberal'. The opposition of one to the other arose in North America, but now the major distinction there is between conservatives – who include Roman Catholics – and liberals and/or secularists. On the other hand, in India where, in the interests of inculturation, many Catholics have defined themselves as just that, they form part of the opposition to the conservative 'Romans'. One implication of this shifting of denominational labels is that world Christianity needs to be studied from an ecumenical or catholic perspective (cf. Hanciles 2006: 378) rather than through the lens of any particular church or confession.

A distinction is often made between 'church' and 'sect' or 'mainline' and 'fringe'; between those who seek credibility and a voice in the political sphere and those which have a more personal and domestic agenda. As we have seen, it is no longer possible to make this distinction along the line of particular denominations. Once Evangelical and Pentecostal–charismatic Christians were fitted entirely into the latter category, but in Africa, Asia and the Americas the terms 'mainline' and 'mainstream' to refer to the historic churches of Europe are no longer appropriate in many cases. From the perspective of this study, it might be better to see a distinction between those concerned to interact at a philosophical level with other world religions and ideologies, and others who are relating to popular belief systems, which include local or tribal religions, 'primal religiosity' and the culture of 'post-modernity'. This is not necessarily a political distinction. Although there are strong movements of the latter type within the older denominations, the hierarchies tend to be nervous of them because of the dangers of enthusiasm to social harmony; they tend to delineate rational and irrational approaches. From the other side, the restrictions imposed by some of the older denominations are often represented as resisting the 'supernatural' dimensions of faith. It is not only Pentecostal–charismatics and Fundamentalists who are in danger of syncretizing the Christian faith. Very often those at the grassroots, like the *dalit* Christians in India, feel betrayed by those who are prepared to dialogue with those whom they experience as oppressors. It is likely that many locally initiated churches will join the more established denominations, or aspire to become so themselves, as did the Methodists in the past. The older churches – Catholic, Protestant and Orthodox – have strategies of accommodation and education to bring them into their fold. In the long run, unless the new churches that have emerged dialogue with the historic Christian tradition, they are likely to diverge so far from it as to become new religious movements outside the Christian fold.

Notwithstanding the above, the chief observation we wish to make about the future is that regional differences and commonalities are likely to assume even greater importance. These regional differences may not necessarily be at the level of whole continents. What we mean is that within regions identified by a common religio-cultural or ideological background, or united against a common neighbour, or sharing particular geographical or ecological environment, common features of Christian confession are likely to emerge which cut across distinctions between Christian groups that arise out of different origins, histories and traditions. When a group of Christians from around the world meet they will differ not only according to the denomination or the trans-national movement to which they belong but also – and perhaps more importantly – according to the social, political and cultural contexts they represent. To show Christianity as it is requires a significant shift in theological education and the study of Christianity in general. Religio-cultural and geographical dimensions and perspectives from international relations need to be incorporated. And, most importantly, the views of Christians from different parts of the world need to be an integral part of any kind of Christian studies. Hearing from one another will help Christians in Europe and North America to recognize that their churches are inculturated and contextual in the same way that African, Asian and Latin American churches are (e.g. Meneses 2006; Ramachandra 2006: 229).

'Religion evolves as the world changes' and this may mean the development of global religion (Juergensmeyer 2003: 10) but it also strengthens local expressions of Christian witness. Africa, Asia, Europe, North and Latin America are each generating new theologies which are challenging one another, and the future of the Christian religion as a whole depends on all of them. As in the early church, theology and practice was a matter for ecumenical (i.e. whole world) discussion between representatives of different parts of the church, so now doing theology is again recognized to be a 'world endeavour' (Vanhoozer 2006: 115). We do not expect a single world Christianity, a world church or a global theology, but we hope for ongoing conversation between Christians, churches and theologies from around the world.

Study Questions and Further Readings

- Is Christianity recognizably one faith? Discuss.
- In what ways do Christians interact with one another globally?
- What are the main issues of discussion between Christians of different continents today?
- How do you see the future of world Christianity?

Briggs, John, Mercy Amba Oduyoye and Georges Tsetsis (eds), *A History of the Ecumenical Movement, Vol. 3, 1968–2000*. Geneva: World Council of Churches.

Cox, H. (1996), *Fire from Heaven: The Rise of Pentecostal Spirituality and the Reshaping of Religion in the Twenty-first Century*. London: Cassell.

Ford, David F. (ed), *The Modern Theologians: An Introduction to Christian Theology in the Twentieth Century* (2nd edn). Oxford: Blackwell.

Ott, Craig and Harold A. Netland (eds), *Globalizing Theology: Belief and Practice in an Era of World Christianity*. Grand Rapids, MI: Baker Academic.

Schreiter, Robert J. (1997), *The New Catholicity: Theology between the Global and the Local*. Maryknoll, NY: Orbis.

Wijsen, Frans and Robert Schreiter (eds), *Global Christianity: Contested Claims*. Amsterdam: Rodopi.

Wingate, Andrew, Kevin Ward, Carrie Pemberton and Wilson Sitshebo (eds), *Anglicanism: A Global Communion*. London: Mowbray.

Bibliography

Abraham, K. C. (ed.) (1990), *Third World Theologies: Commonalities and Divergences*. Maryknoll, NY: Orbis.

Adamo, David Tuesday (2000), 'The use of psalms in African indigenous churches in Nigeria', in Gerald West and Musa Dube (eds), *The Bible in Africa: Transactions, Trajectories and Trends*. Leiden: Brill, pp. 336–49.

Adeyemo, Tokunboh (ed.) (2006), *Africa Bible Commentary*. Grand Rapids, MI: Zondervan.

Aina, J. Ade (1997), 'The church's healing ministry', in John Parratt (ed.), *A Reader in African Christian Theology* (2nd edn). London: SPCK, pp. 104–8.

Ajayi, Jacob F, Ade (1999), 'Mission and empire: the ambiguous mandate of Bishop Crowther'. Henry Martyn Lectures 1999. Avaiable at http://www.martynmission.cam. ac.uk/CAjayiLectures.htm

—(2001), *A Patriot to the Core: Bishop Ajayi Crowther*. Ibadan: Spectrum Books in association with Safari Books.

Allen, Christopher (2004), 'Endemically European or a European epidemic? Islamophobia in a post 9/11 Europe', in Ron Greaves, Theodore Gabriel, Yvonne Haddad and Kane Idleman Smith (eds), *Islam and the West Post 9/11*. London: Ashgate, pp. 130–45.

Allen, Roland (1956 [1912]), *Missionary Methods: St Paul's or Ours?*. London: World Dominion.

Amaladoss, Michael (1981), 'Ashrams and social justice', in D. S. Amalorpavadass (ed.), *The Indian Church in the Struggle for a New Society*. Bangalore: NBCLC, pp. 370–8.

Amoah, Elizabeth and Mercy Amba Oduyoye (1988), 'The Christ for African women', in Virginia Fabella and Mercy Amba Oduyoye (eds), *With Passion and Compassion: Third World Women Doing Theology*. Maryknoll, NY: Orbis, pp. 35–46.

Anderson, Allan (1991), *Moya: The Holy Spirit in an African Context*. Pretoria: UNISA.

—(2000), *Zion and Pentecost*. Pretoria: UNISA.

—(2001), *African Reformation: African Initiated Christianity in the Twentieth Century*. Trenton, NJ: Africa World Press.

—(2004), *An Introduction to Pentecostalism*. Cambridge: Cambridge University Press.

—(2007), *Spreading Fires: The Missionary Nature of Early Pentecostalism*. London: SCM Press.

Anderson, Gerald H. (1974), 'A moratorium on missionaries?', in Gerald H. Anderson and Thomas F. Stransky (eds), *Mission Trends 1: Crucial Issues in Mission Today*. New York: Paulist Press/Grand Rapids, MI: Wm B. Eerdmans, pp. 133–41.

Anderson, Ray S. (1997), 'Evangelical theology', in David F. Ford (ed.), *The Modern Theologians: An Introduction to Christian Theology of the Twentieth Century* (2nd edn). Oxford: Blackwell, pp. 480–98.

Armour, Rollin (2002), *Islam, Christianity, and the West: A Troubled History*. Maryknoll, NY: Orbis.

Armstrong, Karen (2002), *Islam: A Short History*. London: Phoenix Press.

Arokiasamy, S. and G. Gispert-Sauch (eds) (1987), *Liberation in Asia: Theological Perspectives*. (Jesuit Theological Forum Reflections 1). Anand: Gujarat Sahitya Prakash.

Aruldoss, J. (1998), 'Dalits and salvation', in Andrew Wingate, Kevin Ward, Carrie Pemberton and Wilson Sitshebo (eds), *Anglicanism: A Global Communion*. London: Mowbray, pp. 294–300.

Austin-Broos, Diane (1997), *Jamaica Genesis: Religion and the Politics of Moral Order*. Chicago: University of Chicago Press.

—(2001), 'Jamaican Pentecostalism: transnational relations and the nation-state', in André Corten and Ruth Marshall-Fratani (eds), *Between Babal and Pentecost: Transnational Pentecostalism in Africa and Latin America*. Bloomington: Indiana University Press, pp. 142–62.

Ayegboyin, Deji and S. Ademola Ishola (1997), *African Indigenous Churches: An Historical Perspective*. Lagos: Greater Heights Publications.

Baer, Hans A. and Merrill Singer (2002), *African American Religion: Varieties of Protest and Accommodation* (2nd edn). Knoxville: University of Tennessee Press.

Ballhatchet, Kenneth and Helen Ballhatchet (2002), 'Asia', in J. McManners (ed.), *The Oxford History of Christianity*. Oxford: Oxford University Press, pp. 508–38.

Barrett, David B., George T Kurian and Todd M. Johnson (2001), *World Christian Encyclopedia* (2nd edn). Vol. 1. Oxford: Oxford University Press.

Bays, Daniel H. (ed.) (1996), *Christianity in China, from the Eighteenth Century to the Present*. Stanford, CA: Stanford University Press.

Bebbington, David W. (1989), *Evangelicalism in Modern Britain: A History from the 1730s to the 1980s*. London: Unwin Hyman.

Beck, Ulrich, Anthony Giddens and Scott Lash (1994), *Reflexive Modernization: Politics, Tradition and Aesthetics in the Modern Social Order*. Cambridge: Polity Press.

Bediako, Kwame (1992), *Theology and Identity: The Impact of Culture upon Christian Thought in the Second Century and Modern Africa*. Oxford: Regnum Books.

—(1997), 'African theology', in David F. Ford (ed.), *The Modern Theologians: An Introduction to Christian Theology of the Twentieth Century* (2nd edn). Oxford: Blackwell, pp. 426–44.

Belshaw, Deryke, Robert Calderisi and Chris Sugden (eds) (2001), *Faith in Development: Partnership between the World Bank and the Churches of Africa*. Oxford: Regnum.

Beozzo, José Oscar (1990), 'Humiliated and exploited natives', in Leonardo Boff and Virgil Elizondo (eds), *1492–1992: The Voice of the Victims*. London: SCM Press, pp. 78–89.

Berg, Todd M. Vanden (2005), 'Culture, Christianity, and witchcraft in a West African context', in L. Sanneh and J. A. Carpenter (eds), *The Changing Face of Christianity: Africa, the West, and the World*. Oxford: Oxford University Press, pp. 45–62.

Berger, Peter L. (1970), *A Rumour of Angels: Modern Society and the Rediscovery of the Supernatural*. London: Penguin.

Berger, Peter L. and Samuel P. Huntington (2002), *Many Globalizations: Cultural Diversity in the Contemporary World*. Oxford: Oxford University Press.

Bergunder, Michael (2001), 'Miracle healing and exorcism: the South Indian Pentecostal

movement in the context of popular Hinduism', *International Review of Mission*, 90(356–7), 103–12.

—(2004), ' "Ministry of compassion": D.G.S. Dhinakaran, Christian healer-prophet from Tamilnadu', in Roger E. Hedlund (ed.), *Christianity is Indian: The Emergence of an Indigenous Community*. Delhi: ISPCK, pp. 161–77.

—(2005), 'Constructing India Pentecostalism: on issues of methodology and representation', in Allan Anderson and Edmond Tang (eds), *Asian and Pentecostal: The Charismatic Face of Christianity in Asia*. Oxford: Regnum, pp. 177–213.

Berner, Ilse (2001), 'Pakistan', in Scott W. Sunquist (ed.), *A Dictionary of Asian Christianity*. Grand Rapids, MI: Wm B. Eerdmans, pp. 628–31.

Bevans, S. B. (1992), *Models of Contextual Theology*. Maryknoll, NY: Orbis.

Bevans, S. B. and R. P. Schroeder (2004), *Constants in Context: A Theology of Mission for Today*. Maryknoll, NY: Orbis.

Beyer, Peter (1994), *Religion and Globalization*. London: SAGE.

Bisnauth, Dale A. (1996), *A History of Religions in the Caribbean*. Trenton, NJ: Africa World Press.

Boesak, Allan Aubrey (1977), *Farewell to Innocence. A Socio-ethical Study on Black Theology and Power*. Maryknoll, NY: Orbis.

Boff, Leonardo (1986), *Ecclesiogenesis: The Base Communities Reinvent the Church* (trans. Robert R. Barr). London: Collins.

—(1990a), 'The new evangelization: new life burst in', in Leonardo Boff and Virgil Elizondo (eds), *1492–1992: The Voice of the Victims*. London: SCM Press, pp. 130–40.

—(1990b), 'Vatican instruction represents European mind-set', in Alfred T. Hennelly (ed.), *Liberation Theology: A Documentary History*. Maryknoll, NY: Orbis, pp. 415–18.

Bonino, José Miguez (1975), *Doing Theology in a Revolutionary Situation*. Philadelphia, PA: Fortress Press.

—(1997), *Faces of Latin American Protestantism*. Grand Rapids, MI: Wm B. Eerdmans (originally published in Spanish in 1995).

Bonk, Jonathan J. (1991), *Missions and Money: Affluence as a Western Missionary Problem*. Maryknoll, NY: Orbis.

Boodoo, Gerald (2000a), 'The faith of the people: the Divina Pastora devotions of Trinidad', in Hemchand Gossai and Nathaniel Samuel Murrell (eds), *Religion, Culture, and Tradition in the Caribbean*. London: Macmillan, pp. 65–72.

—(2000b), 'Christologies, Caribbean', in Virginia Fabella and R. S. Sugirtharajah (eds), *Dictionary of Third World Theologies*. Maryknoll, NY: Orbis, pp. 52–3.

Bosch, D. J. (1991), *Transforming Mission: Paradigm Shifts in Theology of Mission*. Maryknoll, NY: Orbis.

Boseto, Leslie (1995), 'The gospel of economy from a Solomon Islands perspective', in R. S. Sugirtharajah (ed.), *Voices from the Margin: Interpreting the Bible in the Third World* (2nd edn). London: SPCK, pp. 179–84.

Boyd, Robin H. S. (1974), *India and the Latin Captivity of the Church*. Cambridge: Cambridge University Press.

—(1988), *Ireland: Christianity Discredited or Pilgrim's Progress?* Geneva: World Council of Churches.

—(2002), 'Beyond Captivity?', in Israel Selvanayagam (ed.), *Moving Forms of Theology: Faith Talk's Changing Contexts*, Delhi: ISPCK, pp. 121–5.

Branch, Taylor (1988), *Parting the Waters: Martin Luther King and the Civil Rights Movement 1954–63*. London: Macmillan.

Bria, Ion (ed.) (1986), *Go Forth in Peace: Orthodox Perspectives on Mission*. Geneva: World Council of Churches.

Bright, Bill (1989), 'Personal evangelism: conquering the fear of failure', in Thom S. Rainer (ed.), *Evangelism in the Twenty-first Century: The Critical Issues*. Wheaton, IL: Harold Shaw Publishers, pp. 155–62.

Brook, Timothy (1996), 'Toward independence: Christianity in China under Japanese occupation, 1937–1945', in Daniel H. Bays (ed.), *Christianity in China, from the Eighteenth Century to the Present*. Stanford, CA: Stanford University Press, pp. 317–37.

Brookes, Andrew (2007), *The Alpha Phenomenon: Theology, Praxis and Challenges for Christian Mission Today*. London: CTBI.

Brooks, Sarah (1999), 'Catholic activism in the1990s: new strategies for the neoliberal age', in Christian Smith and Joshua Pokopy (eds), *Latin American Religion in Motion*. New York: Routledge, pp. 67–89.

Brouwer, Steve, Paul Gifford and Susan D. Rose (1996), *Exporting the American Gospel: Global Christian Fundamentalism*. New York: Routledge.

Brown, Callum G. (2001), *The Death of Christian Britain*. London: Routledge.

Brown, Judith M. (2003), 'Who is an Indian? Dilemmas of national identity at the end of the British Raj in India', in Brian Stanley (ed.), *Missions, Nationalism, and the End of Empire*. Grand Rapids, MI: Wm B. Eerdmans, pp. 111–31.

Brown, Peter (1997), *The Rise of Western Christendom: Triumph and Diversity, AD 200–1000*. Oxford: Blackwell.

Brown, Terry (2006), 'Introduction', in Terry Brown (ed.), *Other Voices, Other Worlds: The Global Church Speaks Out on Homosexuality*. London: Darton, Longman and Todd, pp. 1–4.

Bruce, Steve (1995), *Religion in Modern Britain*. Oxford: Oxford University Press.

Brusco, Elisabeth (1995), *The Reformation of Machismo: Evangelical Conversion and Gender in Colombia*. Austin: University of Texas Press.

Bula, Omega (1992), 'Women in mission: participating in healing', *International Review of Mission,* 81(322), 247–52.

Bulangalire, Majagira (2006), 'The consequences of the Enlightenment – a point of view from the churches of African expression in France', *International Review of Mission*, 95(378–9), 293–6.

Burrows, William R. (1993), *Redemption and Dialogue: Reading Redemptoris Missio and Dialogue and Proclamation*. Maryknoll, NY: Orbis.

—(1996), 'A seventh paradigm? Catholics and radical inculturation', in Willem Saayman and Klippies Kritzinger (eds), *Mission in Bold Humility: David Bosch's Work Considered*. Maryknoll, NY: Orbis, pp. 121–38.

Buthelezi, Manas (1976), 'Daring to live for Christ', in Gerald H. Anderson and Thomas F. Stransky (eds), *Mission Trends 3: Third World Theologies*. New York: Paulist Press/Grand Rapids, MI: Wm B. Eerdmans, pp. 176–80.

—(1997), 'Salvation as wholeness', in John Parratt (ed.), *A Reader in African Christian Theology* (2nd edn). London: SPCK, pp. 85–90. Article first published in 1972.

Caipora Women's Group (1993), *Women in Brazil*. London: Latin America Bureau.

Carlson, Joyce (1998), 'First Nations spirituality and the Anglican Church in Canada', in Andrew Wingate, Kevin Ward, Carrie Pemberton and Wilson Sitshebo (eds), *Anglicanism: A Global Communion*. London: Mowbray, pp. 40–5.

Carpenter, Joel A. (2005), 'Preface', in L. Sanneh and J. A. Carpenter (eds), *The Changing Face of Christianity: Africa, the West, and the World*. Oxford: Oxford University Press, pp. vii–ix.

Carter, Richard A. (1998), 'Where God still walks in the garden: religious orders and the development of the Anglican Church in the South Pacific', in Andrew Wingate, Kevin Ward, Carrie Pemberton and Wilson Sitshebo (eds), *Anglicanism: A Global Communion*. London: Mowbray, pp. 45–51.

Chadwick, Henry (2002), 'The early Christian community', in J. McManners (ed.), *The Oxford History of Christianity*. Oxford: Oxford University Press, pp. 21–69.

Chadwick, Owen (2002), 'Great Britain and Europe', in J. McManners (ed.), *The Oxford History of Christianity*. Oxford: Oxford University Press, pp. 349–95.

Chaillot, Christine (1998), *The Syrian Orthodox Church of Antioch and All the East: A Brief Introduction to Its Life and Spirituality*. Geneva: World Council of Churches.

—(2002), *The Ethiopian Orthodox Tewahedo Church Tradition: A Brief Introduction to Its Life and Spirituality*. Paris: Inter-Orthodox Dialogue.

Chandran, J. Russell (1993), 'Methods and ways of doing theology', in R. S. Sugirtharajah and Cecil Hargreaves (eds), *Readings in Indian Christian Theology*, Vol. 1. Delhi: ISPCK, pp. 4–13.

Chant, Sylvia with Nikki Craske (2003), *Gender in Latin America*. New Brunswick, NJ: Rutgers University Press.

Chapman, Audrey R. (2003), 'Perspectives on reconciliation within the religious community', in Audrey R. Chapman and Bernard Spong (eds), *Religion and Reconciliation in South Africa*. Philadelphia: Templeton Foundation Press, pp. 282–301.

Chapman, Colin (2002), *Whose Promised Land? The Continuing Crisis over Israel and Palestine*. Oxford: Lion.

—(2004), 'Israel as a focus for the anger of Muslims against the West', in Ron Greaves, Theodore Gabriel, Yvonne Haddad and Kane Idleman Smith (eds), *Islam and the West Post 9/11*. London: Ashgate, pp. 194–209.

Charles, Rodger, SJ (1998), *Christian Social Witness and Teaching*. Leominster: Gracewing.

Chepkwony, Adam K. A. (2002), 'An African approach to the acquisition of wealth and dealing with poverty', in Peter Kanyandago (ed.), *The Cries of the Poor in Africa: Questions and Responses for African Christianity*. Kisubi: Marianum, pp. 9–32.

Cho, (David) Yonggi (1989), *The Holy Spirit, My Senior Partner: Understanding the Holy Spirit and His Gifts*. Milton Keynes: Word Publishing.

—(1997), *Successful Home Cell Groups*. Seoul: Seoul Logos Co.

—(1999 [1989]), *The Fourth Dimension: The Key to Putting your Faith to Work for a Successful Life*. Secunderabad: Ben Publishing.

Choong, Chee Pang (2008), 'Studying Christianity and doing theology *extra ecclesiam* in

China', in Sebastian C. H. Kim (ed.), *Christian Theology in Asia*. Cambridge: Cambridge University Press, pp. 89–108.

Chopp, Rebecca S. (1997a), 'Feminist and womanist theologies', in David F. Ford (ed.), *The Modern Theologians: An Introduction to Christian Theology of the Twentieth Century* (2nd edn). Oxford: Blackwell, pp. 389–404.

Chopp, Rebecca S. (1997b), 'Latin American liberation theology', in David F. Ford (ed.), *The Modern Theologians: An Introduction to Christian Theology of the Twentieth Century*. Oxford: Blackwell, pp. 409–25.

Chung, Hyun Kyung (1990), *Struggle to Be the Sun Again*. London: SCM Press.

—(1991), 'Come, Holy Spirit – renew the whole creation', in Michael Kinnamon (ed.), *Signs of the Spirit: Official Report of the Seventh Assembly of the World Council of Churches, Canberra, 1991*. Geneva: World Council of Churches, pp. 37–47.

Church, John Edward (1981), *Quest for the Highest: An Autobiographical Account of the East African Revival*. Exeter: Paternoster.

Clapsis, Emmanuel (ed.) (2004), *The Orthodox Churches in a Plural World: An Ecumenical Conversation*. Geneva: WCC.

Cleary, Edward L. (1998), 'Introduction: Pentecostals, prominence, and politics', in Edward L. Cleary and Hannah W. Stewart-Gambino (eds), *Power, Politics and Pentecostals in Latin America*. Boulder, CO: Westview, pp. 1–24.

Cleary, Edward L. and Hannah W. Stewart-Gambino (eds) (1998), *Power, Politics and Pentecostals in Latin America*. Boulder, CO: Westview.

Clegg, Cecelia (2004), 'From violence to peace: reflections from Northern Ireland', in Howard Mellor and Timothy Yates (eds), *Mission, Violence and Reconciliation*. Sheffield: Cliff College Publishing, pp. 61–71.

Coakley, John W. and Andrea Sterk (2004), *Readings in World Christian History, Vol. I: Earliest Christianity to 1453*. Maryknoll, NY: Orbis.

Coe, Shoki (1976), 'Contextualizing theology', in Gerald H. Anderson and Thomas F. Stransky (eds), *Mission Trends 3: Third World Theologies*. New York: Paulist Press/Grand Rapids, MI: Wm B. Eerdmans, pp. 19–24.

Collins, Gary R. (2007), *Christian Counseling: A Comprehensive Guide* (3rd edn). Nashville, TN.: Thomas Nelson.

Comblin, José (1989), *The Holy Spirit and Liberation* (trans. Paul Burns; first published in Portuguese in 1987). Maryknoll, NY: Orbis.

Commission on Theological Concerns of the Christian Conference of Asia (ed.) (1981), *Minjung Theology: People as the Subjects of History*. London: Zed Press.

Commission on World Mission and Evangelism (2005), 'The healing mission of the Church', in World Council of Churches, *'You are the Light of the World': Statements on Mission by the World Council of Churches, 1980–2005*. Geneva: World Council of Churches, pp. 127–62.

Cone, James H. (1990 [1970]), *A Black Theology of Liberation* (3rd edn). Maryknoll, NY: Orbis.

Costas, Orlando (1982), *Christ outside the Gate: Mission beyond Christendom*. Maryknoll, NY: Orbis.

Cousins, Basil (2004), 'The Russian Orthodox Church, Tatar Christians and Islam', in Anthony

O'Mahony (ed.), *Eastern Christianity: Studies in Modern History, Religion and Politics*. London: Melisende, pp. 338–71.

Cox, H. (1996), *Fire from Heaven: The Rise of Pentecostal Spirituality and the Reshaping of Religion in the Twenty-first Century*. London: Cassell.

Cragg, Kenneth (1992), *The Arab Christian: A History in the Middle East*. London: Mowbray.

—(2000), 'Being made disciples – the Middle East', in Kevin Ward and Brian Stanley (eds), *The Church Mission Society and World Christianity, 1799–1999*. Grand Rapids, MI: Wm B. Eerdmans, pp. 120–43.

Cray, Graham et al. (2004), *Mission-Shaped Church: Church Planting and Fresh Expressions of Church in a Changing Context*. London: Church House Publishing.

Curran, Charles E. (2002), *Catholic Social Teaching, 1891–Present*. Washington, DC: Georgetown University Press.

—(2006), *Loyal Dissent: Memoirs of a Catholic Theologian*. Washington, DC: Georgetown University Press.

Dalrymple, William (1998), *From the Holy Mountain: A Journey in the Shadow of Byzantium*. London: HarperCollins.

Daly, Mary (1973), *Beyond God the Father: Towards a Philosophy of Women's Liberation*. Boston, MA: Beacon.

Daneel, Inus (1987), *Quest for Belonging: Introduction to the Study of African Independent Churches*. Harare: Mambo Press.

Davidson, Allan K. (2000), 'Culture and ecclesiology: the Church Missionary Society and New Zealand', in Kevin Ward and Brian Stanley (eds), *The Church Mission Society and World Christianity, 1799–1999*. Grand Rapids, MI: Wm B. Eerdmans, pp. 198–227.

—(2004), ' "The Pacific is no longer a mission field"? Conversion in the South Pacific in the twentieth century', in Donald M. Lewis (ed.), *Christianity Reborn: The Global Expansion of Evangelicalism in the Twentieth Century*. Grand Rapids, MI: Wm B. Eerdmans, pp. 133–53.

Davie, Grace (1994), *Religion in Britain since 1945: Believing without Belonging*. Oxford: Blackwell.

—(2000), *Religion in Modern Europe: A Memory Mutates*. Oxford: Oxford University Press.

—(2002), *Europe: The Exceptional Case. Parameters of Faith in the Modern World*. London: Darton, Longman and Todd.

Davies, Norman (1996), *Europe: A History*. New York: HarperCollins.

Davis, Kortright (1990), *Emancipation Still Comin': Explorations in Caribbean Emancipatory Theology*. Maryknoll, NY: Orbis.

Daye, Russell (2004), *Political Forgiveness: Lessons from South Africa*. Maryknoll, NY: Orbis.

de Gruchy, John W. (1995), *Christianity and Democracy: A Theology for a Just World Order*. Cape Town: David Philip.

de Gruchy, John W. with Steve de Gruchy (2004), *The Church Struggle in South Africa* (3rd edn). London: SCM Press.

Deberri, E. P. and J. E. Hug, with P. J. Henriot and M. J. Schultheis (2003), *Catholic Social Teaching* (4th edn). Maryknoll, NY: Orbis.

Dehqani-Tafti, Hassan B. (1981), *The Hard Awakening*. London: SPCK.

—(2000) *The Unfolding Design of My World: A Pilgrim in Exile* (ed. Kenneth Cragg). Norwich: Canterbury Press.

Dempster, M. W., B. D. Klaus and D. Petersen (1999), *The Globalization of Pentecostalism: A Religion Made to Travel*. Oxford: Regnum Books.

Devanandan, P. D. (1961), *Christian Concern in Hinduism*. Bangalore: CISRS.

—(1964), *Preparation for Dialogue*. Bangalore: CISRS.

Devasahayam, V. (ed.) (1997), *Frontiers of Dalit Theology*. Delhi/Madras: ISPCK.

Dickson, Kwesi (1983), *Theology in Africa*. London: Darton, Longman and Todd.

—(1997), 'The theology of the cross', in John Parratt (ed.), *A Reader in African Christian Theology* (2nd edn). London: SPCK, pp. 75–84.

Dorr, Donal (1992), *Option for the Poor* (revised edn). Maryknoll, NY: Orbis.

Douglas, J. D. (ed.) (1990), *Proclaim Christ Until He Comes: Calling the Whole Church to Take the Whole Gospel to the Whole World. Report of Lausanne II in Manila, International Congress on World Evangelization, 1989*. Minneapolis, MN: World Wide Publications.

Dowley, Tim (ed.) (1990), *The History of Christianity*. Oxford: Lion.

Dube, Musa W. (2001a), 'Fifty years of bleeding: a storytelling feminist reading of Mark 5:24–43', in Musa W. Dube (ed.), *Other Ways of Reading: African Women and the Bible*. Atlanta, GA: Society of Biblical Literature, pp. 50–60.

—(2001b), 'Divining Ruth for international relations', in Musa W. Dube (ed.), *Other Ways of Reading: African Women and the Bible*. Atlanta, GA: Society of Biblical Literature, pp. 179–95.

Dunn, J. D. G. (2006), *Unity and Diversity in the New Testament: An Inquiry into the Character of Earliest Christianity* (3rd edn). London: SCM Press.

Dupuis, Jacques (1997), *Toward a Christian Theology of Religious Pluralism*. Maryknoll, NY: Orbis.

Dussel, Enrique (1981), *A History of the Church in Latin America* (trans. Alan Neely). Grand Rapids, MI: Wm B. Eerdmans.

—(1990), 'The real motives for the conquest', in Leonardo Boff and Virgil Elizondo (eds), *1492–1992: The Voice of the Victims*. London: SCM Press, pp. 30–46.

Ela, Jean-Marc (1988), *My Faith as an African*. Maryknoll, NY: Orbis.

El-Assal, Riah Abu (1998), 'Anglicanism in Jerusalem', in Andrew Wingate, Kevin Ward, Carrie Pemberton and Wilson Sitshebo (eds), *Anglicanism: A Global Communion*. London: Mowbray, pp. 87–90.

Elizondo, Virgil (1997), *Guadalupe, Mother of a New Creation*. Maryknoll, NY: Orbis.

El-Zahlaoui, Joseph (1989), 'Witnessing in the Islamic context', in George Lemopoulos (ed.), *Your Will Be Done: Orthodoxy in Mission*. Geneva: World Council of Churches, pp. 95–104.

England, John C., Jose Kuttianimattathil, John Mansford Prior, Lily A. Quintos, David Suh Kwang-sun and Janice Wickeri (eds) (2002), *Asian Christian Theologies: A Research Guide to Authors, Movements, Sources*, Vol. 1, Asia Region, South Asia, Austral Asia. Delhi: ISPCK.

—(2003), *Asian Christian Theologies: A Research Guide to Authors, Movements, Sources*, Vol. 2, Southeast Asia. Delhi: ISPCK.

—(2004), *Asian Christian Theologies: A Research Guide to Authors, Movements, Sources*, Vol. 3, Northeast Asia. Delhi: ISPCK.

Erskine, Noel Leo (1981), *Decolonizing Theology: A Caribbean Perspective*. Marynoll, NY: Orbis.

Escobar, Samuel (1976), 'The search for freedom, justice, and fulfilment', in Gerald H. Anderson and Thomas F. Stransky (eds), *Mission Trends 3: Third World Theologies*. New York: Paulist Press/Grand Rapids, MI: Wm B. Eerdmans, pp. 104–10.

Esquivel, Julia (1990), 'Conquered and violated women', in Leonardo Boff and Virgil Elizondo (eds), *1492–1992: The Voice of the Victims*. London: SCM Press, pp. 68–77.

Eversley, Shelly (ed.) (2004), *The Interesting Narrative of the Life of Olaudah Equiano or, Gustavus Vassa, the African, Written by Himself*. New York: The Modern Library.

Farhadian, Charles E. (2005), *Christianity, Islam and Nationalism in Indonesia*. New York: Routledge.

Feher, Shoshanah (1998), *Passing Over Easter: Constructing the Boundaries of Messianic Judaism*. Walnut Creek, CA: Sage Publications.

Fernandes, Eleazar S. (1994), *Toward a Theology of Struggle*. Maryknoll, NY: Orbis.

Fiedler, Klaus (1994), *The Story of Faith Missions*. Oxford: Regnum.

Fielder, Caroline (2007), 'Real change or mere rhetoric? An evaluation of the 2005 regulations on religious affairs a year on', *China Study Journal*, Spring/Summer, 33–53.

Fiorenza, Elisabeth Schüssler (1983), *In Memory of Her: A Feminist Theological Reconstruction of Christian Origins*. London: SCM Press.

Fisher, Humphrey (1973), 'Conversion reconsidered: some historical aspects of religious conversion in black Africa', *Africa*, 43(1), 27–40.

Ford, David F. (ed.), *The Modern Theologians: An Introduction to Christian Theology in the Twentieth Century* (2nd edn). Oxford: Blackwell.

Forman, Charles W. (1994), 'The study of Pacific Island Christianity: achievements, resources, needs', *International Bulletin of Missionary Research*, 18(3), 103–12.

Forrester, Duncan B. (1980), *Caste and Christianity: Attitudes and Policies on Caste of Anglo-Saxon Protestant Missions in India*. London: Curzon.

Fraser, Nicholas and Marysa Navarro (1996), *Evita: The Real Lives of Eva Peron*. London: André Deutsch.

Freire, Paulo (1970), *Pedagogy of the Oppressed* (trans. Myra Bergman Ramos; first published in Portuguese in 1968). New York: Seabury Press.

Freston, Paul (2001), *Evangelicals and Politics in Asia, Africa and Latin America*. Cambridge: Cambridge University Press.

Funkschmidt, Kai M. (2002), 'Partnership between unequals – mission impossible? Mission structures revisited', *International Review of Mission*, 91(362), 395–413.

Gajiwala, Astrid Lobo (1998), 'Making a path to the womb: eco-feminism and its implications', in Joseph Mattam and Jacob Kavunkal (eds), *Ecological Concerns: An Indian Theological Response*. Bangalore, pp. 54–67.

Gao, Shining (2003a), 'Chinese Christianity in the 21st century', in Centre for Multireligious Studies, *Christian Theology and Intellectuals in China*, Occasional Paper. Aarhus: University of Aarhus, pp. 51–60.

—(2003b), 'Faith and values: case studies of Chinese Christians', in Centre for Multireligious Studies, *Christian Theology and Intellectuals in China*, Occasional Paper. Aarhus: University of Aarhus, pp. 61–72.

Gaustad, Edwin S. and Leigh E. Schmidt (2002), *The Religious History of America* (revised edn). New York: HarperCollins.

Gebara, Ivone and María Clara Bingemer (1994), 'Mary – Mother of God, Mother of the Poor', in Ursula King (ed.), *Feminist Theology from the Third World: A Reader*. London: SPCK, pp. 275–81.

Getui, M. N. (2003), 'Material things in contemporary African society', in J. N. K. Mugambi and A. Nasimiyu-Wasike (eds.), *Moral and Ethical Issues in African Christianity: A Challenge for African Christianity*. Nairobi: Acton Publishers, pp. 59–72.

Gibbs, Eddie and Ryan K. Bolger (2006), *Emerging Churches: Creating Christian Community in Postmodern Cultures*. Grand Rapids, MI: Baker Academic.

Gifford, Paul (1998), *African Christianity: Its Public Role*. London: Hurst and Co.

—(2005), 'A view of Ghana's new Christianity', in Lamin Sanneh and Joel A. Carpenter (eds), *The Changing Face of Christianity: Africa, the West and the World*. Oxford: Oxford University Press, pp. 81–96.

Gill, Anthony (1999), 'The struggle to be soul provider: Catholic responses to Protestant growth in Latin America', in Christian Smith and Joshua Pokopy (eds), *Latin American Religion in Motion*. New York: Routledge, pp. 17–42.

Gill, Robin (2003), *The 'Empty' Church Revisited*. Aldershot: Ashgate.

Gilroy, Paul (1993), *The Black Atlantic: Modernity and Double Consciousness*. London: Verso.

Gispert-Sauch, George (1997), 'Asian theology', in David F. Ford (ed.), *The Modern Theologians: An Introduction to Christian Theology in the Twentieth Century* (2nd edn). Oxford: Blackwell, pp. 455–76.

Gitari, David (1996). *In Season and Out of Season: Sermons to a Nation*. Oxford: Regnum.

Glasser, Arthur F. (1993), 'Evangelical missions', in James M. Phillips and Robert T. Coote (eds), *Toward the Twenty-first Century in Christian Mission*. Grand Rapids, MI: Wm B. Eerdmans, pp. 9–29.

Gnanadason, Aruna (1988), 'Women's oppression: a sinful situation', in Virginia Fabella and Marcy Amba Oduyoye (eds), *With Passion and Compassion: Third World Women Doing Theology*. Maryknoll, NY: Orbis, pp. 69–76.

—(1993), 'Towards a feminist eco-theology for India', in Prasanna Kumari (ed.), *A Reader in Feminist Theology*. Madras: Christian Literature Society, pp. 95–105.

Goedhals, Mandy M. (2000), ' "Ethiopia shall soon stretch out her hands to God": the Order of Ethiopia and the Church of the Province of Southern Africa, 1899–1999', in Daniel O'Connor and others, *Three Centuries of Mission: The United Society for the Propagation of the Gospel, 1701–2000*. London: Continuum, pp. 382–94.

Goodman, Martin (1994), *Mission and Conversion: Proselytizing in the Religious History of the Roman Empire*. Oxford: Clarendon.

Gooren, Henri (2007), 'Pentecostal conversion careers in Latin America', in Frans Wijsen and Robert Schreiter (eds), *Global Christianity: Contested Claims*. Amsterdam: Rodopi, pp. 157–75.

Gossai, Hemchand and Nathaniel Samuel Murrell (eds) (2000), *Religion, Culture, and Tradition in the Caribbean*. London: Macmillan.

Grant, Jacquelyn (1989), *White Women's Christ and Black Women's Jesus: Feminist Christology and Womanist Response*. Atlanta, GA: Scholars Press.

Grenz, Stanley J. and Roger E. Olson (1992), *Twentieth Century Theology: God and the World in a Transitional Age*. Downers Grove, IL: InterVarsity Press.

Griffiths, Paul J. (ed.) (1990), *Christianity through Non-Christian Eyes*. Maryknoll, NY: Orbis.

Guder, Darrell L. (ed.) (1998), *Missional Church: A Vision for the Sending of the Church in North America*. Grand Rapids, MI: Wm B. Eerdmans.

—(2000), *The Continuing Conversion of the Church*. Grand Rapids, MI: Wm B. Eerdmans.

Gutiérrez, Gustavo (1973), *A Theology of Liberation* (trans. Caridad Inda and John Eagleson; first published in Spanish in 1971). Maryknoll, NY: Orbis.

—(1984), *We Drink from Our Own Wells: The Spiritual Journey of a People* (first published in Spanish in 1983). Maryknoll, NY: Orbis.

—(1988), *A Theology of Liberation: History, Politics, and Salvation* (revised edn). London: SCM Press.

— (1990), 'Towards the fifth centenary', in Leonardo Boff and Virgil Elizondo (eds), *1492–1992: The Voice of the Victims*. London: SCM Press, pp. 1–10.

—(1993), *Las Casas: In Search of the Poor of Jesus Christ* (trans. Robert R. Barr; first published in Portuguese in 1992). Maryknoll, NY: Orbis.

Haas, Liesl (1999), 'The Catholic Church in Chile: new political alliances', in Christian Smith and Joshua Pokopy (eds), *Latin American Religion in Motion*. New York: Routledge, pp. 43–66.

Hackel, Sergei (2002) 'The Orthodox Churches of Eastern, Europe, in J. McManners (ed.). *The Oxford History of Christianity*. Oxford: Oxford University Press, pp. 539–67.

Halsell, Grace (2003), *Forcing God's Hand: Why Millions Pray for a Quick Rapture and Destruction of Planet Earth*. Brentwood, MD: Amana.

Hanciles, Jehu J. (2006), 'New wine in old wineskins: critical reflections on writing and teaching a global Christian history', *Missiology*, 34(3), 361–82.

Hardesty, Nancy (2003), *Faith Cure: Divine Healing in the Holiness and Pentecostal Movements*. Peabody, MA: Hendrickson.

Harding, Vincent (1996), *Martin Luther King: The Inconvenient Hero*. Maryknoll, NY: Orbis.

Hastings, Adrian (1967), *Church and Mission in Modern Africa*. London: Burns and Oates.

—(1976), *African Christianity: An Essay in Interpretation*. London: Geoffrey Chapman.

—(1979), *A History of African Christianity, 1950–1975*. Cambridge: Cambridge University Press.

—(ed.) (1999a), *A World History of Christianity*. London: Cassell.

—(1999b), 'Latin America', in Adrian Hastings (ed.), *A World History of Christianity*. London: Cassell, pp. 328–68.

Hauerwas, Stanley (1999), *After Christendom: How the Church is to Behave if Freedom, Justice, and a Christian Nation are Bad Ideas*. Nashville, TN: Abingdon Press.

Havea, Sione 'Amanaki (1987), 'Christianity in the Pacific context', in *South Pacific Theology: Papers from the Consultation on Pacific Theology, Papua New Guinea, January 1986*. Oxford: Regnum.

Hay, David (2002), 'The spirituality of the unchurched', in Howard Mellor and Timothy Yates (eds), *Mission and Spirituality: Creative Ways of Being Church*. Sheffield: Cliff College Publishing, pp. 11–26.

He, Guanghu (2003a), 'Some causes and features of the "Christian upsurge" among Chinese intellectuals', in Centre for Multireligious Studies, *Christian Theology and Intellectuals in China*, Occasional Paper. Aarhus: University of Aarhus, pp. 43–9.

—(2003b), 'A religious spirit: the hope for transnationalism in China today', in Centre for Multireligious Studies, *Christian Theology and Intellectuals in China*, Occasional Paper. Aarhus: University of Aarhus, pp. 73–83.

Hecht, Tobias (1998), *At Home in the Street: Street Children of Northeast Brazil*. Cambridge: Cambridge University Press.

Heelas, Paul and Linda Woodhead (2004), *The Spiritual Revolution: Why Religion is Giving Way to Spirituality*. Oxford: Blackwell.

Heimann, Mary (1999), 'Christianity in Western Europe from the Enlightenment', in Adrian Hastings (ed.), *A World History of Christianity*. London: Cassell, pp. 458–507.

Hennelly, Alfred T. (ed.) (1990), *Liberation Theology: A Documentary Histroy*, Maryknoll, NY: Orbis.

Hilliard, David (1999), 'Australasia and the Pacific', in Adrian Hastings (ed.), *A World History of Christianity*. London: Cassell, pp. 508–35.

Hilton, A. J. B. (1988), *The Age of Atonement*. Oxford: Clarendon Press.

Hinchliff, Peter (2002), 'Africa', in John McManners (ed.), *The Oxford History of Christianity*. Oxford: Oxford University Press, pp. 474–507.

Hofmeyr, J. W. (Hoffie) and Gerald J. Pillay (eds) (1994), *A History of Christianity in South Africa*, Vol. 1. Pretoria: Haum Tertiary.

Hollenweger, Walter J. (1972), *The Pentecostals* (translated from the German by R. A. Wilson). London: SCM Press.

—(1997), *Pentecostalism: Origins and Developments Worldwide*. Peabody, MA: Hendrickson.

—(1999), 'The black roots of Pentecostalism', in Allan H. Anderson and Walter J. Hollenweger (eds), *Pentecostals after a Century: Global Perspectives on a Movement in Transition*. Sheffield: Sheffield Academic Press, pp. 33–44.

Holter, Knut (2000), 'Africa in the Old Testament', in Gerald West and Musa Dube (eds), *The Bible in Africa: Transactions. Trajectories and Trends*. Leiden: Brill, pp. 569–81.

Hopkins, Dwight N. (1993), *Shoes That Fit Our Feet: Sources for a Constructive Black Theology*. Maryknoll, NY: Orbis.

—(1999), *Introducing Black Theology of Liberation*. Maryknoll, NY: Orbis.

—(2001), 'The religion of globalization', in D. N. Hopkins, L. A. Lorentzen, E. Mendieta and D. Batstone (eds), *Religions/Globalizations: Theories and Cases*. Durham, NC: Duke University Press, pp. 7–32.

Horton, Robin (1971), 'African conversion', *Africa*, 41(2), 85–108.

—(1975a), 'On the rationality of conversion: Part I', *Africa*, 45(3), 219–35.

—(1975b), 'On the rationality of conversion: Part II', *Africa*, 45(4), 373–99.

Hrangkhuma, F. (ed.) (1998), *Christianity in India: Search for Liberation and Identity*. Delhi: ISPCK.

Humphrey Fisher (1973), 'Conversion reconsidered: some historical aspects of religious conversion in Black Africa', *Africa*, 43(1), 27–40.

Huntington, Samuel P. (2005), *Who Are We? America's Great Debate*. London: The Free Press.

Hurbon, Laënnec (1990), 'The slave trade and black slavery in America', in Leonardo Boff and Virgil Elizondo (eds), *1492–1992: The Voice of the Victims*. London: SCM Press, pp. 90–100.

—(2001), 'Pentecostalism and transnationalisation in the Caribbean', in André Corten and Ruth Marshall-Fratani (eds), *Between Babel and Pentecost: Transnational Pentecostalism in Africa and Latin America*. Bloomington: Indiana University Press, pp. 124–41.

Idowu, Bolaji (1965), *Towards an Indigenous Church*. London: Oxford University Press.

Irvin, D. T. and S. W. Sunquist (2001), *History of the World Christian Movement. Vol I: Earliest Christianity to 1453*. Maryknoll, NY: Orbis.

Isasi-Díaz, Ada Mariía (1996), *Mujerista Theology: A Theology for the Twenty-first Century*. Maryknoll, NY: Orbis.

Isichei, Elizabeth (1995), *A History of Christianity in Africa, from Antiquity to the Present*. Grand Rapids, MI: Wm B. Eerdmans.

Jackson, Darrell (2005), 'Pax Europa: crux Europa', in Timothy Yates (ed.), *Mission and the Next Christendom*. Sheffield: Cliff College Academic Press, pp. 85–106.

Jacob, Adai (2001), 'Jacobite Syrian Orthodox Church, India', in Scott W. Sunquist (ed.), *A Dictionary of Asian Christianity*. Grand Rapids, MI: Wm B. Eerdmans, pp. 405–7.

Jacob, Plamthodathil S. (1979), *The Experiential Response of N.V. Tilak*. Madras: CLC.

Jenkins, Philip (1996), *Pedophiles and Priests: Anatomy of a Contemporary Crisis*. Oxford: Oxford University Press.

—(2002), *The Next Christendom: The Coming of Global Christianity*. Oxford: Oxford University Press.

—(2006), *The New Faces of Christianity: Believing the Bible in the Global South*. Oxford: Oxford University Press.

—(2007), *God's Continent: Christianity, Islam, and Europe's Religious Crisis*. Oxford: Oxford University Press.

Jensen, Robert W. (1997), 'Karl Barth', in David F. Ford (ed.), *The Modern Theologians: An Introduction to Christian Theology of the Twentieth Century* (2nd edn). Oxford: Blackwell, pp. 21–36.

Jensen, Tina Gudrun (1999), 'Discourses on Afro-Brazilian religion: from de-Africanization to re-Africanization', in Christian Smith and Joshua Pokopy (eds), *Latin American Religion in Motion*. New York: Routledge, pp. 275–94.

Johns, Jeremy (2002), 'Christianity and Islam', in John McManners, *The Oxford History of Christianity*. Oxford: Oxford University Press, pp. 167–204.

Johnson, Elizabeth A. (1992), *She Who Is: The Mystery of God in Feminist Theological Discourse*. New York: Crossroad.

Johnson, L. T. (1999), *The Writings of the New Testament: An Interpretation*. London: SCM Press.

Johnstone, Patrick and Jason Mandryk (2001), *Operation World* (3rd edn). Exeter: Paternoster.

Juergensmeyer, Mark (2000), *Terror in the Mind of God: The Global Rise of Religious Violence*. Berkeley: University of California Press.

—(ed.) (2003), *Global Religions: An Introduction*. Oxford: Oxford University Press.

Kahindi, Lydia Wakanyi (2003), 'The role of African churches in democratization', in Grace Wamue and Matthew M. Theuri (eds), *Quests for Integrity in Africa*. Nairobi: Acton Publishers, pp. 125–38.

Kamsteeg, Frans (1999), 'Pentecostalism and political awakening in Pinochet's Chile and beyond', in Christian Smith and Joshua Pokopy (eds), *Latin American Religion in Motion*. New York: Routledge, pp. 187–204.

Kanyandago, Peter (1999), 'Management of power and the challenge of democracy in the African church', in Laurenti Magesa and Zablon Nthamburi (eds), *Democracy and Reconciliation: A Challenge for African Christianity*. Nairobi: Acton Publishers, pp. 163–82.

Kanyoro, Musimbi R. A. (2001), 'Cultural hermeneutics: an African contribution', in Musa W. Dube (ed.), *Other Ways of Reading: African Women and the Bible*. Atlanta, GA: Society of Biblical Literature, pp. 101–13.

Karotemprel, Sebastian (ed.) (1996), *Following Christ in Mission: A Foundational Course in Missiology*. Bombay: Pauline Publications.

Kasibante, Amos (1998), 'Beyond revival: a proposal for mission in the Church of Uganda into the third millennium', in Andrew Wingate, Kevin Ward, Carrie Pemberton and Wilson Sitshebo (eds), *Anglicanism: A Global Communion*. London: Mowbray, pp. 363–8.

Kato, Byang H. (1975), *Theological Pitfalls in Africa*. Kisumu: Evangel.

Katoppo, Marianne (1979), *Compassionate and Free: An Asian Woman's Theology*. Geneva: World Council of Churches.

Kavunkal, Jacob (1995), *The 'Abba' Experience of Jesus: Model and Motive for Mission in Asia*. Indore: Satprakashan Sanchar Kendra.

—(1998), 'Neo-pentecostalism: a missionary reading', *Vidyajyoti*, 62(6), 407–22.

Kee, Alistair (2006), *The Rise and Demise of Black Theology*. Aldershot: Ashgate.

Keshishian, Aram (1992), *Orthodox Perspectives on Mission*. Oxford: Regnum-Lynx.

Kim, Kirsteen (2004), 'India', in John Parratt (ed.), *Introduction to Third World Theologies*. Cambridge: Cambridge University Press, pp. 44–73.

—(2007), *The Holy Spirit in the World: A Global Conversation*. Maryknoll, NY: Orbis.

Kim, Sebastian C. H. (2003), *In Search of Identity: Debates on Religious Conversion in India*. New Delhi and Oxford: Oxford University Press.

—(2007a), 'Freedom or respect? Public theology and the debate over the Danish cartoons', *International Journal of Public Theology*, 1(2), 249–69.

—(2007b), 'The future shape of Christianity from an Asian perspective', in Frans Wijsen and Robert Schreiter (eds), *Global Christianity: Contested Claims*. Amsterdam: Rodopi, pp. 69–93.

Kim, Yang-sŏn (2004), 'Compulsory Shinto shrine worship and persecution', in Chai-shin Yu (ed.), *Korea and Christianity*. Fremont, CA: Asian Humanities Press, pp. 87–120.

Kim, Yong-Bock (1981a), 'Korean Christianity as a messianic movement of the people', in Commission on Theological Concerns of the Christian Conference of Asia (ed.), *Minjung Theology: People as the Subjects of History*. London: Zed Press, pp. 80–119.

—(1981b), 'Messiah and minjung: discerning messianic politics over against political messianism', in Commission on Theological Concerns of the Christian Conference of

Asia (ed.), *Minjung Theology: People as the Subjects of History*. London: Zed Press, pp. 183–93.

Kinnamon, Michael (2004), 'Assessing the Ecumenical movement', in John Briggs, Mercy Amba Oduyoye and Georges Tsetsis (eds), *A History of the Ecumenical Movement, Vol. 3, 1968–2000*, pp. 51–81.

Kinoti, Hannah W. (2003), 'The integrity of creation: an African perspective', in Grace Wamue and Matthew M. Theuri (eds), *Quests for Integrity in Africa*. Nairobi: Acton Publishers, pp. 1–16.

Kirk, J. Andrew (1999), *What is Mission? Theological Explorations*. London: Darton, Longman and Todd.

— and Kevin J. Vanhoozer (eds) (1999), *To Stake a Claim: Mission and the Western Crisis of Knowledge*. Maryknoll, NY: Orbis 1999.

Kirwen, Michael C. (1987), *The Missionary and the Diviner: Contending Theologies of Christian and African Religions*. Maryknoll, NY: Orbis.

Kitamori, Kazoh (1965), *Theology of the Pain of God* (5th edn). Richmond, VA: John Knox Press.

Klaiber, Jeffrey (1998), *The Church, Dictatorships, and Democracy in Latin America*. Maryknoll, NY: Orbis.

Knitter, Paul F. (1995), *One Earth Many Religions: Multifaith Dialogue and Global Responsibility*. Maryknoll, NY: Orbis.

Köstenberger, Andreas J., Thomas R. Schreiner and H. Scott Baldwin (eds) (2005), *Women in the Church: An Analysis and Application of 1 Timothy 2:9–15* (2nd edn). Grand Rapids, MI: Baker Academic.

Kotila, Heikki (2006), 'Contemporary worship as an expression of post-modern spirituality', in Kirsi Tirri (ed.), *Religion, Spirituality and Identity*. Bern: Peter Lang, pp. 65–83.

Kozhuharov, Valentin (2006), 'Theological reflections on the missionary activity of the Russian Orthodox Church', *International Review of Mission*, 95(378–9), 371–82.

Koyama, Kosuke (1974), *Water Buffalo Theology*. London: SCM.

Kraft, Charles H. (1992), 'Allegiance, truth and power encounters in Christian witness', in Jan A. B. Jongeneel (ed.), *Pentecost, Mission and Ecumenism: Essays on Intercultural Theology. Festschrift in honour of Prof. Walter J. Hollenweger*. Frankfurt am Main: Peter Lang, pp. 215–30.

Kroeger, Richard Clark and Catherine Clark Kroeger (1992), *I Suffer Not a Woman: Rethinking 1 Timothy 2:11–15 in Light of Ancient Evidence*. Grand Rapids, MI: Baker Book House.

Kumaradas, Vincent (2004), 'Nationalist stirrings in Tirunelvelly and at Madras', in Roger E. Hedlund (ed.), *Christianity is Indian: The Emergence of an Indigenous Community*. Delhi: ISPCK, pp. 3–22.

Küng, Hans (1995), *Christianity: Its Essence and History*. London: SCM Press.

Kung, Lap Yan (2005), 'Reconciliation as trust-building: an exploration of Christian mission in Hong Kong', in Kirsteen Kim (ed.), *Reconciling Mission: The Ministry of Healing and Reconciliation in the Church Worldwide*. Delhi: ISPCK, pp. 176–200.

Kunnumpuram, Kurien, Errol D'Lima and Jacob Parappally (eds) (1997), *The Church in India: In Search of a New Identity*. Bangalore: Indian Theological Association.

Kwok, Pui-Lan (1992), *Chinese Women and Christianity, 1860–1927*. Atlanta, GA: Scholars Press.

—(1994), 'Mothers and daughter, writers and fighters', in R. S. Sugirtharajah (ed.), *Frontiers in Asian Christian Theology: Emerging Trends*. Maryknoll, NY: Orbis, pp. 147–55.

—(1996), 'Chinese women and Protestant Christianity at the turn of the twentieth century', in Daniel H. Bays (ed.), *Christianity in China, from the Eighteenth Century to the Present*. Stanford, CA: Stanford University Press, pp. 194–208.

—(2000), *Introducing Asian Feminist Theology*. Sheffield: Sheffield Academic Press.

Kyomo, Andrew A. (2003), 'Faith and healing in the African context', in Mika Vähäkangas and Andrew A. Kyomo (eds), *Charismatic Renewal in Africa: A Challenge to African Christianity*. Nairobi: Acton, pp. 145–56.

Labi, Kwame Joseph (2004), 'Injustice and prophetic evangelism', in Emmanuel Clapsis (ed.), *The Orthodox Churches in a Plural World: An Ecumenical Conversation*. Geneva: World Council of Churches, pp. 189–91.

Ladd, George Eldon (1981), 'The gospel of the kingdom', in Ralph D. Winter and Steven C. Hawthorne (eds), *Perspectives on the World Christian Movement: A Reader*. Pasadena: William Carey Library, pp. 51–69.

Lafaye, Jacques (1976), *Quetzalcoatl and Guadalupe: The Formation of Mexican National Consciousness*. Chicago, IL: University of Chicago Press.

Lambert, Tony (1991), *The Resurrection of the Chinese Church*. London: Hodder and Stoughton.

—(2006), *China's Christian Millions* (revised edn). Oxford: Monarch.

Land, Steven J. (1993), *Pentecostal Spirituality: A Passion for the Kingdom*. Sheffield: Sheffield Academic Press.

Latourette, K. S. (1971), *A History of the Expansion of Christianity, Vol. 7: Advance through Storm: 1914 and after* (originally published in 1945). London: Eyre and Spottiswoode.

Lee, Moonjang (1999), 'Experience of religious plurality in Korea: its theological implications', *International Review of Mission*, 88(351), 399–413.

Legrand, Lucien and Robert R. Barr (1990), *Unity and Plurality: Mission in the Bible*. Maryknoll, NY: Orbis.

Leung, Ka-Lun (2001), 'China', in Scott W. Sunquist (ed.), *A Dictionary of Asian Christianity*. Grand Rapids, MI: Wm B. Eerdmans, pp. 139–46.

Ling, Peter J. (2002), *Martin Luther King, Jr.* London: Routledge.

Lipner, Julius (1999), *Brahmabandhab Upadhyay: The Life and Thought of a Revolutionary*, New Delhi: Oxford University Press.

Lowe, Chuck (1998), *Territorial Spirits and World Evangelisation? A Biblical, Historical and Missiological Critique of Strategic Level Spiritual Warfare*. Sevenoaks: Mentor/OMF.

Ma, Julie C. (2001). *When the Spirit meets the Spirits: Pentecostal Ministry among the Kankana-ey Tribe in the Philippines* (revised edn). Frankfurt: Peter Lang.

Ma, Wonsuk (2005), 'Asian (classical) Pentecostal theology in context', in Allan Anderson and Edmond Tang (eds), *Asian and Pentecostal: The Charismatic Face of Christianity in Asia*. Oxford: Regnum, pp. 59–91.

Mafico, Temba L. J. (2000), 'The biblical God of the Fathers and the African ancestors', in Gerald West and Musa Dube (eds), *The Bible in Africa: Transactions, Trajectories and Trends*. Leiden: Brill, pp. 481–9.

Magesa, Laurenti (2003), 'Charismatic movements as "communities of affliction" ', in Mika Vähäkangas and Andrew A. Kyomo (eds), *Charismatic Renewal in Africa: A Challenge for African Christianity*. Nairobi: Acton Publishers, pp. 27–44.

Maimela, Simon S. and Dwight N. Hopkins (1989), *We Are One Voice: Essays on Black Theology in the USA and South Africa*. Johannesburg: Skotaville Publishers.

Malik, Alexander J. (1993), 'Confessing Christ in the Islamic context', in R. S. Sugirtharajah (ed.), *Asian Faces of Jesus*. Maryknoll, NY: Orbis, pp. 75–84.

Maluleke, Tinyiko Sam (1999), 'The South African truth and reconciliation discourse', in Laurenti Magesa and Zablon Nthamburi (eds), *Democracy and Reconciliation: A Challenge for African Christianity*. Nairobi: Acton Publishers, pp. 215–41.

Manorama, Ruth (1992), 'Dalit women: the thrice alienated', in T. Dayanandan Francis and Franklyn J. Balasundaram (eds), *Asian Expressions of Christian Commitment*. Madras: Christian Literature Society, pp. 194–8.

Mariz, Cecília and Clara Mafra (1999), 'Family and reproduction among Protestants in Rio de Janeiro', in Christian Smith and Joshua Pokopy (eds), *Latin American Religion in Motion*. New York: Routledge, pp. 205–19.

Marostica, Matthew (1999), 'The defeat of denominational culture in the Argentine Evangelical movement', in Christian Smith and Joshua Pokopy (eds), *Latin American Religion in Motion*. New York: Routledge, pp. 147–72.

Marsden, George M. (1980), *Fundamentalism and American Culture*. Oxford: Oxford University Press.

—(1991), *Understanding Fundamentalism and Evangelicalism*. Grand Rapids, MI: Wm B. Eerdmans.

—(2006), *Fundamentalism and American Culture* (2nd edn). Oxford: Oxford University Press.

Martin, David (1990), *Tongues of Fire: The Explosion of Protestantism in Latin America*. Oxford: Blackwell.

—(2002), *Pentecostalism: The World their Parish*. Oxford: Blackwell.

—(2005), *On Secularization: Towards a Revised General Theory*. Burlington, VT: Ashgate.

Marty, Martin (2002), 'North America', in John McManners (ed.), *The Oxford History of Christianity*. Oxford: Oxford University Press, pp. 396–436.

Masuzawa, T. (2005), *The Invention of World Religions, or, How European Universalism Was Preserved in the Language of Pluralism*. Chicago: Chicago University Press.

Maurice, Frederick Denison (1842), *The Kingdom of Christ: or, Hints to a Quaker, Respecting the Principles, Constitution, and Ordinances of the Catholic Church*, Vol. 2 (2nd edn). London: Macmillan and Co.

May, Melanie A. (2004), 'The unity we share, the unity we seek', in John Briggs, Mercy Amba Oduyoye and Georges Tsetsis (eds), *A History of the Ecumenical Movement, Vol. 3, 1968–2000*, pp. 83–102.

Mbiti, John (1969), *African Religions and Philosophy*. London: Heinemann.

—(1971), *New Testament Eschatology in an African Background: A Study of the Encounter between New Testament Theology and African Traditional Concepts*. London: Oxford University Press.

—(1976), 'Theological impotence and the universality of the church', in Gerald H. Anderson and Thomas F. Stransky (eds), *Mission Trends 3: Third World Theologies*. New York: Paulist Press/Grand Rapids, MI: Wm B. Eerdmans, pp. 6–18.

—(1986), *Bible and Theology in African Christianity*. Oxford: Oxford University Press.

McCullum, Hugh (2004), *The Angels Have Left Us: The Rwanda Tragedy and the Churches*. Geneva: World Council of Churches.

McCullum, Hugh and Terry MacArthur (eds) (2006), *In God's Hands: Common Prayer for the World*. Geneva: World Council of Churches.

McDonnell, Kilian (1975), *The Holy Spirit and Power: The Catholic Charismatic Renewal*. Garden City, NY: Doubleday.

McGavran, Donald A. and C. Peter Wagner (1990), *Understanding Church Growth* (3rd edn). Grand Rapids, MI: Wm B. Eerdmans.

McGrath, Alister E. (2001), *Christian Theology: An Introduction* (3rd edn). Oxford: Blackwell.

McLeod, Hugh (1997), *Religion and the People of Western Europe, 1789–1989* (revised edn). Oxford: Oxford University Press.

McManners, John (2002), *The Oxford History of Christianity*. Oxford: Oxford University Press.

Meneses, Eloise Hiebert (2006), 'Bearing witness in Rome with theology from the whole church: globalization, theology, and nationalism', in Craig Ott and Harold A. Netland (eds), *Globalizing Theology: Belief and Practice in an Era of World Christianity*. Grand Rapids, MI: baker Academic, pp. 23–49.

Meredith, Martin (2006), *The State of Africa: A History of Fifty Years of Independence* (2nd edn). London: Free Press.

Micklethwait, John and Adrian Wooldridge (2004), *The Right Nation: Why America Is Different*. London: Penguin.

Middleton, J. Richard and Brian J. Walsh (1995), *Truth Is Stranger Than It Used to Be: Biblical Faith in a Postmodern Age*. Downers Grove, IL: InterVarsity Press.

Míguez, Daniel (1999), 'Exploring the Argentinian case: religious motives in the growth of Latin American Pentecostalism', in Christian Smith and Joshua Pokopy (eds), *Latin American Religion in Motion*. New York: Routledge, pp. 221–34.

Min, Kyŏng-bae (2004), 'National identity in the history of the Korean Church', in Chai-shin Yu (ed.), *Korea and Christianity*. Fremont, CA: Asian Humanities Press, pp. 121–43.

Miyahira, Nozomu (2008), 'Christian theology under feudalism, nationalism and democracy in Japan', in Sebastian C. H. Kim (ed.), *Christian Theology in Asia*. Cambridge: Cambridge University Press, pp. 109–28.

Moffett, Samuel Hugh (1998), *A History of Christianity in Asia: Vol. I, Beginnings to 1500* (2nd edn). Maryknoll, NY: Orbis.

—(2005), *A History of Christianity in Asia: Vol. II, 1500–1900*. Maryknoll, NY: Orbis.

Mojola, Aloo Osotsi (2002), 'How the Bible is received in communities: a brief overview with particular reference to East Africa', in Philip L. Wickeri (ed.), *Scripture, Community, and Mission*. Hong Kong: Christian Conference of Asia.

Mombo, Esther (2006), 'Kenya reflections', in Terry Brown (ed.), *Other Voices, Other Worlds:*

The Global Church Speaks Out on Homosexuality. London: Darton, Longman and Todd, pp. 142–53.

Morris, Colin (2002), 'Christian civilization', in John McManners (ed.), *The Oxford History of Christianity*. Oxford: Oxford University Press, pp. 205–42.

Moyo, Ambrose (2003), 'Material things in African society: implications for Christian ethics', in J. N. K. Mugambi and A. Nasimiyu-Wasike (eds), *Moral and Ethical Issues in African Christianity: A Challenge for African Christianity*. Nairobi: Acton Publishers, pp. 49–57.

Mugambi, J. N. K. (2002), *Christianity and African Culture*. Nairobi: Acton Publishers.

Mugambi, J. N. K. and A. Nasimiyu-Wasike (eds) (2003), *Moral and Ethical Issues in African Christianity: A Challenge for African Christianity*. Nairobi: Acton Publishers.

Mulago, Vincent (1965), *Une Visage Africaine de Christianisme*. Paris: Présence Africaine.

Mullin, Robert Bruce (1999), 'North America', in Adrian Hastings (ed.), *A World History of Christianity*. London: Cassell, pp. 416–57.

Mullins, Mark R. (1998), *Christianity Made in Japan: A Study of Indigenous Movements*. Honolulu: University of Hawai'i Press.

Mulrain, George M. (1995), 'Is there a calypso exegesis?', in R. S. Sugirtharajah (ed.), *Voices from the Margin: Interpreting the Bible in the Third World*. London: SPCK, pp. 37–47.

Murrell, Nathaniel Samuel (2000), 'Blackman's Bible and Garveyite Ethiopianist epic with commentary', in Hemchand Gossai and Nathaniel Samuel Murrell (eds), *Religion, Culture, and Tradition in the Caribbean*. London: Macmillan, pp. 271–306.

Muzaffar, C. (1998), 'Globalisation and religion: some reflections', in J. A. Camilleri and C. Muzaffar (eds), *Globalisation: The Perspectives and Experiences of the Religious Traditions of Asia Pacific*. Petaling Jaya: International Movement for a Just World, pp. 179–90.

Mwamba, Musonda T. S. (2000), 'The evolving role of the Church: the case of democratization in Zambia', in Daniel O'Connor and others (eds), *Three Centuries of Mission: The United Society for the Propagation of the Gospel, 1701–2000*. London: Continuum, pp. 395–408.

Mwaura, Philomena Njeri (2003), 'African Instituted Churches and socio-economic development', in Grace Wamue and Matthew M. Theuri (eds), *Quests for Integrity in Africa*. Nairobi: Acton Publishers, pp. 75–94.

Nazir-Ali, Michael (1987), *Frontiers in Muslim–Christian Encounter*. Oxford: Regnum Books.

—(1991), *From Everywhere to Everywhere: A World View of Christian Mission*. London: Collins.

Ndung'u, Nahashon (1999), 'Civic education for democracy in Kenya', in Laurenti Magesa and Zablon Nthamburi (eds), *Democracy and Reconciliation: A Challenge for African Christianity*. Nairobi: Acton Publishers, pp. 23–31.

—(2000). 'The role of the Bible in the rise of African instituted churches: the case of the Akurinu churches in Kenya', in Gerald West and Musa Dube (eds), *The Bible in Africa: Transactions, Trajectories and Trends*. Leiden: Brill, pp. 36–47.

—(2003), 'Land as a source of economic sustenance', in Grace Wamue and Matthew M. Theuri (eds), *Quests for Integrity in Africa*. Nairobi: Acton Publishers, pp. 57–74.

Nee, Watchman (1989), *The Normal Christian Life: 'It is no Longer I – but Christ'* (3rd edn). Eastbourne: Victory Press.

Neill, Stephen (1964), *A History of Christian Missions*. London: Penguin.

Newbigin, Lesslie (1986), *Foolishness to the Greeks: The Gospel and Western Culture*. Grand Rapids, MI: W.B. Eerdmans.

—(1995), *The Open Secret: An Introduction to the Theology of Mission* (revised edn). Grand Rapids, MI: Wm B. Eerdmans.

Newman, Las (1998), 'The Church as a source of identity: reflection from the Caribbean', in Andrew Wingate, Kevin Ward, Carrie Pemberton and Wilson Sitshebo (eds), *Anglicanism: A Global Communion*. London: Mowbray, pp. 240–6.

Nirmal, Arvind P. (1988), 'Towards a Christian Dalit theology', in Arvind P. Nirmal (ed.), *A Reader in Dalit Theology*. Madras: Christian Literature Society, pp. 53–70.

Nolde, O. Frederick (1993), 'Ecumenical action in international affairs', in Harold E. Fey (ed.), *The Ecumenical Advance: A History of the Ecumenical Movement, Vol. 2, 1948–1968*. Geneva: World Council of Churches, pp. 261–85.

Noll, Mark A. (1994), *The Scandal of the Evangelical Mind*. Grand Rapids, MI: Wm B. Eerdmans.

—(2001), *American Evangelical Christianity*. Oxford: Blackwell.

Norget, Kristin (1999), 'Progressive theology and popular religiosity in Oaxaca, Mexico', in Christian Smith and Joshua Pokopy (eds), *Latin American Religion in Motion*. New York: Routledge, pp. 91–110.

Norris, Frederick W. (2002), *Christianity: A Short Global History*. Oxford: Oneworld.

Norris, Pippa and Ronald Inglehart (2004), *Sacred and Secular: Religion and Politics Worldwide*. Cambridge: Cambridge University Press.

Nyamiti, Charles (1973), *The Scope of African Christian Theology*. Nairobi: Gaba Publications.

—(1984), *Christ Our Ancestor. Christology from an African Perspective*. Harare: Mambo Press.

O'Connor, Daniel and others (2000), *Three Centuries of Mission: The United Society for the Propagation of the Gospel, 1701–2000*. London: Continuum.

O'Mahony, Anthony (2004a), 'The politics of religious renewal: Coptic Christianity in Egypt', in Anthony O'Mahony (ed.), *Eastern Christianity: Studies in Modern History, Religion and Politics*. London: Melisende, pp. 66–111.

—(2004b), 'Eastern Christianity in Modern Iraq', in Anthony O'Mahony (ed.), *Eastern Christianity: Studies in Modern History, Religion and Politics*. London: Melisende, pp. 11–43.

Ochs, Peter (1997), 'Judaism and Christian theology', in David F. Ford (ed.), *The Modern Theologians: An Introduction to Christian Theology of the Twentieth Century* (2nd edn). Oxford: Blackwell, pp. 607–25.

Oduyoye, Mercy Amber (1986), *Hearing and Knowing: Theological Reflections on Christianity in Africa*. Maryknoll, NY: Orbis.

Oduyoye, Mercy Amber and Hendrik M. Vroom (eds) (2003), *One Gospel – Many Cultures: Case Studies and Reflections on Cross-Cultural Theology*. Amsterdam: Rodopi.

Okeke, Ken (1998), 'The Anglican debate in West Africa on Christian–Muslim relations', in Andrew Wingate, Kevin Ward, Carrie Pemberton and Wilson Sitshebo (eds), *Anglicanism: A Global Communion*. London: Mowbray, pp. 316–22.

Okoye, James Chukwuma (2006), *Israel and the Nations: A Mission Theology of the Old Testament*. Maryknoll, NY: Orbis.

Oleska, Michael (1989), 'Orthodoxy in mission: the Alaskan experience', in George Lemopoulos (ed.), *Your Will Be Done: Orthodoxy in Mission*. Geneva: World Council of Churches, pp. 217–19.

Oliver, Errol (1999), 'Response (to Walter Hollenweger)', in Allan H. Anderson and Walter J. Hollenweger (eds), *Pentecostals after a Century: Global Perspectives on a Movement in Transition*. Sheffield: Sheffield Academic Press, pp. 45–7.

Omenyo, Cephas N. (2003), 'Charismatization of the mainline churches in Ghana', in Mika Vähäkangas and Andrew A. Kyomo (eds), *Charismatic Renewal in Africa: A Challenge for African Christianity*. Nairobi: Acton Publishers, pp. 5–26.

Ong, Eddie (1998), 'Anglicanism in West Malaysia', in Andrew Wingate, Kevin Ward, Carrie Pemberton and Wilson Sitshebo (eds), *Anglicanism: A Global Communion*. London: Mowbray, pp. 172–8.

Orevillo-Montenegro, Muriel (2006), *The Jesus of Asian Women*. Maryknoll, NY: Orbis.

Osthathios, G. Mar (1979), *Theology of a Classless Society*. Cambridge: Lutterworth.

Ott, Craig and Harold A. Netland (eds), *Globalizing Theology: Belief and Practice in an Era of World Christianity*. Grand Rapids, MI: Baker Academic.

Painadanth, Sebastian (1993), 'Towards an Indian Christian spirituality in the context of religious pluralism', in Dominic Veliath (ed.). *Towards an indian Christian Spirituality in a Pluralistic Context*. Bangalore: Dhaemaram Publications, pp. 3–14.

Park, Jong Chun (1998), *Crawl with God, Dance in the Spirit! A Creative Formation of Korean Theology of the Spirit*. Nashville, TN: Abingdon.

Parratt, John (1994), 'Recent writing on Dalit theology: a bibliographical essay', *International Review of Mission*, 83(329), 329–37.

—(1995), *Reinventing Christianity: African Theology Today*. Grand Rapids, MI: Wm B. Eerdmans.

—(ed.) (1997), *A Reader in African Christian Theology* (2nd edn). London: SPCK.

Parrinder, Geoffrey (1949), *West African Religion*. London: Epworth.

Peiris, Jeyasiri (1998), 'The Church in Sri Lanka and relations with other faiths', in Andrew Wingate, Kevin Ward, Carrie Pemberton and Wilson Sitshebo (eds), *Anglicanism: A Global Communion*. London: Mowbray, pp. 337–41.

Percy, Martyn (1996), *Words, Wonders and Power: Understanding Contemporary Christian Fundamentalism and Revivalism*. London: SPCK.

Persoon, Joachim (2004), 'Between ancient Axum and revolutionary Moscow: the Ethiopian Church in the twentieth century', in Anthony O'Mahony (ed.), *Eastern Christianity: Studies in Modern History, Religion and Politics*. London: Melisende, pp. 160–214.

Peters, F. E. (2003), *The Monotheists: Jews, Christians, and Muslims in Conflict and Competition*, Vol. II. Princeton, NJ: Princeton University Press.

Phan, Peter C. (2003), *Christianity with an Asian Face: Asian American Theology in the Making*. Maryknoll, NY: Orbis.

Phillips, James M. (1981), *From the Rising of the Sun: Christians and Society in Contemporary Japan*. Maryknoll, NY: Orbis.

Phillips, Paul T. (1996) *A Kingdom on Earth: Anglo-American Social Christianity, 1880–1940*. University Park: Pennsylvania State University Press.

Pieris, Aloysius (1988a), *Love Meets Wisdom: A Christian Experience of Buddhism*. Maryknoll, NY: Orbis.

—(1988b), *An Asian Theology of Liberation*. Maryknoll, NY: Orbis.

Pike, Frederick B. (2002), 'Latin America', in John McManners (ed.), *The Oxford History of Christianity*. Oxford: Oxford University Press, pp. 437–73.

Pillay, Gerald J. (1994), *Religion at the Limits? Pentecostalism among Indian South Africans*. Pretoria: University of South Africa.

Pinn, Anne H. and Anthony B. Pinn (2002), *Introduction to Black Church History*. Minneapolis, MN: Fortress Press.

Pinnock, Clark H. (1996), *Flame of Love: A Theology of the Holy Spirit*. Downers Grove, IL: InterVarsity Press.

Pirouet, Louise (1978), *Black Evangelists: The Spread of Christianity in Uganda, 1891–1914*. London: Collings.

—(1989), *Christianity Worldwide*. SPCK Church History 4: AD 1800 onwards. London: SPCK.

Placher, William C. (1997), 'Postliberal theology', in David F. Ford (ed.) *The Modern Theologians: An Introduction to Christian Theology of the Twentieth Century* (2nd edn). Oxford: Blackwell, pp. 343–56.

Pobee, John S. and Gabriel Ositelu II (1998), *African Initiatives in Christianity: The Growth, Gifts and Diversities of Indigenous African Churches*. Geneva: World Council of Churches.

Pokrovsky, Gleb (2003), *The Way of a Pilgrim: Annotated and Explained*. London: Darton Longman and Todd.

Pongudom, Prasit, Herbert R. Swanson and Surachai Chumsriphan (2001), 'Thailand', in Scott W. Sunquist (ed.), *A Dictionary of Asian Christianity*. Grand Rapids, MI: Wm B. Eerdmans, pp. 831–4.

Porter, David (2004), 'Bearing witness to the overcomer of violence: reflections from a practitioner theologian in Northern Ireland', in Howard Mellor and Timothy Yates (eds), *Mission, Violence and Reconciliation*. Sheffield: Cliff College Publishing, pp. 73–89.

Porter, Muriel (1990), *Land of the Spirit? The Australian Religious Experience*. Geneva: World Council of Churches.

Prabhakar, M. E. (1988), 'The Search for a Dalit theology', in Arvind P. Nirmal (ed.), *A Reader in Dalit Theology*. Madras: Christian Literature Society, pp. 41–52.

Premanandham, Moses (2004), 'The Bakht Singh movement', in Roger E. Hedlund (ed.), *Christianity is Indian: The Emergence of an Indigenous Community*. Delhi: ISPCK, pp. 331–44.

Prokopy, Joshua and Christian Smith (1999), 'Introduction', in Christian Smith and Joshua Pokopy (eds), *Latin American Religion in Motion*. New York: Routledge, pp. 1–16.

Raboteau, Albert J. (2004), *Slave Religion: The 'Invisible Institution' in the Antebellum South* (revised edn). Oxford: Oxford University Press.

Ramachandra, Vinoth (1996), *The Recovery of Mission: Beyond the Pluralist Paradigm*. Carlisle: MARC.

—(2006), 'Globalization, nationalism, and religious resurgence', in Craig Ott and Harold Netland (eds), *Globalizing Theology: Belief and Practice in an Era of World Christianity*. Grand Rapids, MI: Baker Academic, pp. 213–30.

Ramalshah, Manu (1998), 'Living as a minority in Pakistan', in Andrew Wingate, Kevin Ward, Carrie Pemberton and Wilson Sitshebo (eds), *Anglicanism: A Global Communion*. London: Mowbray, pp. 264–70.

Ransom, Reverdy C. (2002), 'Duty and destiny', in Anne H. Pinn and Anthony B. Pinn (eds), *Fortress Introduction to Black Church History*. Minneapolis, MN: Fortress, pp. 153–8.

Rauschenbusch, Walter (1917), *Theology for the Social Gospel*. New York: Macmillan.

Rayan, Samuel (1983), 'Theological priorities in India today', in Virginia Fabella and Sergio Torres (eds), *Irruption of the Third World – Challenge to Theology. Papers from the Fifth International Conference of the Ecumenical Association of Third World Theologians*. Maryknoll, NY: Orbis, pp. 30–41.

Rev. Kyung-Chik Han Memorial Foundation (2005), *Just Three More Years to Live: The Story of Rev. Kyung-Chik Han*. Seoul: Rev. Kyung-Chik Han Memorial Foundation.

Reynolds, David (2000), *One World Divisible: A Global History since 1945*. New York: Norton and Company.

Ribeiro, Darcy (1990), 'The Latin American people', in Leonardo Boff and Virgil Elizondo (eds), *1492–1992: The Voice of the Victims*. London: SCM Press, pp. 13–29.

Richard, Pablo (1990), '1492: the violence of God and the future of Christianity', in Leonardo Boff and Virgil Elizondo (eds), *1492–1992: The Voice of the Victims*. London: SCM Press, pp. 59–67.

Ro, Bong Rin (1995), 'The Korean Church: God's chosen people for evangelism', in Bong Rin Ro and Marlin L. Nelson (eds), *Korean Church Growth Explosion* (revised edn). Seoul: Word of Life, pp. 11–44.

Robeck, Jr, Cecil M. (1993), 'Pentecostal origins from a global perspective', in Harold D. Hunter and Peter D. Hocken (eds), *All Together in One Place: Theological Papers from the Brighton Conference on World Evangelization*. Sheffield: Sheffield Academic Press, pp. 166–80.

Robert, Dana (2000), 'Shifting southward: global Christianity since 1945', *International Bulletin of Missionary Research*, 24(2), 50–8.

Roberts, J. Deotis (1987), *Black Theology in Dialogue*. Philadelphia, PA: Westminster Press.

Robertson, Roland (1992), *Globalization: Social Theory and Global Culture*. London: SAGE.

Robinson, David (2004), *Muslim Societies in African History*. Cambridge: Cambridge University Press.

Robinson, Rowena (2003), *Christians of India*. New Delhi: Sage.

Ross, Cathy (2005), 'Reflections from "far away" islands', in Timothy Yates (ed.), *Mission and the Next Christendom*. Sheffield: Cliff College Publishing, pp. 147–61.

Rudolph, Susanne Hoeber (1997), 'Introduction: religion, states, and transnational civil society', in Susanne Hoeber Rudolph and J. Piscatori (eds), *Transnational Religion and Fading States*. Oxford: HarperCollins, pp. 1–24.

Ruether, Rosemary Radford (1983), *Sexism and God-Talk: Towards a Feminist Theology*. London: SCM Press.

Saayman, Willem (1991), *Christian Mission in South Africa*. Pretoria: University of South Africa.

Salinas, Maximiliano (1990), 'The voices of those who spoke up for the victims', in Leonardo Boff and Virgil Elizondo (eds), *1492–1992: The Voice of the Victims*. London: SCM Press, pp. 101–9.

Samartha, Stanley (1979), *Guidelines on Dialogue*. Geneva: World Council of Churches.

—(1981), *Courage for Dialogue: Ecumenical Issues in Inter-Religious Relationships*. Geneva: World Council of Churches.

—(1991), *One Christ – Many Religions: Towards a Revised Christology*. Maryknoll, NY: Orbis.

Sanneh, L. (1983), *West African Christianity: The Religious Impact*. London: C. Hurst.

—(1989), *Translating the Message: The Missionary Impact on Culture*. Maryknoll, NY: Orbis.

—(2000), 'The CMS and the African transformation: Samuel Ajayi Crowther and the opening of Nigeria', in Kevin Ward and Brian Stanley (eds), *The Church Mission Society and World Christianity, 1799–1999*. Grand Rapids, MI: Wm B. Eerdmans, pp. 173–97.

—(2003), *Whose Religion is Christianity? The Gospel beyond the West*. Grand Rapids, MI: Wm B. Eerdmans.

—(2005), 'Conclusion: the current transformation of Christianity', in L. Sanneh and J. A. Carpenter (eds), *The Changing Face of Christianity: Africa, the West, and the World*. Oxford: Oxford University Press, pp. 213–24.

Sawyerr, Harry (1968), *Creative Evangelism: Towards a New Christian Encounter with Africa*. London: Lutterworth.

Schoffeleers, Matthew (1994), 'Christ in African folk theology: the *nganga* paradigm', in Thomas D. Blakely, Walter E. A. van Beek and Dennis L. Thomson (eds), *Religion in Africa: Experience and Expression*. London: James Currey, pp. 73–88.

Schreiter, Robert J. (1997), *The New Catholicity: Theology between the Global and the Local*. Maryknoll, NY: Orbis.

—(1998), *The Ministry of Reconciliation: Spirituality and Strategies*. Maryknoll, NY: Orbis.

—(1999), 'Inculturation of faith or identification with culture?', in James A. Scherer and Stephen B. Bevans (eds), *New Directions in Mission and Evangelization 3: Faith and Culture*. Maryknoll, NY: Orbis, pp. 68–75.

Segundo, Juan Luis (1976), *The Liberation of Theology* (trans. John Drury; first published in 1975 in Spanish). Maryknoll, NY: Orbis.

Selvanayagam, Israel (2000), *A Second Call: Ministry and Mission in a Multifaith Milieu*. Madras, Christian Literature Society.

—(ed.) (2002), *Moving Forms of Theology: Faith Talk's Changing Contexts*. Delhi: ISPCK.

Senior, Donald and Carroll Stuhlmueller (1983), *The Biblical Foundations for Mission*. London: SCM Press.

Sepúlveda, Juan (1993), 'Pentecostalism and liberation theology: two manifestations of the work of the Holy Spirit for the renewal of the church', in Harold D. Hunter and Peter D. Hocken (eds), *All Together in One Place: Theological Papers from the Brighton Conference on World Evangelization*. Sheffield: Sheffield Academic Press, pp. 51–64.

—(1999), 'Indigenous Pentecostalism and the Chilean experience', in Allan H. Anderson and Walter J. Hollenweger (eds), *Pentecostals after a Century: Global Perspectives on a Movement in Transition*. Sheffield: Sheffield Academic Press, pp. 111–34.

Shorter, Aylward (1999), 'Inculturation: win or lose the future', in James A. Scherer and Stephen B. Bevans (eds), *New Directions in Mission and Evangelization 3: Faith and Culture*. Maryknoll, NY: Orbis, pp. 54–67.

—(2006), *Cross and Flag in Africa: The 'White Fathers' during the Colonial Scramble (1892–1914)*. Maryknoll, NY: Orbis.

Shourie, Arun (1994), *Missionaries in India: Continuities, Changes, Dilemmas*. New Delhi: ASA.

Siddiqui, Ataullah (1997), *Christian–Muslim Dialogue in the Twentieth Century*. Basingstoke: Macmillan.

Sider, Ronald J. (1984), *Rich Christians in an Age of Hunger: A Biblical Study* (2nd edn). Downers Grove, IL: InterVarsity Press.

Siebers, Hans (1999), 'Globalization and religious creolization among the Q'eqchi'es of Guatemala', in Christian Smith and Joshua Pokopy (eds), *Latin American Religion in Motion*. New York: Routledge, pp. 261–73.

Sizer, Stephen (2005), *Christian Zionism: Road Map to Armageddon?* Leicester: IVP.

Sobrino, Jon (1978), *Christology at the Crossroads: A Latin American Approach* (translated by John Drury from the Spanish). London: SCM Press.

—(1990), 'The crucified peoples: Yahweh's suffering servant today', in Leonardo Boff and Virgil Elizondo (eds), *1492–1992: The Voice of the Victims*. London: SCM Press, pp. 120–9.

—(1993), *Jesus the Liberator: A Historical–theological Reading of Jesus of Nazareth* (translated by Paul Burns and Francis McDonagh from the Spanish). Maryknoll, NY: Orbis.

Song, Choan-Seng (1988), *Theology from the Womb of Asia*. London: SCM Press.

Sørensen, Jørgen Skov (2003), 'Christian theology and intellectuals in China: a historical and theological introduction', in Centre for Multireligious Studies (ed.), *Christian Theology and Intellectuals in China*, Occasional Paper. Aarhus: University of Aarhus, pp. 7–25.

Spickard, Paul R. and Kevin M. Cragg (1994), *A Global History of Christians: How Everyday Believers Experienced their World*. Grand Rapids, MI: Baker Academic.

Stanley, Brian (1990) *The Bible and the Flag: Protestant Missions and British Imperialism in the Nineteenth and Twentieth Centuries*. Leicester: Apollos.

—(1992), *The History of the Baptist Missionary Society, 1792–1992*. Edinburgh: T. and T. Clark.

—(2004), 'Twentieth century world Christianity: a perspective from the history of Christian missions', in Donald M. Lewis (ed.), *Christianity Reborn: The Global Expansion of Evangelicalism in the Twentieth Century*. Grand Rapids, MI: Wm B. Eerdmans, pp. 52–83.

—(2006), 'Defining the boundaries of Christendom: the two worlds of the World Missionary Conference, 1910' *International Bulletin of Missionary Research*, 30(4), 171–6.

Stark, R. and R. Finke (2000), *Acts of Faith: Explaining the Human Side of Religion*. Berkeley: University of California Press.

Steigenga, Timothy J. and David A. Smilde (1999), 'Wrapped in the holy shawl: the strange case of conservative Christians and gender equality in Latin America', in Christian Smith and Joshua Pokopy (eds), *Latin American Religion in Motion*. New York: Routledge, pp. 173–86.

Stendahl, Krister (1976), *Paul among Jews and Gentiles*. Philadelphia, PA: Fortress Press.

Stern, David H. (1991), *Messianic Jewish Manifesto* (2nd edn). Clarksville, MD: Jewish New Testament Publications.

Stinton, Diane (2004), *Jesus of Africa: Voices of Contemporary African Christology*. Maryknoll, NY: Orbis.

Stoll, David (1990), *Is Latin America Turning Protestant? The Politics of Evangelical Growth*. Berkeley: University of California Press.

Stout, Harry S. (1983), 'The transforming effects of the Great Awakening', in Mark A. Noll, Nathan O. Hatch, George M. Marsden, David F. Wells and John D. Woodbridge (eds), *Christianity in America: A Handbook*. Grand Rapids, MI: Eerdmans, pp. 127–30.

Sugirtharajah, R. S. (ed.) (1993), *Asian Faces of Jesus*. Maryknoll, NY: Orbis.

—(ed.) (1995), *Voices from the Margin: Interpreting the Bible in the Third World*. Maryknoll, NY: Orbis.

—(2001), *The Bible and the Third World: Precolonial, Colonial and Postcolonial Encounters*. Cambridge: Cambridge University Press.

Suh, David Kwang-sun (1991), *The Korean Minjung in Christ*. Kowloon: CCA.

Sumithra, Sunand (ed.) (1992), *Doing Theology in Context*. Bangalore: Theological Book Trust.

Sunquist, Scott W. (ed.) (2001), *A Dictionary of Asian Christianity*. Grand Rapids, MI: Wm B. Eerdmans.

Swain, Tony and Garry Trompf (1995), *The Religions of Oceania*. London: Routledge.

Tacey David (2004), *The Spirituality Revolution: The Emergence of Contemporary Spirituality*. New York: Brunner-Routledge.

Tambras, Sotirios (1989), 'Orthodox mission in the Far East', in George Lemopoulos (ed.), *Your Will Be Done: Orthodoxy in Mission*. Geneva: World Council of Churches, pp. 205–9.

Tamez, Elsa (1993), *The Amnesty of Grace: Justification by Faith from a Latin American Perspective* (trans. Sharon H. Ringe). Nashville, TN: Abingdon.

Tang, Edmond (2005), ' "Yellers" and healers – Pentecostalism and the study of grassroots Christianity in China', in Allan Anderson and Edmond Tang (eds), *Asian and Pentecostal: The Charismatic Face of Christianity in Asia*. Oxford: Regnum Books, pp. 467–86.

Taylor, John V. (1963), *The Primal Vision: Christian Presence amid African Religion*. London : SCM Press.

Tempels, Placide (1947), *Bantu Philosophy*. Paris: Présence Africaine.

Thanzauva, K. (1997), *Theology of Community: Tribal Theology in the Making*. Aizawl, Mizo Theological Conference.

Theije, Marjo de (1999), 'CEBs and Catholic charismatics in Brazil', in Christian Smith and Joshua Pokopy (eds), *Latin American Religion in Motion*. New York: Routledge, pp. 111–24.

Theissen, G. (2003), *The New Testament: History, Literature, Religion*. London: T. and T. Clark/Continuum.

Thomas, M. M. (1966), *The Christian Response to the Asian Revolution*. London: SCM Press.

—(1969), *The Acknowledged Christ of the Indian Renaissance*. London: SCM Press.

—(1971), *Salvation and Humanization: Some Crucial Issues of the Theology of Mission in Contemporary India*. Madras: Christian Literature Society.

—(1997), 'Indian theology', in Karl Müller, Theo Sundermeier, Stephen B. Bevans and Richard H. Bliese (eds), *Dictionary of Mission: Theology, History, Perspectives*. Maryknoll, NY: Orbis, pp. 202–12.

Thomas, Scott M. (2005), *The Global Resurgence of Religion and the Transformation of International Relations: The Struggle for the Soul of the Twenty-first Century*. New York: Palgrave Macmillan.

Tiedemann, R. G. (1999), 'China and its neighbours', in Adrian Hastings (ed.), *A World History of Christianity*. London: Cassell, pp. 369–415.

Tiénu, Tite (2006), 'Christian theology in an era of world Christianity', in Craig Ott and Harold Netland (eds), *Globalizing Theology: Belief and Practice in an Era of World Christianity*. Grand Rapids, MI: Baker Academic, pp. 37–51.

Tinker, George E. (1994), 'Spirituality and Native American personhood: sovereignty and solidarity', in K. C. Abraham and Bernadette Mbuy-Beya (eds), *Spirituality of the Third World: A Cry for Life*. Maryknoll, NY: Orbis, pp. 119–32.

Titaley, John A. (2008), 'From abandonment to blessing: the theological presence of Christianity in Indonesia', in Sebastian C. H. Kim (ed.), *Christian Theology in Asia*. Cambridge: Cambridge University Press, pp. 71–88.

Tsetsis, Georges (2004), 'The significance of regional ecumenism', in John Briggs, Mercy Amba Oduyoye and Georges Tsetsis (eds), *A History of the Ecumenical Movement, Vol. 3, 1968–2000*. Geneva: World Council of Churches, pp. 461–8.

Turaki, Yusufu (2006), 'Homosexuality', in Tokunboh Adeyemo (ed.), *Africa Bible Commentary*. Grand Rapids, MI: Zondervan Publishing, p. 1355.

Ugeux, Bernard (2006), 'Questions which new spiritualities pose to evangelization in Europe', *International Review of Mission*, 95 (378–9), 324–8.

Van den End, Thomas (2001), 'Indonesia', in Scott W. Sunquist (ed.), *A Dictionary of Asian Christianity*. Grand Rapids, MI: Wm B. Eerdmans, pp. 374–80.

Van der Merwe, Hugo (2003), 'The role of the church in promoting reconciliation in post-TRC South Africa', in Audrey R. Chapman and Bernard Spong (eds), *Religion and Reconciliation in South Africa*. Philadelphia, PA: Templeton Foundation Press, pp. 269–81.

Van Elderen, Marlin (2001), *Introducing the World Council of Churches*. Geneva: World Council of Churches.

Van Engen, Charles (1991), *God's Missionary People: Rethinking the Purpose of the Local Church*. Grand Rapids, MI: Baker.

Van Ufford, Philip Quarles (2007), 'Religion and development: transforming relations between Indonesian and Dutch churches', *http://www.bezinningscentrum.nl/Religion_Development/ufford.pdf*

Vandana (Mataji) (1982), *Social Justice and Ashrams*. Bangalore: Asia Trading Corporation.

—(1991), *Find Your Roots and Take Wing: Three Essays on Spiritual Formation for the East and the West*. Bangalore: ATC.

Vanhoozer, Kevin J. (2006), ' "One rule to rule them all?" Theological method in an era of world Christianity', in Craig Ott and Harold Netland (eds), *Globalizing Theology: Belief and Practice in an Era of World Christianity*. Grand Rapids, MI: Baker Academic, pp. 85–126.

Vásquez, Manuel A. and Marie F. Marquardt (2003), *Globalizing the Sacred: Religion Across the Americas*. New Brunswick, NJ: Rutgers University Press.

Vassiliadis, Petros (1998), *Eucharist and Witness: Orthodox Perspectives on the Unity and Mission of the Church*. Geneva: World Council of Churches.

Vassiliadou, Anastasia (2006), 'Reception and crisis of the Enlightenment from the 1970s to the present day: an Orthodox point of view', *International Review of Mission*, 95(378–9), 271–5.

Vernooij, Joop (2007), 'Religion in the Caribbean: creation by Creolisation', in Frans Wijsen and Robert Schreiter (eds), *Global Christianity: Contested Claims*. Amsterdam: Rodopi, pp. 147–56.

Verstraelen, Frans J. (2007), 'Jenkins' *The Next Christendom* and Europe', in Frans Wijsen and Robert Schreiter (eds), *Global Christianity: Contested Claims*. Amsterdam: Rodopi, pp. 95–116.

Vischer, Lukas (2004), 'Major trends in the life of the churches', in John Briggs, Mercy Amba Oduyoye and Georges Tsetsis (eds), *A History of the Ecumenical Movement, Vol. 3, 1968–2000*, pp. 23–50.

Visser 't Hooft, Willem Adolf (1993), 'The genesis of the World Council of Churches', in Ruth Rouse and Stephen Charles Neill (eds), *A History of the Ecumenical Movement, Vol. 1, 1517–1948* (4th edn). Geneva: World Council of Churches, pp. 697–724.

Volf, Miroslav (1996), *Exclusion and Embrace: A Theological Exploration of Identity, Otherness, and Reconciliation*. Nashville, TN: Abingdon Press.

Wacker, Grant (2001), *Heaven Below: Early Pentecostals and American Culture*. Cambridge, MA: Harvard University Press.

Wagner, Peter C. (1989), 'Territorial spirits and world missions', *Evangelical Missions Quarterly*, 25(3), 278–88.

—(ed.) (1986), *Church Growth: State of the Art*. Wheaton, IL: Tyndale House.

Wagua, Aiban (1990), 'Present consequences of the European invasion of America', in Leonardo Boff and Virgil Elizondo (eds), *1492–1992: The Voice of the Victims*. London: SCM Press, pp. 47–56.

Wallis, Jim (2005), *God's Politics: Why the Right Gets It Wrong and the Left Doesn't Get It*. New York: HarperCollins.

Walls, Andrew F. (1996), *The Missionary Movement in Christian History*. Maryknoll, NY: Orbis.

—(2002), *The Cross-cultural Process in Christian History: Studies in the Transmission and Appropriation of Faith*. Maryknoll, NY: Orbis.

Walters, Albert Sundararaj (2000), 'Malaysian theology', in Virginia Fabella and R. S. Sugirtharajah (eds), *Dictionary of Third World Theologies*. Maryknoll, NY: Orbis, pp. 134–6.

—(2002), *We Believe in One God? Reflections on the Trinity in the Malaysian Context*. Delhi: ISPCK.

Walters, Philip (1999), 'Eastern Europe since the fifteenth century', in Adrian Hastings (ed.), *A World History of Christianity*. London: Cassell, pp. 282–327.

Ward, Benedicta and G. R. Evans (1999), 'The Medieval West', in Adrian Hastings (ed.), *A World History of Christianity*. London: Cassell, pp. 110–46.

Ward, Kevin (1999), 'Africa', in Adrian Hastings (ed.), *A World History of Christianity*. London: Cassell, pp. 192–237.

Ward, Pete (2002), *Liquid Church*. Peabody, MA: Hendrickson/Carlisle: Paternoster Press.

Ware, Timothy (1993), *The Orthodox Church* (2nd edn). London: Penguin Books.

Warner, Marina (1985), *Alone of All Her Sex: The Myth and Cult of the Virgin Mary*. London: Picador.

Warren, Rick (1995), *The Purpose Driven: Church Growth without Compromising your Message and Mission*. Grand Rapids, MI: Zondervan.

Warrior, Robert Allen (1995), 'A Native American perspective: Canaanites, cowboys, and Indians', in R. S. Sugirtharajah (ed.), *Voices from the Margin: Interpreting the Bible in the Third World* (2nd edn). London: SPCK, pp. 277–85.

Wells, Kenneth M. (1990), *New God, New Nation: Protestants and Self-Reconstruction Nationalism in Korea, 1896–1937*. Honolulu: University of Hawai'i Press.

Werpehowski, William (1997), 'Theological ethics', in David F. Ford (ed.), *The Modern Theologians: An Introduction to Christian Theology of the Twentieth Century* (2nd edn). Oxford: Blackwell, pp. 311–26.

Wessels, Antonie (1994), *Europe, Was It Ever Really Christian?: The Interaction between Gospel and Culture*. London: SCM Press.

—(1995), *Arab and Christian? Christians in the Middle East*. Kampen: Kok Pharos Publishing House.

—(2006), *Muslims and the West: Can They be Integrated?* (trans. John Bowden). Leuven: Peeters.

West, Cornel (1979), 'Black theology and Marxist thought', in Gayraud S. Wilmore and James H. Cone, *Black Theology: A Documentary History, 1966–1979*. Maryknoll, NY: Orbis, pp. 552–67.

Wiarda, Howard J. (2001), *The Soul of Latin America: The Cultural and Political Tradition*. New Haven, CT: Yale Divinity Press.

Wickeri, Janice and Philip Wickeri (eds) (2002), *A Chinese Contribution to Ecumenical Theology: Selected Writings of Bishop K. H. Ting*. Geneva: World Council of Churches.

Wietzke, Joachim (ed.) (1983), *Paul D. Devanandan*, Vol. 1. Madras: Christian Literature Society.

Wild, Emma (1998), 'Working with women in the Congo', in Andrew Wingate, Kevin Ward, Carrie Pemberton and Wilson Sitshebo (eds), *Anglicanism: A Global Communion*. London: Mowbray, pp. 281–6.

Wilfred, Felix (1998), 'Towards a better understanding of Asian theology: some basic issues', *Vidyajyoti*, 62(12), 890–915.

William D. Taylor (ed.) (2000), *Global Missiology for the Twenty-First Century: The Iguassu Dialogue. Papers from the Iguassu Missiological Consultation, Brazil, 1999*. Grand Rapids, MI: Baker.

Williams, Lewin L. (1994), *Caribbean Theology*. Frankfurt: Peter Lang.

Williams, Peter (1990), *America's Religions: Traditions and Cultures*. New York: Macmillan.

Williams, Rowan (2006), Archbishop of Canterbury press release: 'Middle East Christians need support', 23 Dec. *http://www.archbishopofcanterbury.org/releases/061223.htm*

Wilson, Everett A. (1999), 'They crossed the Red Sea, didn't they? Critical history and Pentecostal beginnings', in Murray W. Dempster, Byron D. Klaus and Douglas Petersen (eds), *The Globalization of Pentecostalism: A Religion Made to Travel*. Oxford: Regnum, pp. 85–115.

Wimber, John (1985), *Power Evangelism*. New York: Harper and Row.

Wink, Walter (1984), *Naming the Powers: The Language of Power in the New Testament*. Minneapolis, MN: Fortress.

—(1986), *Unmasking the Powers: The Invisible Forces that Determine Human Existence*. Minneapolis, MN: Fortress.

—(1992), *Engaging the Powers: Discernment and Resistance in a World of Domination*. Minneapolis, MN: Fortress.

—(1998), *The Powers That Be: Theology for a New Millennium*. New York and London: Doubleday.

Wong, Ming-Dao (1981), *A Stone Made Smooth*, Southampton: Mayflower Christian Books.

World Council of Churches (1991), 'Statement on the Pacific', in Michael Kinnamon (ed.), *Signs of the Spirit: Official Report of the Seventh Assembly, Canberra, 1991*. Geneva: World Council of Churches, pp 226–8.

—(2005), 'The healing mission of the church' Available at *http://www.mission2005.org/*

World Evangelical Alliance (2000), 'the Iguassu affirmation', in William D. Taylor (ed.), *Global Missiology for the Twenty-first Century: The Iguassa Dialogue*. Grand Rapids, MI: Baker Book House, pp. 15–21.

Yates, Timothy (1994), *Christian Mission in the Twentieth Century*. Cambridge: Cambridge University Press.

Yi, Mahn-yōl (2004), 'The birth of the national spirit of the Christians in the late Chosōn period' (trans. Ch'oe Ùn-a), in Chai-shin Yu (ed.), *Korea and Christianity*. Fremont, CA: Asian Humanities Press, pp. 39–72.

Yoder, John Howard (1972), *The Politics of Jesus: Vicit Agnus Noster*. Grand Rapids, MI: Eerdmans.

Yong, Amos (2003), *Beyond the Impasse: Toward a Pneumatological Theology of Religions*. Grand Rapids, MI: Baker Academic.

—(2005), *The Spirit Poured Out on All Flesh: Pentecostalism and the Possibility of Global Theology*. Grand Rapids, MI: Baker Academic.

Yu, Chai-shin (ed.) (1996), *The Founding of Catholic Tradition in Korea*. Mississauga, Ontario: Korea and Related Studies Press.

Yung, Hwa (1997), *Mangoes or Bananas? The Quest for an Authentic Asian Christian Theology*. Oxford: Regnum.

Index